HIGH COUNTRY EMPIRE

HIGH COUNTRY EMPIRE

The High Plains and Rockies

Robert G. Athearn

UNIVERSITY OF NEBRASKA PRESS · LINCOLN

First Bison Book printing November, 1965

Most recent printing shown by first digit below:

4   5   6   7   8   9   10

*Bison Book edition reproduced by arrangement with the author from
the 1960 edition published by McGraw-Hill Book Company, Inc.*

For

Ernest Staples Osgood
    A portrait of
    his part of America

PREFACE

This is a book about a section of America. It deals with the stretch of country embracing the great Missouri River drainage, from its southernmost tributaries to those reaching north into Canada. In modern terms, it includes the mountain states of Montana, Wyoming, and Colorado and the plains states of North Dakota, South Dakota, Nebraska, and Kansas, all of which are touched by some part of the Missouri River system.

The land of the high plains and Rockies has figured largely in the history of the American frontier and in the literature written about it. Since it was one of the last parts of the West to feel the effects of civilization, it is generally thought of as America's last frontier. Even before it reached maturity the American people began to romanticize it and it became, to them, all their frontier experiences wrapped up in one. When men spoke of "the West" any time after the Civil War, they meant the high plains and Rockies, for already the Pacific Coast had largely passed through its frontier phase.

I have made no attempt to discuss the rise of the individual states within this region. To do so would be to cut the strands of larger historical movements and "Balkanize" a land whose characteristics and heritage are common. Instead I am concerned with the developments which, regardless of political boundaries, affected this entire inland empire once dismissed as the "Great American Desert." Nor will the reader find a detailed discussion of the processes of settlement, beyond that which is required to provide a backdrop for a general treatment, for this already has been done many times. The principal effort in this work is to view the entire region in broad sweeps in an effort to understand its relationship to the larger story of American growth and to bring out any dominant highlights that characterize its history.

Among these the most persistent theme is that of exploitation and experimentation carried on by remote control from the more settled parts of America. From the day of the mountain men, down through that of the miner, the cattleman, the land speculator, the timber baron, and the oil wildcatter, the region has been regarded as a place to capitalize upon natural resources with precious little concern about what was left when the stripping was finished. Well over a century ago the trapper anointed his traps with pungent orange-brown castor to lure the beaver. Today he is superseded by the prospector whose Geiger counter crackles ominously at the scent of radioactive uranium. Both exploiters had the same thing in mind: to search out the land's riches and retire to some more genteel part of the country. Time's passage has not modified the process; only the method is different.

Thanks are due the Council on Research and Creative Work at the University of Colorado for its financial assistance. Geologist George W. Berry gave his advice on the section dealing with petroleum development and was kind enough to read one of the chapters. Professor Walter Johnson, of the University of Chicago department of history, spent a great many tedious hours reading the manuscript and his suggestions contributed a good deal to its improvement. The author is particularly grateful to the following individuals and institutions for assistance in furnishing illustrations: Michael Kennedy and Vivian Paladin, Historical Society of Montana; Lola Homsher, Wyoming State Historical Department; Glenn H. Johnson, Library, State Historical Society of Colorado; Nyle H. Miller, Kansas State Historical Society; William D. Aeschbacher, Nebraska State Historical Society. Robert Perkin of the *Rocky Mountain News* (Denver) graciously gave permission to use in Chapter 5 material previously published in that newspaper. A very personal kind of appreciation is tendered to A. B. "Bud" Guthrie, the Montana novelist, and to John Starr of the McGraw-Hill Book Company for their enthusiasm and encouragement. It would be unkind to omit reference —now standard in all published acknowledgments—to the author's unfailing helpmate. Her assistance was that of conscript duty, a role she has long since accepted as one of the penalties of academic life.

Robert G. Athearn
University of Colorado

CONTENTS

SECTION I: **THE LAND LIES OPEN**

Chapter 1	Terra Incognita	3
Chapter 2	Traps and Trinkets	27
Chapter 3	The Way West	45

SECTION II: **VANGUARDS OF SETTLEMENT**

Chapter 4	Golden Cornerstone	69
Chapter 5	Picket Line of Civilization	99
Chapter 6	The Cow Kingdom	127
Chapter 7	Web of Steel	152

SECTION III: **THE GREAT INVASION**

Chapter 8	The Sod Busters	179
Chapter 9	Dissension in the Desert	205
Chapter 10	The White Man's Culture	224

SECTION IV: **VINTAGE YEARS**

Chapter 11	Fading Frontiers	257
Chapter 12	Uncle Sam's West	278
Chapter 13	Empire of Dust	297
Chapter 14	A Land in Transition	318
	Index	353

Section I

THE
LAND
LIES
OPEN

Chapter 1   TERRA INCOGNITA

When the United States made the Louisiana Purchase in 1803 it bought the world's largest pasture, considerable mineral rights, one major and several minor rivers—all in working order—and the best-known desert in the Western Hemisphere.

Never before had there been a real estate deal quite like this. The French, who had barely persuaded the Spanish to fulfill the terms of a recent trade, were not at all sure of what they now sold, and the Americans had only a general notion of what they had bought. The only real point of reference demarcating the tract was the Mississippi River. But the Americans, in a promotional frame of mind, were quite willing to take on an area whose title was in doubt and whose boundaries were as vague as the West itself. Details could be ironed out another day and an excellent surveyor named Manifest Destiny would see to it that the purchaser was not shorted.

A glance at a modern map will reveal that the high plains states comprised a major part of the Purchase. Westward from the Mississippi the land slants up until the Rocky Mountains turn it skyward. Tilted though it is, the terrain is generally flat, broken by several major drainages that have controlled the settlement and economy of this inland empire. The Missouri River, tawny, mean and treacherous, snakes its way southward through Montana and the Dakotas, touches

3

Kansas and Nebraska, and then splits Missouri before joining the Mississippi. Old-timers used to say that this was the last river the Almighty cut and He made it by gathering up all the slops left over from other jobs. They despised its unhandsome appearance and cursed its unpredictable meanderings, but it remained the best travel route across a dry and forbidding country. Like a shady lady, it was better than nothing and men used it until something better came along.

The Platte and Kansas rivers etched out the two remaining important drainages in the area but their efforts were so halfhearted that they made little impression, even in the soft and yielding soil. They were useless waterways, unfit for navigation, dangerous to cross and completely unreliable, overflowing just in time to wash out crops and then petulantly going dry when their brackish water was wanted. Southward lay the Arkansas, not much better, but like the others marking off a trail that led to better things.

The eighteenth century failed to divulge much accurate information about the land that Thomas Jefferson was one day to annex. When Le Page du Pratz published his *Histoire de la Louisiane* in 1758, he based his information upon sixteen years' residence and travel in the region and his work indicated a fair knowledge of the lower Mississippi reaches. But the Missouri was something else. He imagined that it arose somewhere near the source of the Rio Grande and speculated that it would make a fine route from the Illinois country to New Mexico. By the time the French government yielded Louisiana in 1763, it knew the country north of the Platte about as well as it knew that beyond the river Styx. A few fur traders had penetrated the plains from the northeast, but they were an uncommunicative lot and had no precise information about what they had seen.

The Spanish were not enthusiastic about the ocean of sod they gained by the Treaty of 1763. In fact, they did not bother to assume control of it for another six years. As they temporized, the Frenchmen who lived along the Mississippi continued to toy with the notion of milking the Missouri River country of its furs. As early as 1714 Etienne de Bourgmont, a French trapper, reached the lower Missouri country, married an Indian woman, and settled down with his new relatives. A few years later, Pierre de la Vérendrye, another trapper

who knew the country around Lake Superior, expressed curiosity
about the prairies to the west. With the assistance of some Montreal
merchants and accompanied by his three sons, he explored the land
in the vicinity of the Lake of the Woods in 1732. A second journey,
in 1739, put him at the Mandan villages, in present North Dakota.
Three years later two of his sons reported that they had pushed out,
clear to the Rockies. About that time Pierre and Paul Mallet visited
the Platte region and then swung south to Santa Fe. None of these
travelers related much of their knowledge to government officials.

By 1764 some French traders had laid out a post near the confluence of the Mississippi and the Missouri and called it St. Louis.
Before long it served as a trap to catch the furs that came downriver.
Stationed at the mouth of the horn of plenty, the fur merchants displayed little curiosity about the origins of their product. Over twenty
years later the Spanish governor of Louisiana, Esteban Miro, drew
up a description of the land to the northwest and proved only that
in two decades little if any new information about it had been produced. Miro explained that so far as he knew no one had been up
the Missouri over two hundred leagues, to the Sioux tribes, and beyond that point geographic knowledge was mere speculation. Nor
was he really curious.

When the Spanish finally moved, it was not because they were
lured into the unknown by the thought of sudden wealth. The British,
who had taken title to Canada in 1763, were on the move westward.
If war came, the Spanish believed they would suffer attacks, particularly since they still imagined that the Missouri had its source in
the region of New Mexico. The British traders who drifted southward posed another threat: their goods were better and cheaper than
those sold by the Spanish. Once the natives made this discovery,
control of the land would be difficult indeed. But the Spaniards were
not given to sudden activity and, worry though they might, they were
affected by a bad case of chronic inertia. Not until the 1790s did
they make any effective moves into the unknown land up the muddy
river. By then it was too late.

A young giant, hungry and dangerous when aroused, but so loosely
built and so distressingly awkward that few feared him, recently had
come upon the international scene. After a few years of tenuous

partnership, the United States had pulled themselves together under a new contract known as the Constitution; suddenly aware that further unconcern about the West would lose them their patrimony, they decided to look across the Appalachians and even to the broad Mississippi River. Such resolve by the newcomer, such a sudden discovery of its equilibrium, alarmed nearby neighbors—and with justification. In its very first year the new government's Secretary of War, Henry Knox, asked General Josiah Harmar if he could not devise some means of exploring a branch of the Mississippi "called the Messouri," to its source. Please find out, he asked, how close this river's southern branches came to the Rio Grande. Lieutenant John Armstrong was selected to lead the expedition; failure to find friendly Indians who would serve him as guides resulted in abandonment of the plan. The officer actually made a start, but of the two Indians he managed to engage one became sick and the other pulled up lame, convincing the leader his task was an impossible one. As he explained to his superiors, "it is a business much easier planed [sic] than executed."

With the country between the Appalachians and the Mississippi virtually unsettled, the nation's southern boundary in doubt, and the mouth of the great river in Spanish hands, Americans still could look hungrily beyond what they owned but had not assimilated and dream about a day when they would own even more. Land hunger, an American characteristic, was not reserved to individuals.

To the south the Spanish Empire drowsed. But times had changed. There was a day when the British had scolded their colonists and told them to stay east of the Appalachians, when only a few Frenchmen cruised the Mississippi. Why worry about the great American midcontinent? No one would disturb it. So the time of opportunity sped by and almost overnight a new nation, whose people were still referred to as Anglo-Americans, had appeared. Too late the Spanish came awake. In belated activity they looked to their child Louisiana, still a stranger to them, and resolved to make up for lost time.

In the summer of 1790 one of their subjects, a Frenchman named Jacques D'Eglise, was sent up the Missouri to study its habitat and characteristics. Three years later he was back. He had been among the Mandan Indians and could relate something of their customs but of botanical or precise geographic knowledge he had little to report. Spanish officials had not bet all their chips on a single Frenchman, however. While D'Eglise was absent Governor Carondelet baited the economic trap by opening the fur trade to any subject who would observe certain restrictions. So violent and immediate was the squabbling among the contestants that the governor was obliged to divide up the trade, by lot, among the merchants of St. Louis. As a result, the Company of Explorers of the Upper Missouri was formed in October 1793. It was hoped that the lure of wealth in furs would send numbers of traders into the barren land.

The new organization, popularly known as the Missouri Company, at once selected Jean Baptiste Truteau to lead an expedition upriver to the Mandan villages, where he was to establish a post. From that point he was instructed to plunge westward and return with some positive information about the mysterious Missouri. Governor Carondelet was delighted. Here at last was action. Louisiana, he said, had something that the United States had not, something that the English would gladly usurp and something the Spanish themselves had too long neglected: furs. So powerful an attraction were these pelts that they alone could enrich the province and even attract an immense population.

The governor's enthusiasm got away from him. For years the French had mined the Canadian wilds of furs and the digging had been rich, but no large population developed. Such was not the nature of the economy. He was right about one thing: the Missouri country would yield many furs and they would be sold for millions. Enough men would be attracted by the trade to strip the country of its furry wealth, but few would stay. They would contribute nothing tangible to the growth of the land and would leave behind only beaver carcasses and perhaps some half-breed Indian children. An official in St. Louis was more realistic when he wrote to Carondelet that even if the upper Missouri trade did not become profitable, at least the country would become well known and that would be more than the Spanish had accomplished to date.

In quest of wealth for itself and knowledge for the government, the Missouri Company's expedition departed for the unknown. The company director set Truteau straight on his objectives before he left. He was to establish his trading post high on the river and make the necessary arrangements for getting the Indians' furs. Be particularly careful to set a high price on all goods traded for furs, warned the director. Of course, when time and business permitted, the matter of discovering the river's source should be looked into. It was somewhere near the "Rocky chain," but how far was as yet a mere guess. Perhaps the traders would be able to improve Governor Carondelet's geographic knowledge. He thought the river rose in some mountains "not more than forty leagues from the South Sea." Even better, he said, there was supposed to be another navigable river leading westward from those mountains and emptying into that same sea. The idea so excited the governor that he offered a reward for anyone who would verify it. A prize of $2000, later raised to $3000, was promised the first man who reached the South Sea via the Missouri River. So the voyageurs went forth with a double incentive: money for furs, money for information.

On a June day in 1794 Truteau and eight men left St. Louis in a flat-bottom craft called a pirogue. After a back-breaking ascent of the river, the men worked their way to where the Crow Creek agency now stands in South Dakota only to be greeted by the Teton Sioux— who promptly appropriated their goods. Such a setback would have discouraged many a trader, but Truteau merely retreated downriver to the future location of Fort Randall and there the group spent the winter. In the spring of 1795 another try was made and despite the fact that his stock was depleted, Truteau pushed his party upriver. He returned to St. Louis later that year without having fulfilled either of his objectives, but he brought back considerable knowledge.

A little less than three hundred leagues from St. Louis lived the Omaha Indians. Farther up were the Arickaras, having among them at least five hundred warriors. There were also Cheyennes in the region; they surprised Truteau by displaying both the maize and the tobacco they produced. Deeper in the interior were the Mandans, numbering about three hundred warriors, and beyond them the Gros Ventres, a larger tribe. The natives he saw lived along the country's great highway, the Missouri River. He wondered how they existed. The waterway itself coursed between two chains of steep hills, with vegetation along its banks, but beyond were the most desolate prairies he had ever seen, "completely sterile; scarcely grass grows there." Far west of the Mandans, at a point along the present Montana–North Dakota border, a new river was encountered. Truteau called the Yellowstone "almost as broad and deep as the Missouri." Its source was somewhere in the mountains, somewhere to the west. Interesting as it might be to find the river's origin, more important was the discovery that its many tributaries "abound in beaver beyond all belief." He recommended the construction of a fort at the Yellowstone's mouth. It would catch not only the furs trapped by Indians along its banks but also those on the upper reaches of the Missouri. The forks of these major rivers, he correctly guessed, would be the most strategic location in all beaverland for a post. Astor's American Fur Company later would take the advice and prove Truteau right. Meanwhile, the Frenchman came back to his Spanish employers with the most accurate information to date on the Missouri from its mouth to that of the Yellowstone. He had charted the way; others would soon retrace his steps.

The Spanish seem to have run out of native conquistadores. First they had relied upon the Frenchmen Jacques D'Eglise and Jean Truteau to explore the river. Not yet satisfied with their findings, the Missouri Company dispatched a Scotsman named James Mackay to follow the river to its source, clear to the Pacific if necessary. He sailed out of St. Louis in the summer of 1795, his four pirogues carrying thirty-three men and a supply of Indian trade goods. The men passed the winter at the Omaha villages, where they built a post named Fort Charles. Early the next year Mackay sent out one of his lieutenants, a Welshman named John Evans, to probe the land beyond and if possible to cross the Rocky Mountains. Nothing came of either effort and by 1797 both had returned. Mackay, a surveyor, brought back some additional geographic knowledge.

The sputtering attempts of the Missouri Company and the unsuccessful efforts of other explorers worried Spanish officials. The governor of Louisiana issued a sharp warning that both the English and Americans, "though unjustly and without the slightest right," were trying to win the Indian trade by promises and gifts. But at the end of the century, most of Louisiana was still a mysterious and un-

tracked waste. The route to the Mandan villages was the only successful penetration to the north; beyond that point little was known
other than what Truteau could tell of the lower Yellowstone country.

On October 1, 1800, Spain suddenly ceded all of Louisiana to
France. The pressure of European politics once more intervened in
the course of America's destiny. It had happened before and would
happen again. Napoleon, now soaring in the political stratosphere,
was in an expansive mood and talked grandly of restoring to France
her earlier glories. Part of that plan was to regain as much as possible of the holdings lost in 1763 and to resume France's position as
a colonial power in America. By dangling a few baubles in the form
of Italian titles before the eyes of Spain's Charles IV, the deal was
as easily consummated as one that involved handing a few yards of
calico to a willing Indian squaw. The Spanish had failed to gain anything from Louisiana, or to discover much of its resources, and all
the king could see was the annual bill for its protection and maintenance. It was so far away and seemed such a frozen asset.

Napoleon shortly discovered that it was one thing to gain title to
his new real estate interests but quite another to take possession. The
Spanish were agonizingly slow about lowering their ensign and hoist-
ing the tricolor. Delay followed delay until the world commenced to
wonder if the Spanish would fulfill their promises. Meanwhile, the
quest for furs up the Missouri slowly moved forward. In 1800 Regis
Loisel requested permission to build a fort four hundred leagues up
from St. Louis and two years later such other fur traders as Manuel
Lisa and the Sarpys asked for a place in the Osage trade. These men
were trying to break into the monopoly held by the Missouri Company and, like any entrenched interest, the company fought back.
Jacques Clamorgan, its director, urged the Spanish further to assist
his organization against both internal and external enemies. Louisiana
was in serious danger, Clamorgan warned. Outsiders not only raided
the commerce in fine peltries, but tried to stir up the residents against
each other.

The early nineteenth-century years found Louisiana's affairs in
a considerable state of flux. Traders sharply warned of outside pres-

sures, but the home governments dawdled and temporized. While the diplomatic flywheel was on dead center in Europe, events east of the Mississippi River were forging a new instrument of power on the American continent. For years residents west of the Appalachians had depended upon New Orleans as an outlet for their trade and by now they were tired of the vacillations in policy that had periodically opened and closed the bottleneck to the Gulf of Mexico. Spain, a weak and declining country, was irritating to deal with but actually no great threat. France *was* a real threat, one that called for action. Its landlordship might result in a permanent closure of the river. The mutterings along the Ohio and down the Mississippi Valley grew loud, and congressmen from the West listened. So did Thomas Jefferson in the White House. When the talk of Kentucky rifles at New Orleans reached a crescendo, representatives of the American government sat down with the French to talk business. But this was no affair that suddenly caused Jefferson to reach for his geography and search out Louisiana. He had thought about that land for some time.

As early as 1783 Jefferson had written to the well-known George Rogers Clark, inquiring if that man of action would be interested in exploring the unknown stretches beyond the great river, provided funds could be raised. Nothing came of the proposal, but Jefferson did not forget. While he was in France, in 1786, he was much interested in the proposals of another young man who talked of a venture more spectacular than Clark had ever imagined. John Ledyard was his name, and he excited Jefferson by proposing a trip across Siberia, over the intervening waters, and eastward through America to its settled regions. But a woman broke up this plan. Empress Catherine of Russia was unenthusiastic. In 1793 Jefferson looked to the western land again. A French botanist named Andre Michaux talked of an expedition through the wilds of interior America and Jefferson was at once suggesting aid from the American Philosophical Society. Jefferson and Alexander Hamilton chipped in $12.50 apiece and George Washington gave $25. Others followed suit, and it began to look as if Jefferson would have his way. He got as far as writing instructions for Michaux, telling him to find the shortest and best route to the Pacific Ocean, observing along the way the terrain, natural resources, flora and fauna. But again, events blunted the edge of the project. Michaux became so involved in Citizen Genêt's intrigues that he was no longer a desirable man with whom to deal and Jefferson had to break off, reluctant though he was.

By 1801 Jefferson was President. His new position thrust upon him many responsibilities but he did not set aside his interest in the West. In the winter of 1802–1803, while Congress was considering a bill for Indian trading houses, Jefferson saw his chance. Why not send out a party to explore the Missouri country? he asked. Could Congress spare $2500? Congress obliged, and plans were at once laid for a scientific exploration through a land that belonged to the French but was still in the hands of the Spanish. Only weeks earlier Jefferson had expressed an interest in the expedition to the Spanish minister, who warned his government that while the President was a man of letters he was also a lover of glory and one who "might attempt to perpetuate the fame of his administration . . . by attempting to discover the way by which the Americans may some day extend their population and their influence up to the coasts of the South Sea." The French were also concerned. That same year one of their officials had commented to Talleyrand on the astonishing increase in American population and warned that their "enterprising genius has excited the ambition or the cupidity in turn of the new inhabitants of the Lakes." To turn back the tide seemed hopeless, since the French and Spanish population of the area was small. Once again the French thought of enlisting the Indians against the Anglo-Americans. They need not have worried. Events in Europe were shaping the sale of Louisiana to the United States.

Elated at the prospect of success for a pet project of long standing, Jefferson chose his private secretary, Meriwether Lewis, to lead the expedition. The young officer asked if his boyhood chum William Clark, the brother of George Rogers, might go along and permission was granted at once. When the President had obtained a French passport for Lewis, he wrote out his instructions. The main aim of the work ahead was the exploration of the Missouri River and its principal streams, with the hope of finding a navigable waterway to the Pacific. As he had earlier instructed Michaux, Jefferson now told

Lewis to notice the Indian tribes, their habits, languages, traditions, and disposition. If any chiefs living reasonably close to civilization wanted to visit the capital, arrange for their transportation at public expense. The date was June 20, 1803.

While Jefferson perfected his plans for the exploration of Louisiana, his agents in Europe were consummating a real estate deal of magnificent proportions. Earlier that year he had instructed James Monroe to join Robert Livingston, our minister to France, in an effort to buy French holdings in the vicinity of New Orleans. The immediate object was a solution of the difficulties arising out of Spanish, and now French, reluctance to give American traders the right to deposit their goods at New Orleans pending arrangements for sale and subsequent ocean transportation. Monroe and Livingston were instructed to offer as much as $10,000,000 for New Orleans and West Florida.

Napoleon, who had entertained ideas of renewing the French empire in America, faced new and increasingly complex troubles at home. The Peace of Amiens, in March 1802, had temporarily removed the threat of the British navy, allowing the French to pursue the quest of American empire. But Napoleon's brother-in-law, General Leclerc, who tried to re-establish control of Santo Domingo, had come a cropper at the hands of the Negro patriot Toussaint L'Ouverture. The Santo Domingo venture turned into a costly military disaster. Unable to put down this rebellion, and faced by the prospect of a renewal of the war with Great Britain, Napoleon now sought a means of disposing of his American holdings. He needed the money and was fearful that the coming war might mean the loss of colonies by conquest. Thus, in April 1803, the French foreign minister, Talleyrand, asked the surprised Livingston how much the United States would give for all of Louisiana. After some haggling a price of $15,000,000 was agreed upon.

On July 3, Jefferson learned that his representatives had bought not only a city, but a whole wilderness empire. While he was surprised, and somewhat apprehensive that so large a purchase might meet opposition in Congress, he wrote with some feeling that it "increased infinitely the interest we felt in the expedition." In retrospect, it was a transaction of daring proportions and of considerable significance. At the stroke of a pen about one third of modern America was attached to the young nation and the land all the way to the crest of the Rockies now was under the Stars and Stripes. Beyond that lay the unknown Oregon country, upon which Great Britain had only a vague claim. Here was the stuff for future dreams.

Of immediate interest was the fact that the land to be explored was American, not French. Young Captain Lewis put aside his passport and prepared for an assault upon the unknown.

Two days later Lewis left Washington for Pittsburgh, where he began to assemble his outfit. A fifty-five-foot keelboat was laid out, but it took shape slowly. Aside from the painstaking deliberation of the workmen, the foreman's chronic inebriety contributed to the annoyance of the delay. Not until the last days of August did the group start down the Ohio. It was the expedition's nucleus, made up of seven soldiers, a pilot, and three young men "on trial." After a slow trip through low water that caused considerable grounding, the men reached Louisville toward mid-September. Here they found Captain William Clark, his Negro slave York (who would later fascinate the Indian squaws), and three Kentuckians. Within a few days six more signed on, including such promising individuals as Nathaniel Pryor, John Colter, and George Shannon. Clark took the group down the Ohio and back up the Mississippi, working north until they were opposite the Missouri's mouth, while Lewis went on to St. Louis to get more recruits. At a camp near the mouth of the Wood River of Illinois the winter was passed as the men readied themselves for a long journey. On the following May 14, the grand start was made, with the keelboat and two pirogues carrying forty-three men and a quantity of supplies.

What they faced was still the great unknown. What little information the Spanish had gleaned about the northern country was highly spiced with all manner of rumors and the unconfirmed reports of those who had been there, or who said they had. There were tales that prehistoric monsters snorted through the land, shaking the earth itself. Others told of the great salt mountain, eighty by forty-five miles in size, that stood a thousand miles upstream. So uncertain was Jefferson of the land into which he sent his young secretary that in the instructions he suggested getting in touch with the American consul at Batavia or the Cape of Good Hope should the explorer want any funds. There was no way of knowing the distance to the Pacific Ocean or—if Lewis found it—that he could get home by the land route.

The Spanish, who knew little more about the great lonely land, fussed about the proposed trip of the "American Captain Merry Weather," and talked of preventing him from trespassing upon their soil. The trouble was they didn't know where he was, or, as a matter of fact, where their own land lay. It was all very confusing. But, determined to clear up some of the mystery, the two young officers disappeared into the maw of the Missouri, cutting loose from civilization as certainly and faced by more trials than Christopher Columbus over three hundred years earlier.

The crew was as interesting as that of any exploration. In addition to fourteen frontier-wise soldiers there were hunters, gunsmiths, guides, interpreters, and a number of colorful French voyageurs. The latter came from a breed that had for years ranged western waterways and whose whipcord muscles could coax a keelboat up the cruelest of currents. Traveling was unromantic, as any of those who had been on the Missouri could have predicted, and the gnats, mosquitoes, and flies provided sufficient torment to keep one's mind off Indian dangers. After a back-breaking trip of sixteen hundred miles that consumed the summer months, winter camp was made among the Mandans near the great bend of the Missouri. During the frozen months, preparations for the push westward were made and when spring came not only had the party come through without loss, but a new member had appeared. Sacajawea, the Indian wife of an interpreter named Charboneau, had given birth to a baby boy.

By early April 1805 the keelboat, loaded with pelts, scientific notes, and specimens, was sent back to St. Louis with part of the crew. The main group, now thirty-two in number, set a westward course and plunged into the unexplored. Clark, who wrote that his crew was "not quite so rispictible" as those belonging to Columbus or Captain Cook, confessed that he was proud of his adventurers and called the moment of departure the happiest he had ever enjoyed. Within a few days they were at the Yellowstone, the deepest point of penetration known to fur traders. From there on, all was new. Mid-June saw them at the great falls of the Missouri, near the present Great Falls, Montana, and when their second summer closed they were beyond the Rockies, following the Snake River. They reached the Pacific at the Columbia's mouth in mid-November and there they wintered, more than three thousand miles from their point of origin. Late in March 1806 the return trip was begun over the original track, and by early summer they were once again on the eastern slopes of the Rockies. The party now divided, with Clark in command of one section and Lewis of the other. Lewis struck north, investigating the region around what is now Browning, Montana, and then headed for a rendezvous with Clark, who had meanwhile explored along the Yellowstone. After the rendezvous the expedition moved down the Missouri, reaching St. Louis at the close of September. The trip from that city had consumed two years, four months, and a few-odd days.

So daring, so courageous, was the Lewis and Clark expedition that it diverted the public view to the northern part of the new purchase. This unprecedented trek was certainly the most dramatic penetration of the Louisiana Territory but it was not the only one, nor the first to be completed. While Jefferson was making arrangements for his private secretary to travel, he also cast a speculative eye at the southern section of his new land. In 1803 he invited a scientist named William Dunbar to direct an expedition up the Red and Arkansas rivers and before the year was out wheedled $3000 from Congress to finance it. Dr. George Hunter, a Philadelphia chemist, was persuaded to join Dunbar and together they set off from Natchez in a flat-bottom boat that had been floated all the way from Pittsburgh. In October 1804, with twelve enlisted men and a Negro slave the leaders moved up the Red River to the Washita and from there to the latter's source. By December 6 they had completed their investigations and by the end of January had floated back downriver. Their report gave Americans the first authentic, scientific view of the recent acquisition's southern reaches.

Still curious about the region through which the Hunter–Dunbar expedition had moved, Jefferson resolved to learn the still obscure source of the Red River. Once again Congress produced funds, and Thomas Freeman, a scientist, was engaged to lead another party westward. Accompanied by an army captain and nineteen men, Freeman and several other civilians set off in the spring of 1805 while Lewis and Clark were still absent. After a tortuous trip of some six hundred miles up the Red River the men were met by a Spanish patrol and sent home. Although they had not moved beyond land already visited by some of the French trappers and had explored little that was not already known, they returned with the first scientific information about that part of the country.

Less than a year later Zebulon Montgomery Pike took his party in the same direction, bound for the headwaters of the Arkansas River. After investigating the Osage, a tributary of the Missouri, he pushed across a barren land he predicted "may become in time as celebrated as the sandy deserts of Africa." Through the blasts of stinging sand the men moved on until the autumn days turned flying dirt into pelting snow. On November 15, 1806, Pike sighted what he called a "small blue cloud" on the horizon. Closer inspection revealed a towering mountain, a landmark that was to bear the lieutenant's name on future maps. After having given "three cheers to the Mexican Mountains," the party continued to follow the Arkansas westward.

A few days' travel brought them to the site of Pueblo, Colorado, where a small log fort was begun. The great peak earlier sighted still enchanted the explorers and they resolved to climb it. Like many who would follow them, they now discovered the bewitching habits of western distances; rather than being part of a day's trip away, the elusive mountain retreated three days before they caught it. Then there was only disappointment. Clad in summer cottons four of the expedition, including the leaders, tried to climb the mountain, only to be turned back by icy blasts that threatened their lives.

Still awed by the unconquered peak's grandeur, Pike and his men returned to the stockade, hungry and cold. Again he turned his attention to the Arkansas River, and at the end of three days of travel reached the now-famous Royal Gorge. As he worked his way deeper into the mountains the explorer realized the task was too great for his resources, considering the time of year. Reluctantly he turned back. He next turned to the second portion of his assignment: to explore the headwaters of the Red River to the southeast of his position. Late in January he camped along what he imagined to be that stream and began construction of another stockade. A few days later, hunting near the new establishment, Pike and a companion were accosted by a Spanish dragoon. Before long the men were being questioned by the dragoon's superiors, who offered to help the lost American. At this suggestion Pike cried out, "What! Is this not the Red River?" It was not; it was the Rio Grande, and would the lieutenant not like to visit the governor at Santa Fe? This side trip resulted in more travel to the south, as Pike suspected it would. He was next taken to Chihuahua, where his documents were confiscated. By July 1807 he and his men were returned to the United States; they had been gone for a year. The "lost Pathfinder" was home.

Not long after his return Pike began preparation for publication of such private papers as he had managed to keep from the Spanish. Within three years the American public was able to read the account. The adventure story, absorbing and filled with examples of personal valor, was well received by its readers, who were pleased to learn more about the mysterious land. As the author's name became famous many other young army officers no doubt speculated upon the new means of achieving notice provided by the uncharted wastes beyond settlement. The coming years would see a number of them probing the unknown, in search of geographic knowledge and hopeful of promotion.

After the War of 1812 the government was free to renew its interest in the plains country beyond the Missouri. In 1820 an expedition headed by Major Stephen Long moved up the Platte River, following the north bank along which the Oregon-bound pioneers, the Mormons, and the Forty-Niners later would go. They found a river that was sandy-bottomed, shifty, and unfordable when at all swollen. On either side lay a rolling plain, sloping upward only fifty or a hundred feet above the water's edge. Dr. Edwin James, a botanist in the

party, called the landscape one "of hopeless and irreclaimable sterility." There were animals in the region but their presence only puzzled the scientist, who wondered what made them stay in such an
inhospitable desert. While the dull beasts would continue in their
error, surely man would not fall into it. The absence of timber itself
seemed proof enough that human habitation was unlikely.

Major Long agreed with James. The commander had failed in his
search for the Platte and Red river sources, but he brought home
some impressions about the high plains that would mightily affect
the course of American thought about the region. While Long's name
is perhaps best known today for the Colorado mountain it identifies,
it was the explorer's confirmation of the desert theory that brought
him into the public gaze during the 1820s. The "desert," as he saw
it, was unfit for cultivation and uninhabitable for an agricultural
people. It was devoid of timber, suitable only for the wild game that
it then supported or as a barrier to further westward settlement. This
latter characteristic, he suggested, was not bad. The spread of our
population would be safely checked and a minimum of contact with
the Spanish would reduce the likelihood of trouble between the two
nations.

The verdict turned in by James and Long was not well received
by an expanding, ambitious America. It ran directly counter to such
predictions as the one made by a Missourian who said that within
a decade the silks of Canton would move up the Columbia, over the·
mountains, and down the Missouri to waiting markets. Westerners
were angry when James promised that the region would forever remain the "haunt of the hunter, the bison and the jackall." Such opinions simply gave ammunition to those Easterners who were already
concerned about the population drainage westward and welcomed
arguments against such a development. Western boosters taunted
Long for not having found the river sources for which he searched
and members of his party fired back, saying they had been miserably
supplied: only six of the thirty-four horses used were government
issue.

After the Long expedition of 1820 the government suspended
exploratory operations on the plains for the time being. More than
two decades later Kit Carson would help John Frémont gain the

name *pathfinder* by probing the mountain passes and a number of
other army men would crisscross uncharted plains regions, but in
the meantime knowledge must come from private sources. During
the Twenties and Thirties fur traders familiarized themselves so thoroughly with major western travel routes that any traveler who wanted
to go out and have a look had little trouble making the round trip, so
far as geographic knowledge was concerned. Now the questions became not how to get there and back, but what was the new country
like, was it subject to settlement, and to what extent were Long and
Pike correct?

Several forces worked against the high plains country. A bad
reputation dies slowly, and the impact of the desert theory upon the
American mind was sharp enough to remain until after the Civil
War, when physical proof of the land's fertility was shown in the
establishment of successful farms. So deep was the necessity of the
tree embedded in agricultural thinking that for years farmers had
avoided grassy little prairies east of the Mississippi in favor of groves
whose blackened stumps would plague them for years in their attempts to work the land. By the time they had moved beyond the
Mississippi and looked across the Missouri, their notions were solidly
fixed. No trees, no crop.

The lack of transportation was, of course, the crowning disadvantage of the western land—but in theory it was not in all cases the
major one. The Missouri River, for example, while not so navigable
as the Ohio, also could carry crops down its muddy course to St.
Louis and beyond. But the country through which the Missouri
moved was too remote, too arid, and in its barren aspect apparently
infertile. Its native population would also prove to be more tenacious
and dangerous than that of the Upper Ohio country. Other valleys,
such as those of the Platte and Kansas, offered the same disadvantages
in addition to their rivers' lack of navigability. Regardless of rainfall
and fertility, anything but subsistence agriculture was out of the question until the coming of the railroad.

During the years that followed Major Long's report, fragments of
evidence about the plains continued to accumulate, much of it only
pricking at the desert theory. Although the traveler John K. Town-
send expressed hope that the country would be more carefully ex-

amined by naturalists who could furnish accurate information about
its resources, during the next few decades most of the knowledge
came from nontechnical observers. Jacob Fowler crossed Kansas
only a year after Long and remarked that while the country was
rolling it was "no wheare two steep for the Waggon or the plow."
Along the Arkansas he saw real hope. The land was not only well
timbered but limestone for building or fencing was also everywhere
in evidence. Beyond the river bottoms the country admittedly was
barren and forbidding, but this did not mean that the whole section
must be ignored. John D. Hunter, who had lived among the western
Indians for some time, supported this optimism. He saw no reason
why the land stretching from the Missouri to the Rockies could not
one day suprort fifty million people. Most of the country along the
lower Missouri was fertile and ready for the plow. Like others, Hunter
foresaw a population along the verdant streams and rivers, the nude
prairies beyond lying untouched until the pressure of population and
consequent rise in real estate prices finally resulted in its settlement.
The Reverend Isaac McCoy, exploring Kansas for the government at
this time, underscored the notion that the tree-lined groves had
promise and said that stories of timber scarcity were exaggerated.
He, too, foresaw a considerable population along the rivers.

Westward travel increased during the Thirties and with it grew
the volume of reports on prospects for the plains. But the advance of
time brought no real changes in opinion. Those who moved up the
Platte, the Arkansas, or any of the other western streams told of
vegetation near the water's edge and arid wastes beyond. As one
crossed the Missouri, there lay a belt of land generally conceded to
be two hundred miles across that held for the farmer an enticement.
Beyond that the rainfall was much less, the land more forbidding.
John B. Wyeth, en route to Oregon in 1832, said that over this stretch
of about six hundred miles man was deprived of two major elements:
fire and water. Not only was wood extremely scarce, but rivers like
the Platte moved toward the sea without "enlivening or fructifying
this desert." As if this were not bad enough, the Indians had a habit
of burning off the prairie, a complaint echoed by Sergeant Hugh
Evans, who explored the region with Colonel Henry Dodge.

The Reverend Samuel Parker followed Wyeth's route several years

later and was much more impressed by what he saw. The Fort Leavenworth area appeared extremely fertile and he predicted that, settled
by an industrious population, it would equal the most favored spots
on earth. Like others, Parker's enthusiasm dwindled as he progressed
up the Platte, but despite the parched landscape he foresaw agricultural possibilities along the streams and the gradual emergence of a
solid population.

Parker wondered if the tree deficiency could not be rectified by
planting. His notion of a man-made tree belt, suggested in 1835,
would be much talked about in the years to come and within the next
fifty years Congress would try unsuccessfully to legislate trees onto
the prairies by granting land to those who would plant them. A century after Parker, the New Deal would try again to follow up his
suggestion. The idea of making the desert bloom with trees was mentioned by a Swiss traveler, Dr. Wislizenus, in 1839. At least half the
great prairie land was capable of sustaining the farmer, he said, and
the lack of wood was not as great as it would seem. Properly cultivated, the land would bear trees just as had the treeless tracts back
in Illinois.

Quite in contrast to the gloomy talk of irreclaimable deserts, the
doctor wrote glowingly of the certain transformation ahead. The
westward movement, a wave of civilization, would lap at sandy plains,
rising higher and higher until it reached the Rockies, inundating the
buffalo, the antelope, and the tribes. Philosophizing on the future of
the white man in this virgin land, Dr. Wislizenus predicted quite accu-
rately that he would "ransack the bowels of the mountains" for
metals, whose presence would ignite the fires of strife, envy, and
"all ignoble passions" until the newcomers would be no happier than
the red brethren who had perished that the white man might live.
Nothing could stop the momentum of westward development. The
existence of wealth in the region, whether beaver or gold, was a magnet of such power that not even hostile Indians, poor transportation,
ignorance of geography, hunger or thirst would deter the enterprising
Americans. Mere lack of trees or infertility of land would constitute
a problem, not a barrier, to these people. So effectively would they
solve it decade by decade that within a hundred years tales of western
life then current would sound like fairy stories.

But that was in the realm of speculation and in all probability Wislizenus was called a dreamer. The high plains, as viewed by the average visitor, did not inspire roseate predictions in even the most optimistic of Americans. The views of Thomas J. Farnham, an ailing young Vermont lawyer who saw the country the same year Wislizenus did, gave what was perhaps a much more typical report. As he headed west, bravely bearing a little flag made by his wife inscribed *Oregon or the Grave,* the attorney crossed what he called "the Great Prairie Wilderness." For two hundred miles beyond the Mississippi the land was rich and alluvial but the next five hundred miles unfolded to him the expected treeless reaches, barren and unpromising, "usually called 'the Great American Desert.' "

The curse of desert seemed permanently fixed upon eastern Colorado and the western sections of Kansas, Nebraska, Oklahoma, and Texas. It would take a good part of the nineteenth century to dispel it. Jefferson had earlier wondered about the value of the southern plains; Pike and Long confirmed his suspicions of its aridity, and for more than half a century the judgment stood. In the Woodbridge and Willard geography of 1824 the notion was perpetuated and in Carey and Lee's atlas of 1827 the Great American Desert was described. Mitchell in his *Accompaniment to Reference and Distance Map* (1835) compared our desert to the Sahara and the same year Hugh Evans, who was on the scene, told how the winds were almost a "hiricane," the sand nearly stifling the men and horses. He too thought of Africa. The *Bradford Atlas* of 1838 and Washington Irving's *Astoria* both made mention of the region's irreclaimability and Greenhowe's *History of Oregon* (1845) underscored the theme.

While government explorers and individual travelers probed the shallow waterways of the great desert, anxious to learn something of the region's economic value, others investigated the great serpentine bow of the Missouri, whose source lay hidden deep in the Rockies. The report of Lewis and Clark excited not only fur trappers, anxious to denude the great river drainage of its peltries, but also men of science, travelers, and the bolder sportsmen. Best known of the earlier visitors were Henry M. Brackenridge and the English botanist,

John Bradbury. In 1811 both were up the Missouri as far as the Mandan villages. Brackenridge, who accompanied the fur trader Manuel Lisa, called the Upper Missouri country a hunter's paradise, a foreign land, another world. Though he was entranced by the magnificent sweeps of country, so limitless that it frightened him and raised the thought that he might never get back to civilization, he saw little chance of settlement. In time settlers might come, but the day seemed distant. This area was too remote, too far removed from communication with the world, to offer any economic attractions. Compared to other parts of America the land was ill served by adequate waterways and devoid of such a necessary resource as timber. Some day Americans might graze their flocks on the grassy plains but never, said the observer, would they turn over the sod. Markets for agricultural goods were too far away. So unpromising a land was it that another century would pass before the Indian would be molested.

John Bradbury, who joined Brackenridge on the return downriver, was more optimistic. He envisaged settlements edging forward, locating along the woody regions near rivers, establishing communities of grazers and perhaps farmers. The botanist admitted that among Americans there was a question whether this forbidding country could be peopled. He recognized that they possessed a mental block, believing that they must have an adequate supply of timber for fuel, building, and fencing, but he correctly predicted that the presence of timber would not be such a necessity as many then imagined. He disagreed with Peter Tabeau, who in 1802 had accompanied Regis Loisel, the fur trader, upriver, when he maintained that the absence of wood alone would pose the insuperable obstacle to settlement. Like many people of his time, Tabeau thought that where no trees grew the soil was inferior. Men like Tabeau and Brackenridge could issue their gloomy predictions; Bradbury chose to dissent. "My own opinion is, that it can be cultivated; in the process of time, it will not only be peopled and cultivated, but that it will be one of the most beautiful countries in the world."

During the spring of 1833 the Upper Missouri received its most distinguished visitor to date, one whose observations would be quoted again and again. The young man, Alexander Philip Maximilian, Prince of Wied-Neuwied, turned up at St. Louis with the announced intention of seeing the plains. Major Benjamin O'Fallon, a nephew of William Clark, persuaded the German prince to enter hostile country by the relatively safe means of a river steamer, and so on its third trip up the river the steamer *Yellowstone* carried a newcomer whose interest in the country was exceeded only by the crew's curiosity about its passenger. At Fort Pierre his party transferred to the *Assiniboine,* a vessel of lighter draft, and beyond Fort Union the means of travel was keelboat. Before the prince turned back, he had gone all the way to the Marias River, deep in the heart of Blackfoot country, a trip not without its dangers from both natural hazards and a thoroughly dangerous tribe of Indians.

Along the lower reaches of the river Maximilian saw timber, grass, and what seemed to be fertile soil. Above the site of modern Omaha the character of the country changed; there were fewer trees and these were somewhat dwarfed. At Fort Union he was told that attempts to raise vegetables had been defeated by drought and high winds. Climatically, the country seemed desirable. Despite the extremities in temperature, people were healthy—thanks in part, he decided, to the fine drinking water. But as others had done before him and would do again, Maximilian voted *no* on the region as a farming country. Aridity and the lack of wood stood between settlers and the realization of an agricultural community. Men of the American Fur Company generally agreed with this, though—as the prince admitted—"Bradbury thinks differently."

But Bradbury was outvoted. Scientists were entitled to their opinions about such theoretical questions as whether the land could be cultivated, but Americans in general failed to see how it would have any practical result. Until well into the latter half of the nineteenth century both the majority and official opinion was that a large section of the Louisiana Purchase would prove to be of extremely limited agricultural value to the nation. Like the earliest colonists from Europe, men looked for more superficial and obvious kinds of wealth, unwilling to consider the slower means of extraction found in the plow. Nor was the small farmer, nestled down in a tree area, attracted by the rolling brown sea of sod to the west. He was willing to regard the great purchase as a national pasture, a home for wild Indians, a back-country preserve.

Time and the pressure of the frontier movement changed the picture. Americans on the move, a restless people drawn on relentlessly by an unexplained and hidden magnet, edged toward the unclaimed regions—ignoring all warning flags thrown up by those who called the land a desert. Traditionally frontiersmen had failed to read official pronouncements, and frequently they disregarded majority opinion. Dr. Wislizenus was right: the pressure of the westward advance might be detoured momentarily by deserts, but it would not be halted. Within a few years the wash of population would lap at the desert's edges, filter into mountain valleys, and ascend the slopes of the mountain chain. Nothing could stop it, not scientific advice, not the warnings of the disappointed who had experimented with plains living, not even the threat of physical violence from the Indians. So persistent was the frontier movement that the American people, schooled in a deep belief that something better must lie just beyond, were destined to search the high plains convinced that some sort of treasure must be found—because it was West.

Chapter 2

TRAPS
AND
TRINKETS

The expedition of Lewis and Clark held great significance for scientists, planners of national destiny, and the more ordinary residents of a lusty young nation on the make. To most of these people the rich experience of the two captains was viewed in long-range terms, as a satisfying body of knowledge that would be useful in the years to come, something to be studied and considered. But to a group of sharp-eyed fur traders around St. Louis, the return of the expedition meant confirmation of earlier reports about four-legged wealth up-river. The beaver pelt, "plew" as they called it, had the virtue of being relatively small and light, high in value, and available in quantity throughout the plains and mountains. These facts stood out as sharply as the cry of *Gold!* in later years, and promised a reward that in its brilliance blotted out distance, danger, and death. The fur traders were the first to respond to the challenge laid down by the reports of Lewis and Clark. Back up the river they went, retracing the explorers' steps, searching out the land for pelts. And with them went the spirit of discovery and exploitation.

For nearly forty years the advance guard of American civilization probed the western watercourses, crossing divides, seeking out new and undiscovered beaver villages—and in the process gaining a working knowledge of geography that others were to write about later. Like that of most frontiers, the day of the fur trader was short and spectacular. It may be said to have lasted from the time of Lewis and Clark's return in 1806 to the establishment of Jim Bridger's post out along Wyoming's Green River in 1843. "Old Gabe," as his contemporaries called him, may not have known that his trading house erected a monument to a colorful chapter in the western pageant, but the fact that its purpose was to supply passing emigrants suggested that a new day had come.

In four fast and furious decades the trapper stripped the land of its rich furs and surrendered its illimitable acres to others only when scarcity of product and the whims of fashion that outmoded beaver hats called a halt. Within this span of years the American public studied the plains from afar, still puzzled as to their worth, and expressed pleasure that Jefferson's real estate deal was able to earn a penny here and there to justify its keep. By the time contemplation was set aside for action and pioneers groped their way toward Oregon, the spaces that once mystified the Spaniards were well known to Americans. In the years to come explorers would go out to make maps, to write of the flora and the fauna, but as to actual discovery they could do little. The trapper already had been there.

The speed with which fur hunters penetrated the midcontinent and bared its secrets might suggest that the accomplishment was less difficult than the Spaniards had imagined. On the contrary, the assault was bloody and filled with crushing setbacks. It was a story of upset vessels, water-damaged furs, attacks by hostile Indians, heavy losses of supplies, bankruptcies, failures—and renewed attempts. Courage, occasional rich hauls in pelts, and an ability generally to get along with the Indians of both sexes provided the necessary drive to propel the fur brigade forward.

The experiences of Manuel Lisa amply portray the difficulties of those who decided to get rich in the beaver trade. In August 1808, after a year in the Yellowstone country, Lisa returned to St. Louis filled with information and desirous of support for an extended stay in the trapping regions. Men whose names were to be synonymous with fur trading came forward with capital of forty thousand dollars. Pierre and Auguste Chouteau, Reuben Lewis (Meriwether's brother), William Clark, Andrew Henry, and others formed a corporation known as the St. Louis Missouri Fur Company which by the spring of 1810 had plunged clear to the Three Forks of the Missouri, deep in dangerous Blackfoot country.

Then came retreat. In a matter of weeks the post was abandoned; the company fell back to the mouth of the Bighorn. Shortly this little bastion was also crossed off and a stand was made at Cedar Island in what is today South Dakota. When stores gathered here were burned, the descent downriver continued. Meanwhile Andrew Henry returned from a tour beyond the mountains with only forty packs of beaver pelts. Thomas James, one of the company's men, was dismayed to learn upon his return that he was three hundred dollars in debt. The firm had charged him six dollars a pound for powder, three for lead, and six for coarse calico shirts. After the sale of his furs, he still owed money, a situation he angrily called "a piece of extortion, fraud and swindling." Contained in the region below the Mandan villages, denied the rich fur-bearing country, and castigated by its employees, the Missouri Company was obliged to reorganize and try again.

New names appeared on the roster—Joshua Pilcher, Andrew Drips, and Robert Jones. After Lisa died in 1820, Pilcher launched a fresh attack upon the fur country, establishing another post at the mouth of the Bighorn, only to suffer a crushing defeat at the hands of the Indians and an ignominious retreat southward. The blow proved to be disastrous for the enterprising company, and characterized a general decline in the fur trade. The first decade, between the time of Lisa's reverse and the defeat of Pilcher, was a marked failure.

The second major attempt to open the Upper Missouri country began with the appearance in the St. Louis *Missouri Republican* for March 20, 1822, of a now-famous advertisement calling for 100 enterprising young men to join an expedition being organized for the fur trade. It revealed that General William H. Ashley, a forty-four-year-old Virginian who was then lieutenant-governor of Missouri, and

Andrew Henry, of the disrupted Missouri Fur Company, had decided upon a new approach to the trade. Instead of offering the natives bright trinkets for their wares, white men would do the trapping
and turn over the fruits of their efforts to authorized agents at speci-
fied rendezvous. The plan eliminated the need for forts, to which the
Indians might come to trade, or to attack, as well as the attendant
expense of construction and maintenance. It also lent a mobility
necessary to follow the furs.

The advertisement of the Ashley–Henry outfit, later to be known
as the Rocky Mountain Fur Company, produced a hearty response.
Niles Weekly Register reported that one hundred eighty adventurers
left St. Charles, Missouri, in April, bound for the Rocky Mountains.
"They are described to be of vigorous and masculine appearance, well
armed and prepared for a three years' tour through this almost unknown and savage country." The editor approved of such young
men, chiding the effeminate sons who chose to stay at home, and he
predicted a profitable trip for those who had signed on. Among the
aspirants for fame and fortune far up the enigmatic Missouri were
names soon to become legendary: Thomas Fitzpatrick, Jim Bridger,
Etienne Provot, and Jedediah Smith. That their journey would be
filled with adversity became apparent almost as soon as it commenced. Of the two keelboats that carried men and supplies, one
failed to get even so far as Fort Osage in the present state of Missouri.
The snag-filled, turbulent river snatched the heavily laden *Enterprize* and in a matter of seconds swallowed a cargo worth ten thousand dollars. Ashley's venture was in the red before a single pelt had
been obtained. The trader was equal to the occasion. He acted with
the courage and the dispatch that predicted ultimate success for his
kind: within eighteen days a new boat and an additional forty-six
men were on their way to replace the loss. By summer a fort, to be
used as a base of operations rather than a trading post, was established at the mouth of the Yellowstone.

The keelboats used by Ashley were larger than those normally
employed. Over a hundred feet in length, they carried an eighty-foot
cargo box that stood more than six feet above the deck, yet the
vessels drew only three feet of water. On either side of the box ran
narrow catwalks to accommodate the polemen who walked along

the vessel's edge, shoving it against the current. Forward of the cabin was a single mast, supporting a square sail that found occasional welcome use. But in the main, propulsion came from pushing or pulling. The latter method, known as cordelling, employed a long rope that was fixed upon the bank ahead and, the bow quartered against the current, obliged the river itself to force the vessel upstream. Sometimes, when the banks were sufficiently free of brush and trees, the cordelle was used to drag the keelboat along, the sailors momentarily acting as towhorses. Whatever the method, it was back-breaking, agonizing labor for which only the hardiest were suited.

Willingness to brave both the elements and hostile tribes paid off. In October Ashley's men came back downriver with cargoes of furs worth twenty-four thousand dollars, a piece of news that was promptly spread across St. Louis newspapers. Encouraged by success, the general once more advertised for recruits and again whipcord-tough young men responded. Among them were men like David E. Jackson, William Sublette (one of five famous brothers), and Jim Clyman—more names soon to be entered upon the rolls as famous fur trappers. Clyman, who was charged with the task of scouring the brothels and grog shops for employees, gathered a collection of hardies in comparison with whom, he said, Falstaff's battalion was genteel.

On this trip, the Indians struck first, but the river was also to have its price. At the Arikara villages thirteen men gave their lives and a dozen more were wounded. Ashley turned back, carrying his wounded out of hostile country on the keelboat *Yellowstone Packet*. At Fort Atkinson, near Council Bluffs, he found Colonel Henry Leavenworth, who listened to his story and promised help. Six companies of the Sixth Infantry at once started for the site of the Ree attack. Leavenworth's naval auxiliary comprised three keelboats, among them the *Yellowstone Packet;* before the group had gone more than one hundred fifty miles the river snags pierced one of the boats, sinking it. Most of the arms and supplies were lost, but quick-thinking river men saved all the whiskey. The expedition pushed on.

The ensuing campaign did little to inspire confidence among the traders. In a strange alliance with the Sioux, who were extremely

anxious to strike their mortal enemies, Leavenworth tried to reduce
the Ree fortifications by siege. It was a bad plan. The Sioux, unused
to such warfare, became discouraged and disappeared after paying
their respects to the Army by stealing some of its horses. Meanwhile,
the troops were unable to dislodge the Rees. Leavenworth, failing by
military methods, tried diplomacy. After lengthy and inconclusive
pipe-smoking with enemy representatives, he decided to go home. As
the troops packed up, happy to be leaving such a godforsaken country, they were subjected to a torrent of verbal abuse from the fur
traders. If they heard their commander charged with imbecility and
incompetence, they must have suppressed their grins. Leavenworth, to
whom it was directed, stubbornly set his course south and returned
to Fort Atkinson's parade ground. Unhappily, it would be a long
time before he would hear the last of his fiasco. No one would have to
remind him that the Army's first major campaign west of the Missouri
had been a signal failure.

   The hostility of the Blackfeet, Sioux, and Arikara along the upper
reaches of the Missouri kept the Rocky Mountain Fur Company, as
well as bands of independent trappers, at bay. As their ally, the
mischievous Missouri snapped at frail keelboat hulls, dragging thousands of dollars worth of supplies to its muddy, uncertain bottom.
The American government, despite the bellowings of oratorical
sponsors for the West, did little about fending off the fur hunters'
enemies. Talk of improving the Missouri and punishing the tribes
died aborning. Colonel Leavenworth's brief experiment with Indian
campaigning closely coincided with abandonment of government
trading with the natives through its official agents or "factors." From
this time on the Great White Father at Washington demonstrated a
reluctance to assist the fur-trading business by supplying soldiers as
protectors. He, also, indicated an early faith in private enterprise in
his willingness to turn the whole business over to individuals who
could take their own chances.
   With the conclusion of the comic Arikara "war," the participants
went their respective ways. General Ashley followed Leavenworth
downriver, bound for St. Louis and a new study of the fur business.

Major Henry packed up the supplies Ashley had delivered and struck off by land for the Yellowstone post where he would suffer further harassment from Indians. The Arikara, defiant and filled with new courage over their test of arms with the white man, once again took up their positions athwart the Missouri River. As far as the Rocky Mountain Fur Company was concerned, the Indians' ferocity and the Army's lack of forcefulness dictated a further modification in methods of fur trading. From now on the river would be abandoned in favor of the horse. Another dimension of mobility had been added.

By its bumbling, Leavenworth's command perhaps contributed more to discovery and exploration on the American high plains than if it had crushed a dozen Indian tribes along the Missouri. Failure to open the river drove the trappers out into the open stretches and from their travels came a sharply increased knowledge of the western terrain. Among Henry's band were men whose names soon would be synonymous with exploration. Edward Rose, its guide and interpreter, had studied the face of the plains back in 1811 with Wilson P. Hunt and the Astorians on their way west. Louis Vasquez, Jim Bridger, and Jedediah Smith now commenced their probings of the buckled, tan sod that sloped up toward the granite barricades of the Rockies. Their findings would allow map-makers to print names of new locations on blank stretches of country. Famous South Pass, whose discovery is claimed for several trappers by various authors, was about to present its extremely flat V as a sight across which American emigrants would aim their westbound wagon trains. Names of rivers such as the Green quickly became accepted terms, handed on to novice emigrants by trappers whose knowledge of western geography was an everyday working tool. The Bighorn, Musselshell, and Upper Yellowstone, later to enter the frontier picture more prominently, would for the moment be reserved to these explorer–trappers as their preserve.

The usual story of the fur traders as the advance guard of civilization is one of intrepid, plains-wise men, who lived in daily danger of their lives, seeking out new locations of wealth, pointing the way for subsequent settlement. True, they were the principal characters, and their names would one day dot the land, but it was a stolid, un-romantic investor who sat in a New York office speaking broken English and shrewdly calculating the financial risks, who put his money on the line and propelled the great movement into the deepest re-cesses of the American West. His very appearance on the scene caused organizations like the Missouri Fur Company and the Ashley–Henry outfit to spread out, seeking better trapping sites for richer furs with which to fight the newcomer. As a result of the pressure, these trappers, as well as countless independents, scattered over the West and discovered every important landmark known today. Far from being a plainsman, a Westerner, or even a former military man, the projector of this new corporate fur extraction was a financier named John Jacob Astor. His weapon was the American Fur Com-pany.

The American Fur Company, incorporated in New York in 1808, was said to be little more than a fiction, designed merely to broaden Astor's fur-trading operations. Its capital, which amounted to the then-impressive figure of a million dollars, was subscribed entirely by himself. After the War of 1812 and British pressure squeezed him out of his trading empire in the Pacific Northwest, the German-born merchant cast his eye upon the Upper Missouri country. After a shrewd appraisal of its economic potential, he unrolled a string of posts clear out to the end of the long and twisting waterway. Carefully he cleared the way by first sending a scouting party of lobbyists in to Congress to press for the abandonment of government trading posts in favor of private enterprise. During the winter of 1821–1822, with the aid of Senator Benton of Missouri, the legislative mission was accomplished. Astor was now ready to begin operations, opposed only by other privately supported competitors.

Astor also furnished an early example of despised "eastern money" taking its chance with nature's resources in an untouched land, crushing smaller bettors, molding an economic empire out of raw materials. This pattern, once fixed, would characterize the develop-ment of the West, with such colorful fixtures as the stagecoach, the river steamer, and the bright railroad locomotive representing little more than the outward evidences of forces that lay beneath the sur-

face. Hated, cursed, feared, fought at every turn, Astor inexorably
fixed his grip upon the American interior and one by one his enemies
were forced to the wall. General Ashley was one of the few to come
out of the fight with any money. After he had made a fortune, he
wisely retired and took up the gentlemanly game of politics. The
Missouri Fur Company finally surrendered the river to its competitors; Bernard Pratte and Company was swallowed by the monster
American Fur Company. During the summer of 1827 the Columbia
Fur Company, another dangerous rival whose competition re-
portedly cost the Astor interests ten thousand dollars worth of injury
annually, was absorbed by the growing giant. Out of the new territory, high along the river, arose the American Fur Company's important subsidiary, the Upper Missouri Outfit. At once the letters UMO
became important in the trade, signifying the advance deep into the
Rockies of a powerful and relentless force.

Astor ruled his enterprise with a firm hand, directing its moves,
fighting off all enemies. One of his biographers freely admits that
"Never in the economic history of this country has a corporation
marched more ruthlessly across the prostrate corpses of opponents
to attainment of monopoly." Those who contested the field were
known simply as "the Opposition," and the personnel of the opposing
camp shifted continually as new gladiators came on the field to replace the fallen. Ashley and Henry carried the banner of defiance
until 1826, when Ashley decided to rake in his chips and get out of
the game while he was ahead. Jedediah Smith, David E. Jackson,
and William Sublette, three experienced and able fur traders, stepped
forward to carry the colors under the firm name of Smith, Jackson
and Sublette. Four years later, tired of struggling against the American
Fur Company, the trio sold out to Jim Bridger, Milton Sublette, Tom
Fitzpatrick, Jean Gervais, and Henry Fraeb, who now formed the
Rocky Mountain Fur Company. The new proprietors represented the
hardiest, most skillful, and most daring of the independent trappers.
Their union, pledged at the annual gathering of the clan, or rendezvous, of 1830, represented the sharpest challenge offered Astor, for
these men were highly respected members of the fur fraternity. From
now on the fight would be one of epic proportions with no holds

barred. With the beaver market at its peak and the number of trappers in the field at a maximum, the race for supremacy would be conducted with craftiness, treachery, and violence on both sides.

Economic warfare is expensive. Competition winnows out the weak and yields riches to the strong, but the wreckage it leaves behind adds a figure to the cost not always reckoned. When the Rocky Mountain Fur Company threw down the gauntlet, Astor redoubled his efforts with both vigor and ruthlessness. To him the land beyond the Missouri was a resource to be tapped; it was endless; it was worthless except for pelts; its value could be equated only in terms of ledger balances in a New York office. So orders went out to his lieutenants, Pierre Chouteau, Jr., and Ramsay Crooks, to push on their men, to drive the opposition beyond the mountains and off the fur map.

To gain an advantage the company converted an old adage into "fight firewater with firewater" on the theory that he who distributes the most whiskey holds the top hand. If the free traders could use alcohol to dissolve the Indians' will power in barter, so could the American Fur Company. So successful was it that in 1831 the Secretary of War would be informed that the company had made fifty thousand dollars in a single year at only one of its Missouri River posts. Diluted in proportions from four to one upwards, the "Indian whiskey" brought between twenty-five and fifty dollars a gallon in trade. The effect upon the natives was devastating. More detrimental than the white man's other contributions of smallpox and syphilis, alcohol not only destroyed those who used it, but inflamed them to a point where murder was an everyday event.

In 1832 the government stepped in to halt the carnage and forbade the further distribution of liquor among the Indians. At once the Hudson's Bay Company, across the international line, renewed its use of liquor as a lure to capture the American trade. The expected result was an open flouting of the law in this country and an unabated flow of whiskey into Indian country. When federal officials managed to check the flow of bootleg whiskey from time to time, more remote trading posts became veritable distilleries, turning out quantities of low-grade "forty rod" for distribution.

Prohibition in Indian country was no more effective than the national experiment in the next century. The Indians craved liquor and white men would furnish it, despite all preventive measures taken by the government. Nothing else worked so well in lubricating business transactions with the natives; it warped their sense of values and made short-weighting easy. That they would readily go in debt for drink was demonstrated by witnesses who told a Senate Committee of debts amounting to sixty thousand dollars incurred by some of the tribes to the American Fur Company. For alcohol the Indians sold their furs, their wives, and their souls. Traders, individual or organized, knew this.

Astor was willing to go further than bootlegging whiskey to the Indians. A latecomer to the treasure hunt in the Rockies, he sought to overcome this disadvantage by dispatching into the country spies who would learn from competitors the best trapping locations. Agents like W. H. Vanderburgh, Andrew Drips, and Lucien Fontenelle, familiar names in fur-trading history, followed Rocky Mountain Fur Company trappers relentlessly. Desperately Fraeb and Fitzpatrick tried to elude them by forced marches and succeeded only after some man-killing days on the trail. But no matter where they went, men of the Opposition encountered American Fur Company agents whose tenacity was to be rivaled only by the future Royal Canadian Mounted Police, who reputedly always got their man. In a final act of frustration Fitzpatrick and Bridger lured Vanderburgh and Drips deep into Blackfoot country, where Vanderburgh was killed by the Indians. Bridger, wounded in the affray, barely made his escape.

The company, ever willing to fight, struck back. Thomas Fitzpatrick, livid with rage, charged that he had been robbed of all he possessed in the fall of 1833 by Crow Indians inspired to the treachery by Astor's men. After both the Crows and company officials confessed, Kenneth McKenzie, in charge of Fort Union, piously offered to pay for the furs, now in his possession, at the same rate any Indian would receive for pelts. With insult piled upon injury, Rocky Mountain Fur Company men resolved to retaliate by any means at their disposal. Shortly, their associate Nathaniel J. Wyeth, on a friendly visit to Fort Union, discovered McKenzie's whiskey still and conscientiously reported the violation to authorities at Fort Leavenworth. It took Senator Thomas Hart Benton of Missouri and others of Astor's powerful friends in Congress to hush up the matter.

By the summer of 1834, the Rocky Mountain Fur Company had had enough. At the annual rendezvous Fraeb and Gervais sold out, leaving Fitzpatrick, Milton Sublette, and Bridger. Within a year the trio signed on with the American Fur Company and the Opposition passed into history. It was only twelve years since Ashley had made his bold move into Indian country, a very short life in the business world, but in a little over a decade his fur traders had opened up a major portion of the West to further exploitation. A leading historian of the fur trade estimated that in that brief time approximately five hundred thousand dollars worth of pelts were returned to St. Louis, with General Ashley and William Sublette getting a lion's share. By any token the small company had done well.

By a judicious application of capital, steam-roller methods, the buying out of any opposition that reared its head, and the use of influence in government circles when and where necessary, John Jacob Astor had spread his fur empire to the limits of the Missouri River and across the central plains to the Rockies. Before he was ready to turn elsewhere, Astor gave Westerners a lesson in successful financial management. Placing the entire responsibility upon the backs of his trappers, he merely furnished them with supplies as an advance against their expenses and then bought their furs upon delivery. It was up to the trader to find the furs, trade for them, and get them to the company's nearest outpost. As one of his biographers concedes, none of Astor's subordinates (with the exception of Crooks, Chouteau, and Pratte) made any amount of money in the fur-trade business. The major part of the profits went to Astor and his son. Pressed for a figure representing the firm's business, son William wrote to the Secretary of War in 1831: "You may estimate our annual returns as half a million dollars." It is estimated that in the decade following 1823 the firm declared dividends of over a million dollars and during his seventeen years as head of the firm Astor made between one and two million dollars. Quietly the financier proceeded, throwing upon others the risks, forcing competitors to spread out in search of new wealth that he might follow and share with them. With his heavy financial artillery he assured himself of superiority in the field.

Astor left his mark upon the West. He founded an impressive string of posts along the Missouri, establishments that sometimes became military posts and, in later years, cities. The pivotal point was Fort Union, first called Fort Floyd, built at the junction of the Yellowstone and Missouri rivers in the fall of 1828; Kenneth McKenzie, widely known as "the King of the Upper Missouri," resided in near-regal splendor at this outer rampart of the company and from it ruled the country lying to the west. When Fort William was erected near Union and operated in competition by William Sublette, Astor once again put his money on the line and bought out the interloper. This much disappointed McKenzie, who wanted for himself the pleasure of breaking anyone who had the temerity to enter his employer's domain.

West of Fort Union, deep in Blackfoot country, stood Fort McKenzie, at the mouth of the Marias River. Up the Yellowstone, at the junction of the Bighorn, stood Fort Cass. With Fort Union, they formed a triangle covering an inland empire over which the Upper Missouri Outfit made its influence felt. "In this manner the Fur Company continues to advance, and firmly establishes itself among nations that are but little known, where the fur trade is still profitable," wrote Prince Maximilian in admiration. As the royal visitor pointed out, the lower reaches of the river no longer abounded in beaver; expansion was a necessity.

South of Union lay Fort Pierre, named for Pierre Chouteau. Thirteen hundred miles above St. Louis, it commanded a vast stretch of land in the heart of Sioux country. George Catlin, who visited the place in 1832, the year of its construction, called it the company's most productive post. Hundreds of miles west of Fort Pierre, tapping another vast section of the Rockies, was Fort Laramie. Built in 1834, it was later purchased by the American Fur Company. Francis Parkman, who visited there in 1846, reacted angrily to the company's monopolistic prices and said that it was "exceedingly disliked in this country—it suppresses all opposition." Letters of introduction, furnished him by Ramsay Crooks and Pierre Chouteau, Jr., did not soften the young historian's feelings about paying a dollar and a half for five cents worth of tobacco. Like many a later entrepreneur, the corporation blandly listened to these and other complaints—and went right on bleeding the customers. When the day of the beaver had passed the firm would sell out to the government (in 1849) and Laramie's name would stand as one of the major military posts of the West.

During the early 1830s Kenneth McKenzie steadily worked at improving the situation for his company in the Upper Missouri country and quite decidedly earned his sobriquet of king. Not only did he successfully outbid the Hudson's Bay Company, whose agents dangled ever-increasing rewards before the Indians' eyes; it was McKenzie who originated steamboat traffic in what is now the Dakotas and Montana. This had an enormous effect upon subsequent American expansion and exploitation of the northern high plains.

As early as 1819 the *Western Engineer,* a strange craft which had a serpentine-shaped bow and belched forth black smoke, had reached Council Bluffs. It was the "flagship" of Major Stephen Long's flotilla and its design was aimed at impressing the natives, which it no doubt did. Council Bluffs was only a steppingstone to the land beyond and in 1830 McKenzie convinced his superiors that not only was steamboat travel to the Yellowstone possible but that it would also be tremendously important to the fur trade. Those who considered his request could view the backdrop of disastrous experiences that keelboats had suffered, and, while the Missouri promised to be no more friendly to larger craft, they did have the advantage of size and speed.

Pierre Chouteau, representing management at St. Louis, approved McKenzie's plan and sent it along to the front office in New York. Certainly, said Chouteau, a suitable vessel could be constructed for about seven thousand dollars and it ought to return its investment rapidly. Accordingly, orders went out to a shipyard at Louisville and in the spring of 1831 the *Yellowstone* appeared at St. Louis, ready to transport trading goods to Fort Union. While the vessel was able to get no farther than the site of the future Fort Pierre, due to low water, it had accomplished an ascent of thirteen hundred miles from St. Louis. Nor were its owners disappointed, for it returned laden with buffalo robes, beaver pelts, and other furs as well as ten thousand pounds of buffalo tongues. It was enough to convince Chouteau that his support of McKenzie had been wise.

By the next year the little steamer met the river after which it was named; its arrival at Fort Union demonstrated the feasibility of steamboat navigation far into the prairie country. Its progress was slow, nearly three months to ascend the river, but the important fact was that it arrived. Merely one hundred thirty feet long, with a beam of nineteen feet, the vessel had a hold only six feet deep. A single engine propelled its side-wheel paddles and when the machinery broke down crewmen were obliged to pole the craft forward. Downriver the going was much better; the *Yellowstone* made as much as a hundred miles a day heading for home port.

Congratulations were in order. Ramsay Crooks predicted to Chouteau that the Missouri's future historians would accord him a place of distinction for having conquered an apparently unnavigable river. Astor, too, was pleased. From Bellevue, France, he told Chouteau how all Europe was impressed by the feat. The plains Indians agreed that such an innovation was indeed impressive and some of them stated that the British were now quite out of the trading picture, having no chance against men who could produce a fireboat that walked on the water. No one seems to have dispatched congratulatory messages to Kenneth McKenzie. Probably he did not mind. He was deeply engrossed in planning his next step, a scheme for the striking of medals for the Indians in order to steal the thunder of the British, who had used this device for some time. He was so successful that the Washington officials ordered the practice discontinued. The Indians were getting the idea Astor was king!

Paramount among Astor's remarkable qualities was the intuitive knowledge of the proper time to quit. In 1834 he sold out to Ramsay Crooks, Pierre Chouteau, Jr., and Bernard Pratte, believing that the end of profitable fur trading was in sight. About that time he wrote from London: "I very much fear beaver will not sell very soon unless very fine. It appears that they make hats of silk in place of beaver."

Shrewdly he saw the handwriting on the wall; it was time to give up the game. Let his successors find out about silk—the hard way.

The decade following 1834 was little more than an afterglow, a time of dying for the once-great quest of the beaver's pelt. With its more colorful characters dispersed and their organizations dissolved, the Opposition gave only fitful struggles against the giant now managed by Pratte, Chouteau, and Company. Grimly the contestants stayed in the field, none of them profiting satisfactorily, none of them willing to leave while others remained. Sublette and Campbell, supported by General Ashley (who was now in Congress), carried the opposition banner, but the former ferocity with which it once waved was no more. By 1842 Bill Sublette decided to follow Ashley's course and enter politics, only to meet failure and a quiet death in bed. Meanwhile, Campbell continued a rather uneventful career at trading.

Finally, after the Upper Missouri Outfit applied the well-known treatment of paying four times the going rate for furs, the most recent opposition followed the pattern set by its predecessors and sold out to the American Fur Company. By now the company had set aside its slogan *ecrassez toute opposition,* no longer afraid of its weakened and dispersed competitors, and rather reluctantly it stayed in the field to mop up what little was left.

Occasional flashes on the scene of battle recalled earlier days of free-for-all fighting. Mysteriously, the American Fur Company urged the re-establishment of the office of Indian agent for the Upper Missouri tribes. When one of its trusted employees, Andrew Drips, got the job and then righteously insisted upon the strict enforcement of prohibition among the Indians in order to strike out at the small traders who used the liquid weapon freely, it was clear that the monopoly was still in the field and had not forgotten earlier training. Ironically, the contest was fought no longer for a rich prize but for a dwindling treasure chest that would yield to the winner only disappointment. The average annual value of furs brought into St. Louis before the Civil War, from both the Missouri and Mississippi valleys, is estimated at from two to three hundred thousand dollars.

However, not far to the west one of the most famous of the mountain men hung up his traps in favor of a new bonanza—the emigrant trade. Jim Bridger—Old Gabe, not yet forty—came out of St. Louis in 1843, laden with goods for the new enterprise and on Black's Fork of the Green River in Wyoming erected the fort that carried his name. As he made ready for the travel season he observed that the emigrants "are generally well supplied with money," and by the time they pulled up along the Green, Jim would have his new traps set. Should they need blacksmith work, horses, or supplies, he would oblige, for money—"cash from the states," as he put it. He was probably surprised to see Jim Clyman, a senior member of the trapping fraternity, turn up in a wagon train, also headed west. But, as Clyman remarked of his former profession, "that once numerous class of adventurers are now reduced to less than thirty men."

With the passing of the mountain men's heyday an economic calm settled over Mr. Jefferson's real estate bargain. It did not mean that overnight furs ceased to flow into St. Louis or that the last dose of pungent castor had been applied to a trap. The investment in outposts, trading stock, and even steamboats was too great for an organization like the American Fur Company to abandon until the last drop of profit had been wrung from the region. As in the later gold-rush days, independent trappers continued to comb the land, if in diminishing numbers, certain that there must remain one last hidden strike that would recoup past losses and yield the ultimate fortune. Economic enterprises, especially those in which large sums of money have been invested, often die a slow and agonizing death, fighting the day of reckoning with every remaining ounce of energy. It took the beaver-pelt industry of the Upper Missouri twenty years to learn that it was dead.

Meanwhile, in the two decades that preceded the outbreak of the Civil War, so far as the general public was concerned the high plains and Rockies lapsed back into a condition of economic worthlessness. Mississippi Valley farmers eyed the high plains with suspicion during the Forties and Fifties, completely uninterested in advancing into the barren, parched country where there was no transportation to carry away their products. Only resources of high value and small weight could attract men into the area, and with the passing of the beaver trade no substitute appeared. Not until just before the war were mineral discoveries made. And not until after that conflict did the cattle-raising business emerge. Before that era the reputation of the midcontinent remained unchanged. It was a desert. A place to be crossed. A barrier between civilization and the green hills of Oregon or the yellow-specked California stream beds.

Chapter 3   THE
WAY
WEST

The migration across the desert regions of America, through the mountain passes, and on to the Pacific arose out of perfectly American origins. That country, then labeled simply *Oregon,* was a land bound to attract frontiersmen. It was far off, therefore both romantic and undoubtedly better than existing tracts open to settlement. It lay beyond the treacherous plains swarming with hostile Indians and there was a serious question as to its ownership. Rumors of a verdant countryside, teeming with fur-bearing animals, possessed of a soil that awaited the plowman's attention, a place eyed by the always-suspect British, proved to be more than the Yankees could stand. They had to go.

A combination of New England promoters and western senators, a partnership that would be much better understood later on, provided the initial spark. Hall J. Kelley, a Massachusetts schoolteacher, and Nathaniel Wyeth, iceman and entrepreneur from the Bay State, sounded the tocsin throughout their homeland, urging the immediate settlement of this western paradise. Without having had the benefit of a visit there, Kelley, the scholar, published a volume called *Geographical Sketches of Oregon.* During the 1830s Boston, seemingly a prolific place for emigrant societies, produced the American Society for Encouraging a Settlement of the Oregon. Kelley's propaganda seeds had borne fruit. And Wyeth stepped forward to lead the first group to the promised land. The spring of 1832 saw him drilling some thirty men in the hardships of frontier life at a camp near Boston harbor, each hopeful pioneer dressed in a loud uniform set off by a broad belt from which dangled bayonet, knife, and ax. The boys at Harvard College, Nat Wyeth's alma mater, expressed a good deal of amusement at the preparations, but the trainees paid them no attention. This was serious business.

As Wyeth's group worked its way west, guided and guarded by William Sublette and his trappers—who were passing that way— applause for such projects were heard in congressional halls. More than a decade before, Congress had appointed a committee to look into the possibility of settling the Northwest Coast. By 1828 territorial government for Oregon, reaching north to 54° 40', was proposed. Debates produce extremes of opinion and the discussion about extending jurisdiction to the Pacific was no exception. One solon arose to decry the whole land westward to the ocean a sterile waste no better than the Sahara and just as dangerous to cross. Another wondered why Anglo-Saxons considered venturing into such a country unless they wanted to become savages.

Most of Wyeth's men, hardened for such travel by rigorous life around Boston, agreed with the senators. After fighting distance, drought, mosquitoes, and finally Indians at a battle near Pierre's Hole, a majority of them deserted and scrambled back home. Those who carried on, and finally reached Oregon with Wyeth, did not stay long. Like their leader they were more interested in extracting furs than tilling the soil. Meanwhile, Kelley the propagandist and promoter, not having experienced western travel, remained firm in his determination to people Oregon. He departed for the Northwest himself during the spring of 1833 and after a long and circuitous journey which took him as far south as Mexico finally reached Oregon, only to give up in disgust and return to Massachusetts after a spell of sickness and a series of misadventures.

But discouragement never seems to have deterred the American westward movement. Instead, it tended to serve as a challenge to those who sought the satisfaction of succeeding where others had not. With Senator Thomas Hart Benton of Missouri shouting that "Nothing is wanted, but a second Daniel Boone to lead the way," and Kelley flooding New England with literature that promised a new life in a new land, America began to believe what it heard and read. Missionaries such as Jason and Daniel Lee, attracted by the possibilities of new worlds to conquer in soul-saving, set forth to work among the savages of the interior. So did Marcus Whitman and his friend the Reverend Henry Spaulding, who established a couple of "firsts" in 1836 by taking both wagons and women over what was becoming known as the Oregon Trail. They were obliged to give up the wagons west of Fort Boise, but by 1840 Joe Meek and Robert Newell proved that wheeled travel west of that point was possible. Pleased by what he saw, Whitman told Newell, "You have broken the ice, and when others see that wagons have passed, they, too, will pass, and in a few years the valley will be full of our people."

He was right. By 1843 another of America's great migrations was in progress and the route over which wagons had first bounced along, feeling their way, now became a roadway of powdered soil, ground fine by the constant pounding of iron rims. And more than dust filled the air; a curious spirit loosely known as Manifest Destiny pervaded the atmosphere, spreading viruslike, affecting all it touched. This ethereal compound took a larger toll among congressmen and newspapermen than from the ranks of the average farmer. Sickness, a malarial climate, or the want of better farmland drove the multitudes westward, but it was the protagonists of empire who took title to the land, provided for law, order, and security and thereby laid out the field for the shock troops of emigration to enter.

In 1843, somewhere between nine hundred and a thousand people passed across the plains, Oregon-bound. With them went about seven hundred oxen and approximately as many beef cattle. By 1845 there were some six thousand people in Oregon; in five years that figure had more than doubled. Most of them had come overland. During the Forties the trail became well demarcated, although caravans generally continued to employ guides. Travel was carried on by caravan as insurance against Indian depredations, but as a rule the natives did not bother those who were merely passing through. Aside from some begging, they stood back and watched this restless people move on, wondering where the big buffalo hunt was to take place.

Life along the trail was one of movement, yet monotony. Once a wagon train settled down to the daily grind, life was carried on almost as it had been at home. There were romances, marriages, and births, causing comment only when they were not carried forth in that sequence. There were deaths. Children died at birth, old men succumbed to the hardships of travel, and cholera struck at all ages. An army officer noted that it carried off whole parties, dotting the way with fresh graves. "When we arose in the morning it was a question among us as to who might fall a victim to it before another sun."

But disease and death were nothing new; the emigrants knew it as a part of their lives at home and were not surprised when it struck them on the trail. On they plodded, keeping diaries, noting the strange country through which they moved, expressing pleasure at finding wood or water, trying not to complain about hot winds one day and sudden mire-making showers the next. The desert was cruel and exacting, but they expected little from it. Something better lay beyond and no reward had any worth without a preceding period of trial. Many a man who worked his way along the Platte, plagued by lame oxen, a sick wife, a shrinking wheel that would not keep its rim, or unbearable heat and blowing sand, wondered why the Maker found necessary so severe a test.

There were others who regarded the land beyond the desert as a haven, a place where things must of necessity be better since they were so bad at home. Members of the Church of Jesus Christ of the Latter-Day Saints, more popularly known as Mormons, fled across the midcontinental wastes to get away from persecution, fear, and physical violence. To them also the desert was a barrier, but it was as well a protective belt that lay between them and an unfriendly United States. Once over it, the arid land offered insurance against further interference from those one-hundred-per-cent Americans who could tolerate no one who did not conform to their own particular pattern.

From the day Joseph Smith founded the Mormon church in 1830, its members were subject to persecution. Strangely enough, in an America shot through with sects and religious splinter groups, these people were not accepted. Driven to Ohio, from there to Missouri, and then to Illinois, they always suffered at the hands of their non-Mormon neighbors. By the spring of 1846, they were once again on the move, this time westward into Iowa and beyond. The spring of 1847 saw them strike out from their winter camp on the banks of the Missouri, bound for New Zion. Brigham Young, successor to the murdered Smith, led them up the Platte along what was to be called the Mormon Trail, on past Fort Laramie and down into Jim Bridger's little oasis on the Green. Old Gabe had little good to say about the country just beyond his roadside post, but to the persecuted group it had one shining virtue. It was beyond the boundaries of the United States. Into the rugged Uinta Mountains they went, and after a rough trip emerged at an opening called Emigration Canyon. Just ahead lay the Great Salt Lake, a place Brigham pronounced good. Along two small streams fed from the Wasatch Mountains they staked out a communal claim and at once prepared to plant crops.

Within a month a party was sent back for the main body of Mormons and when they moved out along the trail the trans-Mississippi West's first mass migration was under way. Nearly sixteen hundred men, women, and children, with herds of cattle and sheep, entered the forbidding plains area and—undoubtedly to their surprise —crossed it with very little difficulty. Others followed and in a few short years Salt Lake City, an attractive town with square blocks divided by wide streets, was the most important municipality between the Missouri and the Pacific Coast. As early as 1848 it had a population of nearly seventeen hundred and there were more than four thousand Latter-Day Saints in the valley itself. Ironically, New Zion found that it was not beyond the reach of the United States at all. A few strokes of the pen and the Treaty of Guadalupe Hidalgo not only ended the Mexican War but attached the present Southwest to a rapidly growing, pushing young nation. The Mormons found themselves catapulted right back under the flag from which they had fled.

This did not stop the migration to Salt Lake. Church leaders set up a fund to aid others who wished to join the group and before long an organized immigration service was bringing settlers from the eastern United States as well as from Europe. Twenty years after the first great movement west the numbers reached impressive proportions. In 1866 nine shiploads of Mormon immigrants crossed the Atlantic, making up 459 wagonloads when they set out across the high plains.

Those who could not afford covered wagons drawn by oxen walked. So anxious were these people to see New Zion that they were willing to risk crossing the desert on foot, tugging at handcarts containing their most precious possessions. Four companies of them, called the Hand Cart Brigade, moved westward in 1856. Mounted on a single axle and a pair of high wheels was a box perhaps four feet long to which was fastened a handle and a crossbar used for pulling and balancing. Made of wood, with the single exception of the wheel rims, the vehicles carried several hundred pounds of goods. As a rule four carts and one tent were allotted to each twenty persons.

The handcart experiment is usually regarded as a failure. Although many deaths resulted from so hazardous an undertaking, the notion of walking across the desert was not so absurd as it may have appeared. Most of the suffering resulted from having started too late in the season. Those who got an early start often crossed with a minimum of difficulty. The first companies of 1856 arrived at Salt Lake City, fourteen hundred miles from their starting point at Iowa City, in a little over two months, having sustained fewer casualties than the average wagon train. Some of the carts were hauled twenty-five or thirty miles a day, double the distance of the daily oxen mileage. Men were learning that if they left the Missouri early in the travel season, stayed on the regular trails, and ignored the natives, they could expect to cross the formidable plains in relative safety.

America, restless since birth, spent most of the nineteenth century on the move. It took little to persuade the professional frontiersman to sell out, pack his few belongings, and strike out for parts unknown. Those who listened to tales of the good life in faraway Oregon required no further persuasion; despite drought, distance, and danger, they were off. Nor has it taken much friction, religiously, to cause movement. From the day of Anne Hutchinson and Roger Williams,

men and women thought moving on justified in order to follow the
dictates of their own beliefs. But each of these cases involved people
who already teetered on the brink of movement, ready to depart with
relatively little urging. Consequently their numbers did not bulk large
in the national population.

Somewhere in the realm of things there is a mover that pulls the
average man out of his home, some compulsion obliging him to leave
a comfortable home, a steady job, even a flourishing profession. In
nineteenth-century America it was gold. Aside from a minor flurry of
gold excitement in Georgia during the Thirties, no mineral deposits of
any consequence had been discovered. It took the California rush
to set in motion a movement that continued to the end of the century
and took men all the way to the Klondike. The thought of yellow
dust disrupted the lives of men who under normal conditions would
have never deviated from their quiet, ancestral patterns. Almost
overnight the beckoning metal drew them westward. They became a
part of one of the greatest population movements in history, one that
would not cease until every inch of the West had been scoured for its
last mineral resource.

The American midcontinent had little direct part in the rush of the
Forty-Niners. Again, it was merely an obstacle, a place to cross,
beyond which lay something worth while. Later, the Rockies would
reveal a treasure that compared favorably with that of the Sierras,
but not yet. Gold in California, however, caused the high plains to be
much better known to the American people. As James Marshall's discovery at Coloma was verified and men came to realize that tales of
wealth in the California hills were not fiction, the entire East Coast
pulsated with excitement.

Maps came out. The long and tortuous route around the Horn
was studied. There was talk of the short cut by way of the Panamanian
isthmus. Most people looked at the direct route, across the American
desert. It had its dangers but was a relatively cheap way to go and
such articles as horses, wagons, and household goods would be in-
valuable once California was reached. The way west was now quite
familiar. Men had gone that way to Oregon; the Mormons had
demonstrated its feasibility as a route. In April 1848, Fort Kearny
was established near the intersection of the Platte River and the

100th meridian. Farther west was Fort Laramie, an army post by 1849. Other posts would soon fill in the gaps, manned by blue-clad troopers ready to aid travelers in distress, whether by protection against the Indians or by mending a broken wagon.

Old-time trappers and Indians alike were amazed at the size of the invasion. Wagon trains lined out along the Overland Trail as far as the eye could see, raising a steady column of dust that floated skyward. At night their campfires gleamed like the lights of a distant city. Legend has it that in a single day an observer counted eight hundred wagons and ten thousand oxen passing Fort Kearny. Captain Howard Stansbury, on the great road in June 1849, told of meeting a French trader bound from Fort Laramie to St. Louis with a wagon trainload of buffalo robes. The trader, who had been on the road forty days, said he had met no less than four thousand emigrant wagons, each carrying an average of four persons. In no time the way was as unmistakably marked as a modern picnic ground. Burned-out campfires, refuse, abandoned household articles too heavy to carry on, broken wagon parts, skeletons of cattle and horses, and freshly patted graves lined the great road. Stansbury called it "already broad and well beaten as any turnpike in our country." Kearny, Laramie, Bridger were part of the western travel language now—stopping places, points of reference, oases in the desert. Any novice on the trail knew of them.

All America seemed to be on the move. During 1850, Independence, Missouri, the most popular rendezvous of departing caravans, saw emigrants from every state in the Union save Texas and Delaware. They formed into groups large enough to provide protection from the Indians, selected a captain, and lunged forward, ready to challenge the barrier ahead. Some were well-planned, almost elaborate, organizations. Semimilitary in nature, they moved with precision and discipline, sending out protective flankers, scouting the terrain ahead, and establishing a night watch. The inclusion of a doctor and a light spring-wagon ambulance was not unknown. Some of the companies even had brass bands for the entertainment of the membership, and the nights rang with both instrumental and vocal music. To many a pioneer, particularly those who crossed the plains with large, well-furnished wagon trains, the way west was less event-

ful than it had been portrayed. Like those who follow them today
over Highway 30, they nevertheless experienced heat, unpredictable
cloudbursts, and hypnotizing miles of monotony. Time has done
little about these characteristics; it has merely shortened the period
of boredom.

Within a decade after the California rush, gold was found in the
Rocky Mountains and plains travel soared to a new high. In the
spring of 1859, William T. Sherman, an unknown army officer who
was to have his date with destiny on Georgia battlefields, wrote from
Fort Leavenworth of the excitement around his military post. The
streets buzzed with emigrants preparing for the trip west, a daily stage
had already announced its schedule to the mountain communities,
and by now the young officer thought more than twenty-five thousand people had departed. Matthew Dale, an ailing young Pennsylvanian bound westward for "health and wealth," was surprised to
learn that Leavenworth was so large. Already it claimed a population of twelve thousand. With enthusiasm he wrote to his father that
"the country what we have seen west of the Missouri is the finest
I ever saw. Am quite in love with it. . . . I like the West. There is a
dash of bold shrewd go-a-head style about every thing which is
entirely unknown in the East. Every thing but river travelling is
fast."

The Colorado gold rush opened new travel routes across the
plains and further popularized the older ones. The well-known Overland Road along the Platte was followed by gold-seekers who turned
off near present-day Julesburg, Colorado, and followed the South
Platte toward Denver. South of this line, through central Kansas, lay
the Smoky Hill road, the future route of the Kansas Pacific Railroad.
It became popular as a freighting and stagecoach route. Best known
of all was the old Santa Fe Trail, leading from the Missouri River
across Kansas to the Arkansas River and along the stream to Bent's
Fort, from which point it went south to Santa Fe. General William
Larimer, famous in the annals of Colorado, called it "the best natural road in the world."

The Santa Fe Trail was the oldest established route across the plains, having been heavily traveled since the 1820s by traders from Missouri. Senator Benton had long since persuaded Congress to put up money for its improvement and as early as 1825 more than thirty thousand dollars went into marking the way and buying up transit rights from the Indians. Thousands of dollars worth of goods were hauled along the road, maintaining a trade immortalized by Josiah Gregg in his *Commerce of the Prairies,* and along it arose such landmarks as Bent's Fort.

This trading post, called the finest in the West with the exception of Fort Union on the Missouri, stood out on the plains as an impregnable adobe fortress, welcoming travelers who wished to replenish their dwindling supplies, trading with the Indians, offering a rest stop for weary U.S. dragoons patroling the region. Its proprietor, William Bent, ruled his domain with all the splendor attributed to "King" McKenzie at Fort Union. When the fur trade fell off, the government tried to buy Bent out the same year it purchased Fort Laramie—1849. But the price was not right and, tired of quibbling, the owner mined his establishment with gunpowder and blew it skyward. When the Fifty-Niners came along they traded with the old gentleman at his new post, forty miles up the Arkansas. Later it would be leased by the Army and called Fort Lyon.

The Santa Fe Trail, like its other western counterparts, was of interest to men only because it led someplace, to a means of gain. The reaction of a trader who crossed it in 1841 typifies that of those who saw it. Beyond Council Grove, he said, "for four hundred miles, there is nothing to be seen but one eternal desert, without one, even one solitary stick of timber to cheer the eye for thirty days." But when the cry of gold was heard from Colorado, men and women poured out over this and other trails without the slightest hesitation, for beyond lay ready wealth. Some went by foot, one of them pushing a wheelbarrow laden with his worldly goods, and a Minnesotan tried dragging his possessions along on a sled. Several attempts were made to use the wind, but windwagons and prairie sailors did not become the order of the day.

However they went, they represented numbers. Albert Richardson, a newspaperman accompanying Horace Greeley, judged that in the spring of 1859 they passed ten thousand emigrants, all struggling westward. One of them inquired of the gentlemen if there were any people still living in the states, so many thronged the prairies. Not all were going west. Some of the early birds were now en route home, discouraged by the fact that they had not been able to gather up bagsful of nuggets in the mountains. They told of depression in the new town of Denver, of picks sold for ten cents apiece, and of town lots traded for revolvers.

Their listeners usually laughed, patted them on the back, and kept moving toward the mountains and what must be wealth despite all rumors to the contrary. Young Matt Dale was representative of this group. As he wrote home, his party had been frightened by tales of "humbug," but were determined to go on at any cost. "My faith was so strong that rich deposits would be found, I was resolved to come through, prospect and hunt part of the season, and then return to the states . . . in fact anything but turning back or joining filibustering expeditions, my antipathy being equally strong against either, as both insured a loss." Although Dale did not become rich in the diggings, he stayed on for more than two years. Of his trip west he wrote, "Our journey across the plains was a most tedious one. We had no adventures that began to pay for the toilsome tramp."

During nearly two decades, between the passing of the fur trade and the coming of the Civil War, most of the high plains and mountain region was little used other than as a transit route. Toward the end of the period, with mineral discoveries in the Rockies, mining towns appeared and an active commerce developed, but for the most part the area remained unsettled. Constant passage over what had been, and still was, called "the Desert" tended to diminish early fears of its hostility to human habitation. It was a mean land, tricky and dangerous, always ready to strike the weak or the careless, but if treated with respect it permitted passage to those who sought it.

The result of this passing acquaintanceship caused many to respect the country and as methods of transport were improved the general region known as desert began to shrink. Curious Mississippi Valley farmers edged forward, cautiously, tentatively, trying out its edges for fertility and productivity. Crusading New Englanders, whipped

into a froth of passion over the great slavery issue, listened to aboli-
tionists who talked of saving Kansas for the Anglo-Saxon race and
consented to carry their "Beecher's Bibles" (Sharps Rifles) and
plows into the new country. Emigrant Aid Societies, armed with
money donated by humanitarians who would fight slavocracy, furnished the financial power for the move.

Although there was no noticeable rush into Kansas and Nebraska
until the more spectacular events of the Fifties shifted the spotlight
of national attention to the area, a slow agricultural infiltration commenced as early as the Thirties. An Englishman who visited Fort
Leavenworth in that period noted that the post bought a good deal
of its beef and other meat from nearby farmers. When Leavenworth
was established in 1827, a result of Senator Benton's pressure for
military protection of the Santa Fe Trail, there were no farmers in
the vicinity. As always, a military establishment had encouraged
local settlement.

From the 1820s, when the Santa Fe trade became an important
economic fact, through the succeeding decades that saw missionary
efforts, military expeditions, and finally the establishment of stage
and mail lines westward, eastern Kansas became famous as a starting
point for travel into the Southwest. The neighboring region to the
north, one day to become Nebraska, meanwhile served as a supply
point for the migration along the Platte, feeding the great Overland
Road, Oregoners, Mormons, Forty-Niners, and Fifty-Niners. Together Kansas and Nebraska provided a general staging area for the
great waves of emigrants that would lap at the Rockies, find their
passes and push westward until they met the sea.

Such activity was bound to bring people who would first furnish
travelers their necessaries, and then turn to other pursuits when the
supply business was gone. Many of them experimented with the soil,
found it not too unfriendly, and stayed on as farmers. That there was
sometimes little choice in the decision is reflected in the popular
couplet "We do not live but only stay, And are too poor to get
away." Meanwhile such names as Leavenworth, Atchison, Independence, Plattsmouth, and Omaha became important in the language of
western travel. In a few years names like Wichita, Ellsworth, and

Dodge City would indicate the irrepressible force of the westward movement and the gradual shrinkage of the desert.

Down into the Fifties, the decade of "Bleeding Kansas," the country just west of the Missouri River remained a launching platform for those who wanted to go to the mountains. Increasing interest in the region, however, led two representatives of the American Reform Tract and Book Society and Kansas League of Cincinnati to visit the place and to write a description of it for the general public. C. B. Boynton and T. B. Mason first made some inquiries of their friends and discovered that the average person had no idea where the place was. One man told them it was about two thousand miles west of Council Bluffs, while another wondered if it were not a newly discovered continent.

Upon their return from this land of mystery in 1854, the men wrote of their findings. Eastern Kansas, they said, "occupies the central position in that line of country which forms the eastern boundary of what is called the American Desert, a belt about two hundred and fifty miles wide, a portion of which is without timber, and almost without rains." Beyond the desert lay a section of country terminated westward by the Rocky Mountains that might one day become both a mining and manufacturing region, a place that must derive its commerce and agricultural products from eastern Kansas.

Thus the hope of Kansas lay in its advantageous geographic location, a situation that gave it a position of primacy in the new western trade. Its boosters looked west, rather than east, for commerce. On the face of it, this looks unreasonable, considering the availability of water transportation in the Mississippi Valley as opposed to the lack of it in the West. But during the Forties and Fifties agricultural discontent was the major topic of conversation in the Great Valley. Flour plummeted from $6.25 a barrel at Cincinnati to $2.51 within a three-year period. Wheat should have brought at least fifty cents to make raising it profitable, but in parts of Illinois it commanded only half that. Low prices at home, coupled with the American dream that something better lay just to the west, made men think in terms of advance, not retreat, across the continent. It was the day of railroad talk, of expansion, of trade with Oregon or even China. And here were places, poised at the edge of civilization, ready to serve those who went beyond, anxious for a connection with the new land. Parched miles intervened, but they could be traversed; men proved that daily.

Nor was the desert so large as had been supposed, the hopefuls told each other. The fertile section of Kansas really extended much farther west than had been generally assumed and "future investigation will very much reduce the dimensions of what has been called the American Desert." Agriculture was bound to move deeper into this forbidden land until finally little if any of Kansas would remain unclaimed. There were those who would contest a recent claim made by a writer for the *Home Missionary Journal,* whose articles appeared in the *New York Tribune.* He wrote that the land of western Kansas and Nebraska was almost totally unfit for ordinary agricultural purposes. To many this view seemed much too pessimistic. Actually, it was not. The belt of land out near the 100th meridian never has been worked by the agricultural methods usual in the 1850s. New techniques were necessary in a semiarid land.

Quite correct was the view, expressed by Boynton and Mason, that without railroads Kansas towns would be isolated. Despite the fact that journalists regarded the prairies quite suitable for transportation, being relatively level, no amount of agricultural products would be hauled over them other than by rail. At least, not in the nineteenth century. But the observers did not exaggerate when they predicted that if these towns became radiating points for railroads, "their future can be easily foreseen."

Accurate, also, was the prediction that frontier communities such as those of eastern Kansas would be melting pots of American and foreign society. "Hitherto, emigration has moved westward, nearly on parallels of latitude, and these streams, except in California, have not met, though running westward on parallel lines. The eastern States have, by emigration, prolonged each itself westward." But in the pre-Civil War decade population movement was deflected, by natural and artificial causes, into Kansas and Nebraska, mingling together Missourians, Kentuckians, Virginians, Tennesseans, and

New Englanders. Together they stood at the threshold of the high plains and joined in projecting the American thrust westward. As time went by they discovered that by new methods, certain concessions to a semiarid climate, and stubborn persistence a living could be made.

At first Kansas farmers grew corn, because they had grown it on their old lands to the east. It was an all-purpose crop, one that could be ground easily for domestic use and also could be fed to hogs and cattle. As early as 1839, at the Shawnee Methodist Mission, experiments were conducted with winter wheat. Wheat culture did not become widely accepted until the 1870s although it was raised not only successfully but in fairly large quantities before that time.

Little by little the newcomers felt out the land and discovered that its treeless and forbidding appearance was often misleading. Experimentations with crops revealed that, while new techniques were necessary, most of the standard cereals could be raised. During the 1850s confidence grew and farmers edged forward in Kansas and Nebraska, probing their way to the edge of the desert, tantalized by the continuing fertility of soil.

Glowing reports drifted eastward. An army officer called the region around Fort Riley "charming and fascinating," rich in soil, building materials, streams, and animal life, "perfect in all its wild beauty and productiveness." A Methodist minister's wife, who lived in the same region, concurred. "We must pronounce this the most charming country our eyes have ever beheld. Beautiful rolling prairie, undulating like the waves of the sea, high limestone cliffs with immense bottom-lands, stretching into thousands of acres as rich as it is possible for it to be, high tablelands, with a soil a number of feet in depth." A New Yorker explained the agricultural possibilities of what seemed to be a barren prairie: "It looks like a country that had been finely cultivated and suddenly every habitation and man swept from it."

None of the early boosters argued with earlier critics about the lack of wood. By staying near streams settlers usually found fuel, but building materials were hard to come by. Some of the early writings reveal that their authors lived in log cabins, but even in mentioning that fact they often allude to the shortage of wood. Two substitutes were available: sod and limestone. The former was universally found, the latter harder to locate.

By various means—mud and brush, sod blocks, or stone—the newcomers managed to throw up habitable dwellings. Somewhat to their own surprise, they were not driven back from the desert's edge. "I am quite prepared to expect," wrote a western supporter, "that the skill and enterprise of American farmers will find the means of obtaining comfort and wealth in those regions, both of Kansas and Nebraska, which many are disposed to condemn as worthless. I am by no means ready to believe that large tracts, in either Territory, are to remain desert and waste, as incapable of affording the means of subsistence." Perhaps, he concluded, some of those who were so harsh in their judgments of this western land might be discouraged with certain sections of New England.

It was not the critics who succeeded; the West was no place for a pessimist. Nor could success come to those who lacked seriousness of purpose. A good many people had rushed into Kansas during the Fifties because it was the thing to do. They came for excitement or out of a spirit of adventure, with no particular purpose in mind. "They have floated into Kansas on the tide, and on the first slight ebb will float out again, or retire in disgust," predicted one who watched the development. No one should listen to reports by these people, he warned. The land was good, as good as any the American frontiersman had seen before, and it would produce if given a chance. That optimism was warranted is eloquently illustrated in the results. Relentlessly civilization crept forward, filling in the more likely spots, then assaulting the more forbidding. While the theorists stood back, pondering the future of the desert, the settler made his invasion, improvising where he had to, learning the tricks of a new agricultural trade, ignoring the pontifications of the "experts."

Propagandists alone did not bring the farmer to the desert's edge. Writers furnished information and lent an initial excitement, but without the practicalities of certain forces little movement might have occurred. Bad times in the Mississippi Valley pushed the settler from behind; talk of higher prices in the West, of trade, transportation, and better opportunities in general urged him on. Political considerations, the tightening slave issue that made of Kansas a crucible in which to sample-test the issue, attracted crusaders. But it was waterways whose fingers stretched out toward the plains that really brought forth men and women.

Water, so necessary in the pioneer's thinking, always attracted the plowman. His first settlements had followed rivers since the early days along the Atlantic seaboard. Across the Appalachians he struck the Ohio, followed it to the Mississippi, and now worked up the Missouri, westward. Branching off, he took to the Kansas and pressed along its course clear out to Fort Riley. It was the transportation offered by these rivers, principally the Missouri, that materially helped push an agricultural spearhead into the desert's front. The bulge of settlement grew until it burst westward and its flanks completely enveloped the forbidden land.

From the day the *Yellowstone* first poked its way up to Fort Union, in 1832, until the middle Fifties, traffic on the Upper Missouri was not heavy. One or two American Fur Company vessels a year comprised the steamboat trade. In 1855 Fort Pierre was established as the Upper Missouri country's first military post. After that time boats other than those owned by the fur company traded upstream, but the number was quite small.

During these years travel on the lower Missouri grew rapidly and with it came great improvements in the vessels used. The Fifties, called the golden era of the steamboat, witnessed improvements in both hull and machinery. Sleeker vessels, drawing less water but hauling more freight, began to ply the waters. The typical craft was about two hundred fifty feet long with a forty-foot beam, featuring a full-length cabin accommodating about four hundred passengers. Atop this deck was perched the officers' cabin, called the Texas (because it was annexed, said a contemporary); above this was the pilot house, commanding a full view of the river. In addition to passengers, the vessels carried from five to seven hundred tons of freight.

As traffic grew the boats increased in elegance. All efforts were bent in the direction of comfort and the main cabin received the greatest attention. Thick Brussels carpets covered its floors and each stateroom was furnished with every modern convenience. The ladies' cabin usually boasted a piano, and if a brass band was not carried certainly a string orchestra might be expected. To top off the luxury of magnificently appointed quarters and continual music and dancing, passengers were served the finest foods and liquors as their daily fare. Those who could afford it now went west in class.

But large amounts of money were not a necessity. One could travel from New York to Omaha for a little over forty dollars at midcentury. The fare from St. Louis to Kansas City was only twelve. Or those who elected to travel under the auspices of Emigrant Aid Societies could go for nearly nothing. One of them offered a ten-dollar fare from Pittsburgh to St. Louis and passage on to Kansas City for an equal sum. Nor did travelers have to wait long for service. In 1858 there were no fewer than sixty regular packets operating on the Missouri in addition to around forty nonscheduled "tramps." At the height of the travel season there was hardly a moment on the river when boats were not in sight. Such places as Kansas City, St. Joseph, Leavenworth, Atchison, Plattsmouth, and Omaha became familiar ports of call and each of them served as a point of embarkation for those crossing the plains to new homes. Truly, Kansas and Nebraska were gateways to the West.

Not content to use only the Missouri River, which turned north to form Nebraska's eastern boundary, steamboats entered the Kansas River and headed for western Kansas. As early as 1831, Peck's *Guide to Emigrants* called it a "large, bold, navigable river," but warned that its channel was fickle and snag-filled. By the Fifties, river pilots were testing out Peck's theories. In the spring of 1854 the *Excel* threaded its way through the snags, its master prepared to go as far west by water as he could. The little stern-wheeler could carry its hundred tons in a mere two feet of water. The river was high that spring and the sailors found themselves navigating Kansas as far out as Fort Riley. Not content with such a victory, they next tried out the Smoky Hill branch and, ignoring the leadman's constant cry of "no bottom," thrashed along that prairie stream, crabbing around tight bends with the greatest of difficulty. When a band of Indians on the hunt came in sight, the steam whistle let out a shrill scream, and the flabbergasted natives looked on in disbelief at the sight of a steamboat lost in the middle of Kansas. They must have wondered what the crazy whites would think of next.

Before long, navigation in such unlikely places was more common. The *Excel* made more than thirty trips to Fort Riley, covering approximately two hundred forty miles in twenty-four hours. Others followed, bringing emigrants and "Cincinnati houses." These early prefabricated dwellings were made in Cincinnati, packaged, and sent west by river boat. Hundreds of ready-made one- and two-story houses were brought out to dot the prairies and form overnight communities. During the late Fifties and early Sixties, a considerable traffic was carried on up the Kansas River and its tributaries, but some years of low water and the coming of the railroad ended that phase of western transportation. In 1866, railroad companies persuaded the Kansas legislature to declare the Kansas, Republican, Smoky Hill, Solomon, and Big Blue rivers to be unnavigable. With the waterways declared legally dead and the right of bridging by railroads secured, steamboats withdrew and sought other western streams to conquer. They had served their purpose, filling a need between the coming of the earliest settlements and the advent of the iron horse.

The years between the day of the trapper and the coming of the Civil War provided a period of training and adjustment to new conditions for Americans who would make the final invasion of the great desert. In the two decades that preceded the war men crossed the plains in growing numbers, making their way to mineral regions in the Rockies, or beyond. California and Oregon became part of the Union, detached though they were for the moment, while the Mormons drew public notice by the miracles they wrought in the Utah desert. Travel routes across the high plains became familiar to thousands during these years. Old roads were improved and new ones appeared. Freight lines went into business and stagecoach companies offered relatively safe passage to the mines. By 1861 the Pony Express had spent its short life and telegraph poles dotted the route, standing as tombstones over a bold and daring venture. By then the reports of railroad surveyors told the American public that there were at least four practical routes to the West. In 1862 Congress said *yes* to the clamors of railroad advocates and chartered the Pacific road. Only the existing struggle between North and South stayed the advance of the rails.

Until the Union Pacific moved out of Omaha, in 1865, the Great American Desert remained fairly intact. White men had crossed it and crisscrossed it, but few settled in it. They came to know its devious ways, learned how to traverse the parched miles of dust and sagebrush. Until the post–Civil War period—for more than sixty years—the American public held the region in low esteem. It served as a barrier, a useless waste, a hindrance to national development, and a problem. All it ever had done to earn its keep was to yield beaver pelts and some gold. Before 1861 the search for mineral wealth was confined to what was loosely known as the Pike's Peak region, and no immense returns were yet produced. To the north, the Missouri River saw one or two steamboats making annual ascents, but not until 1860 did any reach Fort Benton, the head of navigation. That little outpost sent a dwindling quantity of furs down to St. Louis, its real heyday still in the future. The Montana gold rush was shortly to make of it a booming, brawling river town, a commercial gateway to the mines. But not yet.

Until the great horn of mineral plenty poured forth gold dust in quantity, drawing on legions of hopefuls; until the railroads succeeded freight wagons and farmers followed stockmen out onto the plains, the desert remained in the minds of most men a thing to be shunned. Much of it was still unknown. As late as 1858 Lieutenant G. K. Warren reported that settlers had gone as far as fertile lands would permit and they now stood at the desert's edge. "They are, as it were, on the shore of a sea, up to which population and agriculture may advance, and no further." North of the desert lay the badlands, unknown and unwanted by settlers. The lieutenant observed that none of the tributaries of the Yellowstone had been inspected by any exploring expedition. Only the earlier trappers knew anything of that part of the country.

On the eve of the Civil War the opinion persisted. A United States senator, speaking against the admission of Kansas into the Union, charged that beyond the Missouri "there is no territory fit for settlement or habitation. It is unproductive. It is like a barren waste." As before, there were those ready to argue the point. William Gilpin, writing of the region in 1860, insisted that the plains were not deserts. On the contrary, "They . . . form the Pastoral Garden of the world." The writer, who was familiar with the plains, was shortly to be governor of a new territory known as Colorado.

The debate would go on. After the Civil War, General W. T. Sherman, in command of the high plains country, talked of the desert and its irreclaimability. Only when hordes of home-seekers followed the threadlike rails that moved west would he confess error. Even then he wrote to Phil Sheridan that such progress was hard to believe. It was so unlikely. But that was a characteristic of the American frontier movement. It was so often inexplicable. Men like Sherman and Sheridan stood back and shook their heads as the "sodbusters" moved in and made the desert bloom. The poor greenhorns. They didn't know that what they were doing was impossible.

Section II

VANGUARDS OF SETTLEMENT

Chapter 4

GOLDEN CORNERSTONE

Westerners still talk a good deal about the repeated invasions of their land by wealth-seekers from other parts of the nation and how these strangers tore up the countryside in their frantic desire for gain, leaving scarred hillsides, ghost towns, and ugly mounds of tailings in the streams. The descendants of those who remained to till the soil or engage in commerce, after the first flush of prosperity was over, today bear resentment to the "git and git out" philosophy so often employed by earlier residents from more settled parts of America.

Of the many types who have visited the West for extractive purposes only, those in search of minerals received the most unkind comments. As a rule, they brought nothing except essential equipment, dug ruthlessly at the hills, and moved on, contributing only collapsing shanties surrounded by piles of rubbish. If they made a strike, they spent it in the East, or perhaps along the West Coast. If the diggings failed to yield, they said damn such a country and got out. At first glance it appears that the miners did very little for the land they worked. Their existence seemed entirely transitory and artificial.

But all America was wasteful in its years of growth. Never before had so much virgin soil been taken over by Anglo-Saxons in such a brief span of years. Turned loose upon the countryside, entrepreneurs fought against time, each anxious to stake out as big a claim as possible before available resources were all spoken for. They were not concerned with methods of conservation, the requirements of their posterity—or even of tomorrow. The work had to be done today. It had to be finished with a minimum labor force. And while the miners, in particular, were not worried about coming generations of Westerners, unconsciously they provided for them by laying the foundations of permanent settlement.

The lure of gold brought forth great numbers of men. And they in turn brought an economy and a form of society to a new region. Men who worked the mines from sunup to sundown had no time for other projects. They had to be supported, in foodstuffs and other necessaries, from some outside source. They required mail service, telegraph, and express companies for communication with the "states." Freight wagons and railroads were wanted for transportation of minerals to the East and to supply tools, hardware, and later heavy machinery to the mining industry. Subsidiary services, ranging from entertainment to laundry, were required. Law and government were needed, even in a temporary mining camp. Before the mining boom along the Rocky Mountains had spent itself, civilization with all its trappings had come to the new land. Men were used to such things in the East; they insisted upon having them in the West. Gold was the catalyst in the transformation. When the finished product— permanent settlement—appeared, gold was hardly a measurable part of the larger result.

The mining frontier, like that of the fur trader, was short-lived. Placer or gulch mining, in which dust was panned from creek beds, lasted little more than two decades in the mountain West. It began with the rush of the Fifty-Niners to Colorado and ended in the Black Hills. By the fall of 1877 it was common knowledge around Deadwood that local placer mines were playing out and only the introduction of machinery, for use in quartz mining, would keep the industry alive.

During these twenty years the pick-and-pan legion swarmed across Colorado, searched Wyoming, found a momentary El Dorado in Montana, and played a last stand in the Black Hills. Many of the miners had worked their way eastward from California to Nevada, into Colorado, north to Montana and finally into Dakota. Behind them stood dozens of campsites. Some withered on the vine overnight, others lingered in the hope that good times would come again, and others settled down into steady communities fed by grain and beef.

Like the fur trade, the mining industry did not die overnight but suffered a lingering illness. Where it was feasible, heavy machinery was introduced to extract gold by crushing the ore-bearing rock, and the business of mining was carried on in an industrial way, usually by corporate enterprise. This kind of extraction required capital in quantity and was not a kind of business engaged in by the lonely prospector with his burro, pick, and pan. Rather, it resembled eastern or foreign mining, where companies owned the equipment, put up the money, and reaped the benefits. The miners became simply hired hands.

Aside from the gold injected into the national financial blood stream, the mining frontier hastened the development of its own region. The attraction of such wealth resulted in a population that otherwise would have matured only slowly. Growing communities along the mountain front in turn created a demand for transportation and communication, without which the cattleman and homesteader could not have appeared when they did. In short, gold was the key, the cornerstone, to western economic development.

Sometimes this was a fact the Westerner found hard to appreciate. As early as 1859 a Coloradan complained about the Easterners and their octopuslike proclivities in the field of finance. "It is a melancholy fact that we are now too much at the mercy of the east," he wrote in his diary. "Eastern capital builds our railroads—or swindles us out of the value of our bonds; eastern capital makes speculative investments in real estate, which stifles enterprise and deters immigration. . . ." He expressed the hope that the gold of Colorado might be used to develop the West, including the Mississippi Valley, rather than lining the pockets of financiers along the Atlantic seaboard. Rather early, western attitudes were becoming fixed.

The diarist was to be disappointed. The West was tapped, as always, but even in the slops it was accorded—the scraps it gleaned from the most ruthless extraction of resources yet seen in the United States—the region found a basis for subsequent growth. Once men had entered the new country, erected towns, laid out transportation systems, created political structures, it was too late to abandon the field. They had too much invested; they had to stay on and turn to other forms of enterprise.

In 1849 America was stricken by gold fever and the decade that followed discoveries in California witnessed an enormous movement of people. While traces of gold had been found in the Rockies near Denver as early as 1850, the magnitude of the strikes on the Pacific Coast blinded men to the possibilities elsewhere. In May 1858, encamped near Cherry Creek, an army officer recorded in his diary this single tantalizing sentence: "Gold was found by one of the men today." No further comment was made. The writer hurried on to discuss the nature of the weather, apparently unimpressed by the fact he had just set down. That summer William Green Russell, a Georgian with some prospecting experience, led a group of miners into the same region. After a summer's search they sat down to divide up the profits: the sum was a mere eight hundred dollars. Discouraged, most of the men returned home. The nine who remained established a camp on the banks of Cherry Creek and called it Auraria, after a mining town in Russell's native state.

Less than a thousand dollars was enough to start a gold rush. When news drifted back to places like Leavenworth and Omaha that dust had been found in the Cherry Creek vicinity, men disregarded distance, winter weather, and ignorance of the facts. With what supplies they could lay hands on, they started west. Among them was General William J. Larimer, a Pennsylvanian who had suffered heavily in the Panic of 1857. Taking along his son and a small band of followers, Larimer struck off for the diggings, determined to recoup his fortune. Rather than join those at Auraria, Larimer crossed Cherry Creek and established a town named after General James Denver, the territorial governor.

Experience taught the Anglo-Saxons little. Just as the settlers arrived at Jamestown, determined to pick up nuggets and return wealthy, so greenhorns now swarmed along the South Platte and its tributary, Cherry Creek. Many of them had neglected to think about bringing picks, shovels, or even supplies. Larimer estimated that two thousand such hopefuls forlornly searched for concentrated riches and judged that "a more disappointed set had never before been assembled together." Angry cries of "humbug" shortly were heard and large numbers now turned back, and—just as unprepared as they had come—braved the seven hundred miles that lay between them and civilization, hoping somehow to get home intact.

Disappointment did not mean a general exodus. The grim-faced prospectors who elected to go home met a steady stream of west-bound newcomers crawling toward the mountains like a giant ant train. The tiny settlements along Cherry Creek grew, supported by the arrival of Uncle Dick Wootton's wagon train of necessaries, including groceries, hardware, and whiskey. Shortly Larimer could write to his wife about his neighbors, "Oh, how they drink. You cannot conceive of anything as bad as they carry on here." So gay was the village that the General admitted he did not go out after dark.

Other wagon trains soon arrived; as fast as they could be unloaded new stores and saloons appeared. Sometimes prospective merchants were not even granted time to pitch tents from which to sell their goods. Clamorous customers bought directly from the wagons and sped for the mines. A sharp demand resulted in high prices, but the principal cause of inflation was freight rates. The difference between prices farther east and in the mining camps was governed by trans-portation costs. During the summer of 1859 a young miner wrote to his parents that freight rates averaged ten cents a pound. In some cases the figure was as high as twenty-five cents. Shopping in a min-ing camp was therefore expensive. Eggs, packed in barrels of lard, were wiped off and sold at two dollars a dozen. Apples went for fifty cents each. A favorite story, told to illustrate western prices, concerned a Denver housewife who rebelled at the high cost of candles. When the merchant apologized, telling her that Indian troubles on the plains kept freight rates high, she snapped, "What! Are the Indians fighting by candlelight?"

Living costs were a source of complaint from the miners. From the outset, panning was frequently arduous and unrewarding. "We can just make 'grub' by working hard when the weather is fine," said one young man who was trying to borrow money from his parents in the East in order to live. Those who chose to hire out as laborers could expect no more than three dollars a day in wages. Two dollars was much more frequent. It took four men to run a sluice effectively, and small-time entrepreneurs who had the money to buy lumber often erected the boxes and hired men to run them. A sluice box would produce around twenty dollars a day in dust, so even after labor costs were deducted a small profit could be realized. One can understand why men, working for two or three dollars a day and paying enormous costs for supplies, were inclined to use the expression "There's Pike's Peak in it," when referring to humbug or fraud.

Hope kept the miners at their tasks. Frequently, when prospects seemed dim and gloom deepened, news of a fresh strike would spread through the diggings and a new rush was on. One of the most spectacular of the Colorado strikes was that of John H. Gregory, who hit pay dirt early in May 1859. Men working for two or three dollars a day learned that Gregory's location on Clear Creek was yielding that much in a single pan. Just a rumor of such panning was enough; a stampede followed. Almost overnight young Denver was temporarily depopulated. Businessmen boarded up their stores, loaded stocks onto wagons, and headed for the new camp. A newspaperman who saw Gregory Diggings a month after news of the strike was spread reported that five thousand people jammed the place and more were coming in every day.

As usual, the top was skimmed off in a hurry. By the middle of the summer it was obvious that if gold were to be recovered in any quantity, it would have to be taken from the forbidding layers of quartz. That meant machinery for extractions, crushing, and further reduction. Discouraged, many miners decided either to go home or to probe deeper into the hills in search of new placer sites. Late in the summer of 1859 one of them predicted the future of the region's development when he wrote: "Next season we expect the whole thing will be changed by the advent of capitalists, who will take these speculative schemes (most of which will pay) into their own hands." Within a year he revealed that preparations were under way for extensive quartz mining with capitalists buying up claims in great quantity. The individual miner found it increasingly difficult to make a living; the day of the investor was just ahead. "I have not the least doubt of this country's ultimately being a great and profitable mining region," said the same miner, "but time and money are both required to properly prospect it. . . ."

Almost as quickly as it had come, the first placer-mining rush in Colorado was over. By the spring of 1861 one of those who had stuck it out since the days of '59 had to admit defeat: "In my opinion, mining here thus far has proven an entire failure, taking the brilliant expectations formed the first year as a basis. The 'placer diggings' by which term all mines that can be operated with pick and shovel are embraced, such as gulch, bar or dry diggings are so limited, not one tenth part of the miners now here can find employment in them, hence the future prosperity of this entire mining region depends upon further discoveries of 'Placer' or in quartz mines already known." Such a conclusion meant only one thing: *move on.*

The mining frontier was a mobile one. Men moved because they had to. They poured through the valleys and passes of Colorado like water out of a sluice box, finding the most remote recesses of the land, and then relentlessly probing for gold. Little groups of miners' cabins became hamlets, sometimes towns. Central City, Nevada City, Blackhawk, French Gulch, Negro Gulch, California Gulch, and Gold Hill were soon familiar Colorado names. Every strike spawned new settlements, each more remote from civilization than the last. Crude at first, they were like advanced camps of some expedition, and as time passed they in turn acted as supply bases for even newer locations.

The advance of the mining frontier into Colorado meant growth and development for the original cities along the edge of the mountains. Denver, now furnished with a ferry across the Platte, acted as a funnel through which fresh legions of miners moved en route to the diggings. At the mouth of Clear Creek, Golden quickly became a leading rival as a staging area and supply depot for the army of gold-seekers. Boulder, on a creek of the same name, served in a similar capacity. The discovery of gold in South Park called for supply points south of Denver and soon places like Colorado City, Canon City, and Fountain City [Pueblo] appeared. Before 1859 was out, a line of these "valley cities" ran along the plains facing the mountain escarpment immediately to the west, each vying for business from the mines.

A new wave of miners arrived in the spring of 1860, swelling the population figure of ten thousand already located in the mining region. When the travel season reached its height over five thousand newcomers arrived each week, most of them stopping at Denver before entering the mountains. Already, bragged the *News,* over six thousand people lived in Denver. No doubt, speculated the journal, the city would one day be the commercial emporium of the Rocky Mountains. The fact that Denver's first chamber of commerce was organized that year suggested its residents anticipated such a development.

Other valley towns benefited from the influx. By May 1860, Colorado City laid claim to the distinction of being second only to Denver in the Pike's Peak region. That thriving city comprised more than two hundred houses. Canon City also grew rapidly and in September the first issue of the *Times* appeared on its streets. By fall, the population was eight hundred. North of Denver the little town of Boulder, with but thirty log cabins, had built a special building to be used as a school. Its inmates, commanded by Abner Brown, schoolmaster, toiled away in the first building erected in Colorado for purely educational purposes. American cultural equipment had arrived and was in use.

Almost at once agriculture was in evidence around these communities. Miners noticed that the soil was rich, for the banks of their mining canals were quick to turn green. Many a farm boy, whose training had come from the soil rather than hydraulic engineering, abandoned the quest for minerals in favor of raising crops. As early as the spring of 1859 garden vegetables were for sale in Denver and shortly more extensive crops were raised along the mountain streams that flowed eastward over fertile fields. Produce, grains, and hay were easily grown and they fetched prices that caused farmers from the Midwest to wonder if the real bonanza were not at the edge of the Rockies rather than within them.

The earliest towns of the plains and mountain West owed their existence, directly or indirectly, to mineral resources. Gold in California, and later in the Rockies, gave rise to a westward movement of both men and supplies that resulted in a number of commercial points along the way. Some of the trail stops, like those on the Platte River route, lived on after the gold rush was over to become important in the day of the railroad and the automobile. Mountain cities frequently sprang directly from mining camps and, because of the temporary nature of the mineral frontier, just as frequently died an early death. The survivors that ultimately became important cities were usually supply points rather than actual mining camps. The prime example is Denver.

The discovery of gold in the American West altered the nature and characteristics of the nation's frontier movement. Pioneering prior to the mid-nineteenth century was largely an agricultural process; the scattered cities merely proved that the countryside was filling up. Traditionally, the frontier had been a rather slowly moving edge of civilization, dominated by the rural ideal. Then with the electrifying news that concentrated wealth in the remote West merely awaited the miner's pick, the frontier leapfrogged forward in spasmodic hops.

Overnight it was an urban frontier, far in advance of the settlers' frontier, remote and isolated in the mountain fastness. The old process was suddenly inverted. Where there used to be settlement and few or no towns, now there was a town and no outlying settlement. The mining frontier by its very nature was an urban affair. Placer mining was carried on along streams and these waterways frequently ran through very narrow gulches. Property, valued by the foot along creek banks instead of by the acre as on earlier frontiers, became a precious item. The very concentration of miners' cabins, crowded together in an area of highly concentrated wealth, automatically provided an urban type of living.

Frequently the placer-mining camps were figuratively no more than overnight affairs. Once the surface gold was taken off, the population moved on in search of new mineral locations. Oro City, Colorado, located in California Gulch near present Leadville, is a good ex-

ample. It was founded in the spring of 1860, following a strike by
a group of Fifty-Niners who worked their way deeper into the mountains in search of richer diggings. By that fall, over ten thousand people crowded California Gulch, struggling for claims that were limited
by the miners' code to one hundred feet of water front.

During the first season around two million dollars worth of gold
was said to have been produced in the gulch. Legend has it that four
miners, after eyeing the dirt floor of one of the gambling halls with
interest, scraped up a quantity of its surface, took it down to the
stream for panning, and came up with two thousand dollars worth
of gold. Extraction at this mad rate continued during the early Sixties, but like most other strikes its boom period proved to be brief.
By 1865, the panning had run out. In that year there were only
around four hundred residents in the gulch. Two years later it was
almost completely deserted. By that time, many a man had extracted
a fortune from the earth, and some of the girls had done nearly as
well mining the miners. One, who went by the name of Red Stockings,
is said to have departed with more than a hundred thousand dollars.
It was enough to make good girls pause and consider.

By the late Seventies, California Gulch was to have its second
chance, something that did not come to all the mining camps. The
black rock whose presence so long had been disregarded by placer
miners proved to be silver-bearing carbonate of lead. A pair of prospectors who suspected the gulch's potentialities in silver hired a crew
of miners to extract the ore, explaining to them that it contained just
enough lead to keep open their mine. As the men shook their heads
in wonder at people who spent money "on a damn lead mine," the
owners kept their secret. When it was revealed, fabulous Leadville
stepped forth into the world of mineral fame. Unlike its predecessor,
Oro City, the new town managed to gain sufficient root to survive the
coming boom-and-bust cycle.

The spirit of expansion, development, and permanent settlement
found its headspring in the western town. Whether it was a raw mining camp, a cowboy capital, or a homesteaders' shopping center, the
town was the focus of ambitions for the area it served. Through its

newspapers, chamber of commerce, or informal associations of businessmen, the gospel of growth, prosperity, and future eminence was
preached. It was the city fathers, representing local merchants and
nearby farmers, who drew attention to the West's plunging progress
and the need for political recognition.

These places, often microscopic in size, were crucibles in which
great plans were brewed. They were the scenes of constant mass meetings in behalf of this or that improvement; the assembly point for
petitioners who demanded railroad service, prayed for the creation
of territorial or state government, or sought new favor from the
central government; a rendezvous for local volunteers organizing for
battle against nearby Indian tribes. They were dots on the map, in-
dicating the forward progress of the frontier.

Unlike coastal cities that were born as ports of commerce and so
frequently never changed the direction of their growth, mountain and
prairie municipalities gradually altered in composition as new economic forces appeared. They sprang up overnight, usually as the
result of the most recent phase of the general western boom and, if
they were lucky, they lived. Those that survived in the frantic rush to
riches did so because of their ability to adjust to new conditions.
When the first fruits of extraction were dissipated, a more solid basis
for existence had to be found. As a rule the answer was diversification of endeavor, the utilization of as many sources of income as
possible, and willingness to accept the fact that the quick-money days
were over. When the process was complete, western towns took on
the look and attitude of midwestern or eastern villages whose birth
had been somewhat less violent.

· The development of a mountain urban economy whetted the appetites of those who lived east of the desert, along the bend of the
Missouri River. Population of Colorado meant a market for hardware, clothing, and all manner of manufactured items. Missouri,
Kansas, and Nebraska cities looked westward and out of their warehouses came tons of goods destined for sale in the Rockies. The
Mormon "war" of 1857 demanded transportation for army supplies
and from that affair came the great freighting firm of Russell, Majors

and Waddell. By the time of the Colorado gold rush the company owned more than six thousand wagons and seventy-five thousand oxen. During 1860 Alexander Majors had some of his men hard at work building a three-story brick store in Denver. Others were engaged in similar construction, to the delight of the young *Rocky Mountain News*. Speaking of one store, "brilliant with paint relieved by large show windows," the paper proudly asked, "Where is the house west of St. Louis that can beat it?" A new commerce of the prairies was at hand.

The invasion of Colorado by gold-seekers, merchants, and emigrants enormously increased travel routes to that section of the mountains. The first to arrive used older trails, such as those along the Platte or the Santa Fe Trail up the Arkansas. But since these bracketed Colorado to the north and south, additional roads were developed as the traffic grew. To effect a more direct approach and to shorten the distance to the mines, cutoffs from both the older routes were made. There soon were additional roads running almost straight west.

The Smoky Hill route is a good example of the development. Wagon trains leaving the Missouri River towns lined out along the Smoky Hill fork of the Kansas River to eastern Colorado and from there went directly to Denver. It was the shortest way to the gold mines, but it was the most dangerous. Long stretches of arid land, with only occasional sources of wood and water, made the going risky. One miner who completed the trip wrote home that not everyone was so lucky. At one point he saw a party of fifty emigrants who had lost most of their work animals, had burned part of their wagons for fuel, and were now both hungry and sick. "Full 300 miles from any house, without fuel, save a scanty supply of wild sage ... and destitute in almost every particular, it is not to be wondered at, that they should all repent and even curse the day their folly sent them on this desperate chase for filthy gold."

Another of the more direct routes was developed by the Leavenworth and Pike's Peak Express Company. It ran along the Republican River to eastern Colorado, moved over to Big Sandy Creek, and then went straight into Denver. The company, organized by William H. Russell and John Jones, was the first stage line carrying passengers and mail from the Missouri River to the Colorado mines. Service began in May 1859 and was maintained on a weekly basis until the company sold out to the freighting firm of Russell, Majors and Waddell, which changed the route to run along the Platte. While Russell and Jones operated the stage line emigrants tended to follow the coaches, afforded protection by the stage stations, but after the change of route they used the more dangerous but more direct Smoky Hill road. Kansas merchants, anxious to benefit by the outfitting trade, were responsible for publicizing the latter roadway and inducing a large number of people to use it.

By the end of the Civil War, just prior to the entry of the railroad into mountain regions, wagon freighting had become a big business. A Kansas newspaper pointed with pride to the fact that the year 1865 had been notable for trade with the mining communities. Twenty-seven firms or individuals in the little town of Atchison alone were sending wagons westward. Together, they used nearly five thousand wagons, seven thousand horses and mules, and twenty-eight thousand oxen. More than five thousand men were required to keep this livestock and equipment rolling.

Nor was Atchison the only outfitting point. At a place like Leavenworth one could appreciate the magnitude of plains freighting. Horace Greeley's eyes bulged when he viewed the piles of equipment around the headquarters of Russell, Majors and Waddell. "Such acres of wagons! such pyramids of extra axletrees! such employees!" wrote the New York newspaperman in 1859. "No one who does not see can realize how vast a business this is, nor how immense are its outlays as well as its income. I presume this great firm has at this hour two millions of dollars invested in stock, mainly oxen, mules and wagons. They last year employed six thousand teamsters, and worked forty-five thousand oxen."

Strung out along the Missouri were still other towns, each anxious to become a metropolis, a "gateway to the West," or another "Queen City." Transportation was their economic lifeblood and from their warehouse doors poured a steady stream of boat-shaped Murphy wagons, each bearing about three and a half tons of freight. Westward to the Colorado mines went enormous quantities of hardware, bolts of cloth, heavy mining machinery, small household manufactures, and even luxury items. Anything for which there was a market went aboard the canvas-topped prairie schooners. A couple of Germans, catering to those of high taste, loaded one wagon with frozen oysters and peddled them along the way at $2.50 a quart. Others carried apples, selling them in Denver for fifteen dollars a bushel. Perhaps the most interesting cargo was a wagonload of cats, shipped to Denver as mousers. The demand for such services was apparently high, for the cat salesman had no difficulty in disposing of his livestock for a handsome profit.

The miners demanded more than necessities and occasional luxuries. Material things were not enough. One of their earliest desires was for communication, some tie with those who had been left behind. The first arrivals in Colorado discovered that the nearest post office was at Fort Laramie, far to the north. In the fall of 1858 Jim Saunders, a trader, tried to fill the need by hauling mail from Laramie in his wagon, charging fifty cents a letter and twenty-five cents apiece for newspapers. It was too slow and expensive a proposition; by the following summer a new method of delivery was introduced.

By May 1859, with the Leavenworth and Pike's Peak Express Company in operation, mail was carried directly across the nearly seven hundred miles between Leavenworth and Denver. After a few shakedown trips, the distance was covered in six to seven days, putting the mining population in much closer communication with "the states." The new venture was not a complete success. By the end of the first season its proprietors were faced with bankruptcy and were saved only by the intervention of Russell, Majors and Waddell, who bought out the stage line. Under a new name—the Central Overland California & Pike's Peak Express Company—and fortified with a government contract to carry mail, the organization maintained a connection with the mountain communities. In the face of such sarcastic nicknames as "Clear Out of Cash and Poor Pay," assigned by its employees, the C.O.C.&P.P. proceeded. That its services were satisfactory was indicated by a miner who wrote that any mail carried by the company "if put up good would be perfectly safe and come through very expeditiously."

By early 1861 the same miner could boast that Denver was receiving its news by telegraph to Fort Kearny and from there by Pony

Express. "This will give you some impression of Western enterprise," he wrote to his brother. "Receiving news thousands of miles and for six hundred miles and over an almost barren and uninhabited (except by the Indians) region—having them printed and distributed all through the mountains in five days! That is doing things up with a rush, as every thing is done in the West." Within months the telegraph wire would connect Denver to the outside world, ending a period of isolation. Once more the new Westerners had called for a service, and men along the great river had responded by unrolling hundreds of miles of wire.

Whatever the product, eastern Kansas and Nebraska had it or could get it. To the west was a market and gold with which to buy necessaries. The problem was one of logistics. Only the desert intervened and if it could be crossed without a major disaster at the hands of the natives or by the elements, a profit was assured. For this men would, and did, take a long calculated risk.

Like other western enterprises, that of transportation and communication fell to those who had capital. It was no place for small outfits; costs were enormous, profits were subject to a good many variables, and competition was fierce. Like modern airlines, freight outfits bid furiously for government contracts, knowing them to be the most reliable source of income. When Russell, Majors and Waddell secured a contract to furnish General Albert Sidney Johnston's army in the 1857 Utah campaign, it established an advanced supply base at Nebraska City, upriver from Leavenworth. By buying up nearly a hundred fifty lots, erecting shops, warehouses and stores at a cost of nearly three hundred thousand dollars, the firm created a new western boom town at a single stroke.

So the little grains of bright yellow metal threw a bridgehead across the desert, established a front line of civilization along the Rocky Mountains, and drew men from the East farther out onto the arid plains. The glittering prize lighted the way, illuminating the darkness of earlier obstacles, and convinced men that no matter how great the barriers they could be surmounted. After the men came their baggage, both material and cultural. Freight wagons brought them not only necessities but the trappings of civilization, printing presses, the refinements of books, and some art objects. The advance guard of males, the solitary prospectors, found money with which to buy, and out of their spending came roads, civic development, churches, schools, and above all—women. When the family unit came or was locally assembled, permanent settlement was normally assured. With the floating scum gone, those who were serious about the new land settled down to extract their own kind of gold—grain or cattle—and another section of the United States was commenced.

By the time Colorado's placer-mining rush began to decline, news of a big strike in Montana brought renewed hope to prospectors casting about for new locations. As always, the word spread like a grassfire and a hitherto untouched region of the West, barely viewed by a few explorers and known only by the fur traders, was turned into a booming, roistering series of mining camps. As usual, the evidence of gold had widespread repercussions, economically and politically. Almost overnight Montana was catapulted into the status of a territory and traffic to that remote country developed into a human flood.

Actually, the presence of gold was known in Montana some time before the Fifty-Niners invaded Colorado. François Finlay, also called Benetsee, is supposed to have found small quantities in 1852. Either the deposits were of little importance or word of their existence was purposely suppressed by the Hudson's Bay Company, whose representatives still carried on a fur trade in the vicinity, a business they did not want interrupted. In 1858, the year Green Russell made his find near Cherry Creek in Colorado, James and Granville Stuart panned gold in small amounts in Gold Creek, between the sites of Helena and Missoula. After a good deal of delay because of insufficient equipment and the loss of horses and supplies to the Indians, the Stuarts managed to set up sluices in the spring of 1862. The results were not particularly encouraging. The earth yielded only about three dollars a day in gold dust. That same spring a group of Colorado miners camped along a branch of Gold Creek and located a placer they named Pike's Peak Gulch. They fared better than the Stuarts, but there was still not enough "color" to justify a large-scale rush into that part of the country.

During the summer of 1862 another group of Colorado miners, led by John White, stopped at Gold Creek en route to the Salmon River country of Idaho. Sample pans showed an encouraging amount of gold dust and before long the men were making five to fifteen dollars a day. On the site of this, the first really profitable gold strike in Montana, arose the mining camp of Bannack. That city would be the territory's first capital and the home of its first legislative session in 1864.

A miner, fresh from Central City, Colorado, looked the new town over in the fall of 1863 and was disappointed. "It is not much of a place," he wrote in his diary. "It looks now as if it were a wild goose chase to come to this country." There were, as yet, no dry goods stores in town, and only two clothing and three grocery stores. But there was no shortage of saloons. "You can get whisky any time you want it," wrote the newcomer. Refusing two hundred fifty dollars a month to tend bar, the Coloradan ripped out his gloves and used the parts for patterns to make a living manufacturing gloves at nine dollars a pair during his first winter.

Meanwhile, in the spring of 1863, Henry Edgar, Bill Fairweather, and six others worked east of Bannack about fifty miles and made a rich strike in a ravine they called Alder Gulch. Fairweather and Edgar stumbled onto the color while they were guarding camp one day. Panning for what one of them called "enough to buy some tobacco when we get to town," they were astounded to find nearly five dollars in gold to the pan. A few days later the boys were back at Bannack, spending their money for "Salt Lake eggs, ham, potatoes, everything," as Edgar put it. "Such excitement!" he wrote later. "Everyone with a long story about the 'new find.' After I got my store clothes on, I was sitting in a saloon talking with some friends; there were lots of men that were strangers to me; they were telling that we brought in a horse load of gold and not one of the party had told that we had found color. Such is life in the 'Far West.' Well we have been feasted and cared for like princes."

The Alder Gulch news just about depopulated Bannack. As the Edgar–Fairweather party headed back for its claims, Bannack followed. "A crowd awaits us; crowds follow after us; they camp right around us, so we can't get away." Edgar was amused at his sudden popularity. So a new town was born along Alder Gulch. The original founders doffed their hats to Mrs. Jefferson Davis and called the place Varina, only to have a federal judge veto the notion. Into the books went the name Virginia City. Confederate sympathizers in Montana would have to find some other outlet for their sympathies. And they did, by riding past the log cabin that represented the territorial capitol building at Bannack, firing their revolvers, or by applauding a member of the legislative assembly when he positively refused to swear an oath of allegiance to the United States. Confederate or Union in their sentiments, the miners were as one in their economic thinking. A year after the new strike Virginia City had a population of thirty-five hundred and Madison County nearly twelve thousand. Three years of mining would yield nearly thirty million dollars worth of gold, ranking the "tobacco money" strike among the richest of western discoveries.

The golden gifts Montana had to bare were not yet all revealed. In the summer of 1864 a small party, discouraged and tired, made one final attempt in the Prickly Pear Valley and uncovered Montana's last major strike. They gave their location the appropriate name Last Chance Gulch, later to be more widely known as Helena. Before long the new town's inhabitants claimed to have the liveliest town beyond the Missouri, if not in the entire country. Even today, the era of the miner having passed and its principal "diggin's" now found in the state capitol payroll, Helena remains a lively ghost.

Just as in Colorado, the gold miners of Montana now and then were led to deposits of other valuable if less glamorous metals. As early as 1869, William J. Parks was convinced that his Parrot Lode mine at Butte was rich in copper. His three hundred fifty fellow townsmen were inclined to discount the theory and made known their doubts in the form of crude jests about Old Bill. While they laughed, he dug, determined to come up with ore that could be profitably smelted. Working with only a crude windlass and a bucket fashioned from half a whiskey keg. Parks sank his shaft a hundred fifty feet into the earth. As he toiled away, his skeptical friends paid him frequent calls, joking over "Parks' Gloryhole" and offering sarcastic advice.

"I do not mind so much their visits and advice," the miner told a friend, "but every time they come up to the cabin they eat up my grub and drink my whiskey."

Stubborn tenacity paid off. One day in 1876 the miner found what he was looking for—a heavy vein of pure copper. It was rich enough, he said, that "they could ship to hell and back for smelting and still make a profit." Then Bill Parks did something that dozens of other prospectors in the Rockies had done before him. After years of back-breaking toil, he sold out for a mere ten thousand dollars and watched Parrot Number One's new owners take out a million dollars worth of high-grade copper. While he dropped into obscurity, those who had taunted him cashed in on his find.

The immediate vicinity of the Parrot Lode became an anthill of activity as hundreds of miners riddled "the richest hill on earth" with shafts of their own. Individuals like Bill Parks were lost in the shuffle as corporate enterprise, armed with capital and scientific methods, took over. Before many years had passed the Anaconda Copper Company emerged not only as the owner of a city named Butte but also as the manager of a state called Montana. All Montanans today recognize the power of what is generally called "the company," but it is not likely that many of them would recognize the name of Parks. He merely made the discovery.

The Montana gold rush, like all its predecessors, shifted the focus of national attention to a new and undeveloped region. The movement of men and materials resulted in greatly increased travel and consequently much improved means of transportation. Quite aside from metallic considerations, the federal government had, in 1859, directed Captain John Mullan to link Fort Benton to Walla Walla (Washington) by road. The work was finished by 1863, just as the gold rush got under way. Over it poured miners from Oregon and Idaho, bound for the mines of the Rockies. Its eastern terminus, Fort Benton, emerged as a bridgehead between steamer travel and wagon trains moving from the head of navigation to the West.

The Montana mines were accessible not only from east and west, but also from the south. In 1863, a young Georgian who had recently drifted north from the Colorado mines marked off a trail between Fort Laramie and the Yellowstone River. Sometimes called the Powder River road, it was more widely known as the Bozeman Road. Despite objections by the Indians, John Bozeman organized another, and larger, train in 1864, with such success that the new route quickly became a popular short cut. So widespread was its attraction that in 1866 the government established Forts Reno, Phil Kearney, and C. F. Smith to protect travelers.

Yet another road reached Montana. Freighters found it profitable to haul supplies from Salt Lake City, by way of Corinne at the head of the lake. When the Union Pacific Railroad passed by the lake's promontory early in 1869, Corinne took on new significance as a major shipping point into Idaho and Montana. Since this route led through country inhabited by Indians less hostile than the Sioux, the government abandoned its protection of the Bozeman Road in 1868, encouraging those who wanted to approach Montana from the south to use the Corinne route. Until that time Montana was served by four major routes.

Although surprisingly high tonnages were hauled overland, the most popular route was the Missouri River. About five sixths of Montana's mining supplies were brought in by the river route. For over forty years steamboats had worked up and down the Missouri's lower reaches, but not until the eve of the Montana rush, in 1860, did any reach Fort Benton. The decade of the Sixties—Montana's flush period—saw the river travel soar to its peak and then decline. Arrivals at Fort Benton reached their high point in the immediate post–Civil War years and then quickly dropped. By 1870 only a handful of vessels made the trip. The big year was 1867; over ten thousand passengers were carried, and tons of supplies. The two-thousand-mile trip from Omaha to Fort Benton, accomplished in four to five weeks, could be made for an average of one hundred fifty dollars per person.

In the roistering, booming postwar years, when all America was on the move in search of better things, the Missouri River's reputation grew. A main avenue to the northern mines, thousands of men and women watched its muddy banks for days on end as their vessels crawled along. While it was the best means of travel, it was time-consuming, and passengers nodded agreement as the darky roustabouts chanted

> *We's bound fo' de gold fiel's*
> *Fas' as we kin go.*
> *No matter how soon we git dar*
> *Da's still gwine be too slow.*

Travel was not only slow; it was downright tricky. The river had a way of shifting its course and slyly planting new sandbars in former channels of navigation. During the 1830s an army officer had called the river "unimprovable." Not only was the current rapid, he said, but its refusal to stay in one place made steamboat travel hopeless. At that early date he could find few of the many bends described by Lewis and Clark and even those he was able to chart had disappeared before he could make a formal report.

Humorists took up the river's vagaries and employed them as a synonym for instability. "Of all the variable things in creation," said the editor of a Sioux City paper, "the most uncertain are the action of a jury, the state of a woman's mind, and the condition of the Missouri River." Then there is the much-quoted comment by George Fitch: "There is only one river with a personality, a sense of humor, and a woman's caprice; a river that goes traveling side-wise, that interferes in politics, rearranges geography, and dabbles in real estate; a river that plays hide and seek with you today and tomorrow follows you around like a pet dog with a dynamite cracker tied to his tail. That river is the Missouri."

New problems called for new solutions. In order to outwit the capricious river, prairie sailors turned inventors. When a river steamer, thrashing wildly against the muddy current, nosed onto a sandbar, the captain had a choice: back off or go on over the bar. To move forward, the vessel had to be lifted out of the water far enough to clear the obstruction. This was accomplished by a technique known as "grasshoppering," a term that took its name from the long spars, carried on the vessel's bow, that looked like giant grasshopper legs. An army officer, bound for a new assignment on the Upper Missouri, described the operation: "The great spars I spoke of are lowered along side to which are attached pulleys and ropes, and they deliberately lift the boat over, assisted however by a little engine called a 'nigger.' " Once the bow had cleared the sandbar, the paddle wheel at the stern flailed at the water and shoved the craft forward.

Crossing a sandbar was a moment of great tension for both passengers and crew. The drama of the situation is illustrated by a story told of a captain whose vessel was at the critical point, halfway over a bar, with engines straining to the breaking point when a woodchopper came down the bank and scooped up a bucketful of the river. Above the pounding of engines and the groaning of overloaded equipment, the captain's voice was heard as he roared, "Hey! You put that back!"

The river was becoming a part of the American legend. Difficult waterway that it was, it remained the West's greatest avenue of water transportation. It carried heavy machinery to the mines, brought back bullion more safely than land transportation, aided the Army in the movement of its men and supplies, and in its long, winding way served a vast section of the West. As far as Montana was concerned, the river acted as a navel cord, feeding that embryonic community until railroads could deliver it as a lusty agricultural frontier.

All along the Missouri River's twenty-five hundred miles between Fort Benton, Montana, and St. Louis there appeared ports of call, each of whom hoped one day to become a great inland entrepôt of trade. Those located on the southern reaches of the Missouri served as jumping-off places, staging areas in the great mineral invasion to the west. Farther up, they became intermediate supply points that looked down the tawny, muddy waterway toward civilization and a land known to them as "the states." The towns were connecting links between settled regions and the vast, unexplored frontier. The long, crooked pipeline of the Missouri was their only connection with the outside world.

The trouble with being a Missouri River town was that the river was steadily shrinking in length, so far as the river-steamer trade was concerned. Each time a new rail line moved westward, it sliced off a section of the river. In 1859 rails entered St. Joseph, Missouri, and eight years later the Chicago and North Western Line came to Council Bluffs. Within three years the Illinois Central reached Sioux City and steamboat trade south of that point fell off. One by one the river cities of Kansas, Nebraska, and Iowa surrendered to the iron road, just as did their wagon-road sisters farther west. Omaha and Council Bluffs were lucky. They managed to get rail service while many of their Missouri River competitors did not. Frequently this spelled the difference between life and death.

When the Northern Pacific was completed to Bismarck, Dakota Territory, in 1873, more hundreds of miles of trade were taken from the river. The final blow came when the Great Northern Railroad crossed Montana in 1891, bound for the Pacific Coast. With that event, for all practical purposes steamboat travel on the Missouri was at an end. With each of these developments the fortunes of hopeful river ports faded.

The Sixties marked the high tide of river traffic. In the 1865 travel season, a thousand passengers and six thousand tons of goods arrived at Fort Benton by water. Two years later, passenger figures soared to ten thousand and freight tonnage to more than eight thousand. Steamers had all the traffic they could carry at three-hundred-dollar fares for cabin accommodations and seventy-five dollars for deck passage. The *Ida Stockdale*'s trip in 1867 best illustrates the profits that were possible. On one round trip from St. Louis to Fort Benton, the vessel's owners cleared $42,594, not only the largest amount ever earned by a mountain steamboat for a single trip but twice the craft's original cost. A number of other owners made up to forty thousand dollars each. These were very profitable years for the light-draft stern-wheelers and they made the most of their opportunities.

Then the change set in. The fur trade, particularly that in buffalo hides, sagged badly. The placer-mining rush proved to be as evanescent as elsewhere and characteristically the prospectors decamped in favor of new diggings. To make matters worse, and as if conspiring to throttle Fort Benton's very necessities of life, the Canadian Mounted Police dried up the illegal whiskey traffic out of the north and gloom settled over the river metropolis. With the hell-roaring days slipping from its grasp, Fort Benton yielded to respectability. A new class, the merchant princes, took over and names like T. C. Power and I. G. Baker became important. Popskull whiskey, stud poker, and parlor houses were relegated to a lower rung on the social scale as a more permanent kind of wealth sought to recognize culture. "Those who at first were careless of their reputations and desirous only of accumulating fortunes and leaving the country are now eager to become reputable citizens and to establish permanent homes," one of Benton's newspapers confessed.

While the city fathers praised the unaccountable rise of virtue and travelers marveled at the city's transition from a crude frontier outpost to a settled and respectable community, Fort Benton was launched upon its final economic decline. Fewer and fewer sternwheelers appeared at the water front as river trade slackened. Then a new mode of transportation offered the town a reprieve from its death sentence. The arrival of railroads in Montana opened up cattle ranges in that country and a new wave of speculation swept the area. Like the gold rush, the boom was sudden and short. Nature stepped in, during the late Eighties, and the scythe of bitterly cold temperatures mercilessly thinned the herds. Hard on the heels of this disaster came Jim Hill's Great Northern Railroad, hauling in its legions of farmers, distributing them all across northern Montana. Almost overnight Fort Benton was neither a mineral transportation center nor a cowboy capital. It was just another Montana prairie town, selling harnesses and hardware to occasional homesteaders. The railroad, father of so many western cities, was the assassin of the one once labeled the Chicago of the Plains.

Whether it was located deep in the Colorado Rockies or in remote Montana, the western mining camp experienced the early arrival of justice, crude as it was. There was an absolute and immediate need for it. Men who crowded into precipitous gulches, measuring their claims by feet and sometimes inches, were bound to clash over disputed ownership. To prevent chaos if not anarchy, the miners had to adopt a set of rules for the settlement of such differences. They could not, did not, wait for eastern law to catch up with the rampaging westward course of their frontier.

By common consent a mining district was formed; to carry on day-to-day functions a president, a judge, a sheriff, a surveyor, and a recorder were elected. Other trappings of justice such as jails frequently were missing. It took time to build such institutions and their maintenance required labor, a scarce item. Fining, flogging, banishment, or hanging served as substitute penalties. The severity of the punishment doled out was measured by the crime. In the Gregory Diggings of Colorado, the price for willful murder was hanging; the punishment for manslaughter or homicide could be decided by the jury. Not far away, at Tarryall Diggings, a man found guilty of selling stolen property was sentenced to receive thirty lashes, the shaving of one half of his head, and banishment. So the sentences went, harsh and physical but, it was hoped, just.

The situation was much the same in the Montana mining camps. When Bannack was less than a year old, its thousand residents decided the time had come for law and order. In May 1863, more than half the population turned out to elect a set of officers. The successful office-seekers were generally respected men, except for the sheriff, Henry Plummer. A known gambler and killer who had only recently moved to Bannack, the newly elected sheriff soon reverted to type. Before long the people discovered that they had elected only a part-time peace officer. In his off hours, he was the leader of a gang of bandits who showed their patriotism for Montana by trying to prevent any gold from leaving the territory. So successful were their endeavors that most of the roads leading out of the region became quite unsafe as financial arteries.

Montanans quickly showed their resentment for this kind of tight-money policy and soon the limbs of roadside cottonwood trees fairly blossomed with dangling corpses. A sizable number of highwaymen, including their leader, Plummer, were, as the saying went, "jerked to Jesus." Some of the more humanitarian natives had qualms about this kind of justice and, after one execution, a fellow townsman asked the vigilante who had fitted the noose: "Did you not feel for the poor man as you put the rope around his neck?"

"Yes," replied the hangman sympathetically. "I felt for his left ear."

For the moment, the aroused miners were resolved to stick to hemp justice until the more turbulent element settled down or left the country. They had not the slightest intention of deviating from that course even if it meant the defiance of legally constituted authority. When they thought of relaxing this determination, they remembered the Daniels case and their resolve again hardened. James Daniels was arrested by the vigilantes for killing a man in a card game near Helena. They released him to civil authorities, only to see him sentenced to a mere three years. This was bad enough; worse, the prisoner was released after only three weeks' imprisonment by order of the newly arrived acting governor of the territory. As fast as Daniels could get there, he returned to Helena, threatening those who had testified against him. Just as quickly, the vigilantes took him in tow and suspended him from a tree, with the governor's pardon still in his pocket. When the body was cut down a note was found pinned to it, reading: "If our acting governor does this again, we will hang him too." The governor got the point. In the future he was much more cautious with the use of his power of pardon.

The hemp period was brief. All up and down the mountain front, the era of the placer miner quickly passed and with it went the rough-and-tumble existence so characteristic of bonanza-type populations. Some towns died. Others desperately sought a more balanced kind of economy in order to live. A part of this struggle for existence was the quest for civic respectability. City fathers quickly sensed the value of a good reputation and mercilessly hushed any taint of scandal lest it reflect upon the state of local business affairs. General James T. Rusling noticed this as early as 1866 at Denver when he remarked of the city that "the mob-spirit of her early days could not be revived" over a political row then at its height. Residents were obliged to bite their lips and keep holstered their guns for fear of creating any unfavorable publicity that would frighten away prospective investors. Denver, and a host of her sisters, sought conformity to law for the age-old reason—"what would people think?" As one of its other visitors put it, the Colorado capital was "like a reformed rake in broadcloth and fine linen, and resents any allusion to its day of bowie-knives and buckskins."

In the contest for permanent greatness among the Rocky Mountain cities, Denver took first prize. Its business leaders fought for railroad connections with neighboring regions, sought out its share of national trade, furnished the nearby mountain cities with necessities, cultivated commerce with the agricultural communities to the north, east, and south, and became the capital of what one of its newspapers likes to call the "Rocky Mountain Empire." Leadville lived off its patrimony of silver for a few decades and then turned to other mineral deposits. Pueblo gave up its early hope of golden riches and settled for less glamorous excavations from the earth, claiming the title "Pittsburgh of the West" as it became a steel center. Butte, famous for copper, took its place as Montana's leading city.

Most of the other placer-mining camps faded away, leaving only weatherbeaten, crumbling shacks as a withered monument to once young and vigorous dreams. Central City, Colorado, and Virginia City, Montana, after a number of moribund decades, again gasped into life and like old and painted bawds sold their memoirs for a living. Behind reconstructed facades of their early days these mining camps became the haunts of thousands of tourists who make annual pilgrimages to them and little by little put back the gold their forefathers so laboriously extracted. The natives, who recognize the dollar value of nostalgia, each summer comport themselves as quaintly as they know how and patiently mine the strangers until fall —when they may again act more normal. The digging is pretty slow, but it is better than nothing, and it probably will be a long time petering out for, as they know, Barnum was right.

The early gold-mining towns, regardless of how momentary their existence, contributed to a more permanent settlement. In an economic way they gave rise not only to a thriving plains trade but were responsible as well for the rapid growth of a whole string of cities along the mountain front that acted as advance supply bases. This was particularly true in Colorado, where the Rockies rear up with dra-

matic suddenness and the western border of the plains country is
clearly marked. At the mouths of the many canyons—gateways into
the mountains—arose small, hopeful centers of commerce.

In Montana, where the main range of the Rockies does not so
uniformly confront the grasslands, supply towns were sprinkled among
the mining camps somewhat more unevenly. Here it was the
Missouri River, and places like Fort Benton, that fed the mining
population, for Montana was blessed by water transportation, something Colorado never had. Gold was the magnet, and it pulled
steamers upriver across Nebraska and Kansas. When the magnet
lost its power, the newborn centers of commerce struggled on, grasping at any and all alternatives. Some of them managed to survive.

While many of these cities were enjoying a slow but steady growth,
despite ups and downs in the business of mining, prospectors spread
out, searching more remote and unexplored locations with the hope
of finding a new bonanza. In Montana, for example, the mineral
frontier tended to move southward toward present Wyoming, a development that was natural in the light of past experience. The Big
Horn country had shown enough evidence of gold to attract the restless, those who were always ready to find an even better location.
South of Montana, also, lay the Wind River Valley and South Pass.
Sufficient gold was found in that area during 1867 to touch off a fresh
rush from both Montana and Colorado, each of whose placers were
giving out by this time. South Pass City and Atlantic City soon
flanked the famous pass and were swelled daily by the arrival of
miners. When that location proved to be less profitable than had
been anticipated, the Big Horn Mining Association was formed in
1870 to exploit the neighboring country. Army officers, charged with
keeping peace in that region, objected strenuously to the new invasion
and ordered the organized miners to stay out of the Big Horn Mountains. Political pressures, and cries of righteous rage from Cheyenne,
had their effect and the miners proceeded. Within a few months most
of them were back, broke and tired, having found nothing but rough
country and poor hunting.

If prospecting was poor in Wyoming, there was always one bit of
solace for the miner: tales of new finds elsewhere excited his mind
once again and sent him packing for the new discovery. The Black

Hills of Dakota furnished this land of promise in the 1870s. Since before the Civil War there had been talk of hidden wealth in those parts. When that domestic conflict was over, there was a renewed interest in exploiting the Dakota hills, regardless of Indian treaties or any other strictures. Vainly the Army protested, with Generals Sherman and Sheridan going so far as to run out miners who intruded. But as always the pressure was too great and the indecisive Grant submitted to popular demands. By 1877 the Sioux were forcibly persuaded to give up their claims and, with that surrender, settlement proceeded on a legal basis.

Already the miners had carved out temporary empires around French Creek and in Deadwood Gulch. Without noticing that the region was not yet open to settlement, the city of Deadwood was laid out and a provisional government established in the spring of 1876. Early that year a stage line was put into operation between Cheyenne and the Black Hills. The traffic was at once so heavy that not all prospective passengers could be accommodated. Anxious travelers stood around the stage office, ready to pay the twenty dollars, and even more if necessary, for passage to Custer City. Those who were lucky enough to buy a ticket could make the 246-mile trip from Cheyenne in three days.

Within a year there were complaints that the miners were earning little more than bed and board by their efforts. The rush had passed its high point by the spring of 1877 and as always the floating population of prospectors began to disperse and scatter in search of new and better gold fields. Wagonloads of heavy machinery entering the country now met individual miners leaving. Suddenly, with the surface wealth taken from the stream beds, the pick and pan period ended. Behind the crates of machinery came settlers, cautiously poking their way into a new country, ready to apply their own instruments of extraction to the land. When they unloaded their plows and harrows, another phase of economic activity commenced.

So the desert was spanned and then shackled. Gold, and later silver, were the incentives that drew men forward. Once more the high plains and mountains were invaded by wealth-seekers, as in the days of the mountain men. But this time they left their tracks on the land and their little settlements were like seeds planted, forced into germination, then nearly abandoned only somehow to survive. Before the great subsurface treasure hunt was over daring, ambitious, even reckless men had crisscrossed the few remaining unknown portions of the midcontinent, revealing most of its geographic and climatic secrets. These economic storm troopers, as lusty a crew as ever assaulted virgin land, ruthlessly cut their way west, shoving aside animate and inanimate obstacles in their search for gain. When they had had their fill they turned to the cattleman and to the sodbuster with the invitation, "Here, you try your luck for a while."

And the newcomers did. They picked up after the floating population, utilized the established wagon routes, furnished the railroads new business, lived in the new towns or built some of their own, and settled down to the task of making a living. There were readjustments, of course, but the ground had now been marked and staked out for further economic extraction. On a cornerstone of precious metal the building would go forward.

Chapter 5 PICKET
LINE
OF
CIVILIZATION

The national treasure hunt being conducted in their part of the country deeply disturbed the natives. Their concept of land utilization and value did not include subsurface investigations, and their initial curiosity about the white man's probings gradually turned to anger. To the Indians the land was a hunting ground, a game preserve belonging to all hunters, and no individual had the right to claim any part of it for his exclusive use. The early trappers had understood this theory and they had abided by it. Since they were few in number and had goods to trade, there was little objection to such visitations.

But the miners lacked the sociability of the mountain men. They had not come out to do business with the Indians, but to drill holes in the earth or to roil the streams with their picks and pans. Even this could be tolerated by the native landlords, providing it did not get out of hand. It was the magnitude of the rush, the size of the prospectors' armies, and the disturbance caused by their necessary lines of communication with the East that generated a resentment finally translated into violent action.

Western tribes for generations had controlled the plains and mountains with little interference. Small bands of trappers or explorers roamed the land with little or no molestation, certain that if they played the game according to its rules no harm would come to them. From time to time there was conflict, as in the case of General Ashley's traders along the Missouri, but as a rule men passed through the Indian kingdom unscathed. On the northern plains the Sioux, Arikara, Blackfeet, and Crows followed the buffalo herds, engaging in periodic tribal warfare and exchanging beaver pelts for trinkets or firearms with white traders. When there was trouble, it was resolved the best way the whites knew: they absented themselves from that part of the country until things quieted down. Nobody thought of calling for the Army. It would have been a useless request.

Of all the plains tribes the Sioux were the most powerful and, with the possible exception of the Blackfeet, the most dreaded. The Siouan family, large and loosely knit, covered the plains from Canada to Louisiana, but the best-known of the tribes was the Teton branch of the Dakota Sioux. In this group were the Blackfeet Sioux (not to be confused with the Blackfeet nation), the Brules, Hunkpapas, Miniconjous, Oglalas, San Arcs, and the Two-Kettles band. The Oglalas probably were the most famous in western history because of their ferocity and numbers, and their leaders became well known to the American reading public.

The larger Dakota group, including the Eastern Dakota, Santee–Dakota, Teton–Dakota, and Yankton Sioux, made such an impression upon the public mind that it became the prototype of all Indians in the eyes of illustrators and artists. Those who tried to depict "the Indian" to the public came to understand that a native garbed in Dakota-style dress was the surest way. As Clark Wissler remarked in his book *Indians of the United States,* "That is why we see paintings of the Pilgrims landing at the famous rock, greeted by Indians dressed like Dakota, or again Indians receiving Henry Hudson at Manhattan in the same kind of clothes, or Pocahontas in the wedding dress of a Dakota bride." Absurd, of course, but it is the artist's method of telling the viewer that an Indian is being shown.

By the time the white man became a threat to Indian economy the Dakota Sioux dominated much of the northern plains. The Assiniboines, part of the Sioux nation, were enemies rather than allies. Ranging the upper reaches of modern North Dakota and Montana, and into Canada, they made their bid for control of economic resources—the buffalo—and fought it out with the Dakotas. Smallpox came to the aid of the Dakotas during the 1830s by cutting the ranks of the Assiniboines in half. From that point on, the decline of the challengers was rapid. Nor did other cousins of the Dakotas give them much trouble. Warfare against the Crows, constant and bloody, wore away the resistance of that tribe, while the Mandans were never real contenders for plains hegemony. When the white invasion began the Dakotas stood powerful and dominant, ready to contest every inch of ground.

Backed against the Rocky Mountains, west of the Sioux, were the Blackfeet, Gros Ventres, Cheyennes, and Arapahoes, all members of the western Algonkin group. The Blackfeet, divided into the Bloods, Piegans, and Blackfeet proper, dominated what is now the north-central portion of Montana and southern Alberta and Saskatchewan. Under their protection was the smaller Gros Ventre tribe that ranged between the Canadian Belly River country and Montana. Southward, along the mountain front, the Cheyennes and Arapahoes lay in the path of the westward-moving whites, also ready to contest claims to the buffalo country. They tended to spread eastward from the Rockies more than the Blackfeet did.

Contact between the white men and the Blackfeet took place during the eighteenth century and, once armed with the guns and horses, these Indians soon became the scourge of their part of the plains. From the traders' standpoint they were exceedingly hard to deal with and the average trapper chose to give them a wide berth. Thanks to their remote location with reference to the frontier movement, the Blackfeet avoided any general war with the United States, but other and more deadly enemies (including smallpox, venereal disease, and whiskey) contributed to their degeneration. The epidemic that so reduced the Assiniboines also seriously cut the strength of the Blackfeet.

The area of present Nebraska, Kansas, and eastern Colorado was dominated by the Arikara and Pawnee tribes. Just south of them lived the Comanches and Kiowas, whose warriors made life miserable for emigrants and freighters bound for Santa Fe or mining camps in the mountains. Most of the annoyance caused passers-by was in the nature either of begging or, in more aggravated instances, isolated attacks by small raiding parties.

In general there was nothing that could be dignified by the name "war" between the whites and the plains Indians until the period just preceding the Civil War. Even then, the action usually was referred to as a "campaign." As more and more Americans appeared, the Indians' nervousness increased. They showed it in their tendency to raid more frequently and in the viciousness of the attacks. The time of peace was running out.

By the Fifties plains traffic began to get heavy. Oregoners, Mormons, Forty-Niners, and then the Fifty-Niners put tremendous pressure on not only the tribes but also upon their economy. Buffalo herds were scattered by the white assault and hunting became a grim race for existence. Then the Americans began to talk about building railroads to the Pacific. In 1849 the Secretary of the Interior forecast the need of improved transportation facilities to far-western settlements. Not only did the needs of commerce require it, he wrote, but the railroad would also act as an instrument of control over the tribes. In the same department, the Commissioner of Indian Affairs saw the necessity for readjustments. Why not shove tribes like the Pawnee north of the Platte River and confine the Sioux to the line of the Missouri? Then, by pushing back the southern tribes, a broad avenue westward would be freed of mischievous Indians.

The administration saw the point. By 1850 it was obvious that some arrangements must be made for travel along the Platte route. Word was sent to the plains Indians that a grand powwow to discuss the matter would be held out at Fort Laramie in September 1851. At the appointed time Superintendent of Indian Affairs D. D. Mitchell; the editor of the *St. Louis Republican,* B. Gratz Brown (later to be Missouri's governor); and Father DeSmet turned up at Laramie. One by one the tribes came in. Arapahoe, Cheyenne, Sioux, Assiniboine, Shoshone, Arikara, Gros Ventre, and Crow warriors pitched their tepees. When sufficient pipes had been smoked, the Americans made their offer. In return for fifty thousand dollars annually for fifty years, they expected unmolested passage through the region, with full rights to make roads and protect them with military posts. The Indians there regarded this as fair enough. But there was a small hitch. The natives did not reckon with the disposition of the United States Senate. The Solons reduced the time to ten years and sent back the agreement for ratification. But the Indians had gone home. After a fruitless search for all the signatories, the hunt was called off and to this day the treaty stands unratified. Unaccountably, the government decided to honor the agreement as best it could, despite the Senate's intransigence, and it paid for about fifteen years, during which time the Indians generally abided by the agreement.

The Laramie Treaty was an opening wedge. In 1853 the Commissioner of Indian Affairs recommended the extinguishment of land titles in the Kansas and Nebraska region. Already the Kansas–Nebraska question was before Congress, and one of the obstacles to the political subdivision it contemplated was the presence of the Indians. While Congress debated its question, agents were out on the plains, buying off the natives. By 1854 the idea of two great Indian colonies, one lying on either side of the great Platte roadway, was practically in effect.

Transactions with the Indians in eastern Kansas and Nebraska were uneventful, but farther west there was trouble. The difficulty, out near Fort Laramie, originated in something of the manner of the great Chicago fire—from a cow. In August 1854 some of the Sioux came into Laramie to collect their annuities and their visit coincided with the passage of a group of westbound Mormons. Before the party passed one of its cows was killed, presumably by an Indian, although guilt was never fixed. The emigrants complained. Bear-that-Scatters, a Brule Sioux who had signed the Laramie Treaty, offered to give up the accused. Lieutenant Hugh Fleming, temporarily in command of the fort, was inclined to defer the matter until the arrival of an Indian agent, but young Lieutenant Grattan, a hot-headed Irishman just out of West Point, begged for a chance to bring in the Indian. Reluctantly Fleming agreed, on the condition that Grattan take no unnecessary risks. In a state of high excitement the lieutenant gathered together thirty men and set forth, determined to "conquer or die." The latter alternative fell his lot as he tried to storm the Sioux village. When the shouting was over Grattan and his entire contingent lay dead.

Lieutenant Fleming showed himself as equally unaware of Indian affairs as Grattan in his reaction to the tragedy. He recommended that the government at once dispatch a force sufficient in size effectively to punish the natives, believing that if this were done "no hostility from other surrounding tribes may be expected." More than two decades later another young officer named Custer was issuing the same gratuitous advice.

The Grattan massacre, as it became known, touched off sporadic raids along the great western road. There were no general or concerted attacks, just occasional hit-and-run forays led by young bucks out to make a name in their business. Three months later, for example, the Salt Lake stage was attacked and three employees were killed. Because of scattered attacks and a general sullenness on the part of the northern tribes, Colonel William S. Harney was ordered to punish the Sioux. During August 1855 he set out from Fort Kearny, Nebraska, with six hundred men and the threat "By God, I'm for battle—no peace." Moving up the Oregon Trail to Ash Hollow he ran across Little Thunder and his band of Brule Sioux. Declining the Indian's suggestion of a parley, Harney carried out his battle dictum and fell upon the enemy. The affray was unusual not so much for its details as the fact that the round defeat administered to the Indians became known as a massacre. Traditionally this term has been reserved for white reverses. But this time the natives were slaughtered, to the delight of one soldier who wrote "I never saw a more beautiful thing in my life." He was barely apologetic for the death of a number of women and children.

After marching around the Fort Laramie region threatening other

Indians, Harney headed for the Missouri River and camped at Fort Pierre, where he called for a general conference. In March 1856, nine tribes signed on the line, agreeing to keep their hands off all travelers in the future. The government accordingly promised to renew its annuities and supply agricultural implements to all Indians who requested them. Apparently the Sioux campaign was concluded successfully, except for one detail: neither side kept its promise.

The Army next turned its attention to the Cheyennes. Colonel E. V. Sumner, an old campaigner, and Major John Sedgwick were sent out to scour the country for hostiles. Contact was made in July 1857 along the Solomon River in Kansas and after a sharp fight the force of about three hundred Indians was put to flight. Sumner reported that two of his men were killed. Among the wounded was a lieutenant named J. E. B. Stuart, who recovered and in a few years became famous as a Confederate cavalry officer. Pursuing the Indians, Sumner came upon their principal village and destroyed nearly two hundred lodges. As Hafen and Young put it in their *Fort Laramie:* "Thus ended the Sumner campaign against the Cheyennes. It had chastised a few Indians, embittered many more and overawed none."

Fortunately for the Indians, differences among the whites relieved the increasing army pressure on the plains tribes. During the summer of 1857 the natives watched a strange procession move westward. Some twenty-five hundred blue-clad troops, a herd of two thousand beef cattle, and a great supply train were dispatched to Mormon country in the vicinity of Salt Lake. Brigham Young and his followers had lived in their New Zion for a successful decade and their ability to thrive, their independence of mind, and their institution of polygamy appeared to worry the American public. In the election of 1856 the new Republican party had called out for the elimination of the "twin relics of barbarism," slavery and polygamy. Unable to do anything about the matter of Negro slavery, President James Buchanan apparently sought to exercise a more strict control over his polygamous subjects in Utah. In the spring of 1857 he decided to name new, non-Mormon officials to the territory and without any

public announcement he ordered the Utah expedition to insure political control for these appointees.

The Mormons, whose history had been filled with examples of persecution, were understandably exercised over the news that an army
was marching all the way from Fort Leavenworth to stand guard over
them. They were not told that Young was to be replaced as governor;
nothing was said about the general intent of Buchanan's moves. Or-
ganizational delays, the natural barriers of distance across the plains,
and the approach of bad weather obliged the force to winter at Fort
Bridger in the southwestern part of modern Wyoming. Colonel Albert
Sidney Johnston, who soon would lose his life fighting his countrymen
at the battle of Shiloh, arrived that November to take command of
the encamped army and to await the coming of spring. So far as
he knew, there would be civil war in the West when the campaigning
season arrived.

As the soldiers shivered in below-zero weather and complained
about the inadequacy of supplies, a solution to the military problem
was being worked out back in Washington, D.C. There were loud
complaints about the mismanagement of the expedition and bitter
criticisms of Buchanan for having launched it so precipitously. "Old
Buck," as he was called, escaped from his dilemma by accepting the
offer of a philanthropist named Thomas L. Kane to mediate the difficulty. In a series of conferences during the winter of 1857–1858,
Kane and the Mormon leaders worked out a compromise that permitted the new governor, Alfred Cumming, to assume his office
without having to fight for it. In June 1858 the expeditionary force
marched into Salt Lake City unopposed and encamped nearby. There
was no resistance.

Hardly had the "Mormon War" passed into history than the white
men took up arms against one another in a major civil war. This one
was fought in earnest and it lasted four years. It drew no complaints
from the red plainsmen, who sat back and watched with deep satisfaction as the whites counted coups on each other. During the first
half of the Sixties there were no large expeditions against the Indians
because there could be none. Neither the Union nor the Confederacy
could spare men for such enterprises. They were too busy fighting
each other for control of the land. Attentiveness to the natives would

have to await the outcome of the struggle for power taking place east of the Mississippi.

For the most part, people of the high-plains West stood on the side line as spectators, cheering on the participants of the big war along the Atlantic seaboard. The rooting section was by no means a one-sided group; both causes had their fervent supporters. In a few instances the viewers became sufficiently excited over the contest to engage in minor military flurries of their own. Colorado furnishes a good example.

At the outset of the war there was some disposition on the part of Coloradans to remain aloof. The region's leading newspaper, the *Rocky Mountain News,* at first refused to take sides but before long its editor was referring to the "bogus Confederacy" and assuming a strong pro-Union stand. Its rival, the *Mountaineer,* fired off editorial salvos in defense of the Confederacy until May 1861, when its management sold out to the *News* and went back home to don the gray uniform. These journals reflected differences of opinion among their readers. Even before the outbreak of war, two prominent Denverites had put on a civil war of their own. When L. W. Bliss proposed an antislavery toast, Dr. J. S. Stone took exception to its sentiments. Bliss immediately hurled the contents of his glass into the other's face and was as quickly challenged to a duel. The question was settled with shotguns at thirty paces along the banks of the nearby Platte River. In this particular event the South lost; Dr. Stone was killed by a blast of buckshot. The question over which they fought was an academic one so far as Colorado was concerned. The 1860 census showed only eighty-nine Negroes in the entire territory.

The outbreak of the Civil War generated enough excitement around Denver to cause a minor local crisis. On April 24 that city's residents were startled to see the "Rag of Treason," as a newspaper called it, hoisted over Murphy and Wallingford's store on Larmier Street. Accounts of what happened next differ, but it is agreed that the Stars and Bars came down in a hurry. Such occurrences sharpened the issue in Colorado, obliging men who had once dallied with the idea of neutrality to take one side or the other. A majority elected to stand with the federal government. This was something of a relief to William Gilpin, the newly appointed territorial governor, who arrived in

Denver late in May 1861. Without funds and faced by hostile Southern sympathizers, he promptly took advantage of Union sympathy to organize Colorado's armed forces.

Saving Colorado from the inroads of secession was to be no small problem. Gilpin had little trouble in raising volunteer troops, whose patriotism was second only to the need of employment and the prospect of excitement. But the opposition was equally busy recruiting. One A. B. Miller was said to have raised fourteen hundred "secesh" soldiers. While the figure was exaggerated, the existence of a body of troops was not. Miller assembled a train of twenty wagons filled with provisions, a herd of more than four hundred cattle, and a considerable assemblage of men. The organization demonstrated openly in Denver before setting off for an undisclosed destination. It was captured in Kansas during October 1861. Joel McKee, another Southern recruiter, brazenly engaged in an arms race with Governor Gilpin and was accused of trying to corner the percussion-cap market in Colorado. The venture failed when a U.S. marshal arrested McKee in Denver. His followers threatened to rescue him by force, but changed their minds about storming Denver and took up raiding wagon trains until they were run down by federal troops.

Other secessionists came to a more violent end. Charles Harrison, a Denver gambler, and W. P. McClure, local postmaster, crossed the plains to the headquarters of Confederate General Sterling Price in Missouri and convinced him they could raise a regiment of troops in Colorado. On the return trip the little group ran afoul of a band of Osage Indians who had been scouting for the federal Army. In the free-for-all that ensued, most of the erstwhile recruiters were killed and the story has been handed down that the victors proudly returned to their blue-coated friends bearing the heads of their victims as evidence of their efficiency.

More significant than efforts to combat Union forces in Colorado was the Confederate attempt to hijack its gold. In the summer of 1862 a band of guerrillas, led by one "Captain" Madison, prowled southern Colorado to "harass and rob the Government," as the *News* put it. Nothing came of the venture. Better known, although no more successful, was the raiding foray made by James Reynolds and his men in 1864. The raider and several of his followers later were captured and sent to Fort Lyon, in southeastern Colorado. En route they were said to have made the familiar attempt to escape and were shot down. Details of what really happened are tantalizingly absent. At the time no complaints were heard around Denver. Sporadic raids by such gangs as those of Madison and Reynolds posed no real threat to Colorado gold stocks.

The Confederate government, however, put on a raid that was of much larger proportions; although this also failed, the prospect for success was much greater. Under orders from Jefferson Davis, a force led by Colonel John R. Baylor entered New Mexico in the summer of 1861. Before long Baylor had the southern parts of modern New Mexico and Arizona under his control. The plan was to enter Southern California and to infiltrate into the Colorado mining country as deeply as possible. This would have two results: the Confederacy could boast to the world that it was spread from coast to coast and it would at the same time control some valuable mineral resources highly necessary to it in financing the war. By February 1862 Baylor was installed as territorial governor of the newly conquered area and Confederate Brigadier General Henry H. Sibley was in possession of Albuquerque. Very shortly Santa Fe fell. It appeared that the Southerners soon would reach Colorado.

Standing between the Confederates and the Rocky Mountain gold fields was General E. R. S. Canby and his force of federal soldiers. This was not enough. Canby called for help and got it in the form of the Colorado Volunteers, sent down by Governor Gilpin. They were, as William MacLeod Raine called them, "wild, gay, rollicking, tempestuous sons of the frontier, hard drinkers and hard fighters." Led by Colonel John Slough, the Colorado contingent collided with the oncoming force at a place called Glorieta Pass, about twenty miles southeast of Santa Fe. In a wild, hard-charging battle covering two days (March 26–28) the Coloradans provided the spark that is held to have turned the tide. The "Pike's-Peakers" gave a good deal of credit to the exploits of Colonel J. M. Chivington, a preacher turned soldier for the occasion, but folks around Santa Fe had other ideas about his military prowess. They did not, however, take any credit from those hardies who had left their picks and pans to make a man-killing march into New Mexico in Canby's behalf. The retreat they triggered continued until all of "Baylor's Babes" were driven back into Texas, Governor Baylor included. With that the Confederate Territory of Arizona—stretching all the way from Texas to California—evaporated, and Union forces took over for the duration of the war.

After the "Gettysburg of the West," as Glorieta has been called, there was little more than desultory fighting on the plains. The arrival of the California Volunteers, under General James H. Carleton, relieved the Colorado troops, who returned home. Western military activity from then until the end of the Civil War was confined to keeping open lines of communication and warding off occasional Indian forays. Protection of the Overland Trail across Nebraska, Wyoming, and Utah was put into the hands of Colonel Patrick E. Connor, Third Regiment of California Volunteers, who settled down near Salt Lake City and spent most of his time annoying the Mormons, whom he seemed to regard a greater threat than the plains tribes. Toward the end of the war he expanded his operations into present Wyoming and with the help of some "Galvanized Yankees" (Confederate prisoners released from prison to go west and fight Indians) he set about exterminating the natives with a ferocity that had to be curbed by higher authority.

Generally speaking, there were no serious Indian difficulties on the plains during the first half of the Sixties. The government could afford to spare few regulars for such duty. As always, any raids by groups of uncontrolled young bucks generated loud cries from stripling western communities, who invariably insisted that they were about to be wiped out. In some cases there was justification for these complaints. For example, during August 1862 the Santee Sioux went on the warpath in Minnesota, killing a number of settlers. Volunteer troops under the command of Colonel Henry Hastings Sibley [1] took the field, rounding up about fifteen hundred Indians, after which a giant court-martial was held. More than three hundred of the accused were condemned to death but President Lincoln's intercession cut the

[1] Not to be confused with Colonel Henry H. Sibley, C.S.A., who led his Confederates against General Canby in New Mexico in the spring of 1862; see page 109.

number to thirty-nine. This left enough for a good-sized hanging, which was staged late in December.

Out in Colorado the mismanagement of Indian affairs produced long-range difficulties for the entire region. By early 1864 Denver and some of the smaller communities were feeling the effects of Indian hamstringing raids on their prairie commerce. It was not hard to convince the settlers that a mighty red uprising was in the making. Governor John Evans gained government permission to raise a regiment of hundred-day cavalrymen to meet the enemy. Unfortunately they were led by the glory-hunting John M. Chivington, who had attracted some public notice in the battle of Glorieta. Late in November he led his white braves against a group of Southern Cheyenne and Arapaho Indians encamped along Sand Creek in southeastern Colorado.

The nature of the affair that ensued may be understood by the term used to describe it: the Sand Creek massacre. In this encounter Chivington led almost a thousand men against a camp of Indians who supposed they were under the protection of the Indian agent, E. W. Wynkoop. The American flag flew over the chief's tepee to signify that it was under the protection of the federal government. But those who were out to save Colorado from the red scourge were not concerned with such details. They struck at dawn and before the day was over the encampment was strewn with corpses, many of which were those of women and small children. No one knows how many; the numbers of reported dead range from sixty to six hundred, with Chivington claiming the latter figure.

When the blood bath was over the Colonel headed for Denver. His men carried home more than a hundred scalps, some of which were suspended across the stage of a Denver theater as evidence of the Volunteers' patriotism. Early public reaction was favorable, but as the details began to be made known, Chivington's military fame was somewhat diminished.

His defense against criticism for killing children was the comment: "Nits make lice." A few months after the Sand Creek massacre the Civil War came to a close and the Regular Army resumed its task of Indian control in the West. In its absence the Volunteers had muddied the military waters considerably and left professional soldiers with more complicated problems than they ever before had faced.

That the Indians waived the opportunity to drive out the white Americans who had moved gradually in on them is either testimony supporting their peaceful intentions or a sharp criticism of their inability to organize at a time when events promised such a movement success. At any rate, they passed up their final chance to maintain control over the lands they claimed, for once the Civil War was over the western Indians' cause was doomed. No force on earth, not even that of the American government, could stem the tidal wave of settlement that followed the end of the war.

Reverend Chivington's good work among the natives had more widespread repercussions than he imagined. The howl of indignation that went up from humanitarians in the East was overshadowed by the undisguised fury of the plains Indians. As the Southern Cheyennes spread the word about Sand Creek to their brothers, the Northern Cheyennes, and to the Sioux and Arapahoes, pent-up furies broke their bonds. Almost at once there were reprisals. In January 1865, the Cheyennes caught nine eastbound men—who, it happened, were veterans of Chivington's little army—and in a matter of moments dispatched them. Upon opening the dead men's valises they found two scalps identified as belonging to their own people. The discovery stimulated their desire for revenge. Julesburg, Colorado, was attacked and plundered. Out of that frontier town went the Indians, waving captured articles and trailing bolts of cloth behind their ponies. But one bit of loot they threw away. An Army paymaster's strongbox, containing forty thousand dollars in currency, was opened and after puzzled examination the raiders scattered the useless green paper across the prairie, disappointed at not finding something of greater utility.

During the spring of 1865 guns were silenced in the East, but west of the Missouri warfare broke out in earnest. In what became known as the "bloody year" on the plains, the Army grimly fought to check concerted raids by restive bands of Indians. Generals Patrick Connor and Grenville Dodge did their best to hold the line out along the California trail until elements of the magnificent federal army that had forged its victory at Appomattox could send relief. But all that came west was bad news and disappointment. While General Grant presided over the biggest demobilization in American history, his close friend William Tecumseh Sherman took up station at St. Louis, charged with the task of keeping peace on the plains. It was an extremely difficult assignment, for at a time when troops were needed to protect an expanding region there were no men to be had. Three-year volunteers, who served during the war, were glad to go home. Even the "Galvanized Yankees" saw no future in western army life. During this period of flux, conditions in the West became almost desperate.

About the best that could be done was to keep open general lines of travel, protecting the larger settlements and railroads under construction, until more forces became available. Even this was nearly impossible. The dispersed nature of the frontier, with thousands of miners, cattlemen, and small farmers fanning out in all directions, meant that the military was faced by the problem of controlling not only the Indians but also the whites. Emigrants and prospectors were not content to follow the established roads. They sought short cuts, roads with better grazing, or approaches to undeveloped areas.

A good example was the Bozeman Road into Montana. John Bozeman, the Georgia miner who had done some prospecting in Montana, marked off a trail leading northwest from Fort Laramie, along the Big Horns and across to the Yellowstone Valley. The cut-off carried travel from the Platte River route to the mines in a more direct route and at once it became popular. There were immediate demands for army protection and in the summer of 1866 Colonel Henry Carrington moved into the country to establish a string of forts along the way. His approach almost exactly coincided with the visit to the Sioux of Commissioner N. B. Taylor, who solemnly swore that the government had no intention of fortifying the route. News that troops were on the move caused the Indians to break off the talks abruptly and prepare to defend their buffalo range.

As the Sioux scattered into the hills, Carrington set about constructing Fort Phil Kearney. He took great pride in his work, issuing seventy-five special orders in six weeks that dealt with doors, door-keys, soldiers walking on the grass, and other significant details. Sherman had little faith in the officer, remarking later that "the fact that he was a Colonel of the Regulars all the war, and yet never heard a hostile shot was enough," but, he confessed, "we had no choice." And so preparations to defend the Bozeman Road proceeded. In December several bands of Sioux and some Cheyennes struck one of the fort's wood parties and an inexperienced officer named Fetterman was sent to its relief. The Indians used the ancient ruse of putting out a decoy; Fetterman snapped at the bait. Before he knew what had happened his force was annihilated. Within a matter of minutes eighty-one men and officers lay dead, and the American public had another massacre to talk about.

In the spring of 1868 a peace conference was held at Fort Laramie and Red Cloud, of the Oglala Sioux, came down to smoke the pipe. His demands were simple: Close the Bozeman Road. Army men, who had not wanted another roadway to protect in the first place, were glad to agree. The Union Pacific Railroad was approaching Utah at this time and the road from there to Montana went through Bannack country. This route, north from Corinne, was much safer and more desirable in every respect. The Bozeman Road accordingly was closed and the Sioux contented themselves with tearing down what was left of the abandoned forts.

The Laramie Treaty of 1868 and the subsequent abandonment of the Bozeman Road indicated that the government's policy of protecting only major routes had not changed. But the publicity arising from events along that road and others began to alter what had long been called "the Indian problem." The problem itself remained the same—the Indian was in the white man's way—but the possibility of solution was somewhat changed. The universal theory that a good Indian was a dead Indian was now modified by time and circumstance. No longer were any settlements east of the Mississippi in danger. Now that the great crusade against Negro slavery was closed, humanitarians of all kinds sought a new outlet for their emotional energies. Suddenly James Fenimore Cooper's noble red man was revived and placed upon a pedestal for eastern lyceum speakers to admire and pity. Westerners howled their very loudest in derision, but Westerners did not control Congress, or the purse strings, and therefore they did not dictate army policy.

The resurgence of interest in the American native produced a new difficulty for the western Army. Congress now felt pressure to require the soldiers to protect Indians as well as whites. As evidence of its renewed interest in its charges out on the plains, the government invited selected Indians to visit the Great White Father in Washington, D.C. In 1870, for example, Red Cloud and a number of Oglalas were brought back to see military parades, naval cannon, warships, and all the white man's "big thunder." Then they were hauled off to New York where Red Cloud was shoved out onto the stage at Cooper Institute and obliged to speak before a capacity house of fascinated Easterners. Newspapermen were enthralled by the spectacle and a new wave of sympathy for the red knights of the plains emerged. Their stories carried a plea for kinder treatment for the natives. Before the Indians got home they dined with President Grant and his cabinet and were generally lionized by Washington society. When Admiral Dahlgren's wife invited Red Cloud to dinner he flattened her with the remark that he was in Washington on business, not for pleasure. Ladies of the capital city were at once horrified and fascinated by the rebuff.

Army men were dismayed by the turn of events and western editors were apoplectic when they read the eastern papers. The desire of the military to have Indian affairs returned to the War Department, from which they had been taken in 1849, now appeared to have little prospect of fulfillment. The Indian Bureau, in the Department of Interior, maintained that it could solve all difficulties by treaty—arrangements that the Army was expected to enforce. As treaties continued to be broken by both sides, red and white, the press was filled with recrimination and charges of army inefficiency. Then President Grant tossed in an added complication when he refused to support his old friend Sherman, who wanted to use force, and subscribed to what became known as the "Quaker Policy." Churchmen were now sent out to deal with the Indians and the Army was instructed to give the clerics every possible assistance. Since the first of these came from the Society of Friends, the whole policy took the name Quaker.

Sherman and his fellow officers raged at their old comrade-in-arms who had succumbed to the "soft" policy, but they did their soldierly best to follow directives and to try to bring order out of increasing chaos.

Despite all the Quakers and other religious groups could do, the frontiersmen continued their invasion of the land, violating treaties, encroaching upon reservations, and fighting the Indians. Railroad-builders also pushed forward their work, moving generally westward, slicing up buffalo reserves and hunting grounds. Towns appeared from nowhere; cattlemen marked off new claims; farmers appeared, unwinding their rolls of barbed wire, fencing off square plots of prairie. Promises of food and gifts did not pacify the Indians who watched the process. They reacted with violence, raiding white settlements, sniping at lines of travel, driving off cattle herds. Both clergymen and army officers stood by and watched the inevitable clash with a feeling of helplessness and frustration.

As time and the pressure of events aggravated the problems of the plains Indians, the whole region came under the scrutiny of the American reading public. Like the slavery issue, the Indian situation became sufficiently critical to cause a sharp division in public opinion. Westerners, and all men who had either a direct or indirect stake in the new empire, cursed the vacillating policy of the government. Easterners, who regarded developments with somewhat more detachment, tried to support the notion of Manifest Destiny while at the same time expressing great concern for those about to be dispossessed.

The government's tired and badgered servant—the Army—did its best to prevent bloodshed along travel routes in the face of criticism from both sides of the new humanitarian cause. The maddening part of Indian fighting was the tendency of the enemy to disperse and disappear after striking at white settlements. Time and time again small bands, led by ambitious young braves, executed hit-and-run raids, then fled to the sanctuary of the reservation, where the Department of the Interior offered protection against reprisal. After watching the Indian agents and clerics make futile attempts to reform the natives, army officers determined to follow the raiders to wherever they might go, and hunt them out. A Kansas editor signified local approval when he cried out "Militia to the front—Quakers to the rear!"

During the late fall of 1868 General Phil Sheridan drove his men through snow and cold to locate the village of some Southern Cheyennes who had caused a good deal of difficulty in Kansas. One of his dashing young officers, George Armstrong Custer, led the vanguard to the Washita River in Indian Territory (present Oklahoma) where cavalrymen, pounding forward to the tune of "Garry Owen," fell upon the Indians. The Chief, Black Kettle, who had lived through the bloody day at Sand Creek in 1864, fell in the assault. So did a considerable number of his tribesmen.

Washita signalized an all-out fight against the plains Indians. From that point on, continual pressure was applied and as the natives and their buffalo herds were driven and dispersed the final result became crystal-clear. Their brothers to the north were in no better condition. The peace promised by the Treaty of Laramie in 1868 was temporary. By the early Seventies a railroad edged into the Dakotas, pointed at the heart of the Sioux and beyond to the Pacific Coast. Slowly, since the great uprising in Minnesota during the Civil War, those Indians had been shoved westward until they stood now with their backs to the Rockies, with no further avenue of retreat. Like cornered animals they turned and fought. There were no real alternatives. In 1874 young Custer, adorned with plaudits won at Washita, drove into the Black Hills. His confirmation of the fact that gold existed there heaped coals upon an already smoldering situation and did its part in setting off another gold rush. He did not know it, but already he was preparing for his own end. The Sioux, now desperate, took their stand and challenged all comers. He was one of them.

Before the bugles sounded, the government made a final pitiful attempt. Its commissioners tried the standard method of bribe, offering the Indians a substantial sum for part of their land. With deep scorn the Sioux rejected the proposition. Angry government representatives then ordered the nonreservation Indians to come in and join their brothers on the reservations. General Alfred Terry sent word to Sitting Bull that after the first of the next year, if the orders were not obeyed, he would come looking for the Sioux bands. "You won't need any guides," replied the Sioux leader. "You can find me easily; I won't run away." So the gauntlet was thrown down. Each side formed its battle lines and waited.

During the spring of 1876 Americans celebrated their hundredth anniversary as a nation and held expositions demonstrating a century of progress. Dozens of self-congratulatory speeches filled the air, describing hardships along the trail from savagery to civilization. Against this backdrop, military plans were being formulated out in Dakota to insure the victory of which the orators spoke. The campaign against the Sioux, who posed the strongest remaining threat to white advance, was to be a triple-headed affair. General George Crook of Indian-fighting fame in Arizona made ready to march north from Fort Fetterman, Wyoming. General John Gibbon made his approach from Fort Ellis, Montana. Out of the east, from Fort Lincoln, Dakota Territory, came Brevet Brigadier General George Custer—whose participation nearly was prevented by his candid remarks before a congressional investigating committee. President Grant, angered by the young man's criticisms of army methods, finally was prevailed upon to let the cavalryman have his great chance. Grudgingly Phil Sheridan, now in command of the high plains, agreed to Custer's participation, writing to his superior, Sherman: "I am sorry Lieutenant Colonel Custer did not manifest as much interest by staying at his post to organize & get ready his regiment & the expedition as he does now to accompany it. . . ."

Sherman, in command of the Army of the United States, did not manifest as much enthusiasm for the campaign against the Sioux as some of his subordinates. "I suppose now the Indians will lead our troops a will-o-the-wisp circle, until some lucky turn may give one of the columns a chance," he told Sheridan. Time and again he had watched his troops maneuver for the kill only to see the enemy spread out through the hills, evading open battle, to join at some other point and strike unprotected areas. But this time the Indians did not run. On June 25, while some of his army companions were enjoying a reunion in Philadelphia at the Centennial Exposition, George Custer executed what Sherman had called "some lucky turn." Out on Montana's desolate plains he found his prey and in his supreme eagerness to win additional military fame he neglected to consider the magnitude of the enemy's forces. By nightfall the young warrior and a good part of his command were dead and another chapter of American folklore was born. Along with the Bluecoats lay a civilian newspaper correspondent. Just a few days earlier his paper, the *New York Herald,* had forecast events when it said: "In arranging the plan of campaign the military authorities seem to have underrated the importance of the enemy." But no one seemed concerned. Few readers had any doubts about the abilities of the troopers, once contact was made; even fewer had much confidence in the predictions of an eastern paper about events in Montana.

The first practical result of the disaster was an immediate increase in the Army and the determination to vindicate the dead. Congress at once appropriated two hundred thousand dollars and authorized the enlistment of twenty-five hundred additional troops. Terry's command, at the mouth of the Rosebud, was materially strengthened in preparation for a winter campaign against the Sioux. Nelson Miles took to the field and all during the coming winter drove his men with relentless determination, back and forth across the snow-swept reaches of eastern Montana. An officer of the Twenty-Second Infantry later wrote: "Thus passed the winter of 1876–1877, a winter campaign which resulted in Sitting Bull and his bands fleeing to Canada, for tough Miles marched against him whenever he could hear of him. 'General' Bull would not fight; constant worrying though finally drove him from the country. He was wearied out. Some of his squaws said at Fort Peck where they had gone to trade, 'me get no sleep and me tired.' "

By the spring of 1877 Indian affairs in Montana again were quiet. Sitting Bull was in Canada; during May, Crazy Horse and his band surrendered. But before public nerves had a chance to calm down, hostilities flared once more in the same territory. This time it was the Nez Perces, Idaho Indians whose reputation for violence did not compare with that of the Sioux. On the contrary, they had lived quietly for years without causing the whites any particular trouble or concern. It was with considerable surprise that Americans learned of the commotion in Idaho that shortly spread to Montana. When, in 1875, President Grant had opened a part of their reservation to settlement, the move caused hardly a ripple in the nation's press. It was simply another application of the age-old policy of encroachment and one that had been used so continuously that men on the street took it as a matter of course.

The Nez Perces failed to share the apathy. They voiced sharp objections and, after waiting patiently for some response, took to the field. General O. O. Howard happened to be in Idaho during 1877, when the fighting broke out, and in short order his troops were on the march. Joseph, the Nez Perce's young and capable leader, now led his people on one of the most remarkable marches in the annals of Indian wars. With Canada, and refuge, as his goal, Joseph headed across Lo Lo Pass into Montana, on through Yellowstone Park— where his followers scared some tourists half to death and narrowly avoided running into General Sherman, who was visiting there—and then moved north toward the international border. Howard followed as best he could, unable to catch the fleeing warriors, and for his efforts took a severe pelting in the newspapers. Jeeringly the editors called Howard's troops the Indians' best supply line. So enraged was the officer that Sherman was obliged to remind him he was fighting Chief Joseph, not the newsmen.

The inevitable conclusion to the campaign was pitiful. Cornered in the Bear Paw Mountains, just short of the Canadian line, Joseph fought with determination and ability against a combination of army units brought in for the kill. Bitter cold, a lack of food, and overwhelming opposition convinced the chief that his cause was hopeless. Reluctantly he surrendered and prepared for the expected exile. General Miles called him "by far the ablest Indian on the continent" and Sherman agreed; he wrote: "Thus has terminated one of the most extraordinary Indian wars of which there is any record. The Indians throughout displayed a courage and skill that elicited universal praise; they abstained from scalping, let captive women go free, did not commit indiscriminate murder on peaceful families which is usual, and fought with almost scientific skill, using advance and rear guards, skirmish-lines and field-fortifications."

Another phase of the plains struggle was thus terminated. Joseph and his people were shipped downriver to Bismarck, where railroad cars stood by, ready to take them to a strange and humid place called "Indian Territory." Even the Westerners had to salute a brave enemy. Setting aside their normal hostility to Indians, the ladies of Bismarck put on a banquet in Joseph's honor consisting of his favorite dish, salmon, and stood by while the hungry chief had his first good meal in days. It was a final gesture, for the weeks and months of exile ahead were to be as trying as any young Joseph ever experienced.

As the savage Seventies drew to a close, the campaign against the American Indians pressed deep into mountain recesses, probing for the last bit of land they held. For twenty years after the American acquisition of the Southwest the Utes of Colorado were relatively undisturbed. They ranged over the western part of that territory, hunting and engaging in occasional intertribal wars without white interference until 1868, when a reservation was marked off for them. Even then, the terms of the treaty were sufficiently generous to leave the Indians a vast, untrammeled region. But in 1873 they were obliged to cede an additional area sixty-five by ninety miles in extent in the San Juan Mountains. From that point on the pressure for further cessions was relentless.

By 1879 there was trouble. Nathan C. Meeker, a preacher who had founded the colony of Greeley for the New York newspaper owner, was then Indian agent at White River in western Colorado. The pressure of miners, the fact that Indian annuity payments had fallen behind by sixty-five thousand dollars, and more immediately Meeker's dogged determination to civilize the Utes in his own way, caused the Utes to revolt. The agent obliged his charges to abandon their tepees in favor of conventional houses and plowed up the pastures upon which their ponies fed. He moved the agency against their will and threatened to starve those Indians who would not stay on the reservation and toil in the white man's fashion. Then he went too far. He plowed up the racetrack. The White River Utes had over two thousand ponies and they spent a good deal of time racing them and betting on the outcome. The denial of this pleasure was to them the final aggression.

Late in September 1879, a subchief named Douglass and about

twenty of the younger and more warlike braves struck Meeker's agency. They killed all the white men they could find and captured several women and children. Arguments still persist as to the treatment accorded the women, some accounts insisting they were raped and others denying it. While the question caused a good deal of excited conversation at the time it did not alter the situation in which the Utes now found themselves. Rape or no rape, they had attacked and killed whites. It was enough. Chief Ouray, leader of the Ute nation, expressed indignation at the work of his young men, but apologies were lost in the din that arose for the removal of the tribe from Colorado.

In addition to the murder of Meeker and his associates, the Utes committed the unforgivable sin of ambushing a military detachment sent in to quiet the trouble. The death of its commander, Major T. T. Thornburgh, and eleven men drove excitement in Colorado to a fever pitch and very shortly troops in large numbers were on the scene. While army men were anxious to avenge the killing of Thornburgh, not all of them showed great sympathy for the white population they were called upon to defend. One of the officers, writing to his wife, commented upon the rumor that the Meeker women had been violated and at the same time rendered an opinion of Colorado frontiersmen. "I don't believe it," he said of the rape story, "for it is in contradiction of all we have heard before and is gotten up by these people to inflame the public and be one step toward what they are trying to accomplish, which is to have an expensive war and bring in money and eventually to drive out the Utes. These frontier people are wholly unscrupulous. It is an outrage that we of the Army who have all the hardships to encounter should be made such catspaws of, mere tools to ambitious men who care only for their own interests, and cater to the public for popularity."

By June 1880, the desire of the whites to push back the Utes was realized. A new treaty forced the tribe onto reservations in Utah and New Mexico. Except for a forty-mile strip in southwestern Colorado, no Utes were allowed to remain in the state. Manifest Destiny had removed another barrier to white expansion and one more tribe of American Indians was now reduced to the condition of wards. During the coming years, except for minor hunting forays off the reservations, the Utes "walked the white man's path."

In July 1881, the leader of another powerful Indian group acknowledged defeat. Sitting Bull and his hungry followers came into Fort Buford, Dakota Territory, and agreed to go on a reservation. Except for the Southwest, where the Apaches were yet to make a bid for continued tribal independence, the American Indian problem appeared to have been "solved." Grant's peace policy was in the end replaced by a war policy and force dictated final terms in a struggle much older than the Republic itself. Sitting Bull, a symbol of resistance, had come to represent in the public mind all the characteristics of a savage, wily, dangerous people. His surrender signified the end of an era.

But the trouble was not over; not quite. Reservation Indians were not necessarily happy Indians, and their numbers represented a potential danger in the West, whose vast stretches were not yet under the complete control of the new white tenants. Glumly the natives took up their new lives, staying home, collecting annuities, growing restless under confinement. No longer did the excitement of the buffalo hunt occupy their time; instead, they tried to raise the white man's meat, "pinto buffalo," as they called it. The project was a failure. Crops refused to mature as the earth dried up. The cattle died of epidemic diseases; so did the Indians as the ancient enemy, smallpox, invaded their crowded camps. Penned up in small areas, tribesmen talked bitterly of the old days and of the sad state of present affairs. Men without hope grasp at straws. And when material solutions avail them nothing, they turn belatedly to things of the spirit. So it was that as a final, desperate attempt at salvation, the plains Indians embraced the notion of a Messiah.

Throughout the year 1889 word spread among the tribes that wonderful and mysterious things were happening. The Son of God was once again on earth, and this time he had come to save the Indians alone. The Messiah had a name: Wovoka. He was an Indian and lived in Nevada. So the story came to the Sioux. Sitting Bull listened with interest as Kicking Bear, another Sioux chief, revealed that he had seen and heard Wovoka. Before long a new religion was born and Sitting Bull was its high priest. By the fall of 1890 the Ghost Dance, as the movement was called, was in full swing and the Sioux worked themselves to a fever pitch in the excitement.

Sitting Bull's followers introduced some variations into Wovoka's teachings. The Nevada Paiute (who also went by the name of Jack Wilson) counseled patience and nonviolence. The Sioux could no longer wait and hope. In the frenzy arising out of their new belief, they wore a costume made of buckskin called a ghost shirt and made themselves believe it would ward off bullets. With such protection, peace and patience seemed unrealistic.

At a dance held in October, Sitting Bull excited his followers by dramatically breaking the peace pipe he had held for nine years. His explanation for the act was simplicity itself: "I want to die. I want to fight." News of the lengths the movement had reached drove the Indian agent into action. There must be no more dancing. It was an order. But the momentum was too great and the white man's *no* was only a frail reed before a mighty emotional avalanche. Sitting Bull was to have his wish; nothing could prevent it.

Soldiers were called for. The Indian leader ignored the call. "Be ready," he told his followers. "The Messiah is coming. Troops will surround you, but you must dance anyway. The soldiers' guns will not hurt you and all the whites will be destroyed." Sitting Bull's "medicine" was not good, as events shortly proved. Infantry units and eight troops of the Seventh Cavalry took up the challenge, sending about three thousand frightened Sioux streaming into the Badlands to hide. The medicine man did not join the flight. Instead, he headed for Pine Ridge and an anticipated interview with God. Troopers pursued him.

The enemies met at dawn on a December morning. Forty-three Indian police, supported by a hundred cavalrymen, bore down on about a hundred fifty die-hards who stood by the rebellious medicine chief. In a few minutes of fighting six of the Indian police and eight Sioux, including Sitting Bull, were killed. Unceremoniously the corpses of the Indian leader and his seventeen-year-old son, along with others, were thrown into a wagon for a short haul to a lime-filled pit and final disposal.

Meanwhile, late in 1890, almost five hundred soldiers combed the hills and brought in Big Foot along with his band of warriors, women, and children. They were herded to a creek called Wounded Knee. The Indians were ordered to deliver up all manner of arms and reluctantly they turned over a few ancient guns. As the search for additional weapons went on another medicine man, named Yellow Bird, decided to take advantage of the Indians' rising anger and said to his people, "The soldiers can't hurt you. I have made medicine. They will become weak. And their bullets cannot go through the sacred shirts you wear."

Tension mounted. A soldier tried to rip off a blanket one of the Indians wore. Yellow Bird threw a handful of dirt into the air and at the signal one of his warriors fired on a soldier. The dust that filtered earthward was slashed by fire. Four Hotchkiss guns pumped two-pound explosive shells into a small area at the rate of almost fifty a minute. In a matter of moments a mass of writhing, bloody bodies— men, women, and children—lay in the dirt. The "battle" of Wounded Knee was over. Three hundred Indians, two thirds of them women and children, were dead.

Yellow Bird's handful of dirt, tossed into the air, touched off the last real resistance of the plains Indians to the white man. It was a futile, feeble attempt, born of desperation and despair. The struggle was over long before the medicine man made his gesture and most of the Indians knew it. But when one last hope appeared in the mysticism of the Ghost Dance religion, they grasped at it. All else had failed. It also was a failure, as one of the dying squaws admitted. Tearing at her bloody ghost shirt, she said, "Take it off. It was no good after all."

When the plains Indians were finally corralled and turned into government wards living on ever-shrinking reservations, the way was cleared for unrestricted white settlement. The process consumed about twenty-five years following the close of the Civil War. Few Americans approved of the method used, but none suggested a better one. There were debates, emotional outbursts, bloodthirsty proposals, and displays of maudlin sympathy. Like other aspects of the settlement of the West, men had different notions about "progress," and from various interests came somewhat different kinds of force that generally converged in a giant push westward. No one doubted for a moment that the plains would and must be peopled. The original residents were an obstacle and the matter of their removal in a gentle but firm manner constituted a national enigma that made men turn their heads and hope that somehow tomorrow morning would present a ready-made solution. So, for a generation Americans toyed with the conundrum of how to dispossess another race and still look the civilized world squarely in the eye. The outcome brought them no glory. The best they could do was to point to a new area of the globe that was now "civilized." For this contribution the price had been high.

Chapter 6

THE COW KINGDOM

Before the Civil War, the high country empire witnessed two principal types of extraction: furs and gold. In each case the product was of relatively high value, fairly easily transported and in sharp demand. Following the war the nature of extractive industries was heavier, bulkier, and of lower value. Beef, wool, grain, lumber, and lower-grade minerals constituted the bulk of it. In all cases cheap transportation was the key. Without it production of none of them was feasible.

The cattle industry was first in a long sequence of land utilizations. Its appearance was not wholly unexpected; traditionally cattle ranches preceded the settlement of the small farmer on the frontier. During the 1830s, large herds were driven as much as a thousand miles out of the Mississippi and Ohio valleys to market in New York. There was a conviction in the minds of some that this pattern must be broken when the high plains were encountered. As the cattleman looked out on the tawny western sod he was repelled, for the short tufts of "buffalo" or grama grass appeared deficient in nutrition. Appearances were deceptive, as some of the bolder souls who crossed the region discovered. By the 1840s and 1850s, emigrants were surprised to find that their oxen throve on bunch grass along the trail. Of even greater interest was the fact that cattle would paw their way through winter snows to find it, dried but still nourishing. When stray stock was discovered in the spring, sleek and fat, potential cattlemen paid the fact strict attention.

During the years the plains were used primarily as an avenue west, an enormous cattle population was growing in Texas. It is estimated that about a hundred thousand head roamed that region as early as the 1830s and from that time until the end of the Civil War the number multiplied rapidly, encouraged by a free biological democracy and—without fencing, heavy slaughtering, or any control—cattle ran on the Texas plains like wild animals. There were sporadic efforts at marketing the stock during the Forties and Fifties. Some of the beasts were driven to near points like Missouri, or even as far as California. The effort was not a sustained one and did little to deplete the growing number of herds. Then came the Civil War and the end of any further efforts to export beef to the North. There were sales to the Confederacy, but after the blocking of the Mississippi by federal troops this market was also closed.

At the war's end there were thousands of cattle roaming the Texas plains, many of which did not even carry a brand. They were known locally as "mavericks." The term originated in the puzzlement of one Samuel Maverick over why his herds did not increase like those of his neighbors. The answer lay in the fact that his calves were being branded by other owners, a practice that caused all unbranded cattle in the area to be known simply as mavericks. So many of these strays were there, and so listless were their owners about running them down, that it was said a Texan's poverty was measured by the number of cattle he owned.

From time to time in man's experience, economic opportunities fall into place like tumblers in a combination lock. This happened to western cattle-raisers about 1865. Cattle could be picked up in quantity in Texas for four or five dollars a head; they would sell in a place like Minnesota for forty. The animals could be driven long distances. North of Texas, in present Kansas and Nebraska, were open plains rich in grass, a place to fatten the herds. Reaching out to this giant pasture were two principal rail branches, the Union Pacific and what would later be called the Kansas Pacific. It did not take enterprising Americans long to visualize the possibilities and to act. Shortly the Indians watched clouds of dust rise over bands of what they termed "pinto buffalo," as the cowboys hazed their stock toward the railheads. Now, the braves told each other, the invasion was from the south, as well as the east.

The war closed too late in the spring of 1865 for a cattle drive that year, but the following spring saw trail herds on the move northward. The early attempts demonstrated nothing of the organization developed later. The hands were unaccustomed to moving large numbers of animals long distances, the country was strange to them, and residents in the border states still harbored a deep hostility arising from wartime ravages. Faced by such handicaps, the drive of 1866 was not particularly successful. A young Iowan epitomized the difficulty when he wrote of stampedes, rain, food shortage, and discontent among the cowboys. He tried to cheer himself up by writing in his diary, "Have *not* got the *Blues* but am in a *hel of a fix.*"

By 1867 things were much better. Joseph G. McCoy left his stock business in Illinois to capitalize upon opportunities in Kansas. Selecting Abilene, "a small dead place, consisting of about a dozen log huts," because the Kansas Pacific Railroad had reached there, he erected yards capable of holding three thousand cattle. Before long Jesse Chisholm, a half-breed Cherokee who was familiar with the country to the south of Abilene, began to bring in steers for sale. The route he used soon carried his name and later became famous in the annals of the cattle drives. With the way marked and pens alongside the railroad ready to receive livestock, the great movement commenced. It is estimated that thirty-five thousand head of cattle came into Abilene during the summer of 1867. Within the next twenty years over two million of them would plod up the trail.

Abilene was no sudden success. Its first shipment of cattle to the Chicago market, made in the fall of 1867, brought very little profit. The next shipment, to Albany, New York, suffered a three-hundred-dollar loss. Reports that the venture was risky, coupled with the commotion raised about diseased cattle coming in from Texas, put Abilene in a tight spot. Thanks to McCoy's persistence and a large amount of money poured into advertising, the little Kansas town

survived and soon became recognized as the West's principal shipping point for cattle.

Farther north, in Nebraska, the Union Pacific recognized the importance of the new trade and offered attractive rail rates to the
drovers who would push on to meet that road. Schuyler, on the
Blue River Trail, became Nebraska's first "cow town." Its selection
as a shipping point well illustrates the economic impact of the new
industry upon a quiet little frontier village. During the summer of
1870, between forty and fifty thousand longhorns were sold there,
with the result that the city's population rose from less than a hundred
to more than six hundred. Schuyler's claim to fame as a cow town
was short-lived. The Blue Valley quickly filled with settlers who did
not welcome the milling cattle or their boisterous attendants. Within
a year the herds were heading to a more westerly point, Kearney,
where there were rail facilities and fewer farmers to voice objections.

By the early Seventies both the Kansas Pacific and Atchison,
Topeka and Santa Fe roads stretched across western Kansas, hungrily
searching for traffic. The day of the farmer still lay ahead; cattlemen
dominated the scene and, until barbed-wire barriers closed their
domain, livestock was the basis of plains economy. The railroads
were quick to realize the potentialities of the situation and lost no
time in building receiving pens at the appropriate locations. The
convergence of cattle, stockmen, cattle buyers, and transportation
meant an exchange of money; the emergence of a town followed
naturally.

The pressure of farmers in eastern Kansas and Nebraska, their
hostility to trail herds from Texas that trampled and ate their crops,
and the natural congestion of settlement created a westward bulge
in the routes used in the long drive. Hardly had the postwar cattle
boom appeared before problems arose. The stockmen tried to gain
a federal right of way, a six-mile strip of fenced thoroughfare for the
use of their herds, only to have the motion defeated in Congress.
There was no alternative but to use a more westerly route. Places
like Wichita, Newton, Ellsworth, and Abilene lived active but short
lives as "cowboy capitals."

To the west, Dodge City took over and by virtue of its tenure
claimed the title of *the* capital cow town. Dodge was laid out in the

summer of 1872, under the direction of the Atchison, Topeka and Santa Fe Railroad's chief engineer. Colonel Richard Irving Dodge, commanding Fort Dodge, was a member of the town company. But despite these influences the city became famous neither as a railroad nor as a military center. At once, cattlemen saw it as a convenient shipping point and in its very first year a herd of two thousand cattle appeared. When their owner discovered no loading pens, he moved on. The absence of such facilities was only momentary. Within three years herds were funneling into loading chutes, bound for market. Dodge City became a cattle capital almost immediately.

From the outset the new cowboy headquarters was characterized by the normal bawdiness, rowdiness, and violence found in such places. Its inhabitants came from other such places and by now they had well systematized the kind of life expected by the trailhands who stopped there. Buffalo hunters, who were well paid, and cowhands, who were not, came to town for excitement and violent relaxation. The inhabitants of Dodge were perfectly prepared to supply all their needs—from pistols to poker, sowbelly to sex. Whiskey was, of course, a stock-in-trade item. That the process involved some bloodshed was expected by all participants, and they took it in their stride. The expectancy of death lent a zest to life that more settled folk found hard to appreciate.

Only a few years passed before Dodge City started to mend its ways. Late in 1875, the town council passed a number of restrictive ordinances including the prohibition of carrying concealed weapons, a provision later broadened to require the checking of all guns upon arrival. Despite opposition from leading merchants, who opposed killing the goose that laid the golden egg, Dodge tightened up. Andy Adams, whose *Log of a Cowboy* stands as one of the finest personal accounts ever written about trail driving, wrote that by 1882 things were much quieter. An old hand who was on his crew advised the men to watch their step in the famed cow town. "Dodge is one town where the average bad man of the West not only finds his equal, but finds himself badly handicapped," he warned. "The buffalo hunters and range men have protested against the iron rule of Dodge's peace officers, and nearly every protest has cost human life. Don't ever get the impression that you can ride your horses into a saloon, or shoot out the lights in Dodge; it may go somewhere else, but it don't go there."

Already Dodge was losing its reputation. Before long Marshal Bat Masterson would make an unheard-of request and put it into effect. He wanted to close up the saloons! So the liquor dispensers went underground as did the prostitutes, who were the next object of reform. Both were still available, but Dodge wore an outer garment of respectability that warned away some of the more boisterous fun-lovers. Cowboys saved their money until the herds reached some other new and still wide-open shipping point.

North of Dodge lay Nebraska's cowboy capital, Ogallala. It owed its reputation in part to Dodge City, for the Kansas town first attracted cattlemen who were developing the Western, or Texas, Trail in preference to the more easterly Chisholm Trail. Although Dodge City was the end of the trail for many a herd, owners of younger stock tended to go farther north, preferably to Ogallala. By 1873, the Oglala and Brule Sioux Indians were removed to a reservation in northern Nebraska and the road to Ogallala on the Union Pacific lay open. This development coincided closely with the pressure of farmers in the eastern part of the state, whose numbers sent cattle-drivers westward, out of contact with nesters and barbed wire. These negative factors were important, but the Black Hills gold rush in 1876 and 1877, furnishing a new and lucrative market, set the stage for a new cattle empire in Nebraska. Quickly Ogallala took its place among the roistering cow towns of the West, competing in violence with the best of them. Proof of its ascendancy was shown in a news story of 1875 announcing that the city had "the most substantial jail west of Omaha." After 1877, in particular, the lawless element dominated the scene. The period of turmoil was short, however, for by the mid-Eighties trail-driving days were over.

While the boom was on, the cattle business provided Ogallala its principal reason for existence. Evidence of this lay in the seasonal nature of the city's prosperity, for during the warm months its streets seethed with activity and accommodations were at a premium. During the winter, when no herds arrived, gamblers, entertainers, and shady ladies spent their time in more profitable locations, returning, like tourists, for the summer. The rest of the year, activity was desultory as business people awaited the coming of spring.

The day of the trail hand and his boisterous companions was ended by rain and pestilence. Wet years brought hordes of independent-minded sodbusters whose barbed wire and bad dispositions barred the way north. Piled atop this reverse was the epidemic of Texas fever that swept the countryside in 1884, erasing Ogallala as a cow town. Quarantine laws meant the end of Texas cattle, and the demise of another cowboy capital. By the next year that part of Nebraska was so dominated by farmers that newcomers might well have questioned any influence of cattle upon their community. Another kind of frontier had come and gone.

There are two cities on the northern high plains generally recognized as capitals of the vast cattle empires they served. Cheyenne, Wyoming, and Miles City, Montana, early established themselves as important cow towns, a characteristic they maintained longer than some of their sister cities due to the slowness with which the homesteader invaded their respective domains. They were able to resist change and had ample time to establish themselves firmly as stockmen's headquarters.

Cheyenne was not born a cow town. Grenville M. Dodge, the Union Pacific Railroad's chief engineer of construction, located the city during the summer of 1867 as a railroad division point. By November, when tracks reached the infant village, "Hell on Wheels" was already a notoriously rough community. "Here comes Juleburg!" exclaimed the town's founders as they watched railroad construction crews, prospective store- and saloonkeepers, gamblers, and whores pour in. Almost at once the community could boast a population of four thousand.

The railroad construction period was short. Two years after its establishment a traveler, who had been promised a view of hell on earth, complained that Cheyenne was no longer populated by thieves, gamblers, and murderers. He did not doubt that it might have been true once but "the day of its orgies is passed away; the scum of population has moved off to other pastures, and the streets of Cheyenne are as quiet as the streets of other Western cities in which law has conquered license." By 1869, the railroad was completed, Wyoming Territory was organized, and Cheyenne became its capital. The former construction camp might well have become just another stop along the Union Pacific had it not been for the excellent range in the region.

By the early Seventies, the seeds of Cheyenne's later claim to fame began to germinate. Its leading newspaper published the information that in a radius of a hundred miles there grazed somewhere between sixty and eighty thousand head of stock. Before long the chamber-of-commerce spirit took hold and the hopeful cow town advertised itself as a desirable market place for livestock. When the Wyoming Stock Growers Association located its headquarters there, Cheyenne was made, for the association ran Wyoming. Something of the style in which the beef barons would live was indicated by the construction of the Cheyenne Club, built at a reputed cost of twenty-five thousand dollars. That kind of money bought things in those days, and for it members were treated to one of the nation's earliest electric-light systems. The club also boasted the finest cuisine in the land and many a cattleman took advantage of the excellent food and drink for meeting friends and doing business over the dinner table. More than one Wyoming law was conceived at the Cheyenne Club, as legislators and members of the Stock Growers Association met in its rooms.

To the north, in Montana, Miles City laid claim to the title of cowboy capital for its part of the country. Like Cheyenne, its origins were not of the cattle industry, but it quickly turned its attention in that direction. The follow-up campaign after the Custer disaster saw a large body of troops pour into eastern Montana. During 1877, Fort Keogh was built at the confluence of the Tongue and Yellowstone rivers. Almost at once a collection of shacks appeared across the Tongue, where the residents were prepared to serve all the needs of the soldiery. The place was named in honor of General Nelson A. Miles, commander of the Fifth Infantry at the fort.

The city's earliest residents came from the backwash of western society and its younger days were as wild as those in any boom camp located to take advantage of a particular source of income. A Montana cattleman later wrote that he could not remember seeing any hotel accommodations in Miles City. He attributed the absence to the fact that those who visited there were principally interested in staying up to see the sights and had no need for a bed, or even much to eat. They were only thirsty. But, as a cattle-country historian noted, within a year after its establishment the frontier village "had developed in civic experience far enough to have its first wave of reform when the local justice performed a belated marriage ceremony on some one hundred couples." An English sportsman who saw it then described the city as "a miserable little place" whose inhabitants were largely engaged in selling whiskey to the soldiers. One of his friends told him that four years later it was a rapidly growing municipality with all the trappings of civilization—stone houses, a town hall, and a mayor and councilmen.

One of Miles' officers foresaw the area's economic destiny. He wrote in December 1876: "Within a few years all this country will change; it will be occupied by cattle raisers, and domestic cattle instead of buffalo will roam the grassy hills." The development took place more rapidly than the writer supposed. By the end of the Seventies, cattle were pouring down the Yellowstone Valley headed for the terminus of the Northern Pacific at Bismarck. The railroad shortly came to life, after its hibernation resulting from the Panic of 1873, and again took up its westward course. By the fall of 1881 Miles City was connected to the East by rail and its position as a cattle capital was assured. As the northern terminus of the "long drive" from Texas, and a point of dispersal for cattle both to eastern packing plants and to the recently opened northern range, what had once been Fort Keogh's grog shop and brothel now turned to the business of livestock. Its pre-eminence as a cattleman's headquarters is illustrated by Granville Stuart's story of his friend who, having just bought three thousand head of steers in Texas, was asked if he proposed to go south and get his herd. "Hell no!" he replied. "I'm going to Miles City and play poker and be comfortable until those steers arrive."

Not all cattle-drivers were willing merely to drive their stock to a railhead and ship at the going price of beef. Experience taught them that the animals could not only live the year round on the northern plains but that they would put on weight doing it. The cost of maintaining a large herd on the public domain was relatively low, and with free grass available in quantity, only time was needed for a natural increase to occur. By the 1870s, a good many people were interested by this economic fact. Men of the East, not to mention European capitalists, visualized a new kind of gold mine in this West of free and unrestricted rangeland. They heard that in a place like Wyoming each animal increased in value between five and eight dollars a year at a cost of approximately one dollar in maintenance. This set the investors' pocket nerves tingling with anticipation. Westward trooped a number of hopeful financiers ready to execute a new exploitation of virgin land. Before the 1870s were out, the cattle kingdom had developed so rapidly that newcomers in Colorado were advised to move on for that range was already filled.

From Montana and northern Wyoming came word that the winters were not so vicious as reported and that cattle were wintered well. An English sportsman, used to the verdant fields at home, was amazed at the way cattle fattened on sterile-appearing bunch grass. He wrote that "a herd of 5,000 head will feed the year round and grow fat on a stretch of arid-looking table-land, where an English farmer, if he saw it in the autumn, would vow there was not sufficient grazing for his children's donkey." Yet, in this apparently forbidding country, men were making from fifteen to twenty per cent annually while there was talk of even greater profits.

The amount of money necessary to start a small "spread" was not always large. Under the Homestead Act, one hundred sixty acres of land could be obtained for nothing. Here was enough for a base of operations, a place to subsist the cattleman's horses and domestic stock and to serve as a nucleus for expansion. All around the home ranch lay free public domain, claimed by no one, open to anyone who chose to utilize it. The ranchman's first dwelling was often a rude dugout, or cottonwood log cabin, with pole corrals serving as outbuildings. He lived off his own beef, sowbelly, beans, and coffee until his first sales provided money for some of life's luxuries. If nature was charitable, his herd grew by natural increase and, if not, throwing a brand on stray stock was not an unknown method of building a herd. The practice was severely frowned upon in western society but with vast distances, a scanty population, and the difficulty of identifying range cattle to protect him, many a young entrepreneur got his start in this way. Bill Nye, the Wyoming humorist, merely exaggerated the situation when he wrote: "Three years ago a guileless tenderfoot came into Wyoming, leading a single Texas steer and carrying a branding iron; now he is the opulent possessor of six hundred head of fine cattle—the ostensible progeny of that one steer."

Normally the gifts of nature were sufficient and no "running-iron births" were necessary. With free grass, water, and land and the availability of herds from the south, enterprising Westerners took advantage of the situation and prospered. The nation's economy was expanding. While the captains of industry farther east were taking full advantage of natural resources in this circumstance, the possibilities, too, were not lost upon the potential "cattle kings" beyond the Missouri. A good example of the Horatio Alger type on the frontier was John W. Iliff of Colorado. He came west in 1859, with a lot of other young men, in search of sudden wealth in the mines. And, like many of them, he failed to find his big strike along a mountain-stream bed or beneath a ledge. He settled for less, raising vegetables near Denver, for sale in the mining camps. When he had amassed a little capital he set up a store along the old California Trail, near present Cheyenne, and it was here that he met the cattle business.

Like Jim Bridger, who earlier had set up a similar shop farther west, Iliff bartered with the travelers, frequently taking footsore cattle in trade for groceries or other supplies. He was dealing in a buyer's market and consequently acquired the livestock for almost nothing. They roamed near his place of business, eating free range grass, growing fat. Iliff merely awaited the coming of the Union Pacific Railroad and sold his beef to the construction crews. Meanwhile, he picked up steers from herds passing to the north until he became one of the biggest herd owners in the West. At the height of his success he could look back with satisfaction upon an earlier decision. His father had offered to invest seventy-five hundred dollars for him in a good Ohio farm if he would remain in his native state, but the youngster said "No, give me five hundred dollars and let me go west." When he died, in 1878, the once-disappointed miner controlled a whole empire along the Platte River and owned around thirty-five thousand head of cattle, most of which grazed on the public domain. Young men who stood back in awe at the achievements of industrial wizards in the East might have paused to think of the economic potentialities in the "Great American Desert."

So attractive were the profits to be gained from the beef bonanza that the business progressed satisfactorily even during the troublous Seventies. Despite the financial panic, the stock-raising industry expanded enormously—with Wyoming showing an increase from ninety thousand head in 1874 to five hundred thirty thousand in 1880. During those years the Union Pacific Railroad was busy hauling livestock to market, with the animals bringing their owners thirteen to sixteen dollars a head. As the governor of the territory remarked, the cattle literally had raised themselves for market.

By the 1880s, Montana was feeling the pressure of cattle herds. During the next five years, as the industry burgeoned, spreading into new regions, the great glut of cattle in Texas was finally diminished. Demands for cattle by shipping points along the railroads of Kansas and Nebraska, by midwestern feeders who utilized their cereal crops to fatten Texas steers for market, and by stockgrowers on the northern ranges were greater than the source of supply. Western stockmen, searching for young livestock, now commenced to make purchases from the Middle West. Feeders, who had formerly looked to the eastern market, found it more profitable to sell to the cattlemen who wanted to utilize more fully their open ranges. The Eighties witnessed the strange spectacle of cattle moving westward by rail to a new "home on the range." Around the middle of the decade, many of these "pilgrims" were shipped west as other cattle were shipped east.

In 1880, the Northern Pacific Railroad resumed its way west, having been halted by the failure of Jay Cooke and Company and the Panic of 1873. One of the reasons for the renewed effort lay in the prospect of a thriving cattle business in Montana. Before the Northern Pacific could tap the new region, the Union Pacific plunged into Montana from the south, anxious to capture the coming traffic. With the entrance of these two lines into the ranges of Montana, the boom in beef continued to flourish. Railroaders saw a promise of things to come in the fall of 1879 when a trail herd of two thousand cattle from the Yellowstone Valley reached the railhead at Bismarck. A St. Paul editor predicted that the northern range would shortly compete in fame and productivity with the earlier achievements of Texas.

One of the last great natural pastures of the high plains to be invaded by cattle was Dakota Territory. Like other parts of the West, the region became familiar to the public through the discovery of gold, Indian campaigns, and the arrival of a railroad. Texans pushed their herds north into Dakota as early as 1871, selling stock to the government to be fed to both soldiers and Indians. Until the discovery of gold in the Black Hills, no herds grazed west of that section of the Missouri. It was a Sioux reservation. Government explorers, like Major John Wesley Powell and W. P. Jenney, both of whom visited the region in 1875, wrote glowing accounts of the rich grasslands they saw. By the next year ranchers moved in alongside the miners, ready to take advantage of nature's surface riches while their brethren probed beneath the soil. California Joe, one of Jenney's guides, expressed it best when he said: "There's gold from the grass roots down, but there's more gold from the grass roots up. No matter how rich the gold placers in the Black Hills may prove to be, the great business in this region in the future will be stock-raising."

The Black Hills region was opened officially to settlement in the spring of 1877 and a new rush was on. The northward movement of cattle, commenced more than a decade earlier, now pushed toward the Canadian line, filling out the "cattle kingdom." Out of the west, from as far as Oregon, came other herds converging on this last great open range. By the spring of 1880, the Black Hills Live Stock Association was organized and in a little over a year it had a membership of sixty growers who owned most of the cattle in that part of the country.

Enormous herds were driven in during the next several years. During 1882, over a hundred thousand animals arrived in the Black Hills region alone and, in the following year, this figure was advanced two and a half times. The winters were mild, with the exception of that of 1880–1881, and the herds multiplied rapidly. Successful operations in these northern climes tended to cause further expansion. The opening of the Black Hills to settlement saw the ranchers' domain spread far beyond that geographic location as absence of fences and the availability of grass and water offered the traditional attraction to stake out an even larger claim. Soon present North Dakota and eastern Montana were dotted with Texas cattle and "pilgrims" from the Midwest, all fattening on nature's offerings.

The decade of the Eighties was a natural time for such expansion throughout the industry. The effects of the Panic of 1873 had worn off sufficiently to make moneylenders bolder, and they were now willing to make loans at reasonable rates. Cattle prices at Chicago were holding up well, while costs of production were still relatively small. Military campaigns, such as those of Miles and Custer, advertised the region, and the plight of the Sioux suggested that the day of white supremacy in Montana and Dakota was at hand. Easterners and Europeans read stories of the new land and cocked an eye in its direction. As an enthusiastic Englishman wrote: "The dead-meat trade is only in its infancy. Science has not yet been brought to bear fully on the arrangements necessary to make its transport an entire success; and yet, there can be no doubt—for experience has taught us this—that American dead-meat can be delivered in perfect condition in English ports." The development of the refrigerator car shortly proved his prediction accurate.

News of possible profit travels fast and far. Pierre Wibaux, member of a wealthy New York French family, came to Montana in 1883 and spent his first winter in a cave dug from the side of a cliff. Within a year he brought his bride from the East and commenced married life in a sod house. From that beginning, the cattleman saw his herds finally reach a count of seventy-five thousand head and his name used on the map of Montana to designate one of its cities. Residents of his community recognized success when they saw it and changed the name of the town, formerly Mingusville—named for its first citizens, Min and Gus—to Wibaux.

Other Frenchmen saw the point. Such men as the Count de Dorey, Victor Arland, and de Billier settled in Wyoming. Perhaps the most famous of them was the Marquis de Mores, who came to Dakota Territory in 1883 with a large amount of capital, determined not only to raise cattle but also to process the beef on the spot. He founded a town on the Little Missouri River, calling it Medora in honor of his wife, and built a meat-packing establishment that employed two hundred workers. Since the plant operated only part of the year, over-head expenses became extremely heavy. Because of the severe competition of other packers who offered grain-fed beef, whereas the marquis had only a grass-fed product, the plant steadily lost money. By the spring of 1887, the scheme had cost the young Frenchman a million and a half dollars. Disgusted with the whole project, he left for Paris.

The plains cattle boom coincided with a period of British financial expansion. English and Scottish capital, in particular, sought a part of the economic development taking place in the American West. In 1872, W. J. Menzies organized the Scottish-American Investment Company and entered the business indirectly, borrowing money at low rates of interest in Scotland, and loaning it out for much more to hopeful cattle-raisers. Moreton Frewen, of London, directed the Powder River Cattle Company in Wyoming. By the fall of 1883, it had fifty thousand cattle grazing along the Tongue and Powder rivers. The Wyoming Ranch Company, Ltd., operating over two and a half million acres of Wyoming's Carbon County, was also backed by British money, as was the Swan Land and Cattle Company, which was capitalized at more than four million dollars. Colorado's most important cattle corporation, the Prairie Cattle Company, was organized under British laws in 1881. Its holdings in Colorado alone covered nearly two and a half million acres. The value of all of the company's holdings, including those in New Mexico, the Oklahoma panhandle, and Texas, were valued at approximately four and a half million dollars. In Dakota, the Matador Land and Cattle Company sank two and a half million dollars into its venture.

There were others, individuals of somewhat less extensive means, but nevertheless important. An Irishman, Sir Horace Plunkett, ran the EK ranch in Wyoming. Otto Franc, a German, owned the Pitchfork ranch at Meeteetse; his countryman Charles Hetch settled near Cheyenne. So great was the influx of foreign capital on the northern range that, by 1885, the territorial legislature of Montana passed restrictive legislation. The law denied the privilege of owning property in the territory to any corporation of foreigners, or to corporations of which more than twenty per cent of the stock was owned by foreigners. While such a restriction was generally circumvented, in typical western fashion, its existence suggested that the Americans thought the range was getting pretty well saturated.

There is a tendency today to regard the early-day cattleman as a highly individualistic soul who cut out his private empire almost single-handed, fought off the redskins and homesteaders with equal vigor, and clawed his way to success with guts, guns, and grass. Our great body of western fiction finds one of its most common bases of conflict in the difficulties between the rancher and the invading sod-buster. The suggestion is strong that here were two different breeds of man, each struggling for what he thought was just, ready to die for his own particular cause. It is true that each had his own notion of land utilization, but the methods employed had some similarities. Cattlemen were not feudal lords, reigning over western domains with disdain for all others. Like other frontiersmen, they turned to their brothers for assistance and readily offered their own services.

With the enormous growth of the range-cattle industry, coopera-tion became more and more necessary. The multiplicity of problems was so great that no single cattleman could have coped with them, even if he were so inclined. In the vast, unfenced areas over which the stock moved, the difficulty of locating strays was such that the complete cooperation of one's neighbors was a necessity. The digging of wells or building of reservoirs to furnish water was another type of venture that called for joint action. Storage facilities for water were sufficiently expensive to be prohibitive to many an individual cattle-man.

Formal organization among members of the industry was achieved in livestock associations. These were usually made up of local or general associations. The first operated in one's own locality and was normally organized for the specific purpose of mutual pro-tection against thieves, whether two-legged or four-legged. As time went by, the local groups merged into state or regional organizations and thereby gained the advantage of more influence with legislatures and a wider range of effectiveness. These large units were sub-divided into round-up districts, headed by a round-up foreman who was also an officer in the association. Questions about methods of conducting the round-up, the branding of calves, or perhaps the bringing of more cattle onto an already well-filled range were decided by the officers. There were disputes over the extent of range holdings and arguments about where one man's claim ended and another's began that were arbitrated by association representatives. Such a service helped to minimize trouble among ranch owners and was generally welcomed.

One of the most successful of these organizations developed in the territory of Wyoming. The first attempts of the stockgrowers there, in 1871, illustrate the desire of the cattlemen for joint action. The declared purpose of their group, set forth at the first meeting, might well have come from a meeting of the Farmers' Cooperative. They desired "To combine and work together for the attainment of certain objects, among which are to purchase in company upon a large scale, thereby buying and driving cheaper than can be done by persons singly. To form an association which will command influence in securing cheap rates of freight, and other advantages of this kind. To work together for the purpose of improving the breed in cattle, horses and sheep, by the importing of blooded stock in company, the benefit of which can be shared by all the members. To organize for the mutual protection of members against depredations upon stock. To disseminate knowledge in regard to the advantages and resources of this section for stock-raising, and thus induce parties to invest capital in this business among us." [1]

The Wyoming cattlemen developed their organization into a powerful instrument. Historians generally agree that, during the territorial years, the Wyoming Stock Growers Association dominated the local governmental structure. By the mid-Eighties, at least one territorial editor was willing to voice public objection to the extent of the cattlemen's control and to express concern over the dangers of such dominance. The savage winter of 1886–1887, disastrous to so many cattle-growers, large and small, dealt the association a sharp blow. Membership fell off and there was talk of disbanding. After the "big

[1] This first organization, called the Wyoming Stock and Wool Growers Society, and later the Wyoming Stock Grazers Association, was short-lived. It paved the way for the later and better-known Wyoming Stock Growers Association.

die-up," as the winter became known, there was no more newspaper talk about the monopoly of the organization.

The Colorado Stockgrowers' Association, organized much earlier (1867), met rather infrequently during the early years and did not have a permanent headquarters until 1884. The organization kept a record of brands, offered rewards for the capture of rustlers, collected money to fight legislation thought to be detrimental to the industry, and generally promoted the stockman's cause. One of the important services rendered by the association was the recovery of lost cattle. During some years as many as twenty-five hundred head of cattle were returned to their owners.

Montana stockmen were relatively late in organizing. Not until 1885, on the eve of snowy disaster to the herds, did they meet at Miles City to form a territory-wide association. Like their brothers in Wyoming and Colorado, the Montana cattlemen turned to politics and supported a powerful lobby at the state capital. In the manner of other livestock associations, the Montana group worked actively to eliminate rustling, improve the quality of their animals, and in general to bring law and order to the range.

The average homesteader did not resent the cattleman's desire to organize his industry in the interest of more efficient operation. It was the perfection of organization, its rigidity, and—particularly— its power over the legislature that drew complaints. The wealth, the power, and the size of the stockgrowers' association excited the animosity of the homesteader, who felt that he was bucking big business out on the plains. In a day when monopoly was a subject of congressional interest, small operators in the West, whether they were homesteaders or minor cattle-raisers, took exception to the domination of natural resources by one group as opposed to another. It was the old case of who got there first, announced his claim, and was prepared to fight off all newcomers.

The most dramatic and most commonly cited example of clashes resulting from the head-on collision of interests is the Johnson County war in Wyoming. In the fall of 1891, in the northern part of the state, there was a determined attempt by the cattlemen to drive out a group of intruders they indiscriminately classified as rustlers and nesters. The resulting struggle, dignified with the name war, illustrated the determination of those who had come first to retain their stake in the western empire. In the early part of April 1892, matters headed toward a climax. About twenty-five stockmen, accompanied by an equal number of hired gunmen, left Cheyenne for the little cow town of Buffalo, determined to seize the place and make short work of suspected rustlers. They never reached it. Cornered on the TA ranch, fifty miles south of Buffalo, the invaders found themselves fighting for their lives against a group of aroused settlers. In the darkness of night a messenger slipped through the lines and made for Cheyenne to report the plight of the invading stockmen. Three days later, on orders from President Benjamin Harrison, three troops of the Sixth Cavalry arrived to save the erstwhile vigilantes. After lengthy legal maneuvering they were released without trial, although their little expedition cost them $105,000.

The fury of the stockmen that resulted in the invasion of Johnson County was generated only partially by rustling and resentment of the nesters. Much deeper was the unrest arising from hard times in general and the fatal winter of 1886–1887 in particular. In Wyoming, the Stock Growers' Association was rocked by the economic reverses of its members; a number of ranchers and ranch companies went out of business and the industry itself was severely shaken. The same trouble visited other rangeland states but in none of them did violence erupt so dramatically.

These difficulties were symptomatic of deeper maladjustments in the range-cattle industry. By 1880, the vise of geographic limitation and climatic treachery had started to close upon the stockraisers. The already crowded ranges experienced a sample of things to come during that unusually severe winter. The normal losses of from five to ten per cent rose sharply and some owners suffered heavily.

But the warning flag was obscured from view by the shimmer of green promise that brightened the countryside each spring. Westerners always have been optimists; they shake off their reverses and convince themselves that the next year is bound to be better. After the bad winter of 1880–1881, cattlemen rationalized their difficulties by telling each other that risk was a necessary element in so speculative a game. Surely the laws of chance would give them a better roll of the dice next time. And there were outsiders who cheered them on. Eastern and foreign capital simply clamored for entrance into the great beef lottery and made offers sufficiently attractive to entice the most conservative of stockraisers.

Rising prices convinced investor and cattleman alike that they were on the right track to riches. During 1882 range stock was bringing thirty dollars a head, a figure that advanced to thirty-five dollars before the summer was over. Canned and refrigerated beef was shipped to foreign markets while domestic demands mounted steadily. The resulting optimism brought forth a whole new crop of cattle companies as enterprising men with money joined the corporate rush toward what was called the "beef bonanza."

So the game went on. Thousands upon thousands of eastern cattle were shipped in to feed on the dwindling range. By the fall of 1885, western Kansas and Colorado grasslands were saturated and during the ensuing winter, a hard one, cattle died by the hundreds. Nor could their owners take solace in the fact that the survivors would bring high prices, for already the market was softening. The New York stock market had, a year earlier, shown signs of financial distress. The cattle business, among others, was affected and the high confidence of recent years began to fade. By October 1885, Chicago prices for range cattle sank to $1.80 a hundredweight. Then came the snow and cold to underscore depression on the southern ranges.

There were yet other signs that the old days were gone. The long drive, now nearly twenty years old, was at an end. Texas stock-drivers found the way through Kansas closed by law and brandished guns. The Cherokee Strip was also a barrier rather than an open highway. Cattle companies that rented lands from the Indians did not want trail herds passing through, eating the grass, and they made known their displeasure in terms the Texans understood. The drovers took to the courts and won a temporary victory over those who fenced off the land, but the victory was short-lived. Homesteaders, pouring into the country, staked off their allotted acreage and put up their own fences. Western Kansas and Colorado now felt the full impact of the granger and the desert underwent a further shrink-age. Old-time cattlemen shook their heads in dismay and wondered what was to become of the great economic enterprise they had built upon the grassy western expanses.

In the early Eighties an Englishman, who knew and understood the West, predicted some of the difficulties that materialized. "Huge as Uncle Sam's possession available for cattle ranges are," he wrote, "they are nevertheless approaching exhaustion; and indeed, it would be difficult to imagine *what* possibly could resist the energetic onslaughts of his speculative children pressing Westward with unabating impetuosity." He called the movement "a spirit well epitomized in the saying, 'If hell lay in the West, they could cross Heaven to reach it.'"[2] The persistence of such expansion across the American grasslands was understandable. As the same writer admitted, young men could start a flourishing business in the region for as little as three or four thousand dollars. And not a few of these people, he hastened to explain, came from the lowest social rank and "had two or three years ago been railway conductors, hotel-keepers, Western merchants, petty civil servants, and, quite a number, trappers and Indian scouts."

In the fall of 1886, cattlemen were extremely apprehensive. The Chicago market showed no signs of recovering from its downward course, some of the growers were dumping their stock on the market with the intention of going out of business, and there were general signs of hard times ahead. To make matters even worse, the summer had been hot and dry and the grass looked unusually bad. Montana and Wyoming owners struggled desperately against a tightening situation, driving their herds across the border into Canada in search of cheap tracts of grazing land, or "boarding out" some of their animals to settlers who had spare feed. Their only hope was that the winter would be mild, yet wet enough to furnish heavy grass by spring.

Then nature administered the cruelest blow yet. November brought heavy snow and the cattle pawed at it in a vain search for food. January gave a false promise when a chinook wind swept away drifts and warmed the land. The relief was only momentary. Down out of the north came a paralyzing blizzard, driving back the warm air,

[2] William A. Baillie-Grohman, *Camps in the Rockies* (New York, 1882). See pp. 331, 348, and 349 in the 1905 New York edition.

stiffening the countryside in a coat of ice. Men peered out of their bunkhouse windows and watched their stock stand against drift fences, heads down, rumps pointed windward, slowly dying from exposure.

At the height of the crisis a pair of Helena cattlemen wrote to their foreman in the Judith Basin, anxiously inquiring of conditions. While trying to compose an appropriate answer, the foreman tossed the inquiry to one of his cowboys who had shown some talent with water colors. On the back of a postcard the cowhand, Charley Russell, painted a rib-studded steer, standing forlornly in the snow as a hungry coyote looked on. He called it "Last of Five Thousand." The card was mailed without any further comment. Later known also as "Waiting for a Chinook," the little painting brought Russell recognition as a cowboy artist. His last effort sold for thirty thousand dollars.

When spring came at last, cowboys mounted up and rode forth to view the result. Stinking carcasses withered in the spring sun; coulees were lined with dead animals; rows of dead lay along the fences. Men who were hardened to losses were sickened by the sight and smell. Angrily they watched buzzards circling the scene, sinister birds of prey whose presence testified to the enormity of the catastrophe. Granville Stuart, pioneer Montana stockman, later confessed: "A business that had been fascinating to me before, suddenly became distasteful. I never wanted to own again an animal that I could not feed and shelter." The wife of an Englishman who had a ranch near Bozeman voiced the same complaint during the tragic winter. Watching the stock die during bitter January, she wrote: "It's a great shame the way some people neglect their cattle out here. Those which are right back in the hills where the grass is good do well enough; but those which are down among the settlements, where feed is so scarce, ought to be fed. . . . What these cattle live on is a mystery. Certainly they pick over the litter which is thrown out of our stable; that and dry twigs is all they can possibly get. It will be interesting to watch if they get through the winter. If they *do,* I'm sure no one need ever be afraid of cattle not making their own living out here all the year around. I saw in the *Field* the other day, that an English farmer had got three weeks' imprisonment for starving a cow. I shrewdly suspect that a good many Montana cattle-men would spend their whole lives in prison at that rate."

As before, a period of renewed hope followed the wintry disaster. The spring of 1887 saw a good stand of grass and the survivors of the winter quickly fattened on it. New range was opened in Montana during 1888, when the Indian reservation near the Canadian boundary was sharply reduced in size, giving stockmen fresh lands to graze. But these palliatives were not enough. The shock administered during the "big die-up" sent its waves in all directions and washed away a good deal of the confidence that had been built up concerning open ranges. Money was now frightened. Speculators had little desire to bail out failing cattle companies or to invest in new ones. Continuing low prices indicated further deflation in the industry, a fact that also caused investors to recoil from it. Clearly the boom days were gone. There was now sober talk of readjustments, new methods, careful management. No mention was made of enormous and quick profits. An Englishman, writing in the April 1887 *Fortnightly Review,* explained it to his countrymen: "No doubt there is money in cattle yet, but the halcyon days of enormous fortunes rapidly made are past. Well watered and adequately sheltered grazing lands have now become difficult to find. Year by year the acreage over which cattle can range, decreases. The granger with his spade and plough drives before him the cattle-man, who himself in former years drove out the aboriginal Indian."

Like the frontier of the trapper and the placer miner, the cattle-men's frontier spread with amazing rapidity, experienced violent fluctuations, and was relatively short-lived. Similarly, it was founded upon the existence of an enormous tract of unsettled, unclaimed land whose utility was as yet unappreciated by the traditional small settler. The stock grower was simply a latter-day prospector, mining the land in a slightly different way than that used by his predecessors. Unlike them, he was inclined to ignore the facts of economic life. When the open range upon which he had based his scheme of success was gone, the beef baron fought those who were to succeed him in title to the land. He chose not to get out, as had the trapper and the placer miner, but to stay meant facing new conditions and a consider-able readjustment. It was a laborious and painful transition. Gradu-ally he acceded to reality.

While the day of the unfenced range was short, it was of con-siderable significance to American life. Emerging as it did in the years immediately following the Civil War, the cowman's frontier provided an outlet for the restless energies of thousands of former soldiers who were unwilling to return to their quiet villages after four years of campaigning, living out of doors, and developing individual re-sourcefulness. Into the West went the young men, building cattle ranches, operating stage lines and general stores, working on railroad construction crews, or entering various trades that supported the growth of the region. With them went capital, by the millions of dollars, sent along by financial optimists who wanted to share in the building of a new country. Much of the money went into the beef business and, as a single industry, it materially affected the de-velopment of postwar finance.

The cattle business affected more than just the countryside over which the beasts grazed. The Midwest assumed its role as a feeder area, and the resultant demand for grain in turn affected the demand for farm machinery. Alongside the feed pens grew a packing industry, a development whose significance could not have been guessed a few years earlier. Through the packers' doors went processed beef, on its way to tables all over the world, and its labels introduced new names into households: Armour, Cudahy, Swift, Hormel, and Rath.

Less tangibly, the cattle kingdom left its mark upon the land. The affairs of the cattle kings, their "wars," their power attracted atten-tion in the East. So did the activities of the hired hands: the cowboys. Into the realm of fiction went this high-heeled, lasso-swinging, gun-toting knight of the plains and shortly America had a new member in its folk-hero fraternity. The rancher, who struck out into the unknown to capitalize upon nature's offerings, unwittingly set the scene for a population movement unsurpassed in world history. His presence brought forth railroads, established towns, demonstrated methods of coping with extremes in climate and, in general, proved that man could survive and prosper in the desert. The cowman's little vegetable garden was sufficient proof to many a prospective farmer that the soil was more fertile than he had thought. Settlers who earlier had wavered, out of ignorance of the facts, were sufficiently convinced by what they heard to load up and start west.

By the Eighties and Nineties, the cattlemen were being squeezed out by the nester and his accursed barbed wire. The newcomers exercised their legal right to carve out a one-hundred-sixty-acre square, in the middle of a choice range if they so desired, and to box it with a flesh-ripping fence. The inevitable struggle followed, but the stockmen were soon swamped by the agrarian hordes. Long before young Professor Frederick Jackson Turner commenced to talk about the frontier being gone, the cattlemen were telling each other the same thing, if in somewhat less academic language.

Chapter 7

WEB
OF
STEEL

The foundation of high plains civilization was made of steel. Not steel dug from the western earth and processed in the region's mills, but steel brought from industrial America in the form of rails. Spread across the tough sod, they generally preceded settlement. Where they went, towns appeared, and from these grew larger communities. These islands of population not only owed their existence to the railroads, they also looked to them for survival. Steel was the base, the fiber, and the lifeline for an otherwise isolated people.

Before the coming of the railroads, the area's resources were merely scratched. Its pelts were quickly searched out, its more obvious mineral wealth exploited, and its seas of grass just nibbled. That was all. If men had stopped at this, the great land would have remained unmarked for years to come. Without rail service, the main army of frontiersmen—the farmers—could not have braved the arid, wind-swept plains in their search for a cash crop. The earlier frontier, with its wooded acres and navigable rivers, was no more. The plains offered little encouragement for the subsistence economy once practiced. It was devoid of the requisites for such an existence. If the new pioneers were to venture forth beyond the Missouri, they had to be assured of some connection to markets. Their economy would be dependent upon it. In an empire of distance and snarling, shallow rivers, there was but a single solution to the problem of heavy transportation: railroads.

Men of the mid-nineteenth century recognized the fact that the final plunge into America's last frontier would. require new and different weapons. Shortly after the Civil War, Josiah Copley wrote of the problem in his little book *Kansas and the Country Beyond,* and in it he spoke quite frankly of the problem: "To subdue and occupy such a country as that beyond the Mississippi, will require greater forces than were employed in the conquest of the section of our country east of that river, where, although very much aided by navigation on the lakes, and on the Ohio and other rivers, settlement was half a century creeping from the Alleghenies to the Mississippi, as it had been an entire century making its way from the tidewater of the Atlantic to the western slope of the Alleghenies. In the trans-Mississippi regions, where nature assumes vaster and sterner features, and there are few available rivers to aid in the work, artificial means of transportation are imperatively necessary, and must first be supplied." Copley put his finger on the revolutionary change at hand when he said: "The old process must be inverted. The locomotive must precede the plough, and the town and the farm. Even Kansas, with all its fertility—except for a comparatively short distance along its eastern border—could not be occupied in any other way. Colorado, except a few of the best of its gold mines, is practically valueless until reached by rail. New Mexico, with its rich resources, pastoral, agricultural, and mineral is yet almost an unknown land to our people, although we have had possession of it for twenty years."

Westerners had realized these truths for some time. The day of the fur trapper had barely closed, and the day of both the miner and the cattleman still lay ahead, when the first railroad west of the Mississippi began operations. The place was St. Louis, the crossroads of western trade; the time was December 1852. Out of the city toward Cheltenham, five miles away, steamed the initial train of the Pacific Railroad of Missouri. Orators foresaw a connection with San Francisco, and a trade that would supplement the waning fur trade from the Upper Missouri River. They were right. It would take less than twenty years to prove it.

More than a decade elapsed before legal and financial barriers were set aside. During the Fifties, the slave issue cast its dark shadow athwart the paths of railroad planners. Not only was each Mississippi River city, from St. Paul to New Orleans, fighting for the opportunity to become the railroad gateway to the West, but the South itself laid claim to the economic potentialities westward. So fierce was the political struggle that before a rail could be laid on the plains west of the Missouri River, Kansas would have to bleed, Stephen Douglas' political fortunes would be destroyed as he peeped into a Pandora's box of western bees, and a Civil War would be fought. The isolation of the Pacific Coast during the war, the demonstrated ability of the North's railroads to supply military sinews, and the elimination of southern opposition to a central route led the federal government to show an interest in a transcontinental railroad.

At the war's end, financiers, businessmen, speculators, and professional town-builders looked across the Missouri. So did all America. It was ready to turn from years of destruction to the more satisfying task of building. Beyond the river lay an empire almost untouched, beckoning and tantalizing, its golden mountains glittering like sequins, set off by bosomy swells of velvet green that promised interesting things for cattlemen. While most railroad promoters looked across the desert and past the mountains to the Pacific Ocean and the Oriental trade, they had some hope that the intervening arid miles might somehow be made to pay part of the expenses involved. The proportion that the desert ultimately contributed came as a pleasant surprise.

During the summer of 1865 a partnership between private enterprise and the federal government produced the first stretch of railroad west of the Missouri River. The Union Pacific road, chartered three years earlier, moved from the realm of drawing boards and stock certificates into a tangibility more appreciated by westerners. The little steel stub that poked out from Omaha would shortly be the

eastern end of what was for some time called "the Pacific railroad."
Actually, the main road was supposed to have five eastern termini,
spreading out like fingers of the transcontinental line, but in the end
the Omaha Pacific, as General W. T. Sherman called it, became the
principal route. It was Omaha, rather than its regional sisters, that
reached out to touch Sacramento. The means would be new; the
route old. For twenty years wagons had ground through the dust of
the Overland Trail, bound for the West. Now the way was easier,
faster, cleaner.

Stimulated by financial injections from the federal government,
railroad builders now sent the Union Pacific lunging forward. Outright grants of land amounting to every other section on either side of
the track within a twenty-mile belt, plus loans of sixteen thousand
dollars a mile on the plains, thirty-two thousand a mile in the foot-
hills, and forty-eight thousand a mile in the mountains provided
funds with which the builders could work off their pent-up enthusiasms.

To expedite the work, Union Pacific officials hired General Grenville Dodge as chief engineer of construction. The Civil War veteran
willingly gave up his military career to participate in the great national
project. He took up his duties in May 1866, and during that summer
his organization laid more than a mile of rails westward each day. By
the year's end, the road had reached milepost 293, at North Platte,
Nebraska. General Sherman, an old friend, watched the work in
amazement. Anticipating completion of the remaining distance to the
Rockies, Sherman wrote to Dodge early in 1867: "It is almost a
miracle to grasp your purpose to finish to Fort Sanders [Wyoming]
this year, but you have done so much that I mistrust my own judgment and accept yours."

On went the road, giving birth to a litter of towns in western
Nebraska and eastern Wyoming. Most of the track-laying was done
under the direct supervision of the Casement brothers, Dan and Jack,
whose army of workers fought distance, barren plains, and Indians
in the westward course. Thousands of men, including former soldiers
from both Confederate and Union forces, Irish immigrants, muleskinners, mountain men, and midwestern farm boys, toiled all day

while a hardened corps of gamblers, saloonkeepers, and harpies stood by, prepared to offer some of the more recreational aspects of railroad-building in the evening.

While the men made roadbed and laid tracks, troops patrolled the region to ward off raiding Indians. General Sherman, in command of the region through which the railroad ran, did not fear any serious interruptions from the aborigines for, as he said, the number of men at work would offer some threat to the Indians and then, because of the many workmen, enough whiskey would be brought into the country "to kill all the Indians within three hundred miles of the road."

Despite the potency of the whiskey, the Indians posed a constant threat to the road and their lightninglike raids kept the workers in a constant state of nervousness. The tribes regarded the strips of steel as a dagger thrust into the heart of their economy and, as the Union Pacific's tracks began to penetrate the land, they objected. At first the Indians confined themselves to threats. From time to time their anger was translated into action. Upon one occasion, the natives sought to stop a locomotive by stretching a rawhide rope across the track, held by thirty of them on either end. When steel and rawhide met there was a considerable commotion. Surprised bucks were distributed along the right of way for some distance, a response to their scheme that did little to improve their dispositions.

Less humorous was the affair at Plum Creek, Nebraska, in the summer of 1867. A band of Indians found tools laid aside by the workmen and used them to take up part of the rails and lay ties across the remaining track. They also dismantled a section of the telegraph line. When communication was thus cut off the operator at Plum Creek notified the railroad officials. Seven men were sent out, on a handcar, to locate the difficulty. When their car hit the blocks of wood wired to the rails, it jumped the track. At that moment the Indians struck, killing three of the men. One of the wounded, who was thought to be dead and accordingly scalped, survived. The Indian who had performed the hairlifting dropped his prize in the melée and the victim retrieved his top piece. After months in a Chicago hospital the wounded man emerged, carrying the scalp which he had had tanned, and proudly exhibited it to all who would look. While the survivors of the attack were fleeing the scene, a freight train approached and was also stopped. Both engineer and fireman were killed, but a conductor managed to run back along the track to warn another train that was coming. Quickly it backed into Plum Creek and called for help.

During the night, the Indians staged a battleground celebration. By the light of the burning train they circled and danced around the wreckage, some drinking whiskey they found in the cars, others racing their horses across the prairie with bolts of cloth streaming out behind. A few articles they found useful. A consignment of boots was taken, the tops cut off and laced on Indian legs. The bottoms, too restrictive for the native foot, were thrown away as useless affectations of civilization. When General Dodge arrived next morning on a "traveling arsenal," the attackers fled, leaving behind sugar, coffee, and various dry goods spilled all over the sod. The disturbance detained the construction crews only momentarily and served more as an annoyance than a hindrance. Relentlessly, the rails continued their penetration of Indian country. Even bigger wars to come would not stop them.

Despite Indian attacks, engineering difficulties, distances, and supply problems, the road workers pushed on. Sherman was not the only American who was surprised at the progress. All America watched with unconcealed delight and the builders, spurred on by per-mile subsidies and plaudits from the press, fought to break track-laying records set the day before. It became a national game, a contest, a test of endurance and strength. The Platte Valley furnished a natural travel route, one that had been used by wagons for two decades, and track-layers found that very little engineering was required in the way of cuts and fills. A visitor who observed construction crews at work wrote that "the ties in most cases were laid on the grass, a few shovelfuls of earth being put under them when necessary." He was impressed by such speed but admitted that, when storms came, the ties gave way and usually had to be relaid. Nor were the builders always particular about direction. An Englishman, noticing the zigzag appearance of one stretch of road, innocently asked the contractor about it. "Wal, sir, I guess the company were paid by the Government so many dollars and so many acres of land a mile for making the line." The indignant questioner, who saved his wrath for publication, later wrote: "The rascals! so they have gone crooked to increase the mileage."

Americans did not complain much of such methods. The road was being built, and if it was done wastefully, it was in accordance with their tradition of extravagant haste. Soon the *Crédit Mobilier* scandals would rock Congress when financial irregularities in the building of the Union Pacific were uncovered. But the difficulty would be rationalized away by pointing to the unparalleled engineering job done in the West and its general benefit to the nation. More than once America had paid its toll to speculators and it would happen again. Westerners had come to expect it. For the moment, they didn't mind. There were plenty of resources for everyone. To them, now, the main end was to get a railroad. Without it, economic extraction on a major scale was an impossibility. So they joined in celebrating the road's advance and laid plans to get their share of the national patrimony.

Across the Nebraska plains toward the Rockies moved the railroad, pushing before it a city. It had various names, always a new address, but it was usually called simply End of Track. Its population represented more a mining camp city than one whose origin came from an agricultural background. There were no schools, churches, or civic organizations. The population was largely male and its necessities were provided: restaurants, saloons, gambling places, whorehouses, and a newspaper. When the city picked up and moved on, in a giant hopping movement that covered a good many miles at a stride, stage and freight lines adjusted their routes and schedules to the change. All that was left behind were piles of rubbish, abandoned buildings or tent frames, and a memory. Sometimes the camp left roots that struggled and finally grew into a permanent town. Often it left nothing but a lonely signpost, an epitaph to civic hope that would be unnoticed by passers-by.

Some of the permanent cities came perilously close to death. Evanston, Wyoming, is one example. Toward the close of 1868 the young town's newspaper stated that six weeks before not a building had stood where a city now blossomed. Now there were at least a hundred homes with twenty-five more abuilding, most of them substantially constructed. Shortly the railroad appeared, and without pausing continued its westward course. By May 1869 it would meet the Central Pacific's tracks at Promontory Summit in Utah and the Pacific railroad would be complete. Within a year there were only seventy-seven people in Evanston; undoubtedly most of them were certain that the town's days were numbered, now that construction days were over. But, like many of its sister towns in Wyoming, this one-time end-of-track municipality managed to hang on, and today it is an attractive community located not only on a major railroad but along a principal highway. In a like manner, Cheyenne, Laramie, Rawlins, and Green River survived pangs of birth and with the coming of range cattle slowly recovered from post–construction-period depressions.

There are many instances of end-of-track cities that failed to mature. In 1868 the town of Sheridan, located in western Kansas at the end of the Kansas Pacific Railroad, boasted sixty-five business houses and a population of two hundred before it was two weeks old. Not only did Sheridan trade with such cities as Denver and Pueblo, but, like some of its sister cities along that railroad, it acted as a terminus of the still-active Santa Fe trade. For more than a year the town bearing the fiery little cavalryman's name accommodated the long lines of wagons bound to and from Santa Fe. In a single day as much as five carloads of freight were transferred to freight wagons. Naturally, the residents of the new boom town had high hopes that the trade would be permanent; they should have known better. Just as soon as the Kansas Pacific was built farther west, the new town of Kit Carson, Colorado, sprang forth to claim prairie commerce and to threaten even Denver. Within a few months, the namesake of the famous western scout had more than a thousand residents and town lots were selling for seven hundred dollars each. Then the Kansas Pacific moved on to Denver, the city that so eagerly awaited its rails. Kit Carson, struck by economic paralysis, became another small Colorado town.

While the Union Pacific Railroad was pushed westward across uncharted prairies, the Kansas Pacific was lured by a ready-made market at Colorado's capital. The main line, or Pacific Road, as it was called, had little interest in the Nebraska prairies or the Wyoming hills it crossed. Its builders were bent upon reaching the Central Pacific tracks and a connection with international trade. Anything that lay between was just a barrier, something to be passed over. But in the case of the Kansas Pacific, the base of the mountains and Denver was the immediate goal. Denver, a thriving city by the time the first rail was laid west of Omaha, furnished so powerful an economic magnet that it not only deflected the Kansas Pacific from its original course but pulled it rapidly toward the Colorado capital city.

The Kansas Pacific was born under the name Leavenworth, Pawnee and Western in 1855. For nearly a decade it languished, a railroad in name only. When the Union Pacific was chartered, the little road gained its share of the national project by acquiring the right to build from the mouth of the Kansas River to a junction with the main line at the 100th meridian. It was one of the five proposed eastern termini of the greater railroad. During the latter part of 1865 the road, by then known as the "Union Pacific, Eastern Division," crawled out onto the Kansas sod sixty-odd miles west of the Missouri.

Denver businessmen watched the Kansas line as it angled toward a connection with the main road in Nebraska, and they were not happy. Their cries finally gained from the government an agreement that the junction could be made at some point not more than fifty miles west of Denver. Now the road made straight for the Queen City of the Plains, as Denver was called, and residents of the mountain community anxiously awaited its arrival. During 1868 the road moved rapidly across Kansas, bound for the Rocky Mountains. Eastern capitalists like Simon Cameron, the Pennsylvania politician, became interested and made trips to the end of the line to watch the work. William J. Palmer, another former Civil War general, performed a service similar to that of Grenville Dodge when he took charge of the Kansas line's engineering problems.

A hunter named W. F. Cody became famous as "Buffalo Bill"

through his efforts to furnish meat to the more than twelve hundred workers who toiled at building the road. In a period of eighteen months, Cody killed 4280 buffalo to satisfy the crews' appetites and even found time to take Grand Duke Alexis of Russia out hunting. Since the duke was paying a thousand dollars a month for guide services, Cody made a special effort to accommodate the visitor. For that kind of money, he not only escorted Alexis to the hunting grounds, but saw to it that he got his buffalo. It was a mutually satisfactory outing.

By 1869, the name Kansas Pacific was adopted, thereby revealing the ambitions of the road's builders. It was a dream that was not to be fulfilled and Denver became the end of the line for that venture, much to the disappointment of the city fathers. Traffic over the new Kansas road entered Denver in 1870 and then turned hard right, following a branch line north to Cheyenne and a connection with the Union Pacific. The Colorado capital would have to wait until the 1930s and the completion of the Moffat tunnel and Dotsero cutoff before it could say that it sat astride a transcontinental railroad. Its own Denver and Rio Grande Western by then supplied the bridge between the Burlington to the east and the Western Pacific coming from California, providing coast-to-coast service.

Only five years elapsed between the time the first work train crept west from Omaha and the completion of two major rail lines across the central plains. By 1870, the desert was not only twice spanned but the roads were connected between Denver and Cheyenne. The great steel fence set apart a homesteaders' domain and all hostile Indians were driven from the new preserve. Almost at a stroke a farmer's empire was hacked out and furnished transportation. Soldiers, settlers, and businessmen could now go west in comfort and safety.

And go west they did. As early as 1867, General Sherman understood the value of the Kansas Pacific and Union Pacific to the safety of the plains country. "These roads," he said in his annual report, "although in the hands of private corporations, have more than the usual claim on us for military protection, because the general government is largely interested pecuniarily. They aid us materially in our military operations by transporting troops and stores rapidly across a belt of land hitherto only passed in the summer by slow trains drawn by oxen, dependent on the grass for food; and all the States and Territories west have a direct dependence on these two roads for their material supplies."

A year later, as the Union Pacific approached the Rockies, the general wrote that already the route had shifted commercial traffic to the extent that goods were reaching the West from St. Louis, and even Leavenworth, by way of Chicago. With rail connections completed between Chicago and Omaha, and from the latter city westward more than three hundred miles, it was the quickest route of transportation. Of course, he went on to say, Chicago's sudden commercial eminence was highly alarming to St. Louis merchants. But shortly St. Louis would have its connection, via the Kansas Pacific, and its business interests could relax from their temporary fright.

Very soon other lines would knife westward, slicing off new strips of territory, fencing off new millions of acres. The Santa Fe, like its sister roads, received its principal early impetus from governmental land grants. For a decade after its first grant, made in 1863, the road struggled westward. The Panic of 1873 stopped it cold near the Colorado boundary. Another decade and many more meandering miles would be required finally to lead the rails to the sea. Meanwhile, far to the north, another railroad with transcontinental aspirations would have much the same history and experience similar financial difficulties. It, too, hoped to reach the ocean, as its name—Northern Pacific—clearly indicated.

The general movement of railroads was westerly. Within fifteen years after the Civil War southern Colorado and New Mexico were penetrated by the Atchison, Topeka and Santa Fe; the Kansas Pacific and Union Pacific bisected Colorado and Wyoming; and the Northern Pacific crossed Dakota, bound for the Pacific Coast. The projectors of all of these lines thought in transcontinental terms and aspired to international trade.

Out in Colorado a maverick railroader concluded that he would make his stake by running counter to the mainstream. William Jackson Palmer, a veteran of the Kansas Pacific construction, founded his Denver and Rio Grande Railway in 1870 with the expressed purpose of forming a connecting north-south link to interchange traffic among the larger lines. Starting at Denver, he built southward, hoping to reach the Rio Grande River at El Paso and one day to connect with Mexico City. To insure success he planned to build branch lines into the mountain valleys to serve the myriad of little mining communities that sprang forth almost daily.

The scheme worked well enough until Palmer collided with the Santa Fe Railroad, whose managers had an eye on the Colorado mountains as well as on New Mexico. In a railroad war of magnificent proportions, lasting from 1878 to 1880, the little narrow-gauge D.&R.G. slugged it out with Goliath from Atchison. The immediate prize was possession of the Royal Gorge of the Arkansas, a mere keyhole that controlled the way to the fabulous mines of Leadville and to a whole mineral empire that lay beyond. By 1880, a settlement was agreed upon, and like two potentates the railroads divided up the countryside. In return for the Royal Gorge, the D.&R.G. promised to prospect north of a designated line in New Mexico. Grudgingly the Santa Fe relinquished its claims in the Rockies and resumed its southwesterly course toward southern California. So far as the Rio Grande road was concerned, the principal effect of the struggle was to bend it westward in the general direction of Salt Lake City. By 1883 it was doing business with that place, its dreams of tropical climes set aside.

Once again minerals had determined the course of western economic development. Now the narrow gauge became almost wholly a "prospecting railway" as it probed the mountain fastness in search of business. It was, as a Denver paper said, a kind of errant railroad that wandered along deep valleys and over skyline passes like a camp-follower. Each new gold or silver strike caused it to sprout another branch. So sensitive was it to the golden magnet that construction contracts often were let before the engineers could set up their transits and make proper surveys. In many ways the Denver and Rio Grande typified the bonanza qualities of Colorado's growth: when the mining camps played out, turning ghost, so did hundreds of miles of rails whose usefulness also had passed. But like the mineral frontier itself, these hastily built service roads provided a foundation for a later and more substantial growth.

The northern reaches of the high plains were the last part of the region to have transcontinental connections. While the route was one of the earliest considered, having been favored by the early railroad planner Asa Whitney before 1850, financial barriers prevented the realization of rail service until 1883. In that year, the Northern Pacific had its gold-spike-driving ceremony in the Montana Rockies to celebrate the union of St. Paul with Portland.

The fact that the present states of North Dakota and Montana were late in gaining a rail connection with the rest of the nation was not the fault of the planners. Immediately after the Civil War, the Northern Pacific's incorporators sought out the best available financier to help carry their line across the grassy distances to the Pacific Ocean. In that day no name was better known to the American public than that of Jay Cooke, "the financier of the Civil War," and to him the builders turned. For several years Cooke investigated the possibilities, sending out two expeditions to study the terrain. Upon receiving reports so enthusiastic that the region was later jokingly called "Jay Cooke's Banana Belt," the banker in 1869 decided to proceed. Early next year construction was begun and by 1873 it had reached the Missouri River and a place called Bismarck. There it stopped. The Panic of 1873 struck down the mighty house of Cooke and, in the crash, a communication artery feeling its way westward was severed.

Although the Northern Pacific was the victim of a national financial calamity, the result was one of delay, not destruction. When rails met the river at Bismarck, hundreds of tortuous steamboat miles below that point were eliminated, and Minnesota gained a direct connection with the mountain community to the west. Not only was gold still flowing from Montana, but it was shortly to be discovered in Dakota's Black Hills. Quickly, commercial tendrils in the form of stage and freight-wagon lines sprouted from the railhead. Additional traffic was furnished by the Army. Fort Abraham Lincoln, across the

river from Bismarck, now became a major staging area for campaigns
deeper into Sioux country, and the whole military frontier took another step forward.

The coming of the railroad spelled the end of American Indian
civilization. Not only did it bring miners and their camp-followers, as
well as soldiers, but it hastened the grand buffalo hunt already in
progress. The buffalo represented the core and heart of Indian existence; without it they were reduced to absolute dependence. West of
Bismarck, hunters threw themselves at the task of killing the remaining animals. L. A. Huffman, pioneer Montana photographer, wrote:

"Round about us the army of buffalo hunters—red men and white
—were waging the final war of extermination upon the last great
herds of American bison seen upon this continent. Then came the
cattleman, the 'trail boss' with his army of cowboys, and the great
cattle roundups. Then the army of railroad builders. That—the railway—was the fatal coming. One looked about and said, 'This is the
last West.' It was not so. There *was* no more West after that. It was
a dream and a foregetting, a chapter forever closed." [1]

It took the Northern Pacific seven years to recover from the wound
it received in the great panic. By 1880 its rails again moved forward,
across the Missouri and up the Yellowstone Valley. As it swept
through eastern Montana, wiping out photographer Huffman's West,
and headed for a mountain crossing, boom towns popped up all
along its course. A stranger in the little town of Billings noted that,
within three months after its founding, the place was quite impressive. False-front wooden buildings, many of which were saloons, comprised the business section. But beyond these sprawled a promising
residential district. Farther west was Livingston, a typical boom
town. "In every bar-room lay a copy of the local paper," said Rudyard Kipling, "and every copy impressed it upon the inhabitants . . .
that they were the best, finest, bravest, richest and most progressive
town of the most progressive nation under heaven. . . ." The residents had reason to boast. In 1882 there were perhaps fifty people
there; a year later the population stood near twenty-five hundred
"and there are baths, banks, concert halls, and a skating rink. The

[1] Mark H. Brown and W. R. Felton, *The Frontier Years: L. A. Huffman, Photographer of the Plains* (New York: Holt, 1955), p. 26.

electric light and the telephone are, of course, here." Almost overnight Sioux country was downright civilized.

While the Northern Pacific struggled, went broke, was revived and
plodded on across seemingly hopeless distances, a St. Paul merchant
looked on and somehow conceived the idea that he could succeed in
that grim and barren land to the west. James Jerome Hill, better
known as Yim Hill to his Scandinavian farmer friends, was a man of
vision. He was more. Some called him dedicated; others were not so
kind and said he was a fanatic. Bravely and perhaps foolishly, he
sank his savings into the failing St. Paul and Pacific Railroad, whose
dormant tracks across Minnesota attested the violence of the Panic
of 1873. In 1879 the road was reorganized with the help of Canadian
capital and renamed the St. Paul, Minneapolis and Manitoba. Hill
was its general manager. Within four years he gained control and by
1890 a new name—Great Northern—graced its cars. To the horror
of the stockholders the young railroader announced that he did not
intend to stop building until he had reached the Pacific Ocean. But
he could get no land grant. How could he succeed when others had
failed, land grant and all?

But stubborn, one-eyed Jim saw a dream through that single orb.
With the help of the Canadian financiers he pushed his renamed
road into Dakota and beyond, to a great nowhere that paralleled another major road, the Northern Pacific. Amid jeers of "Hill's Folly," he
proceeded, studying the land, talking to farmers, encouraging them
by offering blooded stock to improve their herds, and supplying seeds
to plant crops. He tried not to be discouraged when his friends
slaughtered the expensive animals and ate them. Instead, he gave
more. He fixed the lowest possible rates to encourage travel over his
budding line, and always he pushed westward.

Deep in Dakota he ran into an Indian reservation, and in Montana another. Now, instead of having land granted to him, he had
to buy a right of way. It was a heart-breaking process. As Hill wrote
later: "When we built into northern Montana, and I want to tell you
that it took faith to do it, from the eastern boundary of the state to
Fort Benton was unceded Indian land; no white man had a right

Stagecoach on the road along the Gibbon River
in Yellowstone National Park.

Colorado Indian Chief Ouray "and staff."

A W. H. Jackson photo

The famed Flathead chief, Charlo, (center) who led his people from their Bitterroot reservation near Missoula to the Jocko reservation after years of defying the treaty of 1885.

Historical Society of Montana ph

Fort Laramie. From a drawing by Frederick Piercy in 1853, four years after it became a United States military post.

George Armstrong Custer in camp near Fort Hays, Kansas, in 1869. Custer is the man leaning against the tent pole.

Chinese coolie labor on the Northern Pacific
Railroad in the 1880s. The photograph was taken
along the Clark Fork River in Montana by F. J. Haynes
when he was the road's official photographer.

First Northern Pacific Railroad train from St. Paul to Portland in 1883. Taken near the scene of the "Last Spike" ceremonies in the vicinity of Garrison, Montana.

Villard "Gold Spike" excursion.
thern Pacific Railroad, September, 1883.
inally in the possession of
tana pioneer W. F. Sanders.

Gold-panning in Nelson Gulch near Helena, Montana.

lantic and Pacific Oil Company wells, Spring Valley, Wyoming.

Butte Hill, taken in early 1900s.
From a stereoptic slide
taken by N. A. Forsyth, Butte.

Amethyst and
nce Mines at Creede,
rado. 1895.

The Missouri River Steamer *Golden Gate*.

Going-to-the-Sun Highway, spectacular road over Logan Pass in Glacier Park.

to put two logs one on top of the other. If he undertook to remain too long in passing through the country, he was told to move on. Even when cattle crossed the Missouri River during the first years to come to our trains, the Indians asked $50 a head for walking across the land a distance of three miles, and they wanted an additional amount per head, I don't remember what it was, for the water they drank in crossing the Missouri."

By 1893, Jim Hill had thrown a pair of rails across northern Dakota and Montana, clear to the Pacific Coast. With satisfaction he watched traffic begin to flow over the new line, and could notice that his task not only had been accomplished without government subsidy but also that the same year the Northern Pacific, which had so benefitted, went into bankruptcy. Not content to rest on his laurels, the new railroad giant now bought up the Burlington line, with some of J. P. Morgan's money, right under the nose of Edward Harriman of the Union Pacific, who had intended to make that purchase himself.

To the further amazement of railroad men, Jim Hill induced Japanese industrialists to cross the Pacific and seek him out. He promised to deliver cotton to their mills, without charge if they found that it was in any way short of the high standards he promised. Before long, southern cotton made its way to Japan via the Great Northern and silk was hurtled eastward over the Dakota prairies to American mills. Homesteaders stopped their plowing to watch fast through silk trains speed out of the West to industrial America. Appropriately, one of Hill's trains was called the *Oriental Limited*. More appropriately still, another was known as the *Empire Builder,* after its owner.

Jim Hill's railroading efforts were somewhat unusual. Most of the lines received huge land grants from the sale of which they financed construction. As a rule there were no customers standing around on the prairie, waiting for a chance to buy a farm, and it quickly became obvious that some salesmanship was required. Even before the Civil War railroaders recognized the necessity of populating the routes along which they intended to build. In 1859 a young Harvard graduate, who had recently been charged with the responsibility of forming a land department for the Burlington and Missouri River Railroad, then building in Iowa, wrote a profound truth when he said: "We are beginning to find that he who buildeth a railroad west of the Mississippi must also find a population and build up business." An Iowa newspaper agreed that this was true, but warned against trying to induce settlers by just any terms the railroad chose to fix. Land must be reasonably priced and the method of payment fair, or the incidence of default would run high. The young railroader, Charles Russell Lowell, tried to set aside any fears about gouging and warned one of his colleagues: "Keep it constantly before the farmers that we are a *railroad* company and not a *land* company— that settlers are more important to us than a high price for our land."

Western railroads were to rival the United States government in land distribution. By 1880, the various railroads were granted more than 155 million acres, while individual homesteaders claimed only 55 million from the government. The roads sold their lands to pay for construction costs and to furnish a financial cushion during the period they were building up their traffic. While income was important, price was not the governing factor. The type of buyer was of primary concern to the lines as they searched for successful farmers who would furnish them a healthy traffic when their crops started to pay. Any and all inducements were used to attract tillers of the railroad soil, including the biggest propaganda barrage yet seen in the nation's history.

The American government did not have to advertise its western lands; the railroad companies performed that service for it. Thousands of settlers, many of whom chose to homestead, first heard about the high plains from one of the millions of leaflets distributed both here and abroad by the rail lines. Northern European countries, in particular, were flooded with the literature. Norwegians and Swedes read of a new land of promise in the Dakotas and Montana where their countrymen were busy raising bumper crops for high prices on free or cheap land.

Railroad men now entered the business of land promotion wholeheartedly. Samples of crops, sworn testimonials, pictorial evidence all made their way to the eastern United States and Europe. Modern patent medicine companies and their testimonials, purportedly supported by reputable doctors, were anticipated by a flood of "scientific" tracts swearing to the richness of the western lands. Jim Hill sought out those "scientists" who agreed with him, then spread the word far and wide that such places as the Dakotas and Montana were lands of milk and honey. Newspapers, chambers of commerce, and local supporters fell in with him in his praise of prairie soil and its possibilities. So did the steamship companies, anxious to pack their ships' holds as tight as sardine cans with the oppressed of Europe—for a price.

From all over Europe and from the more settled portions of the United States came farmers, each hopeful that here at last was the golden opportunity. Jim Hill's railroad offered immigrant fares as low as $12.50 from St. Paul to points in eastern Montana. Further to encourage the immigrants, freight rates on farm machinery, household furniture, domestic animals, and other necessities were set as low as a single passenger fare. In other words, a farmer could bring his family and all his worldly belongings west for almost nothing. It is small wonder that thousands regarded it as the bargain of a lifetime and tore themselves loose from their roots to partake of the new life.

If the settler elected to take up a government homestead, land was free. As the saying went, one placed a bet with the government of five years of his life against one hundred and sixty acres that he could stick it out the required time to prove up his claim. For those who chose to buy, perhaps to be closer to rail service, terms were extremely easy. The Union Pacific offered eleven years' credit with only one tenth of the purchase price down. If the purchaser could pay off his obligations within six years, he could buy for one fifth down and get a ten-per-cent reduction in the total cost; an outright cash sale brought a twenty-five-per-cent reduction. In one Nebraska community, in 1872, the good farmland could be had from the railroad for only three dollars an acre.

During the years between 1870 and 1900, the rush continued. In 1878, General Sherman wrote that no place on earth, during any fifty-year period of history, had witnessed so radical a change as the American West during the preceding decade. He called the growth "simply prodigious." Phil Sheridan agreed. "Emigrants are so rapidly taking up land everywhere in the West, and towns and hamlets are so quickly springing up that almost constant additions have to be made to our military maps to enable us to keep posted regarding the spread of our frontiers," Sheridan wrote in one of his annual reports.

High army officers watched the process in amazement as settlers crawled westward steadily. Along the main railroads little nuclei of settlement appeared and bravely labeled themselves cities. Around them grew farming communities peopled by immigrants from Europe intermixed with farmers from eastern states who also had succumbed to advertising. During the 1870s, the movement west of Minnesota was known as the "Great Dakota Boom." Missouri River steamers clogged that muddy waterway while trains shuttled back and forth over the still-uncompleted Northern Pacific. Some people were bound for the Montana mines, others to the newly discovered strikes in the Black Hills. More important, the main body was in search of rich prairie sod that awaited the plow. As the white wave moved forward, the Indians grudgingly gave ground, having no choice but to believe the treaty-makers and withdraw to smaller holdings.

Back from the rivers, back from the rail lines, moved the settler's frontier, ever widening the belt of population, ceaselessly applying pressure upon the natives. Branch lines were built, either to connect main routes, or simply as stubs jutting out to serve a newly opened farm region. In the face of disaster the settlements managed to grow. In 1873, the nationwide panic paralyzed economic sinews; the next two years grasshoppers invaded the Dakotas. Then came drought. Stubbornly the newcomers fought back. Railroads did their best to encourage new settlers, while those already there tried to outsmart the elements by diversifying their agricultural efforts. Part-time employment and new markets stemming from the Black Hills gold rush gave the local economy a badly needed boost.

Depression and climatic adversity did not slow settlement appreciably in Nebraska. During the Seventies, population figures soared from approximately 123,000 to nearly 453,000 and by 1890 the figure had passed a million. The most important factor in such growth was the construction of railroads. In addition to the Union Pacific and Burlington systems, several minor roads tapped otherwise unserved sections, with the result that eastern Nebraska in particular was well supplied with transportation. To the various roads went over eight million acres of land, more than sixteen per cent of Nebraska's total acreage. With the Burlington selling its lands for an average of six dollars an acre and the Union Pacific for a little over four, in each case on long-term credit, it is small wonder that drought, panic, and pestilence failed to keep out the ever-westward-moving farmer.

Nebraska's settlement, rapid as it was, did not keep pace with that of its neighbor Kansas. As early as 1880, the population of Kansas was nearly a million and during the next seven years it grew by another half-million. Likewise in Dakota, a forbidding expanse of land for which early travelers had expressed little hope as an agricultural region, the farmer invasion was heavy. Old theories about the extreme cold and extended droughts were discounted. The chamber-of-commerce spirit now took over, and newly arrived homesteaders in the Dakotas told each other that it was good for the ground to freeze to such unusual depths—it arrested the evaporation of water and stored it for spring needs. They saw no reason why the trackless northern plains should not become America's new wheat belt. They wrote of it to friends and relatives.

Suddenly the Great American Desert theory was a harmless myth; railroad publicity pamphlets said so, and they were believed. Once the movement into the arid regions gained momentum, nothing could stop it. Not drought, not grasshoppers, not depression, and above all, not governmental agencies like the Department of Interior, which in 1879 published Major J. W. Powell's report, *Lands of the Arid Region*. This document, warning that the 100th meridian was the westward limit of reasonably safe agricultural endeavor, was howled down by the promoters who charged that it was a conspiracy against the West.

As a counterblast to such subversive publications, the railroads and their land-company subsidiaries swelled their torrent of literature extolling the virtues of the new promised land. They not only sang its praises but they got down to cases, appealing to both individuals and groups with specific offers of cheap transportation and cheap land to be had on generous credit terms. For the timid, who were interested but still reluctant to go out and "see the elephant," colonization societies financed by the railroads or the states made the temptation almost irresistible.

There was no end to the attractions. In 1874, Kansas went so far as to amend its laws concerning military service, exempting those who opposed it on religious grounds. This was a direct appeal to the German Mennonites in Southern Russia. The Santa Fe Railroad printed the amendments, in German, and distributed them in Russia. It went further; it carried both Mennonites and their household effects from the East Coast to Kansas for nothing. The maneuver paid off. One of the largest groups of the immigrants, about nineteen hundred of them, made their new homes in Kansas. Merchants and railroads watched with satisfaction as their list of customers grew by leaps and bounds.

The arrival of immigrant groups did not end railroad interest in them. Everett Dick, in his *Sod-House Frontier,* described the continuing efforts of the Burlington and Santa Fe roads to assure permanence of settlement by housing the newcomers until they had their own homes. Long barracks, two hundred feet long by eighteen feet wide, were erected to shelter the families during their early days in America. The Santa Fe gave each settlement four sections of land, upon which the barracks stood, as a gift in common. Later the sections were divided into eighty-acre tracts and sold to the poor at an extremely low figure. In cases where such extensive arrangements were not offered, the roads shunted boxcars onto sidings and permitted families to live in them until they could find homes of their own. When the railroads invited the foreigners to come to the plains to live they were in dead earnest. Any immigrant had to admit that the migration was attended to in detail, from departure to arrival, and afterward.

Such facilities brought forth a new kind of frontiersman, one who normally would never have taken the initial step westward. Those who today talk about the intrepid pioneer and his ever-westward movement, despite Indian dangers and a generally forbidding country, should take into account the European farmer who, knowing little English and less geography, was plunked down upon a prairie farm by the rising American businessman. The newcomer was no ax and long-rifle man; he was a transplanted farmer and he wanted no more than to pursue his profession. It was of such pioneers that the president of the Northern Pacific complained when he tried to get them to work on construction gangs. The Norwegians he employed showed first reluctance and then refusal to enter Indian country with the rails. They had come west to farm, not to fight, and they displayed no hesitation in making the fact perfectly clear to the company. Their forefathers had not moved forward on the cutting edge of American civilization, developing a breed of frontiersman who expected to cope with daily violence. They had no tradition of suffering at the hands of the natives and no desire to initiate one. The railroads, whose trains poured forth legions of such people, did more than they realized to create a new kind of West.

As the years passed, the roads discovered that not only had they brought into the West a different breed of resident, but it proved to be, in their eyes, a completely ungrateful one. Like a child who turns upon his parent or sponsor, the transplanted agrarians quickly forgot the original favor done them as the price of their products declined and rail rates rose. The condemnation began with such immediate economic matters and by the twentieth century it had blossomed into a full-fledged bill of particulars. Bruce Nelson, in his *Land of the Dacotahs* (1946) called Jim Hill the land's worst enemy and changed his title from Empire Builder to Empire Wrecker. "The northern plains and its people," said Nelson, "have suffered more, perhaps, through his misguided efforts than through the work of any other single agency. They are still suffering from them." The specific charge was enticing thousands to an arid land with promises of agricultural paradise, and of tearing apart a sod that ought to have remained for other uses. Joseph Kinsey Howard, a native Montanan, wrote that many of his people blamed their state of ruin on Jim Hill and his flamboyant promises about the delights of homesteading on the northern plains. And so on, from the original Populists down to modern muckrakers, charges of deceit and duplicity have been thrown at the railroads. During the years when they furnished many a county its largest tax receipts, the roads remained the prime target for local invective and furnished many a hopeful local candidate for the legislature a plank in his platform.

Yet, in the beginning, the coming of the railroad was heralded as the miracle of the age and the touchstone of American progress and prosperity. The continent, spanned by threads of steel, promised a short cut between Europe and Asia that would revolutionize world commerce. Nothing of the sort happened. Businessmen found that their market was in Dakota or Colorado, not in China.

During construction days, the military jealously guarded the road-beds, watching each westward mile with satisfaction and the knowledge that weeks of hot, dusty, sweat-drenched wagoning or marching would soon be telescoped into mere hours of comfortable riding. Each year of rail extension shrank western distances, and the combination of fast transportation to hitherto remote areas of conflict and the onrush of railborne settlers solved the Army's plains problem. In 1880, when farmers were already beginning to complain about the railroads, General Sherman made a swing around the West, by rail. Upon his return, he wrote that "these railroads have completely revolutionized our country in the past few years, and impose on the military an entire change of policy. Hitherto we have been compelled to maintain small posts along wagon and stage routes of travel. These are no longer needed, because no longer used, and the settlements which grow up speedily along the new railroads afford all the security necessary."

Three years later, the general was even more convinced of the importance of the roads. He admitted that when he had come to a western command, eighteen years before, the country was barren and unsettled, a land controlled by nomadic Indians. But now all that was changed. And he knew the reason: "The Army has been a large factor in producing this result, but it is not the only one. Immigration and the occupation by industrious farmers and miners of lands vacated by the aborigines have been largely instrumental to that end, but the *railroad* which used to follow in the rear now goes forward with the picket-line in the great battle of civilization with barbarism, and has become the *greater* cause."

So the rails came, and with them burghers from Atlantic seaboard cities or from quiet European countrysides. They brought along their customs, habits, and way of life, quieting the boisterous towns they found, forging them into peaceful agricultural villages such as they had known at home. Cattle towns, mining towns, railroad construction towns were transformed to fit the more normal pattern. Old-timers and latter-day historians could talk all they wanted to about the immutable forces of nature enclosing man in a western mold to produce a unique type, but the railroads that brought west the dirt farmer and his eastern-made mental and material equipment sharply mitigated the influences so widely attributed to the American frontier.

Section III

THE
GREAT
INVASION

Chapter 8 THE SOD BUSTERS

The explorers, missionaries, mountain men, miners, buffalo hunters, railroad builders, cattlemen, and sheepherders were what Everett Dick has called the vanguards of the frontier. They were the outriders, the picket line, the cutting edge. Behind them, plodding, drab, and unromantic, came the main body of invaders—the farmers.

It was the farmers, "sodbusters," as the cattlemen contemptuously referred to them, who established permanent settlements, accounted for the erection of political boundaries, insured the future stability of civilization in the area, and replaced a temporary frontier society with a more ordered, if somewhat less romantic, way of life. When the agricultural element took over, the countryside was marked off in precise squares of sections, townships, and ranges, with individual holdings neatly fenced, demarcating the domains of families. The day of the male "git and git out" extractor was largely gone; the family, with full intention to remain, replaced him.

Before the plowman could invade the last great agricultural American frontier a number of barriers had to be removed. Many of these were tangible and real; one of them was that of the mind. For generations the westward-moving farmer worked across a land of trees, streams, and frequently navigable rivers. When he looked beyond the Mississippi, or more particularly, the Missouri, he saw limitless stretches of sod—treeless, arid, and forbidding. All he knew of it, through his reading or by word of mouth, told him that it was a desert, irreclaimable and desolate. It was not a land for his kind. It would not grow the crops he knew.

The planter frontiersman was willing to gamble that the experts were wrong, that he could tame the soil to the plow; but there were additional hazards that often caused him to dismiss the attempt from his mind. Before the Sixties the high plains had no railroads, and without them no connection to markets. Nor was there a river system, with the exception of the Missouri, that was navigable. There were powerful Indian tribes, threatening and savage, ready to block the advance. Supposing he figured out a way to get along without the tree, that gift of nature he had so long fought in laboriously clearing his acres, could the farmer find substitutes for logs with which to build fences, erect houses, make furniture, line his well, or to burn as fuel? What would be the use? The other barriers still stood high before him.

Then the more tangible enemies began to retreat. Distances were contracted by the new railroad network and suddenly a form of rapid and, at first, relatively cheap transportation appeared. With the advance of the rails, accompanied by a white population, the Indian menace diminished. With the promise of personal security outstretched, the farmer gingerly edged westward, trying his hand at raising crops in what had so long been called a desert. To his surprise, and to that of many a gloomy "expert," the land yielded crops.

True, there were few or no trees, and not much water, on the high plains. But American technology offered an answer. Windmills utilized the plains' most constant resource—wind—and put it to work pumping water from subsurface reserves. Grand Rapids, Michigan, and other cities contributed ready-made furniture. Men like DeKalb experimented with a new kind of fencing and sent forth barbed wire to protect growing crops from the ravages of passing trail herds or neighborhood horses. A growing lumber industry furnished boards and shingles with which the homesteader replaced his first home, the temporary "soddy."

Fuel was harder to come by. There were occasional coal deposits on the plains, and along the creeks grew cottonwood trees and willows, a usable but unsatisfactory firewood. When even these items were unobtainable, corncobs, sunflower stalks, or buffalo chips went into the stove. Twists of hay, known as "cats," were a common sight in the settlers' homes. Special hay-burning stoves, fitted with magazines to accept the bulky fuel, appeared on the market and were widely purchased. Such substitutes for wood burned rapidly and in very cold weather just feeding the stove occupied most of the homesteader's time. On these occasions he must have recalled a boyhood east of the Mississippi when his father and grandfather before him had cursed the tree as he hacked away at it, trying to clear the land for a crop. The onetime nuisance would have been a precious item out in the middle of Kansas or Nebraska. The sacrifice paid for this level, unobstructed land, ready for the plow, was high, but there was no haggling with nature over it. It was a take-it-or-leave-it proposition.

But as the "wooden frontier" was passed by, industrial America offered other new tools with which to fight the parsimony of the Creator. A rising young steel industry provided sharper plowshares, scalpels with which to slice the stubborn sod, along with a whole catalog of implements designed for larger-scale farming. Thousands of tons of steel went into farm equipment as another branch of manufacturing appeared in the eastern states.

The American farmer did not simply decide that it was time to move across the Missouri. A whole set of factors and conditions had to develop so that it would be possible, and in the main these were not western in origin. It is agreed that precious metals and lush grazing lands in the West attracted men, and hence called for improved transportation, but it took a good deal more than this to persuade the dirt farmer it was time to try his hand in the desert. He not only had to be sold on the idea and hauled out there to see for himself, but also furnished with the necessary equipment for a new kind of agricultural life. This promotion did not come from the West. It was a real estate deal of magnificent proportions, conceived by financial pioneers whose base of operations might well be, and frequently was, Manhattan Island, Philadelphia, or Boston.

But there was an equally important headquarters in the great promotion—Washington, D.C.

The passage of the Homestead Act in 1862, by which the American government agreed to give to any adult citizen—or anyone who had declared his intention to become one—one hundred sixty acres of land, culminated a movement that had been growing for nearly half a century. The year 1820 was really the turning point. By a law of that year, a settler could purchase an eighty-acre farm for one hundred dollars. It was the lowest price and the smallest number of acres yet offered to those who wanted land. The government here indicated that its policy would emphasize getting people on the land rather than, as before, trying to make money from its sale. From that time on, until 1862, there was a steady growth of what might be called the "social" or "colonization" policy. It reached its ultimate limit in the granting of free farms.

The Homestead Act gave real meaning to the growing farm technology. John Deere had some years before developed his mold-board plow; Cyrus McCormick demonstrated his reaper before 1850. Soon came the harrow and other horse-drawn equipment. But it took the Civil War's demand for food and the passage of the Homestead Act to bring these implements into wide use. Once enticed westward by free land and equipped with machinery for extensive farming, the settler proceeded. Without such agricultural armament and a good deal of persuasion, he would have stayed put.

There were no valid objections to the big handout of 1862. Southerners for some time had complained about the proposed law, not on the ground that anything of value was being given away, but because they feared the growth of northern political power. By the time the law finally got through Congress, the nation had divided and the South no longer had a voice in the matter. The infant Republican party was anxious to make such a present to the American people for obvious political reasons. It hoped that an agricultural–industrial combine would prove irresistible at the polls.

Americans, in general, did not object. During the decade of the Fifties the desert theory was at its height. School atlases still depicted the high plains as a barren void, useless if not downright dangerous. Transcontinental railroad surveys of the period underscored and restated the belief. Even after the Civil War, General Sherman— in whose command the plains lay—reported to army headquarters that "the settlements of Kansas, Dacotah and Iowa have nearly or quite reached the Western limit of land fit for cultivation, Parallel 99° of West Longitude. Then begin the Great Plains 600 miles wide, fit only for Nomadic tribes of Indians, Tartars, or Buffaloes. . . ." As an army officer who had seen the plains, and would see them many times again in the years to come, he wondered why anyone would try to pursue agricultural endeavors in such a place. Conservative Americans agreed with him. Let the farmers go west to free lands, if they were such fools. And the farmers were such fools.

While men like Sherman confided their thoughts to superiors or buried them away in official reports, others set forth different ideas in public print. Eastern newspapers were filled with stories of the Garden of the World, the new Eden just beyond the Missouri. It was a wonderful place, readers learned from journalists who had been out to have a look. Here lay "a garden three times the area of France, with mountains beyond sufficient to supply the ever-advancing world with precious metals, and an ocean beyond them, with more people upon its shores and islands than are found on all the other waters of the globe." Kansas prairies were said to look "as if an ocean, heaving in grand long swells, had become suddenly indurated and clothed with luxuriant grass and flowers. Days after day a man may travel, and still one word will characterize all he sees—*Beautiful!"*

Such powers of description were too much for a good many mid-western farmers whose ancestors had worked westward on the leading edge of civilization, always anxious for something better. Their blood streams were affected by a strange and potent virus that kept them ever restless, and printed words like these served as powerful in-toxicants. Forward they went, a wall of humanity reaching out across the land in search of an agricultural paradise.

Daniel Freeman, a Union soldier on leave, figuratively fired the first gun in the great assault. On January 1, 1863, the day the home-stead law became effective, he filed the first claim in a Nebraska land office. In commemoration of the rush that followed, his farm is today a national monument. This speck of land represents not only a significant step in governmental policy; this was the initiation of the final assault upon the American frontier. When the movement ended, a new nation stepped forth into the family of the world.

Soldier Freeman's experience of filing a homestead claim was not typical. Although he found the town of Nebraska City filled with people whose intention it was to file when the land office opened, his status as a patriot, fighting for his country, worked in his favor. By common consent it was agreed that Freeman should be first and the land office was opened for five minutes on New Year's Day, even though it was a holiday, for the purpose of allowing the soldier to file. Then it was closed until the following morning.

The thousands who followed Freeman learned the meaning of the phrase "a land-office business." Having found a suitable location, prudently marking it by plowing up a bit of land and commencing a well to indicate his intention to settle, the homesteader made for the nearest land office to file his claim. As a rule he found a long line of men, sometimes a double line, standing before that building. Some had spent the entire night waiting. With no alternative but to join the throng, the hopeful farm owner took his place, watching the painfully slow progress toward the door. As he stood there, perhaps he chatted with strangers whose common interest in the new country made them friends before the clerk's desk was reached. From time to time men would drop out of line to get a cup of coffee or to obey a call of nature; by general consent their places were reserved to them upon return. At last the crowded confines of the land office was gained and after a brief struggle before a jam-packed desk, the applicant managed to complete necessary paper work. Weary and perspiring, he had nothing left to do but escape from the crush of humanity that shoved at the office door. Once free, he could return to his claim and start the long task of "proving up."

While more than a million and a third homesteads finally were given to the American people by means of one of the most generous laws ever passed by Congress, the program of land disposition was surprisingly unworkable. Like so many other pieces of legislation, it was passed by an eastern-dominated Congress and supported by legislators from the humid farm belt lying between the Ohio and the Missouri rivers, yet the land to which it was applied was the famed "American Desert."

Agrarians did not proceed very far beyond the Missouri before they discovered the inadequacies of the situation. Despite advance publicity promises that the topsoil was sufficiently deep and absorbent to eliminate worry about moisture, the country showed desert tendencies in its aridity. A hundred sixty acres of land in Dakota was not the same thing as a quarter section in Indiana or Iowa. It did not, could not, yield equivalent produce. When this was revealed to the plowman pioneers, they began to register complaints and accordingly lawmakers sought to remedy the difficulty.

If the plainsman's demand for additional land was to be satisfied, Congress decided there must be some kind of a swap. The farmer was going to have to do something in return. It was the considered opinion of the Land Office Commissioner that the presence of trees induced rainfall and, in 1866, he said so. "If one-third of the surface of the great plains were covered with forest there is every reason to believe the climate would be greatly improved, the value of the whole area as a grazing country wonderfully enhanced and the great portion of the soil would be susceptible of a high state of cultivation." Men who had lived on the high plains and those who had visited there admitted that seedlings would grow in the region. In theory, the Commissioner's notion about a potential forest on the high plains had some validity. In practice it did not work out. Congressmen were willing to give the plan a try and they proposed to offer farmers one hundred sixty acres, in addition to a homestead, for their cooperation. In return all they had to do was plant trees for the government.

In March 1873, the Timber Culture Act became law. Entitled "an act to encourage the growth of timber on western prairies," it provided that whoever would plant, and keep growing for ten years, forty acres of trees would receive the quarter section of land of which the grove was a part. The price was too high, and farmers said so. Trees would not grow *that* easily on the plains. By 1878, Congress reduced the required number of plantings to ten acres, specifying that twenty-seven hundred trees per acre must be planted but only 675 of them need be growing by the time the patent was applied for. Despite this concession, the law was a failure.

Failure resulted not so much because trees were difficult to grow beyond the Missouri as from the fact that Congress could not legislate them on the plains at will. What the Westerners wanted was more land, not groves. By the ancient American custom of circumventing those laws not popular, legal stipulations were sidestepped or openly violated. Fictitious entries were made to keep the land off the market, so that relinquishments might later be sold to settlers. Speculators made a business of buying up fraudulent entries for further sale. Cattle ranchers, in particular, took advantage of the Timber Culture Act's weaknesses by persuading their hired hands to make application for tracts of land. Bits of brush and willow spears were thrust into the ground in supposed compliance with tree-planting requirements. One Dakota outfit by this means obtained twenty-six quarter sections, carefully located along streams, and continued to utilize the land for grazing, not for agriculture. A special agent, investigating conditions in that territory, reported that ninety per cent of the entries were made not for the bona fide purpose of growing timber, but for speculation. The Commissioner of the General Land Office agreed that this seemed to be the case throughout the West. Accordingly, he recommended the law's repeal, and in 1891 it was done.

Meanwhile, Westerners continued their cries for more land, arguing that the Homestead Act was inadequate beyond the 100th meridian. Although President Grant's understanding of a growing America was painfully limited, he was able to recognize the truth of these assertions. In 1875, after a visit to the West, he told Congress that where normal agriculture was not practicable, irrigation was necessary, and, where this was not feasible, the land should be used for grazing. "Land must be held in larger quantities to justify the expense of conducting water upon it to make it fruitful or to justify using it as pasturage," he told the legislators. Congress responded in 1877 by passing the Desert Land Act.

This attempt to adjust land law to western conditions was also a failure. At the time of its passage, both the Land Commissioner and the Secretary of the Interior complained that the law was so loosely drawn that its own provisions would defeat its purpose. The legislators decreed that a settler might claim six hundred forty acres if he would conduct water upon it. But no one said how much water. By paying twenty-five cents per acre at the time of filing, and another dollar an acre at the time of patent (when proof of compliance was required), the applicant gained title to his claim.

Almost at once circumvention of the desert land law began. Stockmen gained control of thousands of acres and held it for three years for twenty-five cents an acre. By means of a tin cup, cowhands "conducted water on the land," thereby living up to the letter of the law. It was reported that in Arizona the holding of four or five thousand acres by stockmen under the new land legislation was not an uncommon thing; and, as the territorial surveyor-general put it, "The desert land act as it stands fosters a wild spirit of speculation." It was the same in Wyoming. Irrigation "ditches" were constructed by plowing a furrow; if the alleged waterways went up and downhill without regard to the contour of the land, the Westerners merely shrugged. They had to do the best they could with the laws Congress conjured up.

Daily violations of the government's land laws by settlers indicated more than a failure on the part of legislators to recognize unique climatic conditions in the neighborhood of the 100th meridian. Such transgressions revealed that the American desert theory was not entirely fictitious and that man's struggle to subdue the plains for his own purposes was to be no easy one. Back and forth the battle surged, with waves of small farmers advancing, only to be driven back in disastrous defeat, and then regrouping for another determined assault.

Bravely the farmers had plunged into Kansas during the Fifties, with no more than the Missouri and the unpredictable Kansas River to serve transportation needs. When they succeeded in raising crops, the settlers found that the great distance from markets made their products almost worthless. "The actual exports of the country—corn, pork and hides—has not yet been enough to pay for the whiskey that is drank every month, and men are living on what they had or the charity of their friends," wrote one disgruntled newcomer in 1860. "A good deal of corn is being shipped this spring, and some hides, but prices are so low that it hardly remunerates the grower for his labor. The best qualities of corn are delivered at the levee in sacks for thirty cents per bushel. Hides command four to six cents per pound. I am inclined to think that we cannot compete with Illinois and the lower states in agricultural produce. They have the advantage of nearer market. . . ."

When the railroads came, and figuratively brought nearer the necessary markets, there were other complaints. Crops failed and recent arrivals who had not yet established themselves turned to the moneylenders, who obliged by offering financial assistance at interest rates ranging from twenty-four to one hundred twenty per cent per annum. Some chose to accept such outrageous terms. Others admitted temporary defeat and went back east to spend the winter with the wife's folks. But—even in the face of scorching summers, cold winters, drought, grasshoppers, and high interest rates—men were still convinced that the land could be domesticated. Where one turned back, two more appeared to take his place. The movement would not be stopped.

For those who sought the safety of numbers, there were mass migrations westward. Back in the Fifties, Kansas had witnessed the appearance of The Vegetarian Kansas Emigration Company, whose "plan of settlement aimed to give the western settler some of the advantages of the East, with the hope of avoiding the hated isolation of the frontier. Each settler would live in a village, enjoy the aid and protection of his comrades, and attain social and educational advantages not otherwise possible." A decade later a group of Swedes bought land from the Kansas Pacific Railroad and established a colony in the Smoky Hill country, hoping for the same kind of security. About that time the Wakefield Colony was established in Clay County, Kansas, by a group of Englishmen. Faced by the usual adversities of the plains, one of the members stated that during 1869– 1870 more than a quarter of a million dollars was poured into this English colony and out of it not a quarter of a million cents could have been collected. There were some Americans in the group, one of whom failed to agree that numbers lent any security. He wrote bitterly: "This state is a fraud on a grand scale. The people are destitute and there is no money. The women are half-clothed and the men are barefooted in the streets."

Such dissatisfactions did not turn back the more optimistic. As a resident of Leavenworth wrote in 1870: "This state is looked to by a great many as affording them an escape from the difficulties that perplex them. . . ." The grass was always greener on the other side of the fence, and despite adverse reports by some of those who tried life on the plains only to find it too much for them, there were some possibilities in the new country. The influx of immigrants furnished at least a momentary market for agricultural produce, and what they did not use the Army bought. Men and women who had had their difficulties in the East believed that things could be no worse in the West and determined to test out the theory.

The frontiersman's traditional answer to adversity was humor. The plains farmer found that it helped him face new and desperate problems. When the land dried up, he laughed over the report that toll-bridge keepers were going broke because teamsters drove their animals across the trickling rivers right alongside the bridges. Or the story of the homesteader who wrote to a wire-fence company, saying: "Send me your terms for fence wire. I am thinking of fencing in Kansas," to which the company gravely answered: "Have consulted the best authorities, and made an approximate calculation of the amount of wire it will take to 'fence in' Kansas. We find that we have *just* enough if you order at once." Much appreciated also was the alleged reaction of a Kansas Indian who saw his first white woman, complete with large hoop skirt. Stepping back in amazement, the native exclaimed: "Ugh! heap wigwam!"

There were plenty of white men who longed for a view of that same hoop-skirted figure. While the farmers' frontier normally was characterized by the family unit, there were a number of young men who set forth to stake out a claim and establish a home before acquiring additional responsibilities. That they soon commenced to think of such things is reflected in contemporary newspapers. School boards, at their wits' end over the marital casualty rate among teachers of all ages and conditions, advertised for candidates who would pledge themselves not to marry for three years. An editor gallantly responded to the challenge by asking for one hundred young girls who would pledge themselves to marry within one year "and who are willing to commence school on one scholar." Hopeful males took to the papers' advertising columns. One Kansas advertisement read: "Wanted: Fifty young ladies to make husbands from fifty well-to-do bachelors residing in and about El Dorado. While our population is increasing very rapidly there is yet half the material here to further comply with the governor's request, if we only had the other half." Another promised that the first "good, respectable young lady" to settle on Slate Creek in Sumner County would be given a fine saddle horse, saddle, and bridle—and even a husband if she wanted one.

Nature's most violent threats could not stave off the invasion of homesteaders, once it gained momentum. A pioneer woman, who lived through troublous times clinging to her toehold in the West, later wrote: "Our attempt to crop and garden was washed out by the flood. The drought followed, and after the drought came the grasshoppers of 1867. They covered the earth and stripped the prairies of everything green, including the leaves of the cottonwoods on the river bank. Food was costly in those days. I paid ten cents a pound for salt, seventy-five cents for poor butter—hard to get at that price. I sold my watch for sixty dollars and bought a Texas cow." The early Seventies were no better. While panic visited the nation at large in 1873, the plains country suffered ruin and a temporary depopulation. Drought and disappointment swelled the ranks moving back east, as men left plows standing in the furrow and abandoned their homes. "The country was a desolate ruin for miles and miles," recalled an early resident. "Not a farmer was left, and the few settlers who remained engaged in the stock business, continually singing the song, 'This is not a farming country, it is only good for cattle.' " Then the retreat slowed and gradually the westward movement regained its momentum.

Western papers again printed stories of long lines of emigrant wagons passing through their prairie towns. Some stopped and looked around, then moved on. One of the newcomers complained that thousands of acres of unbroken prairie lay waiting for the plow but they were held by speculators whose prices were not attractive. "In order to get claims we must then push on, on." Far out on the plains, in advance of the necessary communication and transportation, the same writer informed his wife: "This county though so far West and a long distance from any railroad will be settled up very rapidly. . . . You at home have no idea of the rush to the West. This whole country is full of persons rushing hither and thither in search of homes."

By the decade of the Eighties, the land rush had reached boom proportions. At its height a Congregational circuit rider named Jeremiah Platt related that one of his friends, who had experienced many a similar event, declared that the agrarian invasion of southwestern Kansas was the greatest he had ever seen. Another of his friends told Platt that formerly a mere stake in the ground would hold a claim, but now a man must have a house on it, sit in the doorway with a shotgun, and threaten every man who came along in a covered wagon.

The Reverend was quite aware of the hazards faced by the onrushing farmers. Deep in what long had been regarded the heart of the desert, he watched homesteaders bravely mark off their claims. "While it is quite probable that much of this southwestern country will be parched with drouth in the near future and many of the settlers starved out and obliged to leave," he wrote, "I am more and more convinced that there is a Great Western Kansas which, in fifteen or twenty years from now will be as rich and productive and valuable as is the eastern part of the state, making Kansas the greatest and grandest agricultural state in the union." It was faith such as this that subdued the American desert.

Across the northern reaches of the plains much the same kind of development was taking place. During the mid-Sixties there were feeble attempts to farm in Dakota. Only six hundred seven votes were cast in the election of 1864 when the people elected congressional delegates. Indians, grasshoppers, and distance frightened away most prospective farmers. Settlement during the Seventies mounted steadily, bringing forth an advance guard of cautious homeseekers. Before 1880, however, only a little more than seven million acres of land were claimed. In that year the territory's first land office was opened, and, in the ensuing nineteen months, more than a million acres were filed upon.

Several factors caused the upturn in interest. Rainfall was better than average, land prices and taxes farther east were increasing rapidly, the new roller process of milling sharpened the demand for spring wheat, railroad advertising increased greatly and, perhaps most important of all, in 1883 the Northern Pacific was completed to the West Coast. Added to all these inducements was the discovery that wheat could be grown profitably in those northern climes. Returning travelers reflected the import of that news in their comments about the "wheat excitement" out West. One by one the elements of agricultural success fell into place, giving rise to a new kind of economic empire on the endless plains. To it new hordes of farmers rushed.

Encouraged by farmer interest in Dakota, other railroads reached westward to anticipate new demands and to serve those who had not waited for rail construction. During 1880, the Dakota Southern division of the North Western reached Pierre, producing a number of new agricultural towns as it proceeded. Meanwhile the Milwaukee road extended its tracks to Chamberlain, planting more communities all along the way. During this time, the Northern Pacific, aroused by the fresh surge of homesteaders, had resumed its westward trek to the sea. As the main trunk proceeded, branches sprouted into adjacent farming country, tapping the new and rich wheat belt.

The effect of the immigration is shown in both railroad and governmental reports. In 1881, the land commissioner for the Northern Pacific Railroad reported: "In this region where five years ago there was scarcely a white man, there is now a thrifty population of nearly 35,000 people, hailing from all parts of the world. There were 273,000 acres of land cultivated on the line of the Northern Pacific Railway last year. Barnes County, which is only four years old, has a population of three thousand, with seven hundred farms." By the following year, federal authorities estimated that in the two-year period since the census of 1880 Dakota had grown by at least seventy-five thousand people.

Whole trainloads of prospective farmers rolled westward from such rallying points as Chicago. Some were bound for Minnesota, but the majority headed for Dakota and eastern Montana. Reports from eastern Dakota counties, which revealed that they had no more public land to offer, told a story not only of ascending population figures, but of an advancing agricultural frontier line. Each year filings leaped in number until by the close of the decade that ended in 1889 almost forty-two million acres were taken up. This figure represented approximately half the area of Dakota. As the tempo mounted, population burst out on the end of railroad branches like blossoms. Collections of tar-paper shacks quickly gave way to clapboard buildings. Newly established newspapers trumpeted civic spirit. Outlying settlements teased the branch lines toward them and with their response came new agrarian boom towns. The rail lines, whose management had once pioneered a lonely and forbidding land and looked toward the Pacific Coast rather than at the Dakota sod, suddenly discovered that population had overtaken them. In the richer wheat regions it was now the farmer who beckoned to the railroad. It was then the roads realized that they had built better than they knew.

Within a decade after 1880, Dakota became plural. It was divided into northern and southern political units, and what had been hostile Sioux country was now a land of homesteads looking much like the farming country farther east. Captain Grant Marsh, the well-known river man whose steamer *Far West* once struggled up the Rosebud to rescue survivors of the Little Bighorn battle, was amazed at the transformation of the Upper Missouri country. Returning to central North Dakota just after the turn of the century, having been absent for some twenty years, he was struck by the countryside's change. "When he had left it," wrote his biographer, "it was a wilderness broken only at wide intervals by a struggling hamlet or the half-subdued claim of an adventurous farmer. Now, its towns were many and flourishing and its rich prairies were either under the plow or furnishing pasturage for the flocks and herds of a prosperous people."

Each of the new farming communities had its own capital city—a place in which to buy necessities, to vote, or perhaps merely to visit. The origins of these places frequently were unplanned and unpredicted. When the great homestead invasion swept the plains, towns spilled across the land like seed sown in the wind. Whenever there was the smallest evidence of population concentration, professional townbuilders stood ready to put together a new municipality. They took pride in the new work as they dotted the countryside with quickly built villages patterned after eastern models. Although the results often left something to be desired in the matter of excellence, the work had a most democratic air about it. Almost anyone could create a town in the West. A pioneer from New York admitted that the plains were well supplied with such builders. "This is a great country for cities," he told his brother. "Every neighborhood finds some ambitious man who must straightaway build a *city,* with broad streets, and wide avenues, parks and public squares."

With the exception of Washington, D.C., most American cities were not the result of careful planning, but in the frontier country beyond the Missouri, initial layouts were downright haphazard. Cyrus K. Holliday, who marked out the city of Topeka, Kansas, in the fall of 1854, had no more than a pocket compass, two pieces of rope and some sticks ripped from supply crates. Federal surveyors later pointed out triumphantly that Holliday was 18° 40′ east of true north, a fact that disturbed neither the residents nor the surveyor of young, boisterous Topeka.

Sometimes it was not even necessary to mark off streets and avenues. More than one western town appeared on the map just because some individual erected a building and christened it a city. Ekalaka, Montana, is said to have sprung from such a small seed. As the story goes, a trader whose wagons bogged down in the mud unloaded his stock, principally whiskey, and with the remark, "Hell, any place in Montana is a good place for a saloon," erected a cabin. The town was named after the Indian wife of the bar's first customer, a buffalo hunter. There are many counterparts of Ekalaka in the plains West, some of which never got beyond the one-building stage.

One of the reasons that towns tended to pop up so easily was that there were a number of city folks in the westerly migration. It is customary to think of the great agricultural invasion of the plains in terms of the hardy plowman, but in reality a good many of them never had been farmers. "It is surprising how large a proportion of our emigrants are city men and mechanics," wrote a newcomer from

New York. "A regular bred farmer is a rarity." His comment was frequently repeated in western newspapers, whose editors remarked about the tendency of the people to flock into towns to engage in trade and other "nonproductive" pursuits.

In the rush of settlement the early towns were, of course, exceedingly crude in appearance. Easterners, used to orderly and long-settled cities, expressed surprise at the confusion of the infant western municipalities. One of them, arriving at Lawrence, Kansas, in 1855, later recalled: "We . . . found the town, so widely known throughout the country, a mere collection of shanties, constructed of sods, grass and clapboards, separate or combined, as the skill and ability of the builder permitted; interspersed were some half dozen more substantial rough log cabins."

Some of Leavenworth's buildings were prefabricated in Cincinnati. Salesmen piled them up on vacant lots and sold them like Christmas trees. After being assembled the buildings were coated with a sort of cement, the principal ingredient of which was alcohol. Prairie-home building was frequently delayed by the constant disappearance of this solvent en route to its destination. While no one was mystified by the excessive evaporation, it served as an additional annoyance to the prospective homeowner.

One of the many British travelers who visited the West during the post–Civil War years found the claims of some of the prairie-town builders positively annoying. "At a place called 'La Park,' where there was but one wooden shanty," he wrote, "I heard a gentleman ask its proprietor 'if anyone was then talking about building a second house in that city?'"

The Reverend John H. Blegen, who was searching for a town called Broken Bone, in Dakota Territory, must have had much the same puzzled reaction. Wondering if he had missed his destination, he came to a shanty to which a man was then nailing a sign reading, "Grocery Store and Saloon."

"Where is Broken Bone?" asked Blegen.

"You are right in the heart of the city, sir. This is Main Street, but if you go down the hill, you will find the summer resorts among those trees yonder."

Upon investigation the Reverend found that the "summer resorts" consisted of a couple of small inns. "Thus a store and two inns are called a city out here," he wrote in wonderment.

A good many of the cities were spawned and briefly fed by the great emigration movement. Beginning at the Missouri, where water and land transportation met, they hopped westward with the frontier, outfitting the settlers for each new population movement. River towns of Kansas like Atchison and Leavenworth, both on the Missouri, supplied the Pike's Peakers and the mining camps they founded. Until 1865, Atchison was one of the great overland freight centers, sending forth thousands of wagons each season, but with the coming of the railroad it took its place alongside many another ordinary western town.

Farther out on the plains, towns sprang up as end-of-track cities, knowing full well that construction days would soon pass, but they hoped to become railroad centers after those days were over. "Whenever a railroad reaches a new station," wrote a Leavenworth resident in 1870, "there is an instant rush of population there, town lots become an object of speculation, and values go up to the most fanciful regions." The writer was critical of this boom spirit and lamented the fact that "strangers rush in possessing more money than judgment," hoping to make fortunes in speculation. Infant towns mushroomed with startling speed and shortly the countryside heard loud claims about size. "Census returns prick the bladder of this inflation," announced one realist, "and though they leave us some respectably sized Western cities, they cut in considerably on our assumptions." As boom days faded, former railhead cities tried hard to maintain a position of importance on the line.

Every western town hoped to earn the degree G.R.C., great railroad center. In 1870, a Pennsylvanian who had migrated to Girard, Kansas, told his eastern relatives that on paper there were railroads running through nearly every county seat in the state, but at the moment not one had been commenced. He admitted that since Girard was no longer a railhead there had been some adjustments in population. Construction-camp followers had moved on, leaving around nine hundred permanent residents, who patiently waited for their town to become a G.R.C. Until that day, merchants hoped to prosper from the westward-moving population. "Immigrants are coming into the country in great numbers," wrote a young settler. "Long strings of canvas-covered wagons are continually streaming in upon us, and I sometimes wonder whether the East will not be entirely depopulated. Vast sections of country are being filled up as if by magic."

Like the mining camps and the cattle towns, a good many of the homesteaders' hamlets suddenly bloomed, and then faded away. The ever-optimistic pioneer poured money and enthusiasm into his projects, hopeful that the inflationary trend that characterized all frontiers would somehow last and that the seed he planted would germinate and then flower. The hope of the Sixties and Seventies began to evaporate in the Eighties and Nineties as agricultural prices slumped and depression visited the new land. Thousands of those who filled up the West "as if by magic" silently retreated back to the East, which was not yet quite depopulated, as the writer had feared it might be. Hundreds of little towns shrank in size and some of them disappeared completely.

As the wagon-trade centers and river ports surrendered to the railroad, so many of the hopeful G.R.C.s gave in to the automobile during the twentieth century. There are ghost towns in the mining country and there are ghost towns along the once-busy Missouri River. But there are also skeletons on the prairie where once-thriving communities surrounded the now-lonely railroad water tanks or section houses. The coming of the automobile, and more important, the hard-surfaced highway, spelled extinction to thousands of small-town banks, lumberyards, stores, and newspapers. When roads became all-weather highways, the farmers took their eggs, cream, and other produce to the larger places in their area. There they shopped in bigger stores, with wider varieties of goods, banked their money, outfitted the children, bought Mother a new hat, took in a movie, and went home. Now twenty, thirty, or even fifty miles was no great distance. And the little towns along the way watched hungrily as the new agrarians sped by, en route to "the city." One by one the small-town merchants threw in the towel and moved away.

Today there are numberless agricultural ghost towns, which once aspired to great things, sporting today only a wayside gas station for the tourists. Like their predecessors on the frontier, they are victims of a more perfect system of transportation. Their unpainted and long-neglected structures are monuments to the unfulfilled hopes and the perhaps necessary waste that accompanied the building of the modern West. The land had to undergo a series of violent and occasionally catastrophic readjustments before it settled down. So it was with all of America.

The tidal wave of settlers crested during the Eighties. Its momentum thundered against the Rockies, spilled thousands of farmers through the passes, and scattered them among the high mountain parks. Overnight, Indian tribes were dispossessed, and miners found themselves quarreling with the newcomers over water rights as the greatest movement of the American people reached its climax.

Colorado, in particular, felt the effects of settlement's high tide. Unlike other mountain states, it had in Denver an important city whose ambitious leaders longed to make of it an important railway center. Grandiose plans to connect the Queen City of the Plains by rail to Puget Sound, Duluth on the Lakes, and New Orleans did not materialize in the form dreamers conceived them, yet by the Eighties a number of important links with other sections of the nation were completed. During those years the Burlington, the Missouri Pacific, the Rock Island, and the Santa Fe made a connection with Denver. Meanwhile, the narrow-gauge Denver and Rio Grande, under the direction of General Palmer, plunged into the mountains and sought out Salt Lake City. At the same time a number of other narrow-gauge lines snaked their way through steep canyons, presenting the world with unheard-of engineering feats as they crossed skyline divides. With the way prepared, legions of homesteaders took to the rails and assaulted a barrier that had once defeated men like John C. Frémont.

In western Colorado, where the Utes were hurriedly evacuated in 1881, land boomers took over and commenced the subdivision of a virgin land. Small farms, orchards, and cattle ranches were marked off; to serve them, towns sprang up in the traditional frontier fashion. To the east, on the plains that sloped upward to meet the mountains, there grew an agricultural community fed by an elaborate irrigation system. Since the earliest mining days, residents had understood the water potential generated in the mountains and canal construction dated from that time. But now, with the coming of the homesteader, irrigation projects became big business. In 1884, the Fort Lyon canal was begun. Finished, its hundred-mile length would serve more than a hundred thousand acres of thirsty land. There were others like it, most of them smaller, but each put into production thousands of acres that were once a part of the desert's edge.

The newcomers did not always enjoy a cordial reception. Cattlemen, claiming the countryside by right of priority, fought the advancing farmers at every turn. The contest, the generalities of which are well known to readers of western Americana, represented another phase of the tumult that surrounded the process of settlement. In addition to both threats and deeds of violence against the hated nester or sodbuster, as the stockgrower sneeringly called the plowman, attempts were made to fence off cattle ranges to the exclusion of such interlopers. The farmers set up a howl of protest that was heard at Washington, and, as it would in many later instances, the administration responded. President Cleveland indicated that the beef barons would have to pay more attention to the established rules of financial extraction when, in 1885, he issued an executive order prohibiting such fencing on the public domain. The trappers, miners, and finally the cattlemen had long used federal lands for their own purposes and in any manner they saw fit. By Cleveland's day, the western pastoral was getting a little too crowded for such independence. His action swelled the mournful dirge of earlier residents that, indeed, the Old West was gone.

The doleful notes of lament were drowned out by a new hymn of hope. It was a song of bumper crops on fresh, free lands, and of independence for the poor, the underprivileged, the downtrodden. The land of promise was also a land of unexplained miracles. The rain belt, it seemed, unaccountably had taken up the westward trek and resolutely was moving toward the Rockies. The region of western Kansas and eastern Colorado, formerly a trackless desert, was now so wet that it was unsuited as a winter range for cattle. Where drought once ruled, mildew threatened to take over. No one knew the reason for this marvelous change. Some said the presence of iron rails disturbed the celestial electrical system sufficiently to turn on the

Maker's sprinkling device. Whatever the cause, promoters rejoiced and broadcast the theory. Within a few years drought-plagued farmers would be wondering about nature's fickle ways, or contemplating the wisdom of believing all they had read. But in the wet, booming Eighties, they could not foresee such a development and their optimism more than matched that of the land-hawkers.

Along the mountain front to the north of Colorado, the agricultural invasion was slower. Wyoming, devoid of a rail network, did not see many homesteaders during its territorial days. Apparently the rain belt did not invade that part of the country. At least, no residents were known to have constructed arks.

Montana, to a degree like Wyoming, remained primarily a land of cattle until the Nineties. By that decade, the overflow from the Dakotas reached out toward the Montana Rockies. With both the Great Northern, completed in 1893, and the Northern Pacific to service the state, advancing sodbusters felt their way west, infiltrating the more arable valleys.

Before long civic leaders in Montana, hopeful of a big population and hence a more lucrative tax base, commenced to praise the fertility of the soil. When they referred to agriculture as the "bone and sinew" of the community, an old-time cattleman could contain himself no longer. "Damn such bone and sinew," he roared. "They are the ruin of the country and have everlastingly, eternally, now and forever, destroyed the best grazing land in the world. The range country, sir, was never intended for raising farm-truck. It was intended for cattle and horses, and was the best stock-raising land on earth until they got to turning over the sod—improving the country, as they call it." Almost tearfully he condemned such improvement. "It makes me sick to think of it. I am sick enough to need two doctors, a druggery and a mineral spring when I think of onions and Irish potatoes growing where mustang ponies should be exercising, and where four year old steers should be getting ripe for market. Fences, sir, are the curse of the country." [1]

Just a few years later, the cowboy artist Charley Russell agreed.

[1] Quoted by Merrill G. Burlingame, *The Montana Frontier*, Helena, 1942, p. 35.

Writing to a friend, he said: "Bob you wouldent know the town or the country either it's all grass side down now. Where once you rode circle and I night wrangled, a gopher couldn't graze now. The boosters say its a better country than it ever was but it looks like hell to me I liked it better when it belonged to God it was sure his country when we knew it."

The boosters had their way. Delayed though it was, the westward sweep of homesteaders engulfed Montana. Railroad publicity, the relative scarcity of land in more easterly plains states, and the sheer momentum of the agricultural frontier carried the movement to the Rockies and beyond. By the time the twentieth century was a decade old, more than a million acres of farmland were taken up. It was only the beginning. In little more than another decade the figure stood at ninety-three million, or more than forty per cent of the state's area. It has been estimated that eighty per cent of those acres were, except under unusually favorable conditions, unfit for crop agriculture. It didn't matter. Nothing could stop the onrushing farmers; not sound advice, not arctic winters and scorching summers, not failure itself. They had read of paradise on the plains, had seen samples of its crops, and had talked with some of the more successful settlers. They had to go out and "see the elephant." Many of their descendants are still there, cursing the country among themselves, defending it before strangers, voting Democratic in times of drought and Republican when it rains.

As the nineteenth century closed, the victory of the sodbusters seemed virtually complete. In a single generation they flooded across the high plains and into mountain recesses, wiping out America's last frontier. Their coming heralded the emergence of modern America, for they brought with them a new way of life. Before the arrival of the farmers, the plains West retained its frontier characteristics, and if the homesteaders had moved onto a land similar in humidity and transportation facilities to that farther east, the change might not have been so obvious. But the agricultural pioneers of the plains lived in a new type of economy. Theirs was a cash crop made possible by the railroads, and wherever the rails went so did the farmers. Well connected with eastern markets the homesteaders gave up the near-subsistence agriculture once followed by their forebears. Railroads, rural free delivery, and mail-order houses permitted them to live like and look like Americans in any other part of the land.

The new agrarians modified the frontier's characteristics not only by virtue of their numbers, but also by their culture. They were not, as a rule, the covered-wagon pioneers. They came by train, frequently straight from immigrant ships, and in many cases it was their first pioneering experience. In some parts of the plains there were counties, even states, whose population was dominated by foreign customs and language. It has been said that at one time a man who spoke Norwegian could communicate with more people in North Dakota than if he used English. The typical frontier had disappeared in a linguistic way, for it was no longer dominated by the Anglo-American.

Slowly these foreign-language groups became assimilated, as the younger generation tried hard to hide its accent and sought the conformity of dress offered in the mail-order catalogs. However, as in the commingling of any cultures, each group made its contribution, and much that was desirable rubbed off onto the Yankee settlers. At first they made jokes about the foreigners, but gradually they accepted many of their ideals and customs. After decades of westward movement, the American agricultural pioneer found himself in a new land, living under quite different climatic conditions, and surrounded by neighbors whose pattern of life was not rooted in frontier conditions.

The transformation of the high plains by this polyglot army of plowmen appeared to be a triumph for America's favorite individual, the "little man." By the thousands these people swarmed westward, shoving aside the cattlemen, staking out claims and fencing off the land. Like the locusts they had to combat, the homesteaders spread over the countryside, cutting checkerboard squares from the public domain, infiltrating even the most unlikely farming regions. Reminiscent of the early gold-rush days, they tore up the sod in frantic haste, mining the soil for the golden color of wheat, with absolute disregard of warning signals that predicted failure.

When the sodbuster legion had made its deepest infiltration and was already shouting a song of victory, there came the awful realization that perhaps this was no land of easy conquest but instead a gigantic cul-de-sac, a trap from which there might be no escape. While freight and interest rates soared, the price structure sagged. Boom times, followed by desolate, parched years, caused markets to fluctuate wildly. When the desert struck back at the invaders with sustained viciousness, using all of its climatic weapons, eastern creditors shook their heads in sadness over the plight of their western brethren—and demanded the money due them. Desperately the farmers looked back over their shoulders, but there was no place to retreat. Nor was there any chance to go farther west. The frontier had closed like a vise.

Slowly a great truth dawned. Difficulties that had once appeared temporary in nature were now revealed to be deep-seated, permanent agricultural ailments. Cornered, the agrarians turned upon the East, the government at Washington, the world itself, and snarled like animals at bay. When the first bitterness subsided, they turned to each other and sought a solution to their dilemma. It was at that moment that the high plains truly became a region. Common problems, common hatreds, and common hopes drove together a people who felt they were victims of a giant conspiracy, a hoax, and they resolved to strike back. In some respects, the battle still continues.

Chapter 9

DISSENSION IN THE DESERT

For half a century following the purchase of Louisiana, most of Jefferson's western empire was without formal political organization. While trappers and occasional travelers might argue that it was God's country, most Americans chose to think of it as a barren waste, nice to have but of very little immediate value. Few white people lived there, and those who did had no voice in national or even regional affairs. There were no cities to act as loudspeakers for them and, lacking these civic vocal chords, the countryside remained mute.

Meanwhile, during the first half of the nineteenth century, public attention was focused upon the land lying between the Appalachians and the Mississippi Valley. This was the settlers' frontier, and it was subjected to great pressures of immigration. Growing municipalities in the Ohio and Mississippi valleys stridently demanded the removal of the natives to clear the land for farms in their communities. The plains region was of little interest to agrarian pioneers; their suggestion that the natives be put out onto these grassy reaches had sufficient appeal to the country at large to cause such removals. During Jackson's administration, the enforced migration of Indians was begun, and by 1840 a whole tier of boxlike Indian colonies was marked off on the map just west of the 95th meridian. Into these artificial pens the natives were unceremoniously herded. We now had what was optimistically labeled a permanent Indian frontier.

Almost immediately, emigration to Oregon, the flight of the Mormons, and the California-bound Argonauts knifed wagon roads through the Indian reserve. The discovery of gold in Colorado in 1859, and shortly thereafter in Montana, finished the disruption. Overnight the plains were teeming with travelers and the dream of a western home for eastern Indians was shattered. Crisscrossed by travel routes, its outer edges awash with settlers, the region west of the Missouri commenced to feel pulsations of demand for some kind of political organization. Despite their desire for unfettered economic opportunity, the newcomers wanted a governmental framework to protect that which they hoped to win.

During the winter of 1853, fifty years after Napoleon disposed of his real estate holdings on the North American continent, territorial boundaries were planned for the country beyond the Missouri. While the slavery issue without doubt played its part in the origins of the Kansas–Nebraska Act, western pressure was a powerful force. Missourians and Iowans alike trooped to mass meetings to voice their demands for political organization of the land to the west. Not only would it advertise the potential railroad route to the Pacific, it would also give recognition to the "sooners" of that day who had leapt forward to find themselves living in a political vacuum.

In February 1853, a bill to organize Nebraska passed the House of Representatives but failed in the Senate. At the opening of the new congressional session in December, Senator Dodge of Iowa introduced a similar bill—only to have the Committee on Territories inject the inflammable slavery issue. Westerners were dismayed to see the national emotional crisis focused upon their region, for it threatened to defer a development many of them thought quite apart from the central point at issue. Deeply disturbed, a number of proponents of immediate organization met in convention at St. Joseph, Missouri, during January 1854 and voiced strong objections to further delay. Despite the nationwide crisis produced by the bill, it was passed late in May and President Franklin Pierce affixed his signature to it. Instead of one territory, two were laid out.

With the induction of Kansas and Nebraska into the political fraternity, the way was marked for a similar development in the remainder of the Louisiana Purchase. By 1861, Colorado was formed, largely out of western Kansas and eastern Utah Territory, and William Gilpin, an ardent western enthusiast, became its first governor. During the same year, following demands made by the residents for several successive years, Dakota Territory was created. President Buchanan approved the measure two days before he left office. The new political subdivision, almost a geographic empire in itself, comprised all of present Montana and part of Idaho and reached southward to the Niobrara and Turtle Hill rivers. With its 350,000 square miles it constituted the largest organized territory in the United States.

Dakotans could boast of size for only three years. In 1864, Montana Territory was created, its eastern boundary lopping off Dakota near the confluence of the Missouri and Yellowstone rivers. Sidney Edgerton, Chief Justice of Idaho Territory, became Montana's governor. Meanwhile, Representative James M. Ashley of Ohio, who one day was also to become Montana's governor, tried to divide up the great western expanse further. In 1865, he introduced a bill into the House of Representatives looking toward the establishment of Wyoming Territory. Although he was not immediately successful, events were working in his favor. The Union Pacific Railroad soon approached that section of the plains and shortly there was a booming, if somewhat temporary, populace crying for admittance to the Union. Following the ancient custom, the new residents sent to Washington a petitioner who was possessed of a thoroughgoing chamber-of-commerce enthusiasm. He reported that in 1868 there was a first-class railroad crossing Wyoming, the home of some thirty-five thousand people, and a city named Cheyenne with over five thousand residents. It was high time, he said, that law and order were brought to the community. President Andrew Johnson agreed to this necessity and signed Wyoming's admission papers.

In 1861, the year Colorado and Dakota territories were created, Kansas entered the Union as a state. Already it had a population of more than a hundred thousand and was growing rapidly. Six years later, on the eve of Wyoming's entrance as a territory, Nebraska also attained statehood. Thus, in the early post–Civil War years, all of the northern high plains and mountain region was politically organized.

With the exception of Colorado, admitted as a state in 1876, the area's status remained fixed for two decades. The vast sweep of land north of Colorado and Nebraska was kept as a colonial appendage for political reasons until the admission of the omnibus states in 1889 and 1890. By then the Indian menace was eliminated, railroads served the region, and a population of farmers dominated much of what once had been the domain of the cattlemen. Bitterly Governor Gilbert Pierce of Dakota Territory wrote in 1887: "We have seen people fighting to get out of the union amid the protests of the national government; it is a novel sight to see 500,000 people struggling to get into the union without being heeded or recognized." Reluctantly, in 1889, older members of the political club admitted the two Dakotas and Montana to full-fledged membership. The following year, with the admission of Wyoming and Idaho, the political map of the region was completed.

The nation looked on with approval as atlas publishers busily altered their maps, spreading newly made territories and, finally, states, across what once had been labeled the Great American Desert. The task of building America, at least from the political standpoint, appeared to be nearing accomplishment.

Plains residents also were proud. In a few short years after the Civil War they had built an empire in a land their fathers once called useless and fit only for savages. They congratulated each other, and talked of man's ability to combat nature, of the miracles of modern agriculture, of the realization of the American dream. When statehood was bestowed upon the Westerners, they regarded it as a recognition of their achievements and as a kind of valedictory to the days of pioneering. Now they belonged, in every sense, and the feeling was doubly satisfactory, for they had gone out where others feared to go, had laughed at the doubters, and had won a great economic victory.

What a country! they said. It was indeed a nation where there were opportunities for all, and undeniable rewards for those who persevered. Even a desert could not stop Americans!

But for the desert, the battle was young. It conceded round one to the onrush of those who would subdue it and patiently bided its time. The day of reckoning for the challengers came early. While the invasion was at its crest, the tide began to turn, and almost overnight the jubilant empire builders saw their ramparts of civilization crumble at the edges. The agrarian storm troopers had swept through the desert's defenses with ease and had penetrated its deepest recesses. When the counterattack commenced the advance guard of farmers wondered if the assault had not been too easy and nervously they looked behind them for support. But there was none. The promoters and land-boomers who had sent them forward with a pat on the back were nowhere to be seen.

During the Eighties the momentum of the westward rush carried thousands of farmers to the new country. For nearly a decade before 1887 rainfall in the desert, particularly its western part, was far above average. The wet years seemed to substantiate all the claims made by railroad propagandists, and, convinced that such moisture was normal, countless farmers took the plunge. The belt of land from North Dakota southward to Kansas produced a crop of mortgages that stood near the top in national rankings. In some of these states there was one mortgage for every two people; in others, the ratio was one to three. This meant that there were more mortgages than families and it indicates that the title of more than one farm was graced by multiple encumbrances. With interest rates maintaining their earlier high levels, there seemed to be a never-ending supply of eastern money. Despite warnings of overexpansion, loans remained easy.

Then came the Nineties, which some Americans were to remember as gay, but for hundreds upon hundreds of prairie farm families it was a decade of disaster. The trouble began in the late Eighties and mounted in intensity during the remaining years of the century. With the exception of a few bursts of prosperity, the decline that set in during this period has been continuous. The basic ills are still present.

The first signs of impending trouble came in 1886–1887 when

white disaster brought an end to the day of the open range and froze out many a cattle king. The farmers were next. Crops failed in 1887, and a wave of mortgage foreclosures followed. With the Panic of 1893 the problem was nationwide. During these years, about half the population of western Kansas moved out and whole sections of the country, clear to the Canadian line, were virtually depopulated. Even cities well back from the desert were struck down in the collapse. Years later, houses in Wichita, Kansas, built or partly completed during boom years, rotted away, uninhabited. In a two-year period that city lost thirteen thousand people and Leavenworth suffered a decline of fifteen thousand. As both urban and rural populations fell off alarmingly in the newborn states, talk of the great agricultural bonanza died upon the lips of the enthusiasts. They were too busy scratching for a living to dream.

Desperately the beleaguered farmers fought for their very existence. When the celestial waterworks went dry, they looked back more than thirty years and remembered the parched days in Kansas during the early Sixties. Drought years had come and gone; maybe it would happen again. Frightened men assured each other that the country was basically sound. The cycle would break, the rain would come again. As they waited nervously, eyeing each lonely cloud that drifted by, they made wry jokes about the Garden of Eden the railroad promoters had found for them. Those who lived in Nebraska did not recognize the Platte Valley as a "flowery meadow of great fertility clothed in nutritious grasses, and watered by numerous streams," as the Union Pacific had described it. Dakotans found it hard to laugh over the appellation given their land: "Jay Cooke's Banana Belt." They had come West, listening to Northern Pacific talk of a "Mediterranean climate." The arctic blasts that rocketed in from Canada made them wonder what had happened to the promised Neapolitan zephyrs. But the icy drafts could be tolerated if they would just leave the land some moisture. Instead, subzero temperatures in the winter were quickly exchanged for intolerably hot, dry summers. It was, indeed, a land of extremes.

Climatic problems were hard to solve. As Mark Twain told Americans of his day, everybody talked about the weather but nobody did anything about it. There wasn't much to be done, aside from some experiments in rainmaking. This slight tampering with the elements produced little satisfaction and less rainfall. Besides, it availed a man nothing to cuss the climate or, for that matter, to fight back at such tangible things as grasshoppers. Another villain had to be found, and without much searching around the western farmer fixed the railroads in his political gunsights. Here was a completely satisfactory villain, for not only were the roads guilty of raising their rates, charging more for short hauls than for long hauls, and acting with general arbitrariness, but they had also, said the farmer, engaged in the worst kind of duplicity by enticing emigrants into this economic vacuum to begin with. It was they who had advertised, promoted, wheedled, and propagandized. Like a suitor promising his bride-to-be the moon, the railroads had painted the western picture in rosy hues, and then—said the bitter newcomers—the honeymoon suddenly had ended. Now the railroads were harsh and demanding. Angrily, the victims resolved to punish the perpetrators of this fraud.

What made the railroads a common target was their proximity. In the back of the farmers' minds there was a greater criminal called "the money trust," which was said to be a part of an international conspiracy. But it was intangible, faraway, and hard to attack. Closely allied with these invisible forces were the speculators who used their wealth to engulf large tracts of land by means of unrestricted "entry," keeping away what Westerners regarded as the honest tillers of the soil. Land-law provisions, which allowed such unrestricted entry and temporary monopolization of land, were not corrected until 1888. The result was that the small homesteaders frequently were driven beyond the region of arable lands into marginal areas whose promise of productivity was entirely unreliable except in unusually wet years. Unfortunately, like the money trust, the speculators were also frequently hard to lay hands on.

Some of the disgruntled Westerners blamed fate and circumstance for their dilemma. They believed that the closing of the frontier, and the consequent absence of more rich soil, was to blame. It was not, however, their inability to continue westward toward new lands that caused the trouble. On the contrary, many of them already had moved too far west, beyond a point of adequate rainfall, and traditionally wasteful frontier agricultural methods were now catching up with them. They did not understand the diversity of American soils or the fact that old, humid-area methods would not always work. But to admit this would have been to put blame upon themselves. It was far easier to accuse someone else. The railroads, close at hand, were naturally the first objects of their retaliation.

In little gatherings western farmers began to discuss their common predicament. They recalled that in addition to inducing them to settle upon marginal lands that would produce a living only under the most favorable circumstances, the railroads had persuaded them to finance rail facilities through the sale of bonds. More than one farmer had mortgaged his farm in order to make what appeared to be a necessary investment. Then through some kind of financial legerdemain, performed in eastern offices, road reorganizations took place which mysteriously melted away the value of the stocks and bonds. In addition to declining values in rail investments, as well as in agricultural prices, the farmer-investor found himself faced with higher shipping rates and higher taxes. The latter situation arose because many a town and county had also bought stock and it had somehow to be paid for. It is small wonder that the plowman talked darkly about the captains of industry and the intricacies of high finance. It reminded him of the shell game he had tried at the county fair, an expensive experience.

Before the nineteenth century came to a close, prairie farmers had worked themselves into a mass anger that historians have called an "agrarian revolt." It might better have been termed a dissent, for by and large the farmers did not regard their attitude as revolutionary, at least not in the subversive sense. They were not out to overturn the established system; what they wanted was a major overhaul and a reorientation that would adjust what they regarded as a growing economic inequity. They did not see themselves as any more revolutionary than the Jeffersonians who sought equality of opportunity and showed a hostility to special privilege, concentrated economic power, and vested interests. The Populists' Omaha Platform of 1892 expressed this view when it asked that government be freed from corporate control so that there might be equal rights and equal privileges for all.

The fact that western farmers organized the better to voice their demands caused surprise and concern among urban elements. Traditionally the American farmer has been the most independent, individualistic, and hard-to-organize member of society. When it was revealed that he was prepared to ride twenty or thirty rough miles in a springless wagon to meet with his fellows in some lonely prairie schoolhouse and there to pledge his support to an agrarian cause, Easterners became uneasy. In an era when the courts were solidly antilabor and society in general approved of the suppression of the workingman's demands, it was not hard to frown upon the complaints of the farmer.

America's material prosperity was greater than ever before and the average home was supplied with more of life's necessities, and even luxuries, than at any previous time in the nation's history. It was true, admitted the smaller-town storekeeper or newspaper editor, that industrial America might have some small maladjustments in its magnificent growth, but these were necessary evils attendant on such expansion. Things would even out. People must be patient. These western farmers were a strident lot. They ought to remember that they were but a part of the national family and they could well hold their tongues. So the small-town businessman went on, attending his Monday noon knife-and-fork club, listening to the gospel of "boost, don't knock," and felt a lurking resentment for the wild-eyed plowmen of the plains who seemed dissatisfied with their place in the world's greatest economic system.

Leaders of the agrarians were not apologetic about their position. They were radicals and they admitted it. There was nothing inconsistent between radicalism and the American tradition. The two ideologies had enjoyed a measure of compatibility since the days of Thomas Paine and the Democratic Republican Clubs a century earlier. For decades farmers had railed against the monopolies of money, transportation, and land. When the Populists of the Nineties powered their political drive with the element of antimonopolism they were using a traditional fuel. Through some refinements the propellant had a little higher octane rating, and it was injected into a hotter combustion chamber, giving it a more revolutionary appearance than it really had. In other words, Westerners felt that because of their widespread complaint, now rising to fever pitch, the time and the place were right for an all-out battle. They saw nothing un-American about fighting for what they regarded as their rights.

That the aggrieved chose the railroads as their chief adversary is not surprising. The roads represented but one enemy, it is true, but they were in the West, tangible and subject to punishment. They were not only villains because they held hostage the farmer's crops until he was ready to pay the necessary ransom to get them to market, but they also represented monopoly at large. An Omaha paper stated the case in 1890 when, praising the growth of the Farmers' Alliance, it said that the development was "a gratifying evidence of an awakening among the producers. . . . Organization among the farmers has become an urgent necessity. Confronted on every side by combines and trusts, they are forced to unite to protect themselves from the grasping greed of corporations. It is hoped that strong, conservative men will be placed at the helm of the alliance—men who know the right of the producers and who will demand and secure just treatment from the transportation companies of the state." Radicals, not conservatives, grasped the helm; Nebraska farmers and their brothers in other plains states applauded as the helmsmen steered straight into the storm of eastern disapproval. As the movement gathered momentum, western railroads quailed before the coming onslaught.

The roads had a right to be apprehensive. When "Sockless" Jerry Simpson, the Populist congressman, told his listeners that eight thousand miles of Kansas railroads cost a hundred million dollars to construct but were capitalized at three times that figure in stocks, and a like amount in bonds, road-owners were hard put for an explanation. Nor did they have a satisfactory answer to the charge made by farmer–orators that it took a bushel of wheat or corn to pay freight on the same amount of produce to get it to the market. They also had to admit it was true that western rates were often two to three times higher than those charged for similar distances between places like Minneapolis and Chicago or Chicago and New York, where competition was keen.

Nor was this all. Dakota and Montana farmers angrily trumpeted the fact that Jim Hill not only took them into camp with high freight rates, but he also refused to haul grain from elevators of less than thirty-thousand-bushel capacity. The "Hill system" both milked the shippers for haulage and held them up for elevator-storage and service charges by obliging them to sell their grain at places the railroad operators selected. The elevator operator was king. He could determine the grade, hence the price; could assess the amount of smut and dirt in the grain and dock the price proportionately; or he might charge excessive storage rates if a farmer chose to wait for a better price before selling. It was the redress of grievances like these that farmers sought in their state legislatures.

The determination of the agrarians to enter the political arena to right some wrongs came at an interesting time for some of the farming communities. Four prairie territories—Montana, Wyoming, and the Dakotas—were elevated to statehood with the entrance of the six omnibus states. When Dakota Territory was divided in two, in 1889, and each part given statehood, the farmers did not have to revolt against any established state administration to gain control. It is true that there were territorial political bosses, but the change in political status gave the agrarians a chance to enter the picture with a better opportunity to gain their share of the spoils. The prize was more than mere office-holding. If government could smile upon industry, as it unquestionably was doing elsewhere, it could be made to favor agriculture. And agriculture needed favor, for already there were clouds of doubt in men's minds about their ability to conquer the desert as individuals.

The struggle in North Dakota commenced at the constitutional convention when a delegate submitted a constitution favored by the president of the Northern Pacific Railroad. There was an immediate outcry against it, and the other delegates showed their temper by drawing up a document of their own choosing, including in it a board of railroad commissioners to be elected by the people. The first state legislature followed this lead by enacting additional grain-trade legislation, only to see it thrown out by the attorney general upon motion from the Elevator Association.

After several years of such frustrated attempts to work within the framework of regular parties, the North Dakota Populists entered the field in 1892 with their own ticket and won. This victory was short-lived; within two years they lost political control. In their brief reign they set maximum freight rates on coal mined within the state, established public scales that did not have the peculiar balance of those owned by the private elevator companies, outlawed usury, and made railroads responsible for prairie and crop fires started by their locomotives. Then the forces of Alexander McKenzie, longtime Dakota political boss, resumed control and held it for another twenty years. Patiently the farmers came back. Once, when a delegation of them waited upon the legislators with a request, one of the lawmakers asked what business they had trying to browbeat the legislature. Then, as legend has it, he flatly advised them to "Go home and slop the hogs." It was stories like this one, circulated in western rural areas, that goaded the farmers into fury and deepened their resolve to take over the reins of government as soon as possible.

Railroad owners had to admit that they were in a quandary. They had sent forth their respective lines on a wave of optimism and boom spirit, encouraged by the federal government and cheered by the populace at large. Eager farmers had willingly accepted the attractively low fares and had gobbled up lands offered at reasonable prices. A number of the roads asserted, and probably fairly, that they had profited little from the sale of their land grants. Some of them, like the Santa Fe, offered prospective farmers half fare just to go out and have a look, no strings attached, and many an agricultural prospector finally had chosen to take up government land. The low rates offered emigrants on the haulage of their household goods, machinery, stock, and seeds often resulted in a loss for the railroads. But they wanted traffic that settlement would bring and were willing to take a chance. When the gamble failed, farmers accusingly pointed their fingers at the railroads.

Railroaders were in no better position than the settlers to predict the weather. They prayed just as fervently for rain as anyone; their stake in the game was as important to them as the farmer's was to him. The management's extensive advertising, land promotion, and emigrant travel rates were based upon the premise of agricultural prosperity; when it failed to materialize the vendors of transportation were in serious trouble. With a large initial investment, admittedly overextended, the trap in which they were caught was the same as that of the farmer. Plunging grain prices did not take fixed costs downward with them at the same rate of descent, nor did they lessen the weight or bulk of the bushel. There were still payrolls to meet, equipment to replace, and roadbeds to repair if grain—regardless of its price—was to be moved. There were certain fixed charges, such as interest, that did not follow closely the trend of agricultural income. Furthermore, said the railroads, western farmers who were so bitterly critical did not always remember that in their region freight haulage was frequently a one-way proposition. In order to get cars to haul grain out, many of them had to be deadheaded to the West, completely empty, which doubled the cost of movement.

The railroads, like the farmer, were caught in the bind. Besieged by agrarian legislators in the West and engaged in a bitter competitive fight with other roads to the East, the lines fought with their backs to the wall, grasping in desperation at any means of succor. If they charged three or four times as much for prairie transportation as they did in more humid and populated areas, the roads rationalized it as a necessity arising from the present exigency. Many an official knew that it was wrong to make the farmer pay all the traffic would bear in order to have financial resources with which to fight competing roads elsewhere, but in a life-or-death fight principles had to take a back seat. It was as simple as that. From the standpoint of immediate battle tactics the position may have had a practical aspect, but in terms of long-range strategy it was costly. Many years later, after World War II, when the roads were surrendering their passenger traffic to the airlines, a railroad president sadly remarked: "People think of the airplane in terms of heroes like Lindbergh. But when they think of railroads, they think of robber barons. We're cursed with that reputation." The reputation, which spread from coast to coast, was born largely in the remote and semiarid states of the high plains.

By the Nineties, battle lines were clearly drawn. Western farmers turned their attention from the Indian menace, which was no more, to a new threat—big business in general. After two and a half decades of attempted organization to combat their economic troubles by cooperation within their ranks, the farmers tried politics. Many of them had joined the Grange movement, organized soon after the Civil War, but it was more social than political in purpose. Membership in the organization offered the farmer instruction and encouragement but he was by now more interested in higher prices than in camaraderie. During the Eighties an organization known as the Farmers' Alliance, whose purposes were admittedly political, attracted the distressed Westerners. Here was an opportunity to gain political control and to combat the money of the corporate world with agricultural legislation.

Resolutely the western farmers set about the task of capturing the machinery of government. So successful were they in Kansas that the state came to be regarded as representative of the Populist movement. In 1890, Kansas farmers thoroughly frightened the established parties by electing ninety members to the lower house of their legislature while the Republicans captured only twenty-seven seats and the Democrats eight. Meanwhile, in Nebraska the defection caused the Republicans to lose the governorship and in Colorado to win only by a significantly reduced majority.

While Alliance members in the South showed a greater inclination to work within established party framework, plainsmen of the Northwest chose an independent course. In 1891, encouraged by local successes, the People's Party was organized at Cincinnati and in the summer of 1892 its first national convention met at Omaha, deep in the land of agrarian unrest. Taking a leaf from the Republican book, the Populists sought the magic of a military name by nominating General James B. Weaver of Iowa. Mary Elizabeth Lease, the Kansas crusader who once advised farmers to "raise less corn and more hell," seconded the nomination. Burning western issues such as land, transportation, and finance comprised the major planks in the party's platform. These were problems long in the forefront of the farmers' minds. When a strong free-silver plank was inserted, the plains region was politically welded together, for the mountain states—particularly Colorado—were suffering from the falling price of the white metal.

Although the election of 1892 did not bring national victory to the Populist cause, it gave the country pause. By capturing twenty-two of the available four hundred forty-four electoral votes, the young organization accomplished what no other third party had been able to do since 1860. All the votes came from western states: Colorado, Idaho, Kansas, Nevada, North Dakota, and Oregon. Since Weaver's more than a million popular votes came from states in which Republican strength was great, and because Cleveland defeated Harrison by less than four hundred thousand votes, the Populists determined the election's outcome. The canvass was significant, too, in that the Senate was almost evenly divided between Democrats and Republicans and the Populist senators held the balance of power. The fact that the free-silver issue crossed major party lines also contributed to this control.

The shock of 1892 left a deep impression upon the entire country. The *New York Tribune,* explaining the election, perhaps expressed the East's opinion of the militant Westerners when it said: "The chief cause of Republican defeat and Democratic victory is the modern tendency toward socialism." Readers might have agreed with the editorial when they heard the sentiments of the newly elected Populist governor of Colorado, Davis Waite. Speaking in behalf of the downtrodden poor, he announced: "It is infinitely better that blood should flow to our horses' bridles than our national liberties should be destroyed." The public got the impression that a general repudiation of debts, if not outright revolution, threatened Colorado. Pronouncements like those of "Bloody Bridles" Waite caused a shudder of horror among some of the more conservative elements of the country, and there was nervous speculation about the outcome of this spreading rural radicalism.

General gloom developed as the nation staggered from the effects of financial panic in 1893 and appeared to be slumping into a general depression. The mountain states were near desperation over the drastic downward plunge of silver prices. Conditions in the farm belt worsened as agricultural products went begging for buyers. A leading national magazine bitterly denounced the Populists as "fanatical in the extreme," and possessed of doctrines of advanced socialism. The principal aim of the party, it was said, was "the virtual repudiation of public and private indebtedness, the confiscation of the property of railway and other corporations, and the plunging of the country into a cheap-money debauch," while its elected representatives at Washington were "either fanatics or cranks of limited intelligence and exceedingly pernicious ideas. . . ." Even some of the Westerners were frightened by what they had done in 1892. When they went to the polls in 1894 they turned out most of the Populists up for re-election. The party took the governorship of Nebraska, but it was small consolation for the general reverse in the West.

Undaunted by their setbacks and rationalizing that defeats in the western states arose more out of local complications than a general disapproval, the Populists continued to beat the political drums in anticipation of the next general election. Despite their surrender of some of the western strongholds gained in 1892, they were powerful in other parts of the country, particularly the South, increasing their popular vote in 1894 by forty-two per cent. Aside from such statistical encouragement, the party looked with pleasure upon the silver issue that threatened to divide the major parties and at the same time to become the prime catalyst for bonding together under the Populist banner all the nation's silverites. The demonitization of silver in 1873, accomplished without much uproar, suddenly became the "Crime of '73" when the market price of silver sagged badly. The Populists, whose followers generally favored cheap money, quickly unfurled their "free and unlimited coinage of silver" banner and the crusade was on.

The election of 1896, often referred to as "the battle of the standards," saw a Westerner, William Jennings Bryan of Nebraska, pitted against William McKinley, author of the protectionist tariff. Bryan, in his mid-thirties and known as the "boy orator of the Platte," used his forensic powers to gain the Democratic presidential nomination, and the Populists—who felt that the Democrats' acceptance of their free-silver crusade would offer a better chance to win than as a third party—decided to throw in with that organization. Led by one of their own, Westerners launched themselves into the grand attack upon the "goldbugs" of the East. While Bryan took the electoral votes of every state west of the Mississippi except five, and the South remained generally true to the Democrats, the bid failed. McKinley squeaked by with a mere six hundred thousand popular vote majority, as the eastern states turned back the agrarian hordes led by that political cossack from the steppes of Nebraska. For the Populists it was all or nothing at all. They had surrendered their very existence on one throw of the dice, giving up their political organization for a chance to win with another party. And they had lost. It was the end of Populism and defeat for the farmers until the New Deal came along in the next century to give them much of what they had sought for more than half a century.

The political battle of the century marked the end of an era. While most of the participants did not recognize it, the climactic campaign was another indication that the frontier was gone. For over two hundred years the settlers had edged ever westward, taking up land, exploiting the bounty of resources laid out before them, operating all the while in an atmosphere of individual enterprise. Then the largess of nature ran out. By the Nineties the nation, already near the end of its westward population expansion, had entered a period of adjustment to more stabilized conditions. While the supply of free land was not exhausted, the best had been claimed and henceforth the pickings would be relatively slim. As this period of development came to a close, another already had begun to overlap it. Industrial America was assuming that position of dominance that soon would characterize the nation in the eyes of the world.

Even in the deepest recesses of the Populist stronghold there were Westerners whose innate conservatism made them embarrassed by the flamboyance of the agrarian radicalism. Although they were by no means disciples of the high priests of the industrial cult, they harbored a hidden desire to conform and to assume a more moderate political stand. The best known of them was a twenty-nine-year-old Emporia, Kansas, editor, William Allen White, who soared to national fame by his bitter editorial attack upon the Populists, "What's the Matter With Kansas?" In it he expressed the view that the hell-raising tendencies of the Populists had brought shame and ridicule upon his state and bitterly he twitted them for their leveling tendencies. The acerbity of the attack so appealed to the rest of the country that it was widely reprinted throughout the nation's press and circulated by the Republican campaign committee in the election of 1896. In thousands of middle-class homes the editorial was accepted as a simple explanation that the political renegades of the prairies were fanatics and demagogues.

White, and millions of his fellow Americans, missed the point of the great political crusade. What to them were the ravings of a lot of wild-eyed farmers, were actually warning flags that revealed growing inequities in our system, rumblings at the foundation of the whole economic structure that indicated the need for serious readjustment and predicted the coming of the progressives. In the new order of things, a segment of the population was getting pinched. When the western farmers endured and suffered, and then fought back at the polls—quite within the American tradition—their actions were termed a "revolt." Other third parties had been and would be established, for economic or sectional reasons or both, but no one called it political revolution.

With the passing of the nineteenth century, the appearance of a measure of agricultural prosperity and the sparkling successes of the wizards of Wall Street that made every boy want to be a captain of industry, the Populists folded their tents and silently stole away. They lost their identity through marriage to the Democrats in 1896 and within seven years there were none of them left in Congress. Some of the leaders died, others were relegated to running for unimportant local offices, and the rest went back to the protective firesides of the major parties. It had been a grand, wild, exuberant political fling, a youthful indiscretion, an emotional spree, something they would recall in later years as an exciting adventure.

But it was more. Beneath the tumult and clamor, the schoolhouse orations of bronzed and horny-handed political novices, and the broadcasting of some startling economic theories there lay a fundamental discontent. Smoldering, it burst momentarily into flame once again with the rise of the Nonpartisan League after 1915. Significantly, the new revolt appeared in one of the plains states—North Dakota—and its origins were familiar. When the legislature neglected to carry out the desires of the people expressed in two state referendums, the independent-minded League members infiltrated both parties and for a brief moment dominated Dakota politics. Their success inspired similar movements in Montana, Colorado, and Nebraska, where the results were not quite so spectacular but were nevertheless significant. The League always was a minority, just as are the plains states in the national view, but its ability to strike a balance of power made it a thing to be respected and feared by the major parties.[1]

During the 1920s the League's power faded, particularly when its members tried to act as an independent political party, and as the decade progressed plains farmers who had indulged in yet another political resurgence drifted back into old allegiances. Meanwhile, the disparity between agricultural and industrial incomes grew. In the Thirties there was hope that the gentleman farmer from Hyde Park might find an answer. He and his brain-trusters exerted great efforts, and certainly managed to answer a great many old Populist demands, but after a number of daring departures from the norm there was no evidence that Franklin Roosevelt had discovered a real solution to the problem. Nor did the Republicans find it when they took over in the 1950s. While they talked of free enterprise and patted the farmer on the back, telling him that he must regain his pride by going it alone, they continued to offer him financial support, because they had no better answers than their political opponents.

As the second half of the twentieth century got under way, the plains people watched the East boom, the West Coast flourish, the South industrialize, and then they looked at themselves. Despite the growth of some prairie and mountain cities and an increasing industrialization arising in part from national defense, thanks to the region's very remoteness there was much still to be desired. Agriculture continued to dominate economy; this was undoubtedly the last part of the nation about which this can be said. Somehow, in a nation

[1] Samuel P. Huntington, "The Election Tactics of the Nonpartisan League," *Mississippi Valley Historical Review*, XXXVI, No. 4 (March 1950), 613–632.

known the world over as an industrial leader, there were agricultural surpluses and a tendency toward depressed prices. Problems that plagued the Populists confronted their grandsons, and the resulting frustrations were familiar. Twentieth-century plainsmen gathered together from time to time, snarling their defiance at the "humid-area" folk, and tried to find means of gaining a position of economic equality with the rest of the land. Their talk of aridity, soil blowing, and perverse climatic characteristics would have been quite familiar to Zebulon Pike, Stephen Long, and John Wesley Powell.

It is ironic that, a century and a half after Pike, there were serious proposals that the government buy back part of the desert and then plant it again in grass. To some, the notion meant that the circle had been completed.

Chapter 10

THE
WHITE
MAN'S
CULTURE

The environmental impact of the great plains upon the American frontiersman was probably greater, from a cultural standpoint, than that of any preceding frontier experience. For decades the people of the westward-moving edge of the nation's civilization lived in a humid, tree-covered land of rivers or lakes under rather constant climatic and geographic conditions. The pioneering way of life, once its pattern was established, was carried forward, generation after generation, in much the same manner. The log cabin, the pole-lined well, the split-rail fences, the ever-present task of tree-girdling and land-clearing were characteristics that changed little with the passage of time. Then the frontiersman broke out of the tree belt, into scattered groves that surrounded meadows, and finally approached the prairies that bordered the high plains. Here he held up, aware of transportation difficulties in the land ahead but equally apprehensive about the dramatic changes his way of life would have to undergo if he moved forward.

The hesitation was only momentary. By the middle of the nineteenth century the profession of the frontiersman was well over two hundred years old; the momentum that had gathered during all those years was too great to stop. Pulled forward by the magnetism of precious metals, valuable furs, and free grazing, the vanguard moved out into the hostile land. The farmer, who watched his more adventurous brethren prosper, was meanwhile shoved from behind by a swelling population of settlers who flooded the Mississippi Valley with newcomers. Then the Army and the railroads cleared the way and beckoned him on while the federal government dangled free land before his eyes. When he faltered, wondering what to do without the tree he had so long known and cursed, the industrial East supplied the answers. Barbed wire would supplant the pole fence; sod houses would do until lumber firms could send forward milled timber; new factories promised metal windmills with which to pump subsurface water; Grand Rapids offered furniture; machinery companies displayed their new, sharp sodcutting plows. Confronted by such a convincing prospectus, the farmer's hesitancy was first replaced by cautious optimism and then abandoned entirely in the wild, bold rush into the desert. With these new material armaments he felt that he could make the necessary cultural adaptations.

The transition was not easy. Even though the settlers were furnished with all the implements that were developed in that inventive period, nature's generosity in unrolling endless miles of prairie banked by skyscraper mountains to the west posed conditions that were not quickly surmounted even by the mind of man. Distances themselves called for new concepts that were frequently hard to comprehend before sweat-stained days of experience brought them into their proper focus. Coloradans of the period laughed at the story of the young Englishman who, visiting Denver, announced his intention of strolling over and having a look at Long's Peak. A few delighted natives decided to go along and watch the fun. All morning long the party toiled northward. On into the afternoon they trudged, the elusive peak apparently retreating from them. Then they came to a small stream that could be crossed in an easy leap. Here the Englishman sat down and began to take off his clothes. Asked what he was up to, he said: "I'm going to swim that damned river!"

The exaggerations of nature developed a broad type of humor that came to characterize the Westerner. Violent climatic changes brought forth a whole set of stories about life on the plains. Kansans, obliged to endure unbelievably hot summers, solemnly swore that when their sinners passed away they were buried in overcoats to keep them warm when they reached the cooler region of Hell. Or the story of the mule who stood sweltering in a popcorn field until the corn popped and, thinking the white stuff piled up around him was snow, froze to death. The persistence of wind brought on more legends. A plains visitor, leaning into a near-gale, shouted at one of the old-timers, "Does it always blow like this around here?" and was answered, "No. It'll be like this for days at a time and then it will turn around and blow like hell for a while."

Jokes about the climate did not always originate out of bitterness. People who lived along the mountain front were extremely proud of the high, dry atmosphere and swore that out in those parts so healthy was the climate that it took five minutes longer for a criminal to hang. In one of the towns it was alleged that in order to have a cemetery, like other places, one of the residents had to be shot. In fact, said Coloradans, the air was so pure in their country that one could not get sick if he wanted to. As one of the natives solemnly related to a British visitor: "I once knew a man who tried to make himself ill in order to get off serving on a jury. He ate nothing but fat pork and drank nothing but lemonade for a week, but he couldn't do it, sir. The air that you breathe in Colorado enables you to avoid anything."

Whether the Westerner was in a bitter mood about his conditions or ready to boast about them, he employed his sense of humor to express himself. In a new land, where his life or his fortune could take a new turn in the flick of an eyelash, he had to adjust to the likelihood of sudden change. The ability to accept adversity, and even tragedy, with a smile was much admired. The story is told of two hopeful cattlemen who endured reverses year after year, first from drought followed by flood, then disease among the livestock. At last their luck turned and, as a prosperous season neared its close, one of the partners went into town for supplies. Upon returning to the ranch he found the buildings in flames, the cattle run off, and his partner severely wounded from an Indian attack. Gently he lifted the wounded man in his arms and studying an arrow lodged in the other's back, inquired sympathetically: "Does it hurt much, Podner?" Soberly the victim looked into his friend's eyes and sighed: "Nope. Only when I laugh."

Story after story like this one made the rounds of the West. The yarns were a candid admission of the difficulties to be faced, yet in their exaggeration they served to bolster the morale of those who endured times of tribulation. One observer of this spirit of exaggeration wrote: "In the West it is all-pervading; from cradle to deathbed, through sickness and adversity, it cheers the Western man." And there was need of cheering. Thrust into a situation that was new, faced by forces that were larger than he had ever known before, the Westerner was scared. To laugh at the seriousness of the situation was his best answer to the problem. It was all he could do unless he wanted to quit.

The West was a land of exaggeration not only in its geography and climate, its humor and folklore, but also in its history. Writers of both fiction and nonfiction, yesterday and today, have seized upon the more dramatic events as their subjects, leaving readers no choice but to believe the wild and the woolly. A reputation for disorder, violence, immorality, and general lawlessness is firmly fixed upon the formative years of America's last West. The picture has been warped and twisted. Apparently it will remain so.

The result of such thinking is the belief that the West was naturally irreligious. In the very first days of development, during the concerted rush to the mines, the establishment of infant towns, the beginning of railroads and the initial cattle drives, men of the cloth found the going pretty hard. Itinerants like the buffalo hunters, miners, muleskinners, or cowboys moved about so much and so rapidly that they seldom came into contact with organized religion. The situation gave rise to a saying that there was "no Sunday west of Junction City and no God west of Salina." The phrase, used at the time to indicate the tough character of a new country, is still quoted frequently in modern studies as proof of this condition. A well-known historian of the frontier recently used it to substantiate his flat statement "The West was godless."

One must ask at once, *what* West, and *when?* Hard on the heels of civilization's outriders came the main army—the settlers. Very quickly, in point of time, they unpacked their cultural baggage and set up housekeeping. Among the many treasures of the heritage they brought along was a desire for religious guidance and counsel. Alongside the first newspaper, post office, and school appeared a place of worship. It was as necessary to the settler as any of the others, and he mentioned the fact frequently in his writings.

Even during the very earliest years of the agricultural frontier beyond the Missouri, with a population that was thin and widely scattered, there were opportunities for some kind of worship. Thomas C. Wells, who settled in central Kansas in 1855, wrote to his father that there was preaching each Sunday somewhere within a dozen miles of his isolated farm. He wanted more. "We have no prayer meetings here," he lamented, "and I miss them very much more than almost anything else." A year later, writing from Manhattan, Kansas, he reported that the religious prospects were encouraging. He now had a choice of three churches: Methodist, Congregational, or Baptist. Better still, the Methodists were planning to build a college in Kansas and it was rumored that Manhattan would be its site.

During these years Lewis Bodwell, a preacher at Topeka, recorded: "The interest in religious things increases." He was meeting with his flock from two to four times weekly. In less settled areas the fervor was just as strong. To the north, in Nebraska, newcomers considered the adequacy of religious facilities along with other important considerations. One of them approached a Baptist minister, saying he planned to take up a claim in a particular neighborhood but would not do it until he first determined that a place of worship would be available. George W. Barnes, the preacher, answered the inquiry by organizing a church in the man's neighborhood. He gathered a small congregation of fourteen people around him, and began services in a little log schoolhouse. A Dakota missionary sensed the same impulses when he said that there appeared to be "some seeking after salvation among the people." When no minister was available, church members preached to one another.

Howard Ruede, a young Pennsylvania printer who homesteaded in western Kansas during the late Seventies, made a number of references to desires for religious instruction in his diary. Not long after his arrival he told of attending a meeting at a nearby schoolhouse. The preacher's "true German opera sing-song" manner bothered him, but since it was the first service he had attended since leaving home, he was grateful for the opportunity. His hunger to hear again what he regarded as a really good sermon was soon satisfied by the arrival of an evangelical preacher who, after murdering the English language for a while, "spit out Dutch as fast as he could work his tongue." "He was a preacher!" wrote the young man in admiration.

Later, Ruede told of having heard a Dunkard preacher, who used the "same language in preaching as he does in conversation," which, he allowed, was pretty bad, but it "took" with the people and drew a full house. Before long a local Moravian church was organized, its eleven members holding meetings at one of the settler's homes.

In another reference, Ruede wrote of attending a church meeting held in another schoolhouse. But the preacher's text was "too much for him. He could not expound it, and so he ran off and preached about baptism." When the homesteader went to a Lutheran service he was impressed by the fact that the minister wore a black surplice and white tie, "which are not often seen in this part of the world, and attract notice on that account." The sermon was long, and in German, but it "did not tire us, for we were used to rather long sermons."

When men and women displayed the desire for worship, as they almost always did, the facilities for it somehow made their appearance. The Reverend C. H. Frady, who preached the gospel on the frontier for a half a century, recalled that the Sunday school at Long Pine, Nebraska, was organized in a railroad boxcar. Sometimes even this rude abode was not available and the services were conducted in the shade of some large tree with the congregation sitting on logs. On one occasion the minister helped to build a sod schoolhouse on a Saturday, organized a Sunday school the next day, and on Monday school classes were begun in the new building. In frontier style things happened almost simultaneously, whether dispensing justice, starting a town, or building a place of worship.

There were some settlers who took their religious training almost too seriously. Horace Greeley, the irascible New York editor, approved of the early appearance of places of public worship "and other civilizing influences" he saw out west in 1859, but he criticized Kansas settlers who did not work on the Sabbath. He was angry at one, in particular, who explained that he had no time to build a shelter for his stock, yet admitted that on the day reserved for the Lord he set aside his tools in favor of contemplation. Horace thought it would have been a far greater act of Christianity to have provided for the animals instead.

There were those, of course, who took religious guidance very lightly and helped perpetuate the legend of God's absence west of Salina. Reverend Frady ran into that situation at Chadron, South Dakota, in the early Eighties. A few days after the coming of the railroad to that western city, some cowboys recognized one of the arriving passengers as a minister. They quickly surrounded him, firing their six-guns, generally amusing the residents. When one shot sent the cleric's high silk hat flying, the show was over. He clambered back on the car and headed for civilization. Before the train moved along the boys took up a collection to replace the top piece and advised him that when he next came west he ought to look a little more wild and woolly.

Frady happened to arrive in town the next day and the cowhands, who considered the earlier performance for his predecessor a huge success, staged one in his behalf. "I cheered them on," he wrote. When the boys had had their fill of it, the missionary told them he planned to offer a service and that they were all invited. They answered by riding off without a word. When the appointed time came most of the community gathered to hear the new preacher and in the congregation were the gun-slinging cowboys.

"This morning you had your fun, then you passed the 'buck' to me," Frady told the boisterous members. "The game is still on, it is a dollar ante, and every mother's son of you is expected to chip in." They did. When the money on the table was counted it totaled more than fifty dollars. For the Godless West, the chaplain thought this was a pretty good showing.

There are a number of similar stories about early religious efforts in the mining camps. When the Reverend George G. Smith, a Presbyterian, gave his first sermon in Virginia City, Montana, the affair was characterized by turbulence. Like the Kansas farmers, the miners dropped their shovels on the Sabbath, but there the resemblance ended. For them it was a day of relaxation to their own liking, one of fraternization, drinking, gambling, and entertainment. As the reverend put it: "Business and sin were at their very worst." Next door to the place he performed his service was a gambling hall whose inhabitants were entertained by a brass band. "In the midst of my sermon the band struck up a lively dance tune and the hob-nailed miners began to beat time with their feet upon the bare floor," he later recalled. At a loss to know how to proceed the minister folded his arms and waited. "Just then, the ringleader, a long, lank, lean fellow in buckskin, called out, 'Boys, never mind the music. The elder has the floor. You listen to him. Elder, go on. You shall not be disturbed again.' And I was not. I was patiently listened to until I said Amen."

When Smith returned to the East he recommended that the Mission Board should not expand its work in the West. This was not at all because he was disappointed by his reception in Montana. On the contrary, he was quite pleased by it, but the cost of living was so high that he failed to see how anyone could live there on less than five thousand dollars a year. It was for financial, not religious, reasons that he urged his people to defer their missionary efforts in the region.

In spite of the apparently hostile attitude of men like the cowboys at Chadron, who tried to frighten off circuit-riding clerics, there was a general acceptance of religious representatives in the West. For years the Catholic fathers ranged the land when it was in its most primitive condition and lived out their lives unharmed. The names of Father DeSmet and Father Ravalli, along with dozens of others, were honored by both white and Indian people. Father Dyer, the Protestant "snowshoe itinerant" of Colorado, was widely respected in the mining camps. W. W. Van Orsdel, "Brother Van," who conducted what is thought to be the first Protestant service in northern Montana, was accepted wherever he chose to go in the new, raw country.

It would seem to be a fair generalization to say that where the population was essentially male, and rather closely congregated, the early ministers were accepted rather than sought out. In the farming communities, characterized by a more thinly spread population and a family-type economy, the need for religious organization was greater. Among the miners there was camaraderie, *esprit de corps,* good fellowship, and constant association. It was this craving to belong that, in part, generated a desire among farmers for a local church. Here they met their neighbors, sang together, prayed together, experienced emotional release, and found spiritual satisfaction. It was also a social experience that alleviated the drabness of long, back-breaking, lonely days in a timeless land of distance and monotony. The prairie church was the heart and center of the community, a place to gather and to gain reassurance among one's friends that man did not stand alone against the forces of nature. In it they saw an evidence of civilization and a promise that their chosen part of the country would one day take its place with the rest of the nation.

In new western communities the desire for educational facilities was quite as strong as the desire for religion. Along with the church, the schoolhouse was one of the first needs considered by the community. In one frontier Nebraska county, the settlers voted a tax to build a school before any of them commenced their own homes and at a time when only four claims were filed in the local land office. Their action took place almost upon arrival, while they were still living in railroad boxcars. Within three months the school opened its doors to young scholars.

This was not unique. In dozens of other microscopic settlements, men and women willingly made the necessary sacrifice of time and effort to provide for their children. They regarded it a fundamental part of building a new country and, despite the emphasis on material things in the promised land, they wanted assurance of cultural facilities similar to those farther east. For generations frontiersmen had shown a great interest in education and the schoolhouse was one of their symbols of equal opportunity for all.

Even more than the church, the school's origins were spontaneous. Without waiting for formal governmental organization, early residents made their own provisions for education. While the Fifty-Niners poured through Denver, bound for the placer mines, and that hopeful Queen City was still a disorderly supply base, "Professor" O. J.

Goldrick opened Colorado's first school. Thirteen pupils turned up for instruction one October day in 1859, and for three dollars per head the professor agreed to guide their intellectual growth. For him it came close to being a labor of love. He freely admitted that without an additional twenty dollars per month he earned writing for eastern newspapers he could not have lived. But in a profession so highly revered by Americans and so poorly compensated, such small rewards were not unusual. Five years later the first schoolteacher in Colorado's Larimer County, a housewife, received ten dollars a month for her efforts.

Meanwhile, the progress of education in the new territory was rapid. By 1860, Denver's population had so swelled that three schools were in operation. A few miles away, at Boulder, townsmen raised twelve hundred dollars by popular subscription that year to erect the first building constructed for educational purposes in Colorado. During the next summer, under a clause in the territorial organic act reserving sections sixteen and thirty-six in each township for school purposes, the legislature provided for free public schools. Provision was made for a territorial school superintendent whose annual salary was five hundred dollars. Only two years had elapsed since Goldrick's small flock assembled for its first class.

A frontier public-school system was more difficult to achieve than surface appearances would indicate. School bonds were extremely hard to sell, for until final proof was made and a patent issued on a homestead, it could not be taxed. While many a farmer bought his land from private sources such as land companies or railroads, a great many more of them homesteaded, and in most cases five years elapsed before title was gained. In communities where a high percentage of farms fell into this category, the tax source was exceedingly slight. For example, in 1878 Howard Ruede reported that in his Kansas school district there were only two hundred and forty taxable acres.

In such places the need for schools was answered by popular subscription; they were built by donated labor. Ruede wrote that at a gathering in his community "Everybody promised to work; nearly everybody signed for 6 days—some included their teams." A total of eighty-one days of work was pledged, but when cash subscriptions were solicited only eighteen dollars could be raised. While the average resident was willing to help build the schoolhouse and to pay a dollar a month for each child, in support of the schoolmaster, there was a general desire for free public schools.

In the face of such financial difficulties and the widely scattered population, educational facilities on the plains and in the mountains showed a surprising development. In 1870, a Leavenworth resident boasted that Kansas had "the credit of making the most liberal provisions of any state in the Union for the education of its youth. . . ." This was true, he explained, because the newcomers from the East brought with them "a lively interest in the cause of education." There was want of such facilities, said John Ferguson, an Irish settler who proved it by his own letters. "I sea a nead of it out here," he wrote. "The one fifth of the men out here cant right or cipher."

Lack of education among the newcomers was frequently a barrier, rather than an incentive, to the quest for learning. Untutored newcomers often felt a sense of inferiority and, instead of seeking intellectual elevation, scoffed at their more literate brethren who were "puttin' on airs." In a region where material wealth was a leading measure of success, education and the other arts were likely to find it hard going in some communities. In agricultural areas labor was in great demand, and the larger boys readily used the pretext of being needed at home as an excuse to withdraw from school. Since their ascent up the ladder of learning often was painfully slow, and because the physical maturity of the boys caused problems, the schoolmaster usually gave his consent without hesitation. There are endless stories about the country schoolteacher's first encounter with a crowd of oversized louts, every one of whom was ready to challenge his authority. If the "professor" wasn't as rugged as his pupils, the results were apt to be disastrous.

Like the earliest preachers and newspapermen, the educators normally were obliged to take their places in rough-hewn neighborhoods as best they could. If their methods were direct and emphasized the physical, it was out of necessity. Like the clerics, they worked in rude surroundings and were paid very little, but through the necessity of "boarding around" in order to live they were a good deal closer to the families than is possible today. No P.-T.A. meetings were necessary as devices whereby parents joined with the teacher in joint puzzlement over the mental inertia of the young. Both parties understood the problem and subscribed to the theory of direct action for its cure.

New western states and territories appeared to take more pride in institutions of higher learning than in the common schools. This was due, in part, to necessity. As early as 1870, one Kansan explained that since few eastern teachers wanted to make permanent homes in the unsettled West, it was necessary to provide for a normal school at Emporia to produce their own teachers. Part of the reason was that of pride. Westerners were anxious to show the rest of the country that they, too, had seats of culture. Campuses and buildings were regarded as tangible proof of its presence.

The churches were active in establishing private colleges throughout the plains and mountain regions. Before 1860 the Methodists had commenced two, the Presbyterians one, and the Catholics one, in Kansas. During the next three decades a number of Protestant and Catholic colleges appeared in the plains states, with Kansas having the most. The Methodists, Baptists, Presbyterians, Congregationalists, and Lutherans were particularly active.

Along with them came the universities, colleges of education, land-grant agricultural and mechanical colleges, and normal schools, founded by the states. While these institutions have not been in existence long enough to become as encrusted with ivy-covered traditions as some of their sister schools farther east, western people proudly point to their early origins in a raw and undeveloped part of the country. The establishment date of a number of the church colleges precedes the period of statehood, while state-supported schools frequently appeared almost as soon as that status was achieved.

The type and quality of entertainment demanded by people of a new community furnished another means of measuring its degree of cultural advance. In the mining camps of the Rockies, social life got off to a fast start. Hundreds of men, milling around in a small area in search of wealth, found relaxation in some rather basic forms of entertainment: drinking, gambling, fighting, and frolicking in the brothels. While these time-honored ·forms of male recreation by no means disappeared when the camps settled down, they became less prominent as other types of amusement appeared. The same lure of money that attracted the earliest camp-followers soon brought forth traveling troupes of artists whose repertories usually featured more variety than talent. But the patronage given them indicated that there was a real demand for their offerings.

In the fall of 1859, Colonel Charles R. Thorne, recently retired as manager of Chicago's Metropolitan Hall Theater, brought a small wagon train of props and players into rough-and-ready Denver. He arranged for the use of Apollo Hall, a large second-story room in one of the hotels. The opening night was a huge success. Although there were but three hundred fifty seats, around four hundred tickets were sold, at a dollar each—which, said an observer, "tells well for the patronage, if not for the appreciation, of art in this semi-barbarous region." Typical of frontier programs, Colonel Thorne's company offered *Cross of Gold,* a tragic drama, followed by an afterpiece that included a song, a dance, and a short farce.

Particularly popular with the miners was one of the Colonel's players who was billed as Mlle. Haidie, sometimes spelled Haydee. As a danseuse, claimed a Denver paper, she had no superior. One of Colorado's pioneers in later years recalled that the miners had some difficulty with her French title. They mistook it for her first name and called her Miss Millie. When Thorne returned to the East she took charge of the company and gave performances throughout the Pike's Peak region. In the fall of 1860 it was rumored that she had been kidnapped by a notorious gambler. The aroused miners at once turned out to hunt down the criminal and ominously they made arrangements to hold trial under a tree in Denver. To their great disappointment they discovered that Millie had married her supposed abductor. Broken-hearted, they returned to the diggings to contemplate the perfidy of women.

Mining communities from Colorado to Montana were able to attract such talent at a very early date because of their concentrated population and supply of ready money. Players were willing to make the long trip up the Missouri, or across the plains, for the promise of large audiences. But in the little cities that dotted the farming country, it was a different matter. The desert was to wait for such cultural attractions until the coming of the railroad. Like so many other types of enterprise, stock companies awaited a better means of transportation in the West before venturing forth.

Even river towns, like Omaha, were slow in attracting theatrical people. While occasional performances were offered in that city, beginning in the late Fifties, it did not have a permanent theater until 1867. By that date Denver had long since had its own stock company. During the winter of 1857–1858, Omaha's newly formed Library Association offered some prominent lecturers, among them Mrs. Amelia Bloomer, but the newspapers had to admit that the men were more interested in what it called the "leg-atto movement" of lady performers.

During the Seventies, as the railroad moved across the northern plains, entertainers appeared in Dakota. The offerings ranged from bell-ringers, feats of legerdemain, and musical selections to attempts at drama. While the pioneer residents were grateful for such cultural opportunities, they were selective. When an itinerant troupe offered the people of Grand Forks *Only a Farmer's Daughter,* which poked fun at a rural community, there was sharp resentment, and the local editor predicted that it would be a long time before a similar performance would be allowed in the city. Nor were suggestiveness or crudity welcomed. One western newspaperman criticized a play entitled *Baby,* charging that it was disgusting and made up of dialogue no cultured father would allow his daughter to read. Reception in a farming community was quite different from that in a mining camp, where the audience was likely to be principally male.

On the outer edge of civilization—in end-o'-track construction towns, cowboy capitals, or mining camps—theatrical performances were most likely to be given in concert saloons. These places were combination dance halls and bars, with a stage set up at one end of the room from which a variety of acts were offered. In addition to the usual acts presented, male patrons of the concert saloons particularly appreciated the can-can dancers, whose suggestive and often semi-nude undulations forecast the development of the modern strip-tease. While performances in some of the newer and rowdier towns were gauged for the male tastes, lady spectators were by no means forgotten. The Theater Comique of Cheyenne advertised, as early as 1869, that two evenings a week would be especially designed for the ladies and there would be no smoking. On other nights, the usual beer and cigars would be available during the show.

While a number of well-known troupes played the western circuits, the name of John Langrishe stands out. One authority on the frontier stage has called him the Father of the Colorado Theater. The reception was enthusiastic wherever he took his players in the mining camps. The actors had accustomed themselves to the helpful comments made by members of the audience or by resident stagehands who were sometimes so excited during the production that they forgot themselves. In the middle of a Langrishe performance of *Alice,* given at Central City, the leading man threw himself into the part with all the ability at his command, and turning his wet eyes heavenward begged in agonized tones: "Alice, why don't you speak to me?" Overcome by the plea, a local stagehand who was at work on the beam overhead, answered in loud tones: "Damn it, Alice ain't up here!" The audience was delighted and the management not at all offended.

Some of the entertainers found their audiences a little more demanding. In the spring of 1885, while making a tour of the West, members of the Theodore Thomas Concert Troupe were surprised to have their private car invaded by a bunch of cowboys who, with drawn pistols, ordered the musicians to perform. In tremulous tones they offered "Home Sweet Home," but this was not to the liking of the audience. By request the musicians quickly substituted the "Arkansas Traveler" and their listeners approved.

During the early Eighties, Dodge City, Kansas, produced a brass band presumably composed of music-loving cowboys. The organization made national news when it appeared at the Stockmen's Convention at St. Louis in 1884. After watching the leader beat time with a pistol, a fascinated reporter from the *Globe-Democrat* asked:

"What do you swing that gun for?"

"That's my baton," was the laconic answer.

"Is it loaded?"

"Yes."

"What for?"

"To kill the first man who strikes a false note," the leader solemnly assured the newspaperman.

Eastern readers were fascinated. They were sure that all they had heard about the Wild West was the gospel truth. Westerners, who were proud of any cultural attainment and who welcomed such interest in their band, were disturbed at leaving such an impression. But they knew it was useless to try to correct so firmly embedded a belief, and they tried not to let the notion detract from their enjoyment of the organization's many western concerts.

The early appearance of opera houses, theater buildings, and concert halls in the mining camps and prairie towns indicated a real desire for entertainment comparable to that offered farther east. Far removed from their original homes and lacking in a good many of the cultural advantages of more heavily settled parts of the country, residents of the new region became willing and enthusiastic patrons of the arts. And the performances they attended furnished a much-desired release from long and arduous days of toil in their task of building new communities in a remote part of America.

The coming of civilization to the high plains frontier was frequently a sudden affair. Settlements appeared from nowhere and overnight made great civic claims as "cities." Like newborn babes, they came into the world with lusty vocal chords. The voice of the community was its newspaper, through whose columns the world soon learned of America's newest, boomingest, healthiest, most prosperous, and most promising town.

Occasionally the press preceded the town itself. Such was the case of Leavenworth, Kansas, where in September 1854 a press was set up beneath an elm tree and put into operation before there was a house or any sign of civilization in the town. The scene was described as "four tents, all on one street, a barrel of water or whiskey under a tree, and a pot, on a pole, over a fire. Under a tree a type-sticker had his case before him and was at work on the first number of a new paper, and within a frame, without a board on side or roof, was the editor's desk and sanctum."

In a land of surprising developments this was not regarded as anything startling. In a number of instances the press preceded many of the more ordinary agencies of society. Less than a decade after the event at Leavenworth there appeared a newspaper hundreds of miles westward, out on the lonely stretches of present-day Wyoming. In 1863, Hiram Brundage, the telegraph operator at Fort Bridger, produced the first issue of his *Daily Telegraph,* satisfying the desire for current reading matter in an area far in advance of settlement.

How much the early settlers anticipated the coming of a newspaper in their community is frequently revealed in their letters and diaries. Thomas C. Wells wrote from central Kansas in 1859: "Our Manhattan paper does not get printed yet. I have got most tired of waiting for it. The man they expected to conduct it failed to come. . . ." Three months later his wife wrote that they were still waiting. The next few years brought a rush of settlement into Kansas and with it a great number of papers. By 1870, a Pennsylvanian told the folks at home: "The multiplication of newspapers in Kansas is among the marvels of the age." He explained that whenever twenty or thirty families got together to form a town, one of the first orders of business was to start a newspaper, without which the prospective metropolis would not receive the necessary advertising to attract settlers. Members of the new community, agreeing to this necessity, then sought out a journeyman and subscribed two or three hundred dollars to supply him with a secondhand outfit and a small office. The resultant growth of journals was so rapid that established newspapers gave up trying to keep track of the new arrivals.

Small settlements all over the West told the world of their existence through their newspapers. In the face of statistics that revealed a high mortality among such ventures, newspaper owners were calmly confident of their survival in a growing, booming young town. In one tiny community a stranger once inquired how so small a place could support four newspapers. He was answered promptly that "it took four newspapers to keep up such a city." And therein lay the fact of the matter.

Believing completely in the future of their new communities, newspaper editors vied with competitors in preaching the doctrine of "boost." A Nebraska pioneer woman later recalled the early days of the *Omaha Arrow* and how the editor "wrote many fanciful sketches in his little paper, containing great predictions for Omaha's future." When he forecast the completion of the Union Pacific Railroad by 1870, a great many of his readers laughed at such optimism. To their great surprise, and perhaps to his, the road was finished a year earlier. The accomplishment no doubt sobered some of the jokesters to the realization that in the West there were possibilities unlimited.

Plainsmen needed all the courage that their newspapers could give them. In the days of drought, they grasped at predictions that good times would come again and took solace from even the most visionary of projections. Henry King, editor of the *St. Louis Globe Democrat,* later told a college graduating class in Kansas that but for the newspapers the state might have been depopulated during those trouble-packed years. He confessed that in their search for facts to bolster the declining morale of the people, the editors frequently came close to bearing false witness, but he justified it as a necessity.

Plains editors were extremely outspoken and direct. There were few subtleties in their writings. Westerners were accustomed to speaking simply, sometimes bluntly, and they appreciated this quality in their reading. The local paper told the nation how its subscribers felt about matters and when the editor rushed into battle, presumably in defense of his community, they approved. His ability to launch literary roundhouse punches brought applause, and if he descended to kicking and gouging it was quite within the frontier tradition. In an era of personal journalism, western editors took full advantage of their opportunities.

Wars between editors in rival towns delighted patrons on both sides and the contestants, cheered on, entered the fray in earnest. Sometimes the free-for-all turned into a Donnybrook, and resulted in fist fights, "cowhidings," and offers to duel. Usually, the battle was confined to exaggerated name-calling, emphasizing the use of the hyphen. Take, for example, the blast sent forth by the editor of the *Jacksonian,* at Cimarron, Kansas. "We are 'onto' the lop-eared, lantern-jawed, half-bred and half-born whiskey-soaked, pox-eaten pup who pretends to edit that worthless wad of subdued out-house bung-fodder, known as the Ingalls *Messenger*. He is just starting out to climb the journalistic bannister and wants us to knock the hay-seed out of his hair, pull the splinters out of his stern and push him on and up. We'll fool him. No free advertising from us."

The violence with which the editors attacked one another was matched by the editorial heat generated in preaching local causes that were popular. From the onset, western papers displayed an impatience with the federal government, the political parent of the territories, who, it was made to appear, was neglecting its younger children. Governmental representatives, civil and military, were roundly cursed when the policies they carried out did not please local folk. Newspapers which did not have the patronage plum of public printing were particularly fearless in the attack. The papers' cries of righteous indignation were a useful avenue to a larger circulation.

In their quest for popularity and increased sales, the papers frequently were guilty—as editor Henry King openly admitted—of dallying with the truth. Those that did not purposely slant their news were often careless about checking stories they printed. The result was the propagation of rumor and consequent difficulties for those about whom it was written. Rather than admit their mistakes the editors were given to blaming "the lying telegraph" from which they received their reports.

As a rule, the newspapers were guilty of no more than intense local or regional patriotism and their transgressions are perhaps best explained as arising from this source. Most of them were motivated by the best of intentions and their long-run contribution to the community cannot be denied. A good example is the *Rocky Mountain News* of Denver. It was Colorado's first newspaper, having beaten out the only other claimant to that distinction by twenty minutes. From his office in the leaky attic of Uncle Dick Wootton's cabin, William Byers launched a journalistic venture in April 1859 that has been continuous to date. Through the ceaseless efforts of Byers to be accurate and truthful the paper became an important influence in the life of the young mining community.

Byers' attributes were never fully appreciated. Not only was he challenged to duels, and once abducted and threatened with death, but his journalistic brethren in other parts of the nation were not inclined to believe his stories. As Douglas McMurtrie has put it, he was regarded by his eastern editors "as one of the most capable and dangerous liars in the country." Despite these handicaps the editor went ahead with his work, faced by a shortage of paper, a lack of communication with news sources, financial difficulties, and all the limitations of a new, undeveloped community. For fifteen years he boosted local railroads, carried on a successful crusade for Colorado's statehood, fought for and got a post office in Denver, and personally toured the nearby mining country to gain useful information about conditions, the better to advise hopeful prospectors in their quest. In 1878, two years after the Centennial State was admitted, Byers retired from publishing but not from a continuing active participation in Denver's civic affairs. In retrospect, he stands out as one of Colorado's most respected pioneers.

The establishment of the *Rocky Mountain News* was an unusually successful venture. A large majority of the mining-camp newspapers lived short lives for, as in the case of the miners, the "diggin's" petered out on them. Many an editor rushed westward with the prospectors, hoping to get in on the bonanza and to make his stake from the news-hungry miners. This was true from the Montana camps all the way down the Rocky Mountain front. The *News* was fortunate to have a founder who picked a place that did not fade away into a ghost town.

One of the most interesting western newspapers of the post–Civil War era was the *Frontier-Index,* owned and operated by itinerant newsman Leigh R. Freeman. Like others who sought to take advantage of the boom days, Freeman started his paper at Julesburg, Colorado, in 1867, but to avoid the fate of the ghost-town journals he moved westward with the advance of settlement. He was a kind of journalistic camp-follower who sold his literary wares to the builders of the Union Pacific Railroad. When the end-o'-track camps moved, he picked up his outfit and went along. In July 1867 he was at Julesburg, in October at Cheyenne, and before the year was out he was operating at Fort Sanders (near present Laramie). The summer of 1868 found him at Green River, Wyoming, and by fall he had moved on to Bear River. Here his attempts at survival failed, for his printed invective was too strong, even for the construction crews. A mob stormed his office in November and destroyed the press.

Like so many of his frontier colleagues, Freeman was tough. In later years, he explained the affair at Bear River by saying: "Our press had always been remarkably bold and fearless in behalf of right." It was his exposure of the *Crédit Mobilier,* the financial organ of the Union Pacific Railroad, that presumably caused his downfall. According to the editor, several thousand road-graders led by thugs in the pay of the railroad staged the riot, burning his office "to a grease spot," and causing the type to run down the hillside in a molten mass. When the free-for-all was over, Freeman left the smoldering ruins of his newspaper and started anew at Ogden where he carried on a running fight with editors of other papers in the region. From there he moved on to Butte and made several successive attempts in other Montana towns. In 1882 he went to Yakima, Washington, and after several years dropped out of sight.

There were a great many Leigh Freemans in the plains and mountain country. And like other men who sought their fortune in the land of plenty, the journalists were frequently highly peripatetic individuals. Whether they moved about, or settled down at one place, they answered a need of the time and in more cases than not made a lasting contribution to the region. As a class they were courageous, hard-fighting prophets whose publications were quite in consonance with the optimism of the western people.

Each of America's successive frontiers has had a fascination for authors. From James Fenimore Cooper, Washington Irving, and Francis Parkman to Bret Harte and Mark Twain, the West—wherever it was—offered an attractive field. But the land lying between the Missouri and the Rockies came to typify *the* West in the minds of a large group of fiction and even nonfiction writers. This was the region passed over in the rush to Oregon and California. In point of time, it became the last frontier. As Americans watched it disappear, they realized that they faced a new era in national development, and like parents watching the youngest child grow up and leave home, they tried mentally to hold back time. Almost overnight they commenced to view yesterday with nostalgia and recall the glamor and the excitement that surrounded the physical growth of the nation.

It was not unnatural that their minds turned to the country of the plains and Rockies: this was not only the best-known frontier, it was one that represented a culmination of decades of frontier experience. Over this land had ranged the fur trapper, the intrepid scout, the cavalryman, the cowboy, the stagedriver with his colorful if sometimes unprintable language, the steamboat captain who was a kind of royalty in his profession, the gambler, the lady of easy morals, the railroad builder, and the dangerous plains Indian. It was the biggest, the most diverse, and the busiest of the frontiers. The magazines—from pulps to slicks—the book publishers, movie makers, and television networks have accepted it as their "West."

During the latter half of the nineteenth century, at the height of high plains country development, the dime novel became the first literary vehicle to convey eastward the story of a rampaging frontier. That type of book, widely read by troops during the Civil War, now displayed a new kind of heroics the scene of which was set somewhere "Out West." Ned Buntline (Edward Zane Carrol Judson) used his vivid imagination to fix a pattern for the kind of material widely published by Erastus Beadle. Beadle's Dime Library, written by both men and women, included such titles as *The King of the Lariat, Deadly Eye and the Prairie Rover,* and *Bigfoot Wallace.* In the Half-Dime Library, readers found never-ending adventure in E. L. Wheeler's Deadwood Dick stories.

In these cheaply printed, lurid works the heroines were always breathtakingly beautiful, all heroes were possessed of a startling virility, and each villain was the most black-hearted cuss who ever dry-gulched an honest settler or wrested the virtue from a wide-eyed, innocent (and no doubt surprised) maiden. One gained the impression from this literature that western women were rare articles indeed, and those who resided there were unfailingly beautiful, highly cultured, invariably unmarried, and always of spotless reputation. "Fair Edith" of *Mustang Sam,* was "slender and lithe, with a peculiar willowy grace in her every movement, the perfection of delicate symmetry. Her hair, luxuriant and waving, was a rich golden brown." This by no means completed the inventory. Her complexion was of dazzling clearness, her eyes were soft and lustrous and, best of all, she had "lips that needed no artificial coloring, ripe and moist." And Edith was not unusual. She was par for the course.

The most surprising part of the dime novel was the hero's ability to live long enough to participate in the story. It was a poor beginning if he were not left for dead in chapter one, to reappear several chapters later with the explanation that the bullet miraculously had missed a vital organ and that his wounds had been attended by an old hermit who unaccountably was a surgeon of the rarest skill. This was just the beginning. The central figure could be expected to be retrieved from the dead several times more before he put on a strong finish in a breathtaking climax. That these characters were sufficiently drawn to strain the credulity of a small child bothered no one of the Victorian era. Instead, the readers continued unperturbed at the impossible and were happy to believe the improbable.

While these literary efforts could be, and were, criticized on the ground that they were badly written and stressed a portrayal of violence, they had the virtue of high morality and the lesson of right triumphing over wrong. Obscenity never was used, sex was not even hinted at, and the highest ideals of manhood were thrust at the reader. Authors rarely made much effort to refute the charge of loose plotting and inept use of the language. More than one of them produced a dime novel a week and in such a schedule there was little time to achieve the ideal of literary art.

Of all the individuals who passed across the western scene of the last frontier, the cowboy came to have the greatest appeal to the writers of "westerns." The era had almost passed before anyone came along to tell his story and then, ironically, it was a gentle Philadelphian, come west for a vacation, who was to make the cowboy the presiding hero of the western scene. In what is often called the first "western," Owen Wister endowed the working cowhand with convincing humanness and set him off with a background of Wyoming country such as American readers had not yet seen in print. The book had a simple title, *The Virginian.*

Wister wrote a good many other pieces about the West but, as in the case of the poet Robert W. Service, fate and a tough-minded reading public determined that he should be known for but one work. The story of *The Virginian* promptly was accepted by the theater, just as another generation had insisted upon the dramatization of *Uncle Tom's Cabin*. Wister himself wrote the stage version and it became a standard piece for stock companies until as late as 1938, when Henry Fonda played the leading part in a road company. The first movie of *The Virginian* appeared in 1914, and there have been three versions since. The novel itself was translated into German, Czech, French, Spanish, and Arabic. It still sells in the United States.

While the book has its limitations in the eyes of modern critics, it bestowed upon Wister the title of "father of the westerns," just as Eugene Manlove Rhodes was the progenitor of fiction about the cowboy of the Southwest. Wister himself entertained doubts about the story and admitted in a letter to his mother: "I wish this book was 20 times better than it is. I'd already like to have it back to make certain things better. But I think it is very much of an advance on its predecessors." On this last point the American buying public agreed, and the author's fortune was made. Were the author alive today some of his misgivings about the book might be modified; a look at a good many modern attempts to portray the cowboy would reveal that nothing has been added to Wister's basic notions.

Action is still the main ingredient; without action a novel about the West would be refused the title "western." Throughout the 1920s and 1930s the formula of conflict and physical violence provided what seemed to be a never-ending component. When Walter Webb wrote his *Great Plains* in 1931, he could report that one publisher of a western pulp claimed a weekly circulation of a million and a half copies. Why this particular form of literature enjoyed a reading audience that even included ranch bunkhouses is perhaps explained by the desire of all Americans, regardless of local address, to identify themselves with a day of action, individualism, and personal valor.

During the years immediately following World War II this type of fiction continued to sell well, thanks to the device of the paperback book and the age-old desire of readers for excitement. A former general, who found himself in the Presidency of the United States, joined his fellow Americans in taking this avenue of escape. He may even have noticed that *The Virginian* was dedicated to another President, Theodore Roosevelt, who also had a great affection for that great outdoors that was the West.

One explanation of the American reading public's long-time fascination with the cattle business, as it was practiced on the high plains, is that it was unique in the frontier experience. As Walter Webb has suggested, both authors and readers for generations had known something of trail-making, hunting, or other frontier practices through reading or occasional practical experience. But not so with the cow country. Only a few classic contemporary accounts, such as Teddy Blue Abbott's *We Pointed 'Em North* and Andy Adams' *The Log of a Cowboy*, were the genuine article. Adams' work, in particular, stands today as a classic, superior to anything else written about the cow kingdom during the nineteenth century. Generally speaking, the world of the cowboy remained a mysterious, little-known phase of American development that readers seized upon as romantic. Here was a way of life to them that was fast-moving, colorful, dangerous, and supplied with all the elements of individual heroism required by those who were anxious to take momentary flight from their humdrum world. By combining the dramatics of Ned Buntline's heroes with the background of a new and interesting phase of western life, the new school of native writers was developed. Their portrayal of this broad-hatted, bechapped, and six-gun-decorated knight of the plains—real or imaginary—found instant acceptance in an America whose last real excitement was the Civil War.

Out of the Wister school came novelists like William MacLeod Raine, Luke Short (Fred Glidden), Ernest Haycox, Wayne Overholser, and Norman Fox. These men and others sought to give their stories a sense of reality. They knew the country well and were quite familiar with the type of people about whom they wrote. They understood and properly used rangeland terms. When they spoke, it was with authority. While this breed of writers is frequently criticized for an apparent inability to rise above Wister, they are not always entirely at fault. Attempts to write about the cowboy and his way of life are still hampered by the idealized version of the cattle country that came into existence in a day when the East drew its own mental picture of the West. Editors and publishers who worship before financial altars and themselves study such fiction as best-seller lists, require strict adherence to a faded daguerreotype that portrays what people long ago thought was the West.

Perhaps the Westerners have no room for complaint. The fiction-alized West not only sells well in their country, but worse, they have gone along with the myth. Unblushingly western towns that had but a slight acquaintance with the cowboy stage rodeo extravaganzas that too often feature celluloid bronc busters. They carry on with Pioneer Days parades that frequently so prostitute the genuine article as to embarrass anyone even slightly acquainted with the facts. It has made attempts of the western writer to tell the truth almost impossible. Nobody wants to hear it.

Out of the cow kingdom there also came a native poetry, usually packaged in ballad form. These folk songs of the profession were, as a rule, indigenous. The cowboy ballad arose, in large part, from the restless disposition of the herds whose need of tranquilizing was met by the tuneless doggerel of the mounted herdsman. These offerings, often hard on human nerves, apparently satisfied the restless rumi-nants and may have helped the night herdsman pass the time until dawn. Gradually the cowboy developed songs and ditties based upon themes of his everyday life and through them he told his story.

Several characteristics of western life are revealed in the range ballads. The element of exaggeration—borrowed from the long-used "tall tale"—was simply the Westerner's expression of his belief in himself. The broad humor he employed illustrated his liberal, indi-vidualistic attitudes. Some concern with the next world was shown in such songs as "The Cowboy's Lament" or "The Dying Cowboy," whose opening lines make the plaintive request "O, bury me not on the lone prairie." A happier note was struck in W. L. Chittenden's "The Cowboy's Christmas Ball." Early in the twentieth century John A. Lomax collected and published a number of cow-country folk songs. His *Cowboy Songs and Other Frontier Ballads* appeared in 1910. Later generations accepted these and more modern bits of "western music," as radio announcers classify it. In the more recent past, the popularity of "Home on the Range"—a favorite song of Franklin D. Roosevelt—was recognition of the continuing interest in western themes and gave rise to a whole new group of folk songs.

A western locale is the subject of occasional efforts on the part of those writing "intentional poetry." Vachel Lindsay's "Ghosts of the Buffaloes," "When Gassy Thompson Struck It Rich," and "What the Miner in the Desert Said," are examples of work by a man whose principal interest was in more general subjects. Stephen Vincent Benét's *Western Star* deals with the westward movement. Such Westerners as John G. Neihardt, the Nebraska poet laureate who wrote "The Song of Hugh Glass," or the Montanan Frank B. Linderman, whose "Bunch-Grass and Blue-Joint" told of pioneer days in his state, became known nationally for their efforts. Colorado's Thomas Hornsby Ferril, playwright and poet, employed gold mining and early narrow-gauge railroading as a part of his portrayal of the western experience. He is without doubt the finest exponent of western-based verse of the mid-twentieth century. To the pleasure of his friends, he is a native who stayed put, becoming an exception to the rule that successful western boys always go east.

Most of the better regional authors have shied away from the plains-cattle business. A possible explanation is that the field has been so pre-empted by the pulp writers that they are afraid of having their work, which they intend as serious, placed in the general category of a "western." Bernard DeVoto, who wrote so extensively about the region in his *Year of Decision, Across the Wide Missouri,* and *Course of Empire,* vowed that he never would write about cowboys. And he never did. The great regional novelist, A. B. Guthrie, Jr., after attracting national notice with his *Big Sky,* a story of the mountain men, and winning a Pulitzer prize with *The Way West,* which dealt with the trail to Oregon, ventured to write of the cattle frontier in *These Thousand Hills.* No one accused him of writing a "western," but the book attracted far less acclaim than his earlier efforts and seemingly demonstrated some of the hazards of trying to produce a serious work in this field. More recently Mari Sandoz, recognized as one of our finest regional writers, tackled the same subject in a volume called *The Cattlemen,* and she too dropped her over-all grade average by doing it.

There are a number of novelists who have written successfully about plains life without using cattle as the main theme. Ole Rolvaag's *Giants in the Earth* stands today as one of the great portrayals of life on the homesteader's frontier. When the Norwegian–American author described the bitter loneliness, the struggle for existence in a cold and forbidding land, and endless personal privations, it was not as a casual observer. He had experienced those things of which he wrote. Hamlin Garland's realistic description of agrarian communities a little to the east of Rolvaag's country told similar grim truths of nature's eroding effects upon man. In *Main-Travelled Roads, Prairie Folk,* and his "middle border" stories eastern readers learned about a West that departed sharply from established myth. Willa Cather established herself with portrayals of the same theme—hard, dreary prairie life capped by ultimate success for the individual who stuck it out. *O Pioneers, My Antonia,* and *The Song of the Lark* are examples of the vehicles she used to tell her story. In this general category *The Rim of the Prairie,* by Bess Streeter Aldrich, might be added even though it fell short of the others in depth of perception.

No appraisal of the plains country by a local author was more penetrating or bitter than that of E. W. Howe. The Kansas newspaperman's *Story of a Country Town* drew laudatory comments from such well-known writers as William Dean Howells and Mark Twain. Twain, who could appreciate a caustic pen, said: "His picture of the arid village life, and the insides and outsides of its people, are vivid, and what is more true. . . ." While the story's nineteenth-century maudlin sentimentality makes for nervewracking reading today, it is sufficiently interlarded with pithy commentaries to justify the effort. Representative of Howe's cynicism is his explanation of western town growth. "Most of the citizens of Twin Mounds," he wrote, "came from the surrounding country, and a favorite way of increasing the population was to elect the county officers from the country, but after their terms expired a new set moved in, for it was thought they became so corrupt by a two years' residence that they could not be trusted to a re-election. The town increased in size a little in this manner, for none of these men ever went back to their farms again, though they speedily lost standing after they retired from their positions."

Howe's frankness about the unattractiveness of the plains ought to have made him a security risk in the eyes of any chamber of commerce. "Haven't you noticed that when a Western man gets a considerable sum of money together, he goes East to live?" he asked.

"Well, what does it mean except that the good sense which enabled him to make money teaches him that the society there is preferable to ours. . . . If I should get rich I would leave this country, because I know of another where I could live more comfortably. I stay here because it is to my interest; all of us do, and deserve no credit." He concluded that the westward movement was largely made up of the lower classes who "came here to grow up with the country, having failed to grow up with the country where they came from."

William Allen White took a more optimistic view. While his earlier fiction was said by H. L. Mencken to contain "a flavor of chewing gum and marshmallows," White was not as convinced as was Ed Howe that intelligent self-interest was the only vital human motive. He was not afraid to criticize his prairie neighbors, but in doing it he was more gentle and took a more cosmopolitan view than did the tough-minded, provincial Howe.

More recent years have been rather barren of substantial novels about the plains. Among the better ones are Milton Lott's *The Last Hunt* and Hal Borland's *The Amulet*. Montana appears to have produced more and better regional novelists than any of its neighboring states. A. B. "Bud" Guthrie attained national recognition for his work and forever fixed his position in the West's literary "hall of fame." More recently Dorothy M. Johnson and Dan Cushman came into prominence in the field. Miss Johnson's *The Hanging Tree* was widely recognized as an accurate and well-written portrayal of an early placer-mining camp. Cushman's *Stay Away Joe* convulsed readers with his uproariously funny yet poignant story of the Rocky Boy Indians' attempts to cope with modern economic life. He followed it with his prize-winning novel of early Montana quartz mining, *The Silver Mountain*. If stage and screen acceptance of fiction is any measure of achievement Guthrie, Johnson, and Cushman were howling successes.

The high plains and Rockies have fared better—numerically speaking—in the field of nonfiction. Stanley Vestal (Walter Campbell) wrote a great deal on Indian life, mountain men, and general regional subjects. Joseph Kinsey Howard earned a widespread reputation with his *Montana: High, Wide, and Handsome* and numerous articles on western life. At the time of his early death he had just finished

Strange Empire. It told a story of Canadian and American breed-Indians, the Metis, and their struggle for survival in the westward rush of civilization. Paul Sharp, after several earlier regional studies, produced his solidly written *Whoop-Up Country,* an account of plains life in northern Montana and Canada. Geographically, he and Joe Howard covered much of the same country. David Lavender's *One Man's West, The Great Divide,* and *Bent's Fort* are primarily about the country lying athwart or near the Rockies. While his work lacked the depth or permanency of some of the others, it was a welcome and useful addition to regional literature. Real contributions were made by Mari Sandoz, whose *Old Jules* quickly became a standard. In recent years her *Crazy Horse, Cheyenne Autumn,* and *The Buffalo Hunters* confirmed earlier predictions that the author's place in western literature was to be a permanent one.

Toward the end of the 1920s historian Charles A. Beard stood behind the cultural ramparts of his New England surroundings and peered down his nose at the less fortunate parts of America. "What contributions have serfs, landlords, freeholders, peasants and land toilers as such ever made to letters, arts and sciences?" he asked. "How many of the inventions that have revolutionized American life —contributed to American development—have come directly from farms and plantations, are due to the free land or the frontier?" From the title of his article, "Culture and Agriculture," and from the tone of his queries, he suggested that the only kind of culture to be found in the newer, and agrarian, parts of the land was agriculture. As one of the members of his own profession later confessed, the article did not reveal the eminent teacher at his best. But it did disclose an attitude. And it suggested that a much earlier notion about the cultural depravity of America's less thoroughly developed sections had not died.[1]

No Westerner ever claimed that after a dawn-to-dusk tour behind the plow he was prepared to sit down before the lantern and write the

[1] For a discussion of Beard's article, see Fred A. Shannon, "Culture and Agriculture in America," *Mississippi Valley Historical Review,* XLI, No. 1 (June 1954), pp. 3–20.

great novel or reach immortality as a playwright. Nor could he be a hayloft Edison or Marconi under such conditions. Perhaps no part of America made significant cultural contributions while it was yet in a state of construction. Yet, certainly there was present in the West the same productive roots that once grew along the Atlantic seaboard. If prairie-born writers, artists, or inventors tended to migrate to larger population centers better to take advantage of their talent, their places of origin cannot be accused of sterility. For a land that is still young, the West has proved itself capable of cultural development and the appreciation of life's refinements.

Section IV VINTAGE YEARS

Chapter 11 FADING FRONTIERS

By the time Americans made ready to welcome the twentieth century, their nation had undergone some dramatic changes. The great political commotion of 1896, culminating in the "battle of the century," was over. The agrarian hordes, with their frightening economic and political theories, had been turned back. McKinley was President, the Republicans were in firm control of the apparatus of government, and the country was safe. Suddenly, too, the money question was set at rest as supplies of gold flowed into financial arteries from new discoveries in Alaska and South Africa.

Then, in 1898, after the nation's maudlin sympathy for struggling Cuban revolutionaries had jumped the banks of emotional control, America plunged into what John Hay called a "splendid little war" with Spain. To the surprise of many, who thought the conflict was being fought for the rights of man in the Caribbean, the country came up with possession of the Philippine Islands, eight thousand miles west of Washington, D.C. There were other strange names in the papers—Guam, Wake, Porto Rico. It seemed that we had also acquired these bits of real estate. During that summer of American blitzkrieg against Spain, Congress approved the annexation of Hawaii, which had nothing at all to do with the war, but we were in an acquisitive mood.

Suddenly the American people were thrust upon the world scene. They had an empire. Europeans, who had long been in the business of imperialism, nodded understandingly. Some of the homefolks were not quite so sophisticated. They did not understand. The forces that had built up since the Civil War were tangible yet subtle. The wealth of material things pouring out of eastern factories, the resulting consolidations in business, the perfection of communications were so welcomed by a people who admired progress and efficiency that they did not fully anticipate the end result. By the close of the nineteenth century the builders of economic weapons had not merely matched the demands of western agricultural imperialists but had surpassed them. When the crest of plains expansion was reached, the manufacturers were just realizing their own potential. If western markets could not absorb the supply, other places of disposal must be found. In short, industrial America had burst out of its continental bounds.

So fascinated by these new developments were the nation's political and business leaders that they tended largely to forget the scenes of their recent triumphs. The plains and mountain West now took a back seat, from a national point of view. There were new worlds to conquer, and the businessman was not one to lose sight of fresh opportunities. True to the pattern of American history, the entrepreneurs leapfrogged with the hope of tapping some richer source. That the "diggin's" they left behind were not quite panned out was of no moment in the continuing rush for riches.

Men of that day realized some of the implications. "The true opportunity of the American people lies not in the tropical islands of the Pacific and Caribbean, but in the vast unsettled regions of their own country," wrote a former Omaha newspaperman in 1899. "The advocates of colonial expansion abroad argue that hitherto we have been engaged in the conquest of this continent, and declare that this work is now done. But it is *not* done. There is room for one hundred million people in the States and Territories between the Missouri river and the Pacific Ocean." The author lamented the nature of our new expansion and argued that mere profit was not a strong enough motive to cause the abandonment of the West in favor of investment abroad. There was more than material opportunity in the arid part of America, he contended. "It offers the best field in all the world for the expansion of ideas and the development of institutions. This is no less important to mankind than the expansion of trade and the development of natural resources." [1]

From even the material standpoint there was a good deal of opportunity in the West. By 1900, when the United States was shopping around the world real estate market, there were nearly six hundred million acres of public domain still open to entry and settlement within its boundaries. This was almost half of the original public domain. Of the lands yet available to homesteaders, not quite two hundred million acres, or one third of the nation's remaining free land, lay in the seven plains and mountain states under consideration. Frederick Jackson Turner could write that the frontier was gone, but this did not mean that the West was settled. Millions of acres were to be claimed after 1900.

Twentieth-century settlers were obliged to operate under different conditions than their predecessors. They discovered, as had the Johnnies-come-lately of the mineral frontier, that the first fruits had been plucked. To farm the residual lands successfully, new methods and the application of larger amounts of capital were required. A great deal of the undeveloped farming land that remained lay west of the 100th meridian, deep in the heart of the old American desert. While the farmer had made significant adjustments when he crossed the Missouri, there were limits to the flexibility of older, long-accepted methods. Without a reasonable amount of moisture the land would not respond to the traditional type of tillage.

There were two possible solutions. The first was irrigation, known to man for centuries but little used in American agriculture. Until the farmer reached the semiarid and arid regions of his country, there was no real need for the artificial induction of water. In the humid parts of the country the annual measure of rainfall was adequate and steady. Mississippi Valley farmers moved out across the plains on the supposition that, with some limitations, the same source of moisture

[1] William E. Smythe, *The Conquest of Arid America* (New York: Harper and Brothers, 1900), pp. xiii–xiv.

would be available. By a twist of fate many of them homesteaded during years exceptionally wet for the plains, which tended to reassure them in their beliefs. When the supply failed, a good number of them attributed it to the perversity of nature and to abnormal conditions. They were wrong. There was nothing unusual about aridity on the high plains.

Those who stayed to fight for economic survival considered the possibility of irrigation. While it was not common in the region, it was known. The Mormons had produced a thousand miles of irrigation ditches within a very short time after their arrival in the Salt Lake area. Soon men were pointing to the experiment that made the desert bloom. On the eastern slopes of the Rockies irrigation commenced as soon as the Fifty-Niners arrived. It is estimated that by 1866 the ditches were serving over one hundred thousand acres in Colorado. General William Tecumseh Sherman, who traveled along the foot of the mountains to Denver that year, was impressed by the possibilities. "I would not be surprised if these mountain streams would irrigate and make most fruitful one fourth of all the land from the base of the mountains out for fifty miles," he reported to army headquarters. Just as many other of the general's predictions suffered from his conservative nature, so this one fell far short of ultimate accomplishments.

A little more than a decade after Sherman's prediction one of Colorado's rivers, the Arkansas, was watering the lands of western Kansas. In 1878, during the great rush into that part of the country, some enterprising businessmen at Garden City decided to build a grist mill beside the river. Dry winds withered the crop away before the mill had a chance to be of any use. Among the men who did not decamp in the face of this disaster was one who had lived in California and Colorado, where irrigation was practiced. He asked for permission to use the water from the now-abandoned mill-race and to the delighted surprise of his neighbors, an enormous crop resulted.

The news of the "Garden City experiment" spread rapidly. By 1890 Kansas had over four hundred miles of large canals, built at a cost of about three million dollars, and she had earned the title "mother of irrigation on the plains." The happy discovery made at the useless millrace was like a lot of others that Westerners had experienced. It was too good to be true. After making some heavy investments Kansans, along with some English investors, stood helplessly by and watched their ditches dry up. Coloradans, to the west, claimed prior use of the Arkansas and used its waters freely during the growing season. The development was a crushing blow to residents of the desert, who had been certain that at last they had found the answer to their problems.

There was one more way to get water: dig for it. Farmers along the Arkansas River found that by going down between eight and twenty feet they could tap subsurface supplies. By harnessing the most abundant resource of the plains—wind—the precious liquid was hauled to the surface. Thousands of windmills pumped water into storage reservoirs where it could be ladled out to the thirsty land. The alternative method cost about double that of canal irrigation and necessitated the use of intensive methods of cultivation in limited acreages.

Though expensive and limited, the use of irrigation spread throughout the plains states. Nebraskans had experimented with it as early as the Sixties, but it took thirty years to convince them that the celestial waterworks were not reliable. There were less than twelve thousand acres under irrigation in that state in 1890. Then came the terrible, dry years and realization that the desert theory was more than an army officer's report, filed away and forgotten. Skeptics, who had long scoffed at the artificial induction of water on the land, were convinced. The amount of irrigated acres in Nebraska jumped more than twelvefold in a decade. By the turn of the century the hydrographer for the United States Geological Survey could write that in the western states and territories most of the readily available sources of irrigation had been utilized.

Where irrigation was not feasible there was another possibility of coping with nature's miserliness with her water. Crop failures west of the 100th meridian obliged owners of nonirrigable land to seek some method whereby they could husband what rainfall they were lucky enough to receive. The answer was dry farming, sometimes referred to as "horse-leg irrigation."

One of the leaders of the experiment was Hardy W. Campbell. The Vermonter came to South Dakota in the late Seventies and in 1882 raised twelve thousand bushels of wheat on three hundred acres of land, using normally accepted methods of tillage. Next year's crop was a total failure. This sobering event resulted in considerable thought on the newcomer's part. Out of his deliberations came the Campbell system of dry farming that featured a subsurface packer, an instrument used for conserving moisture. The new implement was at first widely used on the plains but successive experiments showed that in topsoil cultivation it was not necessary. Campbell, however, had pointed the way toward summer-fallowing and cultivation methods of moisture conservation.

The plains farmer, who had hesitated, confused and undecided about his future, again took heart. If he lived in a region where irrigation was possible, he diversified his agricultural endeavors and made a profit, despite the increased cost of operations. If he lived in a nonirrigable part of the plains, he continued extensive methods, putting in a maximum crop with a minimum of cost. By letting part of his land lie fallow for a season he found that it maintained a sufficient moisture content to give some assurance of a crop the following year. The method was by no means foolproof, but its results were sufficiently encouraging to make a man stay in the game and gamble.

Fortunately for farmers of the arid lands, there was an almost ideal grain. Wheat is a frontier crop that is capable of withstanding drought. Thanks to the development of the roller process of milling, northern spring wheat, hardy and high in protein, came into great demand. The cold, dry region of the Dakotas and Montana now had a grain compatible with its topography and climate. By the application of machinery to large amounts of land, wheat farmers engaged in extensive agriculture much as the cattle barons had utilized the vast rangelands of the West.

As always, the desert was a temptress. It responded to dry farming methods just enough to regenerate the frontier farmer's enthusiasms and again send him forward to the front line of battle. As before, he did not know where to stop. The new method of tillage, widely heralded in the arid regions, was accepted as a panacea and the new immigration pushed out into marginal and submarginal lands, certain that the worst was past. Irrigation enthusiasts suffered from the same

Wide World Photos

soner of the Dust—Merle Frazzee, owner of a farm in Colorado's
st bowl, inspects partly buried disk plow. His section was among
se hardest hit by wind storms.

Courtesy Wyoming State Historical Department

Irrigation division
boxes in the Wheatland,
Wyoming, irrigation
district. This particular
project never was
particularly successful.

Wagon train at Denver, Colorado, in 1866.
The location is Market Street between 15th and 16th.

ants coming into the Loup Valley,
r County, Nebraska, in 1886.

Sod dugout in the Loup River Country of Nebraska.

Courtesy State Historical Society of Col

Steam threshing outfit in Kansas, about 1909.

Courtesy Kansas State Historical Society

A modern sugar-beet crop set off by
the Colorado Rockies in the background.

"An Even Twenty" is the title of this picture
taken by Montana's best-known photographer,
L. A. Huffman. For more of his work see Mark
H. Brown and W. R. Felton, *The Frontier Years*
(1955).

Colorado cattle-branding scene.

Modern beef on the hoof
at a Denver stock show, 1945.

Southwestern Kansas cattle roundup in the nineties.

Chuck-wagon scene on the eastern Montana cattle range.

illusion. No one could convince them that the problem had not been solved, that much of the region was unsuited for such agriculture. For half a century, through private and governmental agencies, water was conducted to parched acres in a determined effort to "make the desert bloom." The effort was much publicized and the impression was lent that the West was being reclaimed. But little more than a start had been made. By 1940 only a little more than five million acres of the vast Missouri River drainage would be under irrigation, a very small percentage of the land.

But American optimism is hard to dull. Where plains irrigation was at all feasible, men merged their resources to form cooperative districts and engaged in intensive agriculture. They became a minority for several reasons. Their numbers were small in relation to the plains population, because the amount of land adaptable to their cause was limited. The crops they raised, the large amount of seasonal labor required, and heavy requirements in capital set them apart from the dry-land farmers. Railroads, farm equipment manufacturers, and businessmen in general were attracted by the possibilities of this type of farming. Their sympathies helped the irrigationist minority to achieve national publicity, and hence the passage of federal legislation that aided them.

The dry-land farmer was not forgotten by industrialists who were interested in the new agriculture. The extensive nature of this method not only tended to affect federal land legislation, but it also made new technological demands. After the long, cold winters of the northern plains, the land must be put to crop as quickly as possible to take advantage of residual moisture and a short maturing season. With the size of farms steadily increasing it soon became obvious that better tools were necessary. The horse was too slow a motive power for use on large tracts. The steam tractor pulling a gang plow offered something better, but this meant a heavy investment, one that only the larger operators could afford. Where these tractors were used their very cost tended to make the owner till even larger acreages in order to justify the outlay. When American industry finally offered the farmer a smaller, less expensive gasoline-driven tractor, the same effect was had upon that group of people as came to the nation with the introduction of the Model T Ford.

Speed was just as important at harvest time. When the crop was ripe, every day of delay meant an additional risk of loss by wind, hail, or grasshoppers. By the Seventies, binders were given up in favor of the header, which worked better where wheat stalks were short or uneven due to withering dry weather. Rather than being made into shocks the wheat was now piled into large stacks to wait for the threshing machine. The transition to the combine was a natural development. With that machine the entire process, from cutting to threshing, was done in a single operation. By the 1920s the combine, developed before the turn of the century, was in general use throughout the plains region. With the appearance and improvement of the truck, grain was often in the elevator only minutes after the harvesting process commenced.

Progress is not without its costs. In solving one problem, others are often born. Farmers of the arid West made this discovery when they turned to mechanized extensive farming and the intensive methods characterized by irrigation. In both cases much larger amounts of capital were required than ever before employed by the average homesteader. Like the cotton planters of the ante-bellum South, Westerners were faced by steadily declining prices for their product and mounting expenses. Like them, they made a desperate effort to escape the inevitable trap by producing more. The attempt only magnified the inescapable disaster of mountainous surpluses.

When the prairie farmer forsook his semisubsistence type of existence for mechanized agriculture, he crossed an economic Rubicon. Any possibility of survival from "eating off the land" disappeared with the coming of the machine. In some cases the typical farm life so long understood by the American people disappeared. When the modern day dawned it revealed a picture of land literally "mined" by machinery, land upon which frequently not a living animal, not even a dog, was seen. Though it is perhaps the extreme example, there were farms on the plains that could not even claim a dwelling. Instead, into barbed-wire enclosures of a half-section or section of wheat land there moved a gasoline-driven train composed of tractors pulling a wheeled cookshack, a fuel tank, drills, harrows, discs, and plows. After the soil had surrendered to steel, the train would move on to another tract in an industrialized kind of agriculture. When the process was complete and the crop was in, the owner went back to town to spend the winter.

The system invited peonage. That fate was avoided so long as crops materialized, but when they failed and cash reserves dwindled, the farmer was faced by steely-eyed creditors who expressed the same sympathy displayed by Calvin Coolidge when he snarled at the Europeans: "They hired the money, didn't they?" The tiller of the soil was now introduced to the agonizing results of overextended credit and financial dependence: foreclosure. He came to know the term "repossessed tractor" just as his city cousin learned of it when he failed to meet his Morris Plan payments and surrendered his vacuum cleaner.

Major difficulties for the plains farmers were deferred until the 1920s, thanks to an unexpected reprieve. The temporary upturn in their prospects arose from the two coincidences: international war and an unusually favorable crop year. Up to 1913 the price of wheat —the principal plains crop—had been in a long-range decline, with a slight upturn after 1897. After the turn of the century, in particular, exports of that grain had declined considerably. Then, as the shadows of agricultural gloom began to return, events in Europe altered the situation.

When the events of war closed the Dardanelles and denied western Europe its customary supply of wheat, new markets appeared for the Americans. Demand quickly affected the price level which, in early 1915, advanced more than sixty cents a bushel. By May, farmers were getting $1.40 for their wheat and the nation exported around fifty-five million dollars worth each month. Then nature took a hand. In that year the American farmers harvested their first billion-bushel crop. This tended to depress the price temporarily, but when production dropped again the next year, it once again advanced. By the spring of 1917 it stood at $2.40. Despite a very good crop again in 1918 the price stayed at two dollars or slightly above.

The result was an agricultural boom reminiscent of the early mining days. Farmers ransacked the earth for more land to work. By 1919, wheat acreages in the plains states of Nebraska, Kansas, Colorado, Oklahoma, and Texas had increased by more than thirteen million acres. Minnesota, Montana, and the two Dakotas added over four million more new acres under cultivation. The Secretary of Agriculture explained. "This crop expansion was brought about by plowing up some pastures and meadows in Minnesota and North and South Dakota, but more especially wild pasture lands in the semi-arid sections of the western part of the Dakotas and in Montana."

Again the plains farmers had pushed their luck too far. Under the most favorable climatic and price conditions the marginal lands whose sod they had ripped off would yield a favorable return. When one of these conditions was not present, the result was disaster. Montana farmers experienced it in 1919. For the first sixteen years of the new century their prairie farms had averaged twenty-five bushels per acre; in that tragic year the average was just under two and a half bushels. Even with the price still above two dollars this meant a return of only about five dollars an acre. One Montana historian estimated that in a single season the state's farmers lost fifty million dollars to drought. As he pointed out, "loss of that much money would constitute a spectacular financial disaster even in New York."

And so it was, across the northern high plains. Like cowhands on piebald buckers, the farmers hung on, desperately waiting for the ten-second whistle. Perhaps next year would bring rain. But often next year's crop was one of mortgage foreclosures. Then came the final blow. Agricultural prices collapsed. Old-timers may have remembered the remark a cowboy once had made about their country: "I wouldn't give a pair of boots for the best section up there. Matter of fact, just before I left, I swapped two sections of the best land you'll find anywhere on them plains for these boots I've got on." By the late 1920s the comment carried a good deal more cogency than at the time of its utterance.

While farmers of the plains struggled for survival in their battle with the elements, residents of the mountain region were also faced by changing economic conditions. In many ways the problems were parallel. When the miners had skimmed from the earth's surface the immediate and obvious wealth, they, too, were confronted with the necessity of making heavy investments in equipment to continue their extraction. In Colorado, where silver-mining finally surpassed that of gold, the curse of nature's generosity sent prices plummeting just as it did in the wheat belt. Both groups of extractors were plagued by rising costs of production and lower returns.

The decade of the Eighties was one of great prosperity for Colorado miners. Gold was mined in greater quantities than in previous years, yet the value of such an unexciting mineral as lead exceeded it by a million dollars annually. Silver, however, was king, yielding more than fourteen million dollars a year during those years. Leadville was still the mining capital but other, newer, camps made their bid for pre-eminence. Aspen rose to a city of five thousand out of rumors of rich silver-bearing ore. When its Mollie Gibson mine showed an average yield of six hundred ounces of silver per ton, the white metal gained new respect in the eyes of the miners. A single ore car of twenty-four tons returned $76,500. Even gold-hunters could appreciate this kind of mining.

By the early Nineties Colorado's boom in silver was attracting worldwide attention. During the first three years of that decade the mines earned more than twenty million dollars annually. Concern about the gradual decline in price during the preceding few years was soothed by continued high production figures and new strikes. In the spring of 1890 a rich find was made at Creede. Into narrow Willow Creek canyon hundreds of prospectors jostled each other and perched their little cabins on precipitous sites. It was the old, roistering mining frontier, alive again. Cy Warman, the local newspaper editor, fixed the scene in poetry:

> *Here the meek and mild-eyed burros*
> *On mineral mountains feed—*
> *It's day all day in the daytime,*
> *And there is no night in Creede.*

> *Here's a land where all are equal—*
> *Of high or lowly birth—*
> *A land where men make millions*
> *Dug from the dreary earth.*

Then came the toboggan ride. Supply far outstripped demand and the price of silver skidded sickeningly. By 1893, with a national panic in progress, the "Silver State" was thrown into a turmoil of bankruptcies, unemployment, and general depression. The repeal of the Sherman Silver Purchase Act in August appeared to etch the epitaph on Colorado's gravestone. Perhaps it was just a symbol. Compared to the production figures, the amount the government tried to buy under that legislation was like bailing out a sinking ocean liner with a coffee can. But to Westerners, President Cleveland's action was the final betrayal.

The only ray of sunlight that pierced the gloom was a cowboy's discovery of gold-rich ore at Cripple Creek, thirty-five miles from Pike's Peak. For three decades prospectors had combed the area but none had found the key to riches until Bob Womack made his find in 1891. The first year the new diggings yielded a half-million dollars, the next two years two million each, and in 1895 the production tripled. By 1900 the annual figure was eighteen million dollars.

Rich as the new field was, it was a local affair and its injections of gold into the economic blood stream did not rouse the state from its general moribund economic condition. The maladjustment was too deep to be remedied by palliatives. When the full force of the panic hit Colorado, there were scenes of disorder that places like Denver had not seen since the days of its infancy. Ten banks closed their doors within three days in that city. The story was the same in other parts of the state. Thousands of unemployed miners and other laborers roamed the streets of towns and merchants fought desperately for survival. In a land of gold and silver there was no money. Cripple Creek and all its treasure appeared to provide no answers. It was incredible, men told one another, simply incredible. But it was true.

Word came down from Montana that things were no better there. The mines of Butte had shown a steadily increasing output of silver through the Eighties—and then came the prostrating blow to that market. Overnight the silver mines closed down, never to recover. Some struggled on for a few years, but 1893 marked the end of the bonanza era. It was never again of any significance in Montana. New methods and a new metal had to be found. The metal was copper; the method corporate enterprise. The day of the prospector and individual enterprise was no more. From now on it was to be a matter of capital and labor. As elsewhere in America, the change in methods would have its moments of friction and violence.

Even the unique prosperity of Cripple Creek could not buy peace in the troubled days of the early Nineties. Into that camp poured unemployed silver-miners, anxious to work the new gold mines for wages. Three dollars a day was the going rate. Some of the Fifty-Niners had worked for that amount; it had not changed by 1880, despite an unsuccessful strike for more money at Leadville that year. But now, in August 1893, with the country in financial distress and wages falling, Cripple Creek mine owners tried to extend the daily working hours from eight to nine with no raise in pay. The change would be effective February 1, 1894. Labor objected on the ground that conditions at Cripple Creek were not typical. Wood was selling for $4.50 a cord, water at forty cents a barrel, and the cost of freight elevated the price of food at the camp by nearly fifty per cent. The mine owners were adamant. They recalled the affair at Leadville when Governor Pitkin had called out the state militia to break that strike; they were sure of themselves now.

But this was a new day. In May 1893, in turbulent, depression-ridden Butte, Montana, the Western Federation of Miners was born. One of its organizers, a Scot named John Calderwood, now appeared on the Cripple Creek scene, with the blessing of his old friend Populist Governor "Bloody Bridles" Waite. The mine owners made their play and Calderwood called them. Out of the mines came five hundred of his followers. Management answered by having the sheriff deputize a force to protect property and those who wanted to work. The two small armies eyed each other, one waiting for the other to move. Then Winfield Scott Stratton, one of the earliest prospectors at Cripple Creek and its first millionaire, did what his colleagues down at Colorado Springs regarded a downright traitorous thing. He entered into negotiations with Calderwood and agreed to a scale of $3.25 for a nine-hour daytime shift and the same amount for eight hours of night work. The other holdout mine owners gasped in disbelief. Management actually had stooped to talk with the hooligans from a branch of the Western Federation of Miners! They shuddered and thought of the French Reign of Terror a century earlier.

With Stratton's acquiescence the owners' defensive line was wedged in. But the local masters of capital were not ready to throw in the sponge. Like their brethren in the East they took to the courts and fired away with salvos of injunctions. The Union was enjoined against interference with the operation of the mines by scab labor. The striking workers responded by fortifying Bull Hill, the site of the affected mines, and even rigged up an ingenious bow–gun that could rocket forth beer bottles filled with dynamite. When more strike-breakers were brought in from Denver to accomplish what the injunctions had not, all hell broke loose. Members of the "defending" army staggered forth under a heavy load of bourbon and threatened to blow up every mine in the vicinity. Class warfare now broke out, full scale. And owner Stratton regretted his fraternization with representatives of the working man.

There were explosions and a few fatalities. But before civil war seriously reduced the population, Governor Waite stepped in and laid down the law. The owners reluctantly consented to a truce. They agreed to an eight-hour day for the sum of three dollars and amnesty for strike leaders. The end came on June 10, 1894, after one hundred thirty days of turmoil that cost around three million dollars. Out of it came the first great victory for the Western Federation of Miners and the introduction to the West of such modern labor battle weapons as injunctions, blacklists, spies, and dynamite. The new land was becoming quite sophisticated.

Successful strikes breed more strikes. It was true in the industrial East toward the end of the nineteenth century; it was also true in the Rockies. Leadville miners, who had lost their battle against management in 1880, watched the recent affair at Cripple Creek with interest. Then they tried it. At this camp capital and labor had an agreement that wages would be two and a half dollars a day so long as silver sold for less than eighty-three and a half cents an ounce. However, in order to get better workers, the owners generally ignored the arrangement and paid three dollars. When there was talk of returning to the lower figure in the spring of 1896, a strike resulted. As at Cripple Creek, there were explosions and deaths, but there the parallel ended.

The strike was a failure and once again the Leadville miners gave in.

In 1901 trouble broke out at Telluride, when the owners tried to institute a contract system based upon how much digging the worker accomplished, rather than pay by the hour. That strike, of two months' duration, was characterized by strikebreaking, assassination, and warfare. It resulted in a victory for the W.F.M. and increased prestige for that organization among the miners. Encouraged, the union set out to nail down its control by going to war against the smelters at Colorado City, where most of the Cripple Creek ore was refined. Its leadership ordered thirty-five hundred men out of the mines during the summer of 1903. Accordingly, the owners brought in strikebreakers who were promptly attacked and, as usual, the call went out for troops to protect management. A thousand strong, the militia invaded Cripple Creek, ready to crush the malcontents. National Guard General Sherman Bell made no bones about the purpose of the soldiers. "I came here to do up this damned anarchistic federation," he stated simply.

Big Bill Haywood, secretary of the Federation, decided to counterattack with a reign of terror that would drive off the strikebreakers and intimidate the mine owners. Happily, there was a newcomer to Cripple Creek who was just the man for such work. Harry Orchard, who would soon come to national notice by blowing the former governor of Idaho sky-high, was at liberty. He volunteered his services. For two hundred dollars he would put on a demonstration by dynamiting the scabs in the Vindicator mine. Through an error he set his charge at the wrong level, and no harm came to the workers, but when the mine superintendent and foreman entered the charged area they were blown to bits. "You got two good ones," Haywood told him, much impressed by such talent.

The strike spread to Telluride where, in the winter of 1903–1904, Federation leaders casually debated whether to poison the town's water supply or launch dynamite-filled barrels upon the place from a nearby mountain. Telluride was under militia rule. While they talked Harry Orchard experimented with new bombs, artfully designed to look like lumps of coal that could be secreted in the mills' fuel stocks. When he planted two boxes of dynamite under the depot platform at Independence in June 1904 and blew thirteen scab workers to shreds, not to mention wounding a score, public sentiment revolted. There were general deportations of union leaders into Kansas, New Mexico, and the more remote parts of Colorado. The Federation, which stubbornly refused to call off the strike, suffered enormously. The blast at Independence signaled the beginning of its decline.

Labor unrest, hatched in the gold fields, spread to other industries. The United Mine Workers of America called a strike in the coal mines of southern Colorado in the fall of 1903 that lasted nearly a year and was unsuccessful. For nearly a decade after that there were mutterings of discontent, particularly in Boulder County. By 1913 coal miners in the Trinidad district again walked out, demanding higher wages and recognition of their union. United Mine Workers, national in scope, rushed in its best organizers, including the eighty-two-year-old woman Socialist "Mother Jones," who had a great deal of influence among the miners. The owners resorted to their traditional reliance upon strikebreakers and troops. Both sides poured out a flood of propaganda leaflets.

Colorado, so recently in the national limelight through violence at Cripple Creek, again appeared in headlines across the country. The most dramatic incident of the strike, and the one that went into the pages of history, was the Ludlow massacre. The striking miners removed their families to temporary tent colonies, to keep them from harm. At Ludlow station, about eighteen miles from Trinidad, there were twelve hundred people in one of these encampments. On April 20, 1914, Colorado National Guardsmen fought a pitched battle with the Ludlow miners and in the course of the fighting the flimsy dwellings were set afire. When the affair was over, five miners and one militiaman lay dead. For those used to labor strife, this was simply the price of the contest. But what aroused the nation particularly was the fact that in the charred ruins of Ludlow lay the bodies of two women and eleven children who had been unable to escape the conflagration. Now, fifty years after Chivington's attack at Sand Creek, Colorado had another massacre on its record. As a result, federal troops were sent into the state and President Woodrow Wilson personally interceded. The United Mine Workers abandoned any further attempts to organize Colorado miners and the frightened state legislature hastily enacted a workmen's compensation act, a mutual liability insurance act, and an industrial commission act. Slowly the mines resumed normal operations.

During the spring of 1914, while Colorado was in the throes of Industrial warfare, Montanans watched Butte add to its reputation as the toughest mining town in the country. Here too, the union was experiencing a great deal of difficulty in maintaining its power, but in this case the trouble was internal. By now the Western Federation of Miners was exacting a day's wages per month for dues from its members and there were rumblings of discontent from the ranks. Open rebellion occurred when a glib young miner named Muckey Mc-Donald persuaded some of his followers to break away from the union; the mine owners, fearing that organization, barred the men from entrance. The result was immediate and violent civil war among the miners.

Butte now treated the nation to an orgy of labor upheaval that matched anything the East had seen. Even a seasoned French revolutionary, accustomed to tearing up the cobblestones of Paris and barricading the streets, would have fled for his life. Butte's police chief, Jerre Murphy, tried to do his duty. He and his men moved against the crowd and the chief was promptly beaned with a bottle. Then the insurgent miners yelled "To the Miners Union Hall—Tear it to hell and get the records! Wreck the house of the grafters!" The forces of law and order were engulfed by a howling mob that moved toward the building where the union's records had been kept since 1888.

Out of the headquarters windows flew typewriters, cash registers, packets of records, furniture, and everything else that was not nailed down. One burly raider ripped off the piano's keyboard and sprinkled ivory keys over the crowd below. The acting mayor foolishly tried to intervene and was promptly heaved out a second-story window. Then the miners went to work in earnest, pounding away at the big burglarproof safe that held money and records. They were interrupted by the arrival of the police, who brought along a large van with which to rescue the container. The rioters drove off the officers and confiscated the vehicle, which they used to haul the safe to the edge of town. Liberal use of dynamite brought forth a thousand dollars in cash and a number of account books and contracts. Their objectives reached, the rioters calmed down and there was peace again in Butte.

But not for long. A few days later Charles Moyer, president of the Federation, came to town to mend the rift. He was faced by a new, rival union headed by Muckey McDonald. Moyer refused to recognize the result of the recent revolution and called for a meeting of the stalwarts. It was a mistake. McDonald's followers, armed to the teeth, surrounded the hall and when one of the late arrivals to the meeting tried to enter the building, a union card clenched in his fist, he was shot through the shoulder. That touched off a new riot and the cry went up, "Blow them to hell out of the hall! Get dynamite!" Stick after stick of the explosive was inserted into the walls. After twenty-five blasts nothing remained but crumbled bricks and rubble. Then Butte went back to work. As one of the miners later wrote, it had been a trying time. All the saloons were closed during the warfare. "It was a sad period," he said. "Almost like prohibition."

For the high plains and mountain West, the time between the passing of the Populists and the day of Woodrow Wilson was one of reappraisal and attempts to find a normal place in the national economy. Like the rest of America, the region was mightily affected by the forces of the new industrialism and the accentuation of urban trends.

In the case of the mountain country, geographically and politically isolated, mining still dominated the economy. In such communities the cleavage between capital and labor was great, and members of all subsidiary types of business were obliged to stand on one side or the other; there was no middle ground. The result was united labor versus united business. Here the transition from frontier conditions to those of modern industrialism was rapid and violent, as the bloody strikes in Colorado demonstrated.

In an earlier day miners worked for wages no higher than those offered in the Nineties and paid high prices for food and supplies. But it was in a different milieu. Then there was hope that the situation would be temporary, that a small grubstake could be accumulated through labor, and that he who worked and saved had the privilege of setting himself up in the mining business. As the century came to a close it was obvious that, except in rare instances, this opportunity was gone. There were those who had struck it rich and were now millionaires, but they were rare. Most of the mines were operated by corporations and the personal relationship between employer and employees was absent. In its place had arisen class-consciousness and the attendant animosities.

The average Westerner, who had found no gold mine of his own, regarded the development as undemocratic. All he had ever asked for was a chance. Now, it appeared, even that was not available. The day of the placer miner had long since disappeared, but worse, so had that of the small quartz miner who could no longer compete with corporations and their expensive machinery that probed the bowels of the earth. For the mining industry it was now the turn of the small businessman to be squeezed out. It came at a time when all America was reading the charges of the muckrakers and pondering the cost to the nation of its management by the masters of capital.

Those who were not miners regarded the new scene with mixed feelings. As they watched the western labor–capital struggle, they felt as many Americans had a century before when the French people arose to strike down a privileged class. At first there was sympathy with the cause of the common man, but when the struggle turned to excesses of violence, public opinion was forced to take a stand on the side of law and order. It was this abhorrence of disorder that finally crushed the miners' uprising. The unions pushed their cause too far. Their use of violence, and even some of their less drastic notions, met with disapproval from a western people who had long known conflict but whose basic sense of orderliness was strong.

While one major industry, mining, was suffering from internal conflict and declining profits, the West's other principal form of economic endeavor experienced a period of temporary respite. Beginning about 1897, the price of farm products crawled upward and for two decades gave the farmer some encouragement. There were several reasons for the improvement: increased international supplies of gold and a resultant inflation, a rapid urban growth that meant more American mouths to feed, a relative decline in the number of farms, and, finally, the artificial stimulation of a world war. A recent student of the period has perhaps overenthusiastically called it "the golden age of American agriculture," but there is no question about the fact that, for the moment, agrarian times were better. To the plains farmer, ample rainfall and favorable prices go a long way toward the solution of his problems. But these are variables, subject to sudden change without notice, and he who plants crops beyond the Missouri under the impression that this is not the case has no business living there.

During this era plains farmers made a better adjustment to the new industrialism than did their brothers in the mountain mines. Thanks to the availability of machinery they were able to expand their operations without any significant dependence upon additional labor. The average farm family continued to supply those needs, and there was no labor–management clash on the harvest fields. But just as the American Indian economy had become dependent upon the white man's metal—hatchets, knives, kettles, and guns—so the farm culture was affected by the iron puddling at Pittsburgh. The marvelous new farm machinery that poured forth from the womb of the industrial giant was welcomed by the farmer who saw in it a means of expansion and more efficient methods. Under favorable conditions he could afford it. The trouble came when he could not afford these instruments but was unable to operate without them.

For the American farmer of the Midwest, or of other humid sections of the country, the years immediately before and after the turn of the century were those of consolidation, attempts at more efficient agricultural results through education and improved techniques, and the increased use of business methods in the financial realm. The plains farmer tried these things too, but his part of the country was in some respects still a frontier. He had to anticipate greater variants in rainfall and more extreme conditions, generally, than his midwestern brothers. He was still fencing with the elements, probing for their weak spots. Most dangerous of all was his advance into marginal and submarginal lands. The only way to find out if they would yield a living was by trial and error. It was this "golden age" of agriculture that encouraged him to try.

By the time the boys were singing "Over There" and "Goodbye Broadway, Hello France," pioneer conditions on the high plains had pretty well disappeared. Armed with their new weapons and heady from the lyrical pleas of the public for more wheat to help make the world safe for democracy, farmers ripped up sod, anxious to do their bit in the name of patriotism and profit. This did not mean that they abandoned their traditional isolationism. Much of the grain-growing plains country was peopled by first- and second-generation Americans whose fathers had demonstrated their lack of interest in European problems by emigrating. On one hand there was a vague, half-hearted loyalty to the Old Country that bred an unconscious opposition to international conflict, and on the other hand there was the lurking feeling that old-world entanglements had no place in the new mecca out West. Sandwiched in was the general western opposition to big business, whose minions now were about to make a fortune in war contracts. Local moneymaking in a time of national involvement was one thing, but eastern profiteering was quite another matter. As one Kansas farmer said, he and his neighbors would fight when America was invaded, but "The honor of the country doesn't get outside our boundaries that we can see." [2] So the farmers went to work, furnishing agricultural products for the great crusade, for local and immediate reasons. It lasted only a few months. Then the boys came home, ready to take up membership in the "lost generation," and overnight, it seemed, the beautiful dream of an agricultural seventh heaven beyond the Missouri faded. Suddenly the plains farmers were shoved into a kind of lost generation of their own.

The nation, plagued by unemployment, financial panic, bank failures and the general economic distress of postwar adjustments, could find no time to sympathize. For the business world the days of trouble were temporary, and after a short period of distress it launched upon its own brief golden age. The roaring Twenties brought the western farmer only dry years and sagging prices. When the big crash came in 1929 he was already launched upon his own depression. Then came the "dirty Thirties," and the lament of displaced persons in the industrial wastelands, "Brother can you spare a dime?" Onetime wheat kings had their own query: "Pardner, could you use some four-bit wheat?" For them the golden age of agriculture wasn't really gold at all. It was gilt.

[2] Ray Allen Billington, "The Origins of Middle Western Isolationism," *Political Science Quarterly*, LX, No. 1 (March 1945), p. 56.

Chapter 12 UNCLE SAM'S WEST

For a century after the Louisiana Purchase the land stretching from the Mississippi westward across the Rockies was subjected to exploitation with a minimum of control. Trappers, prospectors, cattlemen, sheepmen, tie-hackers, lumbermen, and farmers moved about at will, using nature's facilities as recklessly as tourists in a public campground. Individual and corporate entrepreneurs worked frantically to beat out competitors in a race for riches. Extraction of resources, without consideration of preservation or conservation, stood uppermost in their minds. It was the heyday of laissez faire.

By 1900 it was time for the federal government to take stock and to learn what the advocates of free enterprise had left of their patrimony. Millions of free acres still remained but much of the land was unsuited for traditional agriculture, or even dry-land farming, and some was not arable at all. Timbered regions were being stripped at an alarming rate. Dams were being built privately to gain a source of power rather than to prevent flood or erosion. Suddenly Americans started to ask themselves how best to utilize the residual public domain. Already some of the more thoughtful had commenced to lodge complaints about the rate of depletion and pessimists talked darkly of the day when actual shortages and material want would face the nation.

Westerners were in general not particularly concerned about conservation in its narrowest sense. Development was, and still is, the key word in their book. As sons of frontiersmen they inherited an abiding faith in the ability of the land to produce. The problem that faced them was how to proceed in the light of new circumstances. They had predicated their earlier hopes for success upon movement, fluidity, inflation, and fresh opportunities. Now, as frontier conditions were replaced by more static ones, considerable readjustment was necessary. The question was one of technology rather than land availability.

As always, they appealed to the generosity of the federal government and asked for further assistance. It had encouraged them earlier through a number of modifications of the Homestead Act—some of which had been helpful while others had not. If the western farmer were going to take advantage of what remained to him in the way of land, additional help would be required. For example, private enterprise had been proved inadequate in the case of major irrigation projects. Here was a place, said the farmer, where the government could be useful. It could help to open a yet-undeveloped portion of the country and at the same time furnish homes to the landless in a nation rapidly losing sight of the agrarian ideal.

Congress was willing. It had tried continuously since 1862 to give away western lands. When the Desert Land Act of 1877 proved to be a failure, the Carey Act was passed in 1894. Under its provisions certain states were guaranteed as much as a million arid acres within their borders for irrigation and settlement. Ten years would be allowed to fulfill the offer. But after seven years less than a million acres out of a possible eleven million had been applied for, and only 7648 were actually patented. Again the giveaway plan had failed.

By 1900 it seemed clear that neither private enterprise nor the states were able to handle so large an undertaking. By then a good many supporters of irrigation had abandoned their demands that remaining public lands be turned over to the states for final disposal. Even Easterners were ready to go along with the idea of federal management. The talk of saving what was left of America's forests had made them conscious of conservation and it was generally agreed that the larger task of reclamation was national in scope. Both major parties recognized it as a political fact when they included recommendations for federal sponsorship of irrigation in their platforms that year.

General interest in reclaiming arid western lands did not emerge spontaneously. Hiram M. Chittenden, engineer and historian of the Missouri River, urged governmental participation in irrigation in his *Reservoirs in the Arid Regions,* published in 1897. He wanted the government to acquire any improvable reservoir sites, build dams, and distribute water without charge. The National Irrigation Association, formed that year in Kansas, agreed. Its leader, George H. Maxwell, at once began a propaganda campaign, financed by the numerous industrial and transportation interests who would benefit from increased western agricultural output. When the Ninth Irrigation Congress met at Chicago in 1900, it wholeheartedly backed the Chittenden recommendations. Maxwell's educational campaign was so successful that politicians were obliged to take notice of it, hence the appearance of the matter in national platforms. The result was the United States Reclamation Service.

The passage of the Reclamation Act was attended by a political battle greater than that produced by any land legislation since the Homestead Act forty years earlier. The initial bill, the draft of which was prepared by Frederick H. Newell of the Geological Survey, was introduced into Congress by Representative Francis G. Newlands of Nevada early in 1901. It provided that the money received from the sale of lands in sixteen western states, except that promised by prior legislation to the land-grant colleges, should go into a revolving fund to be used for building irrigation projects. Any lands valuable as irrigation sites were to be reserved.

The notion that land sale receipts were to be earmarked for reclamation raised a storm of protest from those who felt that it was a treasury raid. They held that these moneys traditionally had gone into the general fund and when this source was cut off it would be the same as supporting the new project by direct subsidy. Others argued that the government was now bent upon disposing of the remaining public domain, or reserving it, and such action would cut off monetary sources upon which the agricultural colleges depended under the terms of the 1890 Morrill Act. Finally, the three million dollars that the government proposed to spend upon projects annually caused complaint from people who objected to federal funds being used to benefit any particular part of the nation. The public lands and money obtained from their sale belonged to the people as a whole, went the argument.

Fortunately for the irrigationists and conservationists, a powerful sponsor came to their aid. Shortly after McKinley's assassination, young Theodore Roosevelt went before Congress with his annual address. Among other things he told his listeners, "The western half of the United States would sustain a population greater than that of our whole country today if the waters that now run to waste were saved and used for irrigation." He called the water problem one of the most vital internal questions of the day. When the Newlands bill was under attack he entered the fray with his customary vigor, arguing that the government had as much right to make arid regions useful by storing water in their streams as it did to improve rivers and harbors in more humid sections.

Midwestern Congressmen fought back, relating in tearful tones how their people had pioneered the land unaided and alone, without governmental aid, and had built up the value of their farms through endless toil. Now, the lament continued, the planned-economy boys proposed to erect a new farming section to the west that would enter competition with the fathers of agricultural free enterprise. Both sides shouted accusations of self-interest. Then the industrialists stepped in between the battling farm sections and threw their support with the West, an area where they hoped to tap new markets. Meanwhile the proponents of the bill played hearts-and-flowers background music, using the old, old theme of securing the little people on farms of their own where they could pass their days in peace and plenty. The bill passed, and in the spring of 1902 it received Roosevelt's signature.

Plainsmen received the victory with mixed feelings. They welcomed the additional federal support, but some thought the price was high. While the law was designed to promote settlement, it also provided for the reservation of certain lands, and this was something Westerners had long opposed. In places where Uncle Sam was the principal landowner, the tax base was necessarily reduced and the ultimate settlement of the land was delayed or prevented. The law itself announced the beginning of the end. Despite its strong homestead theme, so popular to land-seekers, the bill's very provisions suggested that settlement of the public domain soon would be a thing of the past. In short, to gain one final injection of settlers, Westerners were willing to support a law that, in effect, closed out the books in the old business of federal land-granting.

In Colorado the federal government turned its attention to irrigable lands lying west of the divide, where less than half the potential was served by private companies. The Uncompahgre project, located in the southwestern part of the state, was the first federal reclamation attempt.

By means of the Gunnison Tunnel, nearly six miles long, water was diverted from that river to the Uncompahgre Basin. The work was completed in 1909 and within fifteen years the government had almost five hundred miles of canals in operation. It cost more than six million dollars. In terms of gain to the region, land values shot up from around two dollars per acre to as high as eight hundred when it was used for fruit raising.

A second early Colorado project was developed in the Grand River Valley during World War I. By a system of canals, flumes, and tunnels water was carried more than sixty miles to the region around Palisade and Grand Junction and distributed to waiting users. The two projects cost around eleven million dollars, a sum that was equaled in crop values in a three-year period during the Twenties. Farmers could well afford to pay for the water received under these conditions.

In Wyoming the Jackson Lake project, the construction of which is so amusingly described in Elliot Paul's *Desperate Scenery,* was built in 1910–1911, to irrigate portions of Idaho. A half-dozen years earlier the Shoshone Dam and reclamation project was constructed to the east of Yellowstone Park to irrigate lands in the vicinity of Cody. Just to the north, in Montana, the Huntley project in the Yellowstone Valley put into cultivation some thirty-three thousand acres of otherwise marginal land. As in the case of the Colorado undertakings, those in Wyoming and Montana resulted in sharply increased land values and the development of agricultural communities that otherwise would not have existed.

Similar success attended the development of the Sun River development in central Montana and the Lower Yellowstone project near Glendive, in the eastern part of the state. In the latter case, around sixty thousand acres in Montana and eastern North Dakota were served by sixty-six miles of main canals and almost one hundred fifty miles of laterals. Meanwhile, Wyoming and Nebraska took advantage of water from the Platte River. Water stored behind the Pathfinder Dam, one of the largest masonry constructions in the world at the time it was built, was doled out to serve a hundred thousand acres in the two states.

There have been criticisms of the government's attempts. The Uncompahgre development made possible high returns from agriculture during the first few years of its operation, but after World War I the per-acre income dropped considerably, causing one student of irrigation to remark that the water was piped in by gold plumbing. Despite adjustments made in the repayment schedule, it will be 1979 before the debt is paid off. Similarly, there has been some taxpayer complaint against New Deal enthusiasm for the Big Thompson scheme in Colorado, to pump water through the Alva Adams Tunnel from the west slope of the Rockies to the east side. The Northern Colorado Conservancy District, comprised of some eight thousand members, agreed to pay for half of this bit of engineering, up to an amount not exceeding twenty-five million dollars. By the time the first water crossed the divide costs had gone well over a hundred million and there was talk that before the job was finished another eighty million would be required. The government's only hope to come out even was through the sale of hydroelectric power, a by-product.

Results of reclamation efforts have been varied; disappointing in some cases but quite rewarding in others. Thousands of acres have been brought under cultivation, and although they do not make a great impression on the western map, their contribution cannot be underestimated. As early as 1913, Theodore Roosevelt said in his autobiography that "The population which the Reclamation Act has brought into the arid West, while comparatively small when compared with that in the more closely inhabited East, has been a most effective contribution to the National life, for it has gone far to transform the social aspect of the West, making stability of the institutions upon which the welfare of the whole country rests. . . ."

It remained for the New Dealers to attempt the mightiest irrigation and flood-control project of all. Their subject was the Missouri River and the project spread across the northern plains to affect directly every one of the seven states here considered and indirectly a number of others. This long and tortuous murky ribbon meanders southeastward out of the Montana Rockies, across the Dakotas, touches Kansas and Nebraska, and then empties into the Mississippi just above St. Louis. Its tributaries, long and crooked fingers, stretch out across a whole arid inland empire, catching the mountain drainage from Montana to Colorado.

The river system has been more cursed than praised by the white man. Except for the Missouri itself, none of the waterways have been practically navigable. Shallow, treacherous, and unpredictable, they have on the whole done mankind more harm than good. Their low banks are subject to easy flooding and with great frequency they have jumped their confines to wash away those who ventured too close in trying to work the alluvial bottomlands. Few rivers in the world have offered water engineers a greater challenge.

Even before the Civil War engineers tried to carry on what one author has called "first-aid work" to patch up the river's leaky and wandering banks. As early as 1838 snags were removed in an attempt to make the waterway usable. In 1852 the first appropriation was granted for channel improvement. From then on until the Eighties, money was spent continuously to keep the channels clear and navigable. The principal result was magnificent pork-barreling by river communities and spotty attempts at improvement. After the turn of the twentieth century businessmen, community leaders, and navigation lines continued their efforts to deepen the channel along the river's lower reaches, particularly between St. Louis and Kansas City. In

1912 Congress kicked in twenty million dollars to help achieve this goal.

In 1922 Charles G. Dawes, Director of the Budget in the Harding administration, tried to reduce the amount to be appropriated for rivers and harbors, only to have lobbyists talk legislators into restoring the funds. Instead of suffering, those who were interested in correcting the errant river had more money than ever. The parsimonious Coolidge administration recognized a vote potential when it saw one. In the fall of 1925, Coolidge's Secretary of Commerce, Herbert Hoover, talked of a sixteen-hundred-mile waterway from Pittsburgh to Kansas City whose depth would be nine feet. The secretary also recommended the completion of projects on the upper Missouri. The result was more money, particularly for the waterway below Kansas City. From then until Franklin Roosevelt's time in office neared its end, the Lower Missouri area never got less than two million dollars a year in appropriations.

The first major attempt to control the Upper Missouri began in eastern Montana during the early, free-spending days of the New Deal. In 1933 a sum of twenty-five million dollars was handed over to the Public Works Administration for the construction of an earth-fill dam near the Fort Peck Indian reservation. After ten years of effort there appeared a two-mile stretch of dirt and gravel piled two hundred forty feet high equipped with hydroelectric facilities. During 1943, the year the first generators went into operation, there was an unusually destructive flood that covered more than two million acres of land below the dam and damaged five large cities. Congress decided that to control the Missouri's tail was not enough; the whole animal had to be domesticated.

In the spring of 1944 Roosevelt's crotchety Secretary of the Interior, Harold L. Ickes, told his chief that two plans of control had emerged. As a result of the disastrous floods the Army Engineers produced a triple-headed scheme, designed by Colonel Lewis A. Pick, that envisaged a system of levees, some reservoir dams high up the river system, and five major dams on the Missouri itself. The Bureau of Reclamation offered its solution in a plan devised by W. Glenn Sloan of its Billings office. Its first goal was irrigation, with a secondary benefit to be derived in flood control. While it proposed to contain about the same amount of water as the other proposal, the Sloan plan would accomplish it by a series of some ninety reservoirs much closer to the river tributaries' source.

Mr. Ickes reported that while these plans were not identical, he thought that they could be successfully coordinated. The secretary had forgotten his history. For years the War Department and Interior Department had been arch-rivals over various plains problems. Their battles about who would save the Indians had reached dramatic proportions. Now they selected for adoption an equally sullen and dangerous pet: the Missouri River.

Ickes was overly optimistic about "successful coordination." The battle that now broke out between the two agencies of government was loud and acrimonious. It was only when the President suggested to Congress the creation of a Missouri Valley Authority, superseding both plans, that the quarreling brethren suddenly stopped shouting at each other. Aware of a common danger, they sat down at the "Treaty of Omaha" in October 1944 and agreed to compromise, rather than coordinate. With characteristic lack of realism the government permitted them to draw a line down the map, in effect dividing their domains. The fateful 98th meridian, publicized by Major Powell, was the line of demarcation. Waters originating west of the designated boundary would be reserved to that area for "consumptive use." Presumably, irrigation would take precedence over navigation.

Then, as the indulgent father, Congress gave each of the squabbling departments two hundred million dollars to play with, and told them to see what they could do about getting along nicely thereafter. "A shameless, loveless, shotgun wedding," cried the president of the National Farmers Union when he heard of the Pick–Sloan match. But the victors ignored such comments. Unblushingly they proceeded, duplicating wondrously, spending their patrimony like celebrating cowboys. As of 1950 these saviors of the plains had been allotted nearly six and a quarter billion dollars for their hydrological missionary work in the West.

In answer to the shotgun wedding allegations, Mr. Sloan could only protest that at least such a ceremony had occurred and the offspring—flood control and reclamation works—was legitimate. Examination of their brainchild does not yet reveal a particularly lusty creation. More than a decade after the wedding, the projects had added less than twenty-eight thousand new acres to the total irrigated area. Census figures for 1950 showed a greatly increased interest in irrigation on the high plains, but only about a tenth of the newly served acres could be credited to Pick–Sloan projects. Much of the water came from ground water, brought up by electric pumps. On the credit side of the ledger, the Bureau of Reclamation has greatly increased the stability of water supply in areas previously under irrigation, but from the standpoint of a larger picture the Missouri Basin project has been a typically American political extravaganza whose price has been high.

The great interest in the West manifested by the advocates of irrigation and planners of national conservation aroused suspicion among some of the natives. For decades Westerners had complained that their region was an orphan, a forgotten child, neglected by its guardian at Washington and obliged to shift for itself in a cold, hard world. From the time of the first settlers, who cursed the government for its failure to furnish sufficient military protection against the Indians, to the years when the northern plains territories fought for admission into the Union, the feeling persisted that there was prejudice against the West. Then came the government engineers followed by contractors and large payrolls. At first, plainsmen watched with delight as federal funds were lavished upon dams and reservoirs, built to serve water upon thirsty acres. Then followed a period of doubt.

The trouble was, the nation's legislators were a little too enthusiastic in their work. The words *reclamation* and *conservation* were inseparable in the public mind, and the policy of setting aside certain lands to be held in trust for posterity had a great deal of popular appeal. Congress, after years of search for new methods of giving away lands, now turned miser and began withholding tremendous tracts under a policy of reservation. Startled Westerners watched the process with mounting anger and allowed as how Uncle Sam was about the biggest landgrabber they had ever seen—and they had watched some experts at work.

One of the biggest landlords in the new regime was the Forest Service. Roosevelt, in his boundless enthusiasm, became a great admirer of Gifford Pinchot, "the nation's first forester," and he readily approved of Pinchot's plans for timberland withdrawals. In 1902 there were already over sixty million acres reserved and in the next three years another fifteen million were added. As Westerners howled their complaints Roosevelt tried to cover up with one of his famous blanket statements, asserting that the administration had the unbroken support of the people in its policy. In June 1906 a sop was thrown to those who charged governmental monopolization of land. The Forest Homestead Act permitted agricultural use of the lands within forest boundaries that could be proved more valuable for crop-raising than for timber usage. A similar arrangement was made for the extraction of minerals in federal forests. The joker was that much of the land judged by individuals to be more useful for farming or mining was not so regarded by the Department of Agriculture, or its division of Forest Service. Meanwhile, during 1906 the government reserved an additional twenty-one million acres of forest lands.

In 1907 Westerners struck back. Senator Charles W. Fulton of Oregon fastened an amendment to the Agricultural Appropriation Bill that forbade the President to set aside any more national forests in six northwestern states, three of which were Montana, Wyoming, and Colorado. Fulton reflected the views of many trans-Mississippi residents when he argued: "I deny that it is wise public policy that the Government shall engage in business within the limits of a State." Such withdrawal prevented the states from utilizing the lands for their industrial and commercial growth. "They are robbing the State of its resources, hampering it in its development," he charged of the conservationists. The appropriation bill passed with its rider, and the President's enemies appeared to have won a major victory.

Roosevelt acted with characteristic aggressiveness by reserving more than forty million additional acres two days before the new law took effect. He proudly described the feat in his autobiography, saying: "The opponents of the Forest Service turned handsprings in their wrath; and dire were their threats against the Executive; but the threats could not be carried out, and were really only a tribute to the efficiency of our action." By the end of his term, he could well talk about the efficiency of his actions. During his time in office, more than a hundred forty-one million acres of the total one hundred sixty-eight million acres that make up the national forest reserve were set aside.

By the spring of 1910 the opponents of conservation had another opportunity to cripple the movement. During April, Representative Charles Pickett of Iowa introduced legislation aimed at authorizing further withdrawals and approving those already made. President Taft had suggested that this be done in order to make clear the power of the departments to take such action. Western legislators shot up the bill with their oratorical six-shooters, determined to kill it. Senator Clarence D. Clark of Wyoming took the old homestead point of view when he requested that agricultural lands should be excluded from the reserves. "Our view is that the agriculturist who goes upon a piece of land and thinks he can make a home upon it and thrive upon it and raise his children is the best man to determine whether or not the land will make a farm." The arbitrariness of Forest Service officials in determining what land was good for farming still rankled. Colorado's Senator Charles Hughes launched his attack from another direction. Coal lands were being withdrawn, he said, on the theory that monopolistic entrepreneurs were trying to corner them. As a Westerner who wanted to see the region's resources developed, even at the risk of exploitation, he took another view. "I . . . object to the acceptance by well-meaning people of wild stories which are told of wicked men in the West who are pictured as gobbling up these natural resource possibilities and rendering them useless." Weldon Heyburn of Idaho joined his colleague in complaint, crying out: "Conservation to what end? For whom? For what purpose? Conservation against the rights of those who are entitled to enjoy them, or conservation in favor of a strange outside interest that the future may have in these conditions?"

Eastern members of Congress listened in bored silence as the old grievances were aired and then they cast their votes for a nationally popular conservation movement. Once again the West was told what was good for it and, as always, it had to take the medicine prescribed.

While conservationists urged the withdrawal of forest, mineral, and oil lands from the public domain in the interest of the nation's future requirements, a strong movement developed to set aside part of the land purely for recreational purposes. The "national park" idea probably was born beside a campfire in modern Yellowstone Park in the fall of 1870. An exploring party led by General Henry D. Washburn, surveyor-general of Montana, and Lieutenant G. C. Doane of the United States Army spent about a month in the area that year. One night members of the party were discussing the wonders of nature they had seen and some of them speculated upon the wisdom of picking up nearby land for private exploitation of a potential tourist business. Cornelius Hedges, a Montana pioneer who had come west from Yale law school during the Sixties, objected. He thought it should be utilized for the enjoyment of the American people, under public maintenance. Two years later President Grant signed an act creating Yellowstone Park. Nearly thirty-five hundred square miles in extent, it is the largest and probably the best known of the national parks.

Shortly after 1900 other parks were established in the region of the plains and Rockies. South Dakota's Wind Cave Park dates from 1903; Sullys Hill, in North Dakota, from 1904; Mesa Verde and Rocky Mountain, in Colorado, from 1906 and 1915; and Glacier, in Montana, from 1910. The Dakota parks are small and were set aside primarily as game preserves. Glacier Park, fifteen hundred square miles in size, contains without doubt the finest alpine country in the nation, far surpassing Yellowstone in natural beauty. Wyoming's Grand Teton National Park (1929), in the Jackson Hole region, is the West's closest scenic rival to Glacier. Rocky Mountain National Park's four hundred square miles straddle the main range of the Rockies and offer a massive grandeur that has attracted visitors since the 1870s. This park has sixty-five named peaks that tower skyward more than ten thousand feet.

These national vacation spots have been maintained by the Department of Interior's National Park Service since its establishment in

1916.[1] With the development of the automobile and the steady improvement in highways, these vacation spots have attracted a mounting number of tourists each summer. In 1950 more than thirty-two million people visited some part of the national park system. No one has tried to estimate the amount of annual income the western states gain from those who come to look upon the marvels of nature set aside for their pleasure, but most of the residents are well aware that it is considerable. For example, Yellowstone Park alone, during its short summer season, has four times as many people pass through its gates as live in the State of Wyoming.[2] Glacier Park, only a minute part of Montana, has more visitors each season than live in the state—the fourth largest state in the Union in land area. These people know that in the long haul the land so reserved will yield a larger return as tourist attraction than if it had been turned over to their land-hungry forebears.

The national forests are another matter. Much more extensive than the parks, they are set aside as a reserve for future consideration rather than being developed for tourist use. In some western states rather large regions have been blocked off as the "king's preserve." Colorado, for example, has fourteen national forests in addition to cne that crosses over into Utah. The total size is thirteen and a half million acres. About one seventh of Wyoming is considered forest-land, yet almost none of it is privately held. The twelve national forests in this state cover more than nine million acres. Approximately a fifth of Montana, twenty million acres, is tree-covered; of that extent about sixteen million acres are set aside in twelve reserves.

[1] In addition, the Interior Department maintains a number of national monuments, national historic sites, national memorials, and national recreational areas in the region under consideration. Lumped together, there are two in Montana, three in Wyoming, seven in Colorado, two in North Dakota, four in South Dakota, and two in Nebraska.

[2] In 1958 officials reported that for eleven consecutive years more than a million visitors had passed through Yellowstone Park each season. The figure for 1957 was 1,595,875.

Even the plains states of North and South Dakota each have more than a million acres administered by the Forest Service. For the region under consideration, the total acreage controlled or in the process of acquisition by the Forest Service is in excess of forty-two million acres.[3]

Another category of land withheld from the pioneer plowmen was that reserved to the Indians. During the Eighties and Nineties the extent of Indian lands shrank considerably but after about 1910 reservations remained nearly the same in size. For example, in 1881 more than twenty-nine million acres of Montana were under the control of the Indian Bureau. By 1900 this had dropped to nine million and after 1910 it stood at around six million acres, the figure today. Using Montana as the example, this represents about six Glacier Parks taken out for Indian reservations in that state.

By the early Eighties over thirty-six million acres of Dakota Territory were still reserved to the Indians, but that figure now stands at only about five and a half million for South Dakota and less than a million for North Dakota. At present, the total number of acres withheld for the Indians in all seven states here considered is just over fifteen million, with a state like Kansas having less than thirty-five thousand acres of Indian reservations and Nebraska just under twenty-nine thousand. Regardless of the great diminution of Indian lands, states like Montana and South Dakota still have an appreciable area unavailable to the tax assessor.

When Easterners complain about the condition of western highways or of the small amounts of money applied to state-owned holdings such as universities, prisons, museums, or state office buildings, the homefolks get annoyed. Their first reaction is to point to the large amount of land owned by the federal government in Indian, forest, and national park reservations and for other purposes. In the mountain states the federal government is a very large owner. For example, it controls over thirty per cent of Montana, thirty-six per cent of Colorado, and almost forty per cent of Wyoming. When one looks at a large state like Wyoming and notices that less than three hundred thousand people, who have tax access to only about half of

[3] *National Forest Areas,* Department of Agriculture Forest Service Bulletin, June 30, 1956.

their land, must maintain statewide services, some understanding of the problems peculiar to the West are apparent.

Conservationists point out that the situation is not as bad as it is painted. To begin with, thousands of acres in the plains and mountain states are today in federal hands because the government was unable to give them away. The ogre at Washington, D.C., hardly can be charged with hoarding when it tried for three quarters of a century to rid itself of these tracts. Nor can it be fairly accused of preventing state governments from realizing any revenue from the federal domain. True, the lands are not taxable, but the states get substantial amounts of money from lease payments each year. The national forests turn over twenty-five per cent of their gross receipts to local governments. Leased mineral lands pay thirty-seven and a half per cent. Grazing districts, under the control of the Bureau of Land Management, yield twelve and a half per cent of gross receipts, and other lands under that bureau pay fifty per cent. What does this mean in terms of dollars? In 1951 Wyoming received four million dollars from mineral leases; Colorado collected nearly two millions. Added to this, there are indirect benefits. Public-land states get a higher rate of federal highway aid. Whether these federally controlled empires within western states would yield more money if taxed is a question that can be argued. It would depend upon their degree of agricultural or industrial development. During the day of free lands they were not asked for. With the passage of time this condition undoubtedly will be altered.

Westerners are proud of their land; rather than having objections to those who visit it, they are pleased to welcome them. They won't deny that the mainspring of their hospitality arises from tourist dollars, but aside from that there is a perhaps less tangible satisfaction gained from watching strangers admire some of America's most beautiful sights. Few of the natives object to the existence of national parks, for their total acreage is not large in so big a land and they do offer an economic attraction. But federal reservation of forest and mineral preserves continues to be a source of complaint from those who want to exploit resources.

Back in 1913, as the nation left behind the Roosevelt–Taft regimes and watched a Princeton professor move into the White House, a western paper voiced an opinion typical of that held by its readership: "The problem of the West is to get the lands settled and cultivated, the water powers appropriated and developed, and the forests logged and made into lumber. Yet the government is directed by the conservationists in the East to withhold its land, streams and forests from use on the extraordinary ground that the way to make a nation great is to balk and to stigmatize as criminals the men who by their labor and their money reclaim the wastes, populate the wilds and utilize the water powers." [4]

The newsman was hopeful that Woodrow Wilson did not share the Roosevelt and Pinchot enthusiasm for nationalizing the West. He and those who agreed with him must have been happy when the President-elect stated: "A policy of reservation is not a policy of conservation." Even more encouraging to them was the appointment of Franklin K. Lane, a Californian, and Clay Tallman, of Nevada, to the posts of Secretary of the Interior and Commissioner of the General Land Office. The new administration made one attempt to carry out Wilsonian land policies when it passed the Stock-Raising Homestead Act of 1916, providing for tracts of six hundred and forty acres to those who sought additional grazing areas. But it failed to satisfy demands for liberalizing the use of mineral resources. Instead, it continued to withdraw coal and mineral lands, reserving in one case about three million acres of phosphate lands in the mountain states. Critics of Wilson were quick to point out that the conservation policies of Theodore Roosevelt and his successor, Taft, had not undergone any material change with the coming to power of the opposition party.

The return of the Republicans in 1921 and the administration of Harding did not help the West. A typical Westerner, one who thoroughly believed in the exploitation of the region's natural resources, was appointed Secretary of the Interior. But the difficulties into which Albert Fall got himself, with regard to oil reserves in Wyo-

[4] *Portland Oregonian,* January 15, 1913, quoted by Roy M. Robbins, *Our Landed Heritage: The Public Domain, 1776–1936* (Princeton, 1942), p. 380.

ming and California, did nothing to promote the West's claim against the government lands held in trust. Nor did the story of private power companies during that decade. In 1930 the government still owned more than three hundred forty million acres of land, most of it in the arid and semiarid West.

Then came the election of Franklin Roosevelt, a strong conservationist. His Secretary of the Interior, Harold Ickes, not only believed in continuing the policy of governmental control, but in addition he wanted to take out of cultivation about twenty-five million acres of submarginal land then being farmed. His was a policy of irrigation and rehabilitation and of the resettlement of those people who were trying to work inferior lands. Rather than turn over more acres to private enterprise he advocated the enlargement of national parks and forests and the absorption of the remaining 173,000,000 acres of public domain into the government's own western homestead. By 1935 the latter proposal was enacted into law and the remnants of the great national pasture, so long a political football, passed beyond the reach of the individual. Professor Ray M. Robbins concluded: "Thus ended an era. The land of opportunity—opportunity measured in terms of free land—had officially closed its doors."

Perhaps the door was only partially closed. With the return of the Republicans to power in 1953, the business world cocked a hopeful eye upon government real estate and made ready to welcome back the G.O.P. as their Grand Old Patron. Less than two months after Eisenhower's inauguration the U.S. Chamber of Commerce produced, for local distribution, a radio program script called "The Public Lands." It was part of the businessman's campaign to seize natural resources for private exploitation and this particular tract was aimed at the Forest Service. The propagandists tried to shock their readers by reciting such well-known facts as the percentage of land held in the West by the federal government. They compared the figures to those of Sweden— "a country where socialistic ideas are popular"—and triumphantly revealed that by this token we were far more socialistic.

The cries were not without some effect. As Eisenhower's first administration drew to a close the charges of giveaway reached significant proportions, and they might have been even more serious had it not been for the control exercised by a Democratic Congress. Even so, the handouts were large enough to cause public concern. For example, the National Wildlife Refuges, normally inviolate, were opened up to the oil men. In August 1953, Secretary of the Interior Douglas McKay promised to halt this practice, yet between that time and the end of 1955, two hundred seventy-four additional leases were granted by the department. Forest lands in Minnesota and Oregon were turned over to private companies and in Idaho private power won the Hells Canyon contest with the advocates of public power.

The contest is by no means over. In the years immediately ahead the lines of battle will tighten as the demand for further utilization of national resources grows. The Rocky Mountain West, an area called by one economist "America's Last Frontier," will be the scene of increased industrial development as scientific advances shrink national boundaries and oblige America to take another look at what it once regarded as its wasteland. Then the question to be resolved will be one of finding the most equitable and economically sound method of land utilization. The history of America's public land policy does not promise intelligent answers.

Chapter 13 EMPIRE OF DUST

The plains farmer has been doubly cursed by fluctuating rainfall and instability of prices. From the very beginning of agricultural effort in the region these threats to his security have haunted his fight for survival. Bad years brought discouragement and dogged attempts to hang on, hoping for better times. Good years were almost as treacherous. They caused the horn of plenty to erupt with such violence that the hungry agrarian forgot his troubles and, always the optimist, convinced himself that happy days were here to stay. Periods of prosperity almost always resulted in attempts at expansion, high-priced mortgages, and a double-or-nothing attitude about the future.

The era of World War I brought to the plains a boom that overshadowed anything ever seen there before. Old-timers regarded the prices given for agricultural products as preposterous, even downright unbelievable. But they soon got used to the new condition. Many a plains farmer harvested crops of only average yield but their monetary value made things look exceedingly rosy. Even in the northern reaches of the area, in Montana and North Dakota, where harvests were below average, there was prosperity. It was easy to rationalize that there were good years and there were bad years with regard to rainfall. The dry cycle would pass and the rains would come. Meanwhile, the strange conviction grew that somehow high prices were here to stay. And upon this assumption thousands of new acres were put to crop. With demand high, the day of salvation seemed at hand.

The trouble with the Twenties was that the demand for agricultural products faded during a period of industrial boom. Postwar America headed for what Harding quaintly termed normalcy, but the farmers were not included on this expedition. After a brief postwar panic had passed, the nation entered what writers have called the "seven fat years." It was the day of industrial know-how at its best, of the Morris Plan—which introduced buyers to the delights of credit buying—and of paper prosperity whose foundations were built upon financial quicksands. As the stock market rocketed to dizzy new heights and young businessmen romped through hitherto undiscovered fields of financial clover, the farmers sat on the side lines and watched. Nobody seemed concerned over the fact that purchasing power was steadily shrinking in this heyday of mass production and industrial might. When, in 1920, the Northwest experienced a seventeen-percent rise in railroad rates, there was no great uproar, even from the farmers who still felt the effects of wartime inflation. Even the fact that during the preceding four years the price of farm machinery had doubled did not cause much immediate comment. But as the decade of the Twenties proceeded and greatly increased industrial production failed to lower prices on manufactured goods, the effect upon agricultural areas was significant. Faced by sagging farm prices and increased costs, the farmers learned a new word: disparity. To the economists it meant a condition of price and income inequality. To the farmers, it sounded very much like another word they knew: despair.

It was a time of serious difficulty for American agriculture as a whole. European nations made successful efforts at self-sufficiency and that market, so hungry during the war, was soon cut off. Domestic consumption of grain products dropped away sharply as urban America turned to the light lunch, the slim waistline, and nonstarch foods. Prohibition—the "great experiment"—further reduced demands upon grain supplies. Even old Dobbin, the oatburner, was supplanted by automobile and tractor. Suddenly corn, wheat, rye, and other grains appeared to have no buyers.

Once again, the western farmers found themselves in a helpless position. They could do nothing about the world supply of grain, or the office girl's desire to eat salad for lunch, or the disappearance of the horse, or even prohibition. All they could do was what they had tried before: raise more to make up for low prices. And that was, of course, inviting ultimate disaster. Nebraska farmers watched with dismay as wheat dropped from above two dollars in 1919 to a dollar thirty-one a year later, and on down to eighty-three cents by the end of 1921. Their neighbors, the Kansans, suffered a fifty-per-cent decline from the wartime price peak, a slump that kept crop values even below the level of that received by other American farmers during the early Twenties.

Things were no better in Montana and the Dakotas. The price drop, about fifty per cent, struck down banks and business firms that had carried the farmers through the dry years. Credit dried up and pressures for the repayment of loans heightened. Retrenchment was not enough. By 1924 more than five hundred banks in those states had closed their doors. Between 1921 and 1925 half the farmers of Montana were said to have lost their farms through foreclosure. During those years twenty thousand of them failed, a figure representing nearly sixty per cent of all foreclosures in the state's history. "In Jim Hill's county," wrote Joseph Kinsey Howard, "there were 120 foreclosures for every 100 farms—more than one mortgage per farm, or more foreclosures of parcels of land than there were farms—in 1920–25; and half of the county's farm land was seized by creditors. When the wave of liquidation finally ended in the '30's, 90 percent of all the farm mortgages in Hill County had been foreclosed."

During the days when hundreds of small farm-community banks were locked in a death struggle with an unstable postwar financial situation, the Federal Reserve System came along to administer the *coup de grâce*. Suddenly the German menace to world peace was gone, and with it went not only the requests to western farmers to be patriotic and grow more wheat but, also, the demand that they buy Liberty bonds. The Federal Reserve System was alarmed at the large holdings of these bonds by rural banks because they were used as collateral for further borrowing. So the financial agency "set out coldly and deliberately to smash prices, including the inflated agricultural values its wartime credit policy had helped establish; and despite its protestations to the contrary, it did this with brutal haste."

By raising re-discount rates to seven per cent, agricultural paper was squeezed out of country banks. The final wringer was applied through the additional-collateral policy, a device that forced bankers to put up extra security on previous loans. The excuse was that the rapidly dropping value of agricultural paper made the move necessary. Western bankers knew that the farmers' notes were of less value during drought years, but that this was one of the inherent risks, and a better crop next year restored the worth of such paper. This was a point of view not shared by moneychangers in the city. Without any signs of emotion, they turned down the screws and ignored the howls of pain borne in by the west wind.

If there is any quality that has characterized the farmer of the high plains it is that of almost incurable optimism. Straight into the teeth of the economic gale he went, determined that the trouble was only temporary and that sooner or later nature would relent. Where his grandfather and his father before him had expanded operations in the face of falling prices, trying to make up for the loss by increased production, the latter-day frontiersman based his hope on the utilization of modern machinery. By the mid-Twenties plains farmers reasoned that the postwar deflation was due to end, that wet years were upon them, and that given the efficiency of their mechanized methods they could make a living at this ancient game of soil-tilling. As a matter of fact, there was a price upturn about this time, and in states like Kansas the rainfall was about average, but this was not to be enough.

It was enough, however, to make it tempting. Old-timers bought expensive combines, new and more powerful tractors, one-way disks, and anything else that meant farming more acres with a minimum of labor. In addition, there was a new class of immigrants. They were, in the words of Vance Johnson, "the Chicago policemen, the retired schoolteachers, the dentists, the stenographers, businessmen, maiden aunts, and even the plug-uglies who bossed the prohibition-era underworld. . . ." They came, bought land, and "took a flyer," with no intention of staying. Many of them did not last long, but they left behind a new term: *suitcase farmer*. Before the new assault was finished, thousands of acres of sod were ripped up and "shotgunned" into crop. Not since the earliest days had the plowup been so all-encompassing. Between 1925 and 1930 more than five million acres—an area seven times larger than the state of Rhode Island—were torn from the southern end of the plains.

It was not only the suitcase farmers who came, saw, and tried to conquer. Native sons, boys who had grown up in the plains country, were excited by the golden color of wheat. One of them wrote "from the time I was in knee pants my one and only ambition had been to be a farmer." At the age of nineteen he moved onto a place owned by his father in southwestern Kansas, determined to become a wheat king. For almost a decade, in the late Twenties and early Thirties, he pitted his strength against the elements. During most of that period he experienced one disaster after another and when finally the climate favored him, his wheat brought only twenty-five cents a bushel, less than the cost of production. He admitted defeat and surrendered with the remark, "My own humble opinion is that, with the exception of a few favored localities, the whole Great Plains region is already a desert that cannot be reclaimed through the plans and labors of men." [1] His decision to quit came just before the outbreak of World War II, and a new era of inflation prices and wet years on the plains.

In the course of America's history its people have from time to time experienced periods of financial distress and suffering, but no decade of its span stands out more sharply in that respect than the 1930s. All preceding times of economic trouble are labeled panics, violent but relatively short in duration. The Thirties are set aside as the Great Depression, and nothing like that era ever had visited the nation. The trouble was widespread, visiting industry and agriculture alike, and striking at all elements of society in all parts of the land. But it would be hard to find a section of the country that was more persistently bombarded by adversities of every kind than the high plains.

In some western areas the farmers had been in difficulty for more than a decade before the advent of a general depression. They had

[1] Lawrence Svobida, *An Empire of Dust* (Caldwell, Idaho, 1940), p. 203.

fought drought, hail, grasshoppers, high interest, low prices, a growing income disparity, increasing costs, rising taxes, and just about everything else that made life difficult. Then came the national slump of 1929 and another decade of distress. As if this were not enough, the land began to blow away and the Great American Desert surrendered its old title for a new one: the Dust Bowl. Now the agrarians paid the price of ambition. Millions of acres, turned grass side down, swirled off in "black blizzards" more violent than any man ever before had witnessed. Modern methods of shallow tillage left the soil finely pulverized and highly susceptible to wind. Too late, the farmers realized that in some respects they had outsmarted themselves.

Heroic efforts were made to fight even so powerful an enemy as the wind. They tried strip farming. But working the land in alternate strips, giving it a zebralike appearance, gave no sure-fire results. Another means was that of strip-listing, or running deep furrows twenty to thirty feet apart across the path of the oncoming wind with the hope of catching the dust as a snow-fence does snow. It was not enough. The winds were of gale velocity and the furrows proved as ineffective as a sheet anchor in a major storm at sea. Topsoil, seed and all disappeared, leaving only the hardpan, bare and sterile as concrete. In the face of average winds these methods usually worked; but these were not average times on the plains, in any respect.

By the fall of 1932 the people of the high plains and Rockies had reached a point of deep despair. A great many of them concluded that theirs was the most desperate situation yet experienced in that part of the country and they were ready to accept almost any plan that promised action. The leader did not spring forth from among them. This time no William Jennings Bryan appeared to lead a crusade against the bastions of the financially entrenched East. It was a New Yorker, whose only claim to agricultural experience was that of being a gentleman farmer, who pointed out the serious maladjustments in American agriculture and promised to do something about it. To Franklin Delano Roosevelt the fact that twenty-two per cent of the population gained its income from agriculture but received only seven per cent of the national income was sufficient proof of this disparity. He regarded the farmer's diminishing purchasing power as a major factor in the nation's deepening economic distress and made known his intention to take corrective measures if elected. The Westerners—"sons of wild jackasses," as Senator Moses had called them—set aside their suspicions of Easterners long enough to cast their votes for Governor Roosevelt. He offered them a "new deal," and they were more than ready to throw in their old cards and look at a new hand.

Critical situations call for swift and sometimes dramatic measures. The nation's economic health was bad enough during the campaign of 1932, but the winter that followed was worse. Not since the election of Lincoln in 1860 had a people waited so nervously for the inauguration of a new administration. An agricultural capital like Omaha watched with dismay as its grain and livestock markets disintegrated. In early 1933, during the milk strike, the roads leading to the city were picketed by angry farmers to waylay milk trucks and overturn them. Farmers marched upon the Nebraska capitol resolutely demanding relief on farm mortgages. By March 4, Inauguration Day, Westerners shared the nation's tense apprehension concerning the future; all those who could get to a radio gave it strict attention as the new President prepared to reveal his plans.

"This nation asks for action, and action now," Roosevelt told his listeners. Plains communities listened with particular interest when he talked of "definite efforts to raise the values of agricultural products and with this the power to purchase the output of our cities." They applauded when he promised measures to prevent further losses through farm and home mortgage foreclosures. They plucked up courage when he told them "the only thing we have to fear is fear itself." Aside from his references to the solution of problems that plagued the agricultural West, the descendants of early homesteaders liked the new man's courage, optimism, and willingness to experiment. In this respect they found in him a brother.

When Congress met, its first efforts in both agriculture and industry were directed at relief. For the plains, primarily an agrarian region, this meant relief from the threat of foreclosure, from dependence upon local money markets for credit, and—if possible—from the distress occasioned by falling income. The first two problems were attacked at once. During the preceding five years about ten per cent of the nation's farms had been sold at public auction. To alleviate an unfavorable mortgage situation Congress authorized the Federal Land Bank to issue bonds up to two billion dollars, to be issued and used in making new loans or refinancing old ones. It also directed the Reconstruction Finance Corporation to allot the Farm Loan Commissioner another two hundred million for the purpose of making first or second mortgage loans to farmers or for use as working capital. Congress further protected the indebted farmer by passing the Frazier–Lemke–Long Farm Bankruptcy Act, which permitted him to file for bankruptcy without relinquishing possession of his property. As a means of solving the third problem, falling income, Congress passed the well-known Agricultural Adjustment Act.

The Triple A, as it became generally known, was aimed at both immediate and long-term aid. When the new administration took over, wheat was selling for a trifle over sixty-eight cents a bushel and beef for five and a half cents a pound in the New York market. Pork was bringing a little better than seven cents. These were eastern prices. Out beyond the Missouri the return was materially less. When legislators attacked the problem of low prices brought on by surpluses, they addressed themselves to a matter that had plagued the agricultural West for years. What the farm experts now advised was to try something manufacturers had long since discovered: control the output and you control the price. The first AAA tried to do just this. By agreements with individual farmers, not one of whom was coerced, some eight million acres of wheat were removed from the market the first year. The land that became idle was rented by the federal government, the funds for the rental raised by means of a processing tax laid upon wheat at the mills. During the summer of 1933 a premium was offered for all pigs weighing less than a hundred pounds, with the result that about six million of them did not live to a ripe maturity of five or six hundred pounds. Further to reduce the surplus, about a million sows were slaughtered.

This porcine infanticide and birth control brought immediate howls of protest from a number of Americans and constituted one of the earliest condemnations of the New Deal. When Roosevelt talked of action, he meant action. But for America, wasteful as it had been, this ran contrary to the tradition of more and better. William Allen White, to be a leading corn-belt critic of Roosevelt, turned his trenchant pen upon the agricultural planners in Washington. "What is to be done with the young sow of subnormal intelligence and bad home environment—or the headstrong individualist who would set her own impulses above the somber judgment of the Party and insist upon having eight or ten little piggies instead of the allotted six?" he asked.

A young farmer from White's own state of Kansas told of criticism directed at the AAA in his neighborhood. "There were mouthy individuals who seized every opportunity to run down this entire program, talking as long as anyone would listen to them, condemning it as useless, crooked, revolutionary, or dictatorial; but it was noteworthy that when the first AAA payments were made available, shortly before Christmas, these same wordy critics made a beeline to the courthouse. They jostled and fell over each other in their mad scramble to be the first in line to receive the allotment money. . . ." As the farmer remarked, "There were very few wheat farmers who failed to sign under the AAA program." [2]

The immediate relief granted farmers by this means was a lifesaver to thousands of them. Like many another and earlier frontier, cash simply had fled the country. The injection of benefit payments into farm communities affected agriculture and business alike as new life flowed through shriveling financial arteries. Outstanding bills were paid off, equipment received necessary repairs, and seed wheat for a new effort was purchased. Better yet, the farmers naturally set aside their submarginal land and the agricultural effort that proceeded on better parcels had much more chance of normal and steady crop return.

In long-range terms, the New Deal planners tried to control the old bugbear—the eternal surplus. They sought to maintain a balance between production and consumption that would give the farmer a relatively constant and equitable return. In order to restore his purchasing power the Act of May 12, 1933 declared the period of August 1909 to July 1914 as a time when farmers' purchasing power

[2] Svobida, *op. cit.*, p. 45.

was "normal." This desired price was explained in a now-famous word: parity. This was the goal toward which agricultural planners proposed to work.

It was well that they took the long view. The agricultural problem was serious and the maladjustment deep. Money might be poured in as it would have been in the case of local disaster by fire or flood, but this was a palliative, not a cure. Nature's rampage had robbed the high plains people of their earthly belongings and their very spirit to survive. In 1932 the national average price of wheat was only thirty-eight cents a bushel, but for western farmers, who paid the highest freight rates, the per-bushel income was not even this much. By 1935 a quarter of Montana's population was on relief. Cattle ranchers and dry-land farmers alike were broke. Beef now brought a third of what it had only five years earlier and the price of sheep had declined similarly. In Nebraska, where rainfall in the Thirties was subnormal, farm prices had sagged to record lows. Using the parity figure of 100 (based on the 1910–1914 average) purchasing power in that state had slipped to 54, while as late as 1932 costs were up around 107.[3]

At the same time, one county in Colorado had mortgages on its crops that approximated their total probable value, based upon average yields in previous years. Men who had long been successful in the community were on relief. These were not shiftless sharecroppers who had never owned anything before. But in times such as these they could put up no better a front than the most indigent. The great leveler, poverty, had dragged them to the lowest reaches of the economic ladder despite their bravest efforts. These are the things that tear the guts out of a man and leave their mark upon him for the rest of his days. It would take more than a monetary handout to get the patient back on his feet.

But for the moment the emergency called for shots of financial adrenalin straight to the heart. Convalescence could come later. Instead of the upturn that farmers traditionally expected, conditions became worse. During the winter of 1934–1935 drought conditions worsened and even the hardy jackrabbit found life impossible in his native habitat. Thousands of rabbits and birds died that winter, unable to survive the dust and aridity. Then came spring and new dust-

[3] James C. Olson, *History of Nebraska*, Lincoln, 1955, p. 300.

bowl records. Parts of Kansas got no measurable rainfall during the critical month of April and it appeared that once again there would be no crop. May and June offered only a spit of rain here and there, just enough to pluck up hope, but this bit of dampness was quickly erased by searing winds that shriveled wheat in the hull.

The crop season of 1935 will long be remembered on the plains. In short, all hell broke loose as nature reached down to the bottom of its bag for its worst climatic weapons. Dust storms that caused old-timers to shake their heads in amazement swept the countryside, stopping trains, grounding planes, blocking highways, closing schools, and claiming human lives. Day was turned into night, obliging house-holders to burn their lights at high noon. Life came to a standstill. In one college gymnasium the dust was so thick that officials had to halt a basketball game. Scoopshovels replaced brooms on the kitchen floor, bedding was heavy with dirt, and the simple matter of breathing became a problem. It developed into a fight for survival.

When the plains farmer had lost everything else, he fell back upon his sense of humor. It was a quality that had helped to carry his fore-fathers through their times of trouble in this same unpredictable country. Now farmers tried to cheer each other by telling yarns such as the one about the bachelor who utilized the dust storm by holding his pots and pans against the keyhole until they were sandblasted clean, or the pilot who was obliged to abandon his plane and after parachuting out had to spend six hours shoveling his way back to earth. Or the one about a man who fainted from shock upon being hit by a drop of water and was revived only after two buckets of sand were thrown at him. A grim-faced Kansan summed it up when he scrawled upon a dusty windowpane these bitter lines:

> *Ashes to ashes and dust to dust;*
> *The menfolks raved and the wimmin cussed.*
> *Take it and like it; in* GOD WE TRUST.[4]

With grim humor, stubborn faith, and sheer guts, most of the high

[4] I have drawn heavily from Chapters 5 and 6 of Fred Floyd's *A History of the Dust Bowl* (Ph.D. thesis, University of Oklahoma, 1950) for descriptions of the Dust Bowl. Both he and Vance Johnson (*Heaven's Tableland*) recount the examples of humor used here.

plains farmers managed to hang on. Some moved out and sought new pursuits elsewhere. Others took advantage of the government's re-settlement policy, giving up marginal lands for a fresh start in more promising soil. The process was not new. Settlement had come to the country in waves, with the wash of frontier effort eddying and withdrawing during troublous times. But the movement was persistent and a hard-bitten cadre of tillers always remained, ready to welcome and recruit among the uninitiated who were bound to venture forth in better weather. So it was now.

Meanwhile, the federal government bought into the game, confi-dent that the run of bad luck could be turned aside, fearful of national consequences if it were not. There have been many criticisms of the heavy spending that took place and charges that parity prices were unrealistically high. Conservatives, and even some who called them-selves liberals, complained of the wastefulness of haste, of the dupli-cations of effort, of intergovernmental rivalries, of boondoggling. These first charges were heard after times were somewhat better, after the nation began to get its nerve back, and when the immediate crisis had passed. But during that dusty decade when all hope had fled from the plains West, those who stayed behind to fight a rear-guard action reached out for the preferred help and were grateful.

From one point of view the government's AAA program did not live up to the hopes of its originators. The stated objective was to adjust the production of basic crops with the view of obtaining both parity prices and parity incomes for farmers. Despite the withdrawal of land from production and regardless of light crops in particular regions, national surpluses could not be cut sufficiently to drive the price level to parity goals. Compared to parity, or to even the 1929 level, prices were low at the outbreak of World War II in 1939. Dur-ing the decade of the Thirties nonfarm income had recovered some-what from its historic low in 1933, but it was still sixteen per cent lower than the 1929 figure. By the outbreak of the Second World War farm income was even less favorable. It was twenty-four per cent lower than that of ten years earlier, having made a slower recovery from the disastrous year 1933.[5]

[5] Walter W. Wilcox, *The Farmer in the Second World War* (Ames, Iowa, 1947), pp. 8–9.

The plains farmers themselves contributed to the failure of agricultural surplus reduction. Their dustbowl years had taught them a great deal about coping with the tricky climate and little by little they discovered methods of combating the elements. The result was consistently better crops and fewer outright failures.

One of the big lessons learned during the parched years of the early Thirties was the absolute necessity of retaining what moisture nature grudgingly granted them. They used well-known methods, such as that of terracing and contouring and found that unless conditions were at their very worst their efforts paid off in higher yields. Summer fallowing was another commonly known practice. By allowing a tract to rest for a season and cultivating it enough to destroy the moisture-hungry weeds, the probability of a better crop next year was improved. A substantial number of farmers questioned its worth, however, convinced that the added return was not high enough to justify the effort. Frequently these men preferred to till their soil after the harvest, which increased its powers of moisture absorption, controlled the weeds, and checked wind erosion.

More attention was now paid to methods of holding the soil. Listing, already mentioned, was effective against all but the most violent winds. The planting of row crops gave much the same effect as the list furrows in minimizing soil movement and obliged the farmer to engage in a diversification that had other benefits. On a larger scale, strip farming resulted in both diversification and the reduction of wind damage. Added to these efforts was the renewed attempt to halt blowing through shelterbelts. During the 1870s the government had tried, under the Timber Culture Act, to encourage the planting of trees on the plains, but those were days when the farmer wanted more land, not better methods, and the legislation failed. New Dealers, who encouraged the shelterbelts, were confronted by the same fact that had faced earlier planners: trees require more water than the plains customarily receive. However, by locating the trees along roadside ditches, or other places where abnormal amounts of water were apt to collect, the program attained some success. Some seven thousand miles of belts were successfully planted and maintained.

Adversity was a severe and demanding teacher, but through it the farmers of the high plains learned a good deal about agricultural survival during the parched years. Paradoxically, considerable help and encouragement came from the federal government, which at the same time was trying to cut mounting surpluses. So the government, in effect, was opposed to itself and when the AAA fell short of its announced goal it was denounced, not only by the white-collar worker in the East, who had never been on a western farm, but even by many of the dry-land farmers themselves, who suddenly remembered such worthy phrases as "rugged individualism" and "private enterprise."

By 1939 the Roosevelt administration was beginning to entertain doubts about solving the farm problem. Despite colossal and expensive efforts to reduce the surplus, thus raising prices, millions of bushels of wheat and other grains piled up to confront the New Dealers. During the summer of 1938 exports shrank in the face of foreign competition and relatively higher domestic prices. To stimulate exports, large subsidies on wheat exports were now offered. Well over a hundred million bushels went abroad—with the assistance of a twenty-nine-cent-a-bushel subsidy. Again, the planners were merely rubbing salve on the deep sore of permanent surpluses. By the summer of 1939 the world wheat supply was more than five billion bushels, and in the face of that fact the American government continued to stimulate the local market through artificial respiration.

Then in September the Germans' panzer divisions moved into Poland and another world war was under way. This, combined with predictions of a smaller American crop in 1940, acted as a sudden stimulus to the market. By the following spring farmers were receiving seventy-five per cent of parity prices, something they had not expected to experience. This sudden pleasure was temporary. By the spring of 1940, with Hitler's sweep through western Europe and the resulting British blockade of the continent, wheat prices took a downward turn. Before long, however, lend–lease and then America's participation in the war drastically altered the demand picture and soon agricultural leaders were fighting off attempts to place a ceiling on the prices of their products.

For some time the New Deal had offered the farmer a percentage of the parity price as a loan upon his grain, which, in effect, was price support. Now, with wartime demands at a high, the government used this method as an incentive to grow more. The guarantee was set at eighty-five per cent of parity, and soon it was raised to ninety. Prices quickly soared beyond this "floor" and then agriculture was once again walking by itself, unaided by crutches of any sort. For the first time in a decade, it was on its own.

Suddenly, trouble appeared to be over in the plains country. About the time the war broke out Montana and the Dakotas experienced a wet cycle. All during the war bumper crops were raised and sold at prices that farmers had dreamed about for years. According to Bruce Nelson (*Land of the Dacotahs*) the average gross income per farm in North Dakota for the year 1945 was approximately eight thousand dollars. Much the same was true in other plains states. Nebraska's annual average rainfall rose from sixteen inches in 1939 to as high as twenty-seven during the war and postwar years. Corn production soared from around 157 million bushels in 1941 to 261 millions in 1952 while wheat rocketed from thirty-six to over ninety-eight million bushels. Livestock, particularly cattle, grew to nearly four million in number by the war's end, even though hogs and sheep did not respond as readily. Total farm income showed a startling increase in Nebraska, passing the billion-dollar mark after the war. During the Twenties it never reached half that amount. Prosperity also visited neighboring Kansas where, by 1948, price levels had reached 338 per cent of parity, or about forty-one per cent above the highs of World War I.

The new bonanza had old results. The plainsmen became intoxicated by high prices and good crops. Once again they played agricultural poker with the same reckless abandon they had known in World War I. With the appearance of better times and an unprecedented demand, land values shot upward. Land that Colorado farmers had abandoned during dustbowl days sold for forty dollars an acre. In Kansas it brought anywhere from sixty to a hundred dollars. Now there were again winter vacations in California and Florida, or Las Vegas. Money was easy and spending it easier. Those who elected to stay around for the winter moved to town—"sidewalk farmers." Townsmen looked, and blinked their eyes in amazement as the golden harvest grew crisp green currency. Dentists, doctors, lawyers, teachers, and preachers bought in, and the suitcase farmer was back in business. Men who did not know the difference between a farrow and a furrow suddenly became gentleman farmers, determined to make their fortunes from this warborn boom.

Patiently the New Deal had persuaded farmers to give up marginal lands, to plant cover crops in windswept areas, and to refrain from breaking new sod. Owners readily agreed, during the bad years, for the crop to be harvested from the AAA office was much more certain than that offered by the land. Now it was different. Uncle Sam's allowance was a pittance compared to what might be had at the local elevator. In almost every county landholders who had for some time participated in the government's program now got out of that game and turned to something more promising. To soil-conservation districts, where the land gradually had been restored, and to new and unbroken areas, the plowmen turned with the enthusiasm of a hunter stalking his kill. The result: millions of acres plowed up in the old Dust Bowl, a land that had just begun to heal.

Man, in his cupidity, helped to make the Dust Bowl of the Thirties. The federal government spent millions trying to help him rectify the error. Then, when some of the sores were healed over, man could not refrain from picking at the scabs. During the war any soil that would germinate seed was put to use. And after the war, in the day of the Marshall Plan and of economic aid to less fortunate parts of the world, the demand for grain stayed high. So the Westerners kept at their task of ripping up sod, searching for more soil in which to plant. A conservation writer, visiting near Cheyenne Wells, Colorado, in the spring of 1946, watched them at work and remarked: "They were plowing again the land reclaimed from the dust by Government help and sowed back to grass in the 1930's. They were also turning over native sod on shallow soils never before plowed. This was but a sample of the mischief going on in a dozen other localities along a 600-mile front." Disgustedly, he wrote that this had been the situation for a half-century. "Greenhorn settlers have pushed out into the arid plains beyond the established farming zone. They have messed up the place, gone broke, and vacated it to lie idle again until a new crop of suckers got ripe." [6]

The farmers were only partly to blame. Land speculators, their eyes fixed upon a new generation of "pilgrims," were anxious to sell as many acres as possible. Well-financed companies owned land they had acquired at giveaway prices during the Thirties and now they wanted to cash in. In a state like Colorado, where early conservation laws had set up conservation districts, there were restrictions against the plowing up of soil that was too shallow. But absentee owners quickly voted out such strictures and placed upon the market some decidedly inferior farmland at plush prices. The speculators went a step farther when they organized a congressional lobby to obtain legislation looking toward the return to private hands of those tracts purchased by the government for restoration to grass.

Prosperity, and the prospect of quick money, brought back old desires of exploiting everything that could be had. A few moist years and high wheat prices made it hard for greenhorn and veteran farmer alike to appreciate the long view. They were deaf to arguments that during the Thirties about ninety per cent of marginal land sowed to crop was blown out while only eight tenths of one per cent of the best land was seriously damaged by wind. Convinced that this was a coincidence, that it was all past and would never happen again, they plunged ahead in their attempt to pan from the earth a quick fortune —and then get out, if necessary. In the American tradition, they insisted upon the God-given right of free men to go broke, regardless of the greater danger to society.

For a time, during the mid-Fifties, it looked as though the latter-day boomers were going to be frozen out of the game. Most of the region, with the exception of parts of North Dakota and a bit of Montana, was deficient in rainfall during the first half of the decade. Some counties in Colorado and Kansas endured the most severe drought known there to white men, one that exceeded even that of the historic Thirties. Once more the powdered land began to move. In 1954 nearly seventeen million western acres were damaged by wind erosion. Winds in eastern Colorado and Kansas averaged fifty miles

[6] H. H. Finnell, "Pity the Poor Land," *Soil Conservation*, XII, No. 2 (September 1946), p. 27.

an hour for periods up to six hours, with occasional gusts as high as ninety miles an hour. Wheat was ripped out of the ground, tumble-weeds gathered along fences to collect the dust in small mountains as the old Dust Bowl ogre again raised its head. The Soil Conservation Service urged farmers to return some of their fields to grass, to strip-crop, or otherwise to prepare for the worst, as they warned that twenty-six million acres were in a condition to blow during the 1955 season. "Only a near miracle will prevent widespread wind erosion in a parched area extending all the way from West Texas to the Nebraska panhandle," said one reporter.[7] Fortunately for the modern plainsmen, fate dealt out the required near-miracle. Necessary moisture, in the form of rain and snow, came to the region.

This time, however, the farmers had not relied entirely upon rain as an ace in the hole. The Thirties had taught them something, and they now put the knowledge to use. With powerful tractors they dug deep into the soil, turning up clods that kept it from extreme blowing. With newer methods of tilling, contour plowing, terracing, and strip-farming they stabilized the land. The shelter belts of New Deal days gave added protection and cut the damage done by hot winds. During the period of trial they had something else that spelled the difference between ultimate victory and defeat: higher prices.

The farmers knew other valuable things at midcentury. The arid years taught them that rain deficiency was probably more normal than wet cycles and that moisture was a precious commodity, to be hoarded by every known means. It was a game of percentages, one that required a backlog in cash and capital goods to tide one over the rough spots. It had taken a long time to knock out of the plains farmers' heads the notions gained in more humid climates farther east. The economic beating they took during the Thirties did a great deal to change their thinking. It is surprising that the lessons stuck at all, considering the boom times that came during World War II and immediately after. The suitcase farmers, of course, were not interested in such precepts. It was the professional tillers, the men whose lives were dedicated to the high plains country, who profited from the lean

[7] "A New Dust Bowl in West," *U.S. News and World Report*, Vol. 38 (January 21, 1955), pp. 71–72.

years. When the dry years of the early Fifties came along, they were much better prepared for survival combat.

They understood the odds they faced, and there was a better chance than ever to alter them. Long-range weather forecasts were no longer in the farmer's-almanac category. While they were still far from perfect, the predictions were getting better all the time. Even attempts at rainmaking had ceased to be a joking matter. While there was still doubt about the value of extensive cloud-seeding, so far as the plains were concerned, the practice of artificial induction of rain made great strides, particularly through the work of Dr. Irving Krick of Denver.

The political climate was more favorable for the farmers of the Fifties than it had been twenty-five years before. Despite Republican complaints about the New Deal's "socialism," that party went right along with agricultural price supports and the domestic allotment program when it came to power in the election of 1952. With these guarantees, as well as generous government crop insurance, the farmers had backing not available to their plains predecessors. In effect, no matter how long the gamble, the house still furnished part of the chips. It gave the agriculturists an opportunity to experiment with cover crops, to diversify, to utilize flexibility in their efforts, with the knowledge that federal help was ready, in the wings, in case of trouble on the stage.

Such paternalistic interest generated complaints from other members of the national community. In the beginning conservatives, most of whom found their political home within the Republican party, voiced strenuous objections to New Deal attempts at farm aid. They refused to accept the thesis that farming was a special interest requiring special consideration. And they had serious objections to the application of so revolutionary a notion, crying out that the wheel was fixed. In so large a program it was a simple thing to single out instances of duplication, misapplied law, and outright fraud. Election time saw these bits of dirty wash prominently displayed to the public, as the party out of power cried out against the high incidence of graft and the passing of free enterprise.

A change of parties did not materially alter the situation. The

Eisenhower administration quickly revealed that it accepted the assumption of agriculture's special position. The Agricultural Act of 1954 provided a flexible price support, ranging from eighty-two and a half to ninety per cent of parity to be applied to the following year's crop, after which there would be a return to the seventy-five to ninety per cent of parity provided by the Agricultural Act of 1949, passed during the Truman administration. Murray Benedict, writing about the agricultural dilemma, explained that "The new act was a victory for those who favored a more flexible program but it did not change drastically the main features of the farm program." [8] Nor did it silence the howls of complaint from nonfarmers. By the fall of 1957 the Washington bureau of *Look* magazine could charge the Eisenhower administration with "Fraud, Graft and Folly in the Farm Program." Reviewing a quarter-century of government aid to agriculture, the writers alleged that Agriculture Secretary Ezra Benson's department was "the welfare state in miniature, if anything costing almost 30 billion dollars since 1933 can be called miniature."

The attack upon Republican efforts followed the familiar pattern they themselves had once employed against the Democrats. Examples of individual attempts to defraud the government were recited in an attempt to prove the whole notion of supports was wrong. They pointed to the Kansas farmer who leased four hundred and twenty acres of government-owned land from the Corps of Engineers for $1475 and collected $2500 for not growing wheat on the tract. In Saline County, Kansas, a similar incident happened with the rental of a quarter section of the Smoky Hill Air Force Base.

The writers illustrated how the conflict of bounty laws made North Dakota "an Alice-in-Wonderland." In that state the Soil Bank Act paid farmers to reduce their wheat production while at the same time the Durum Wheat Act offered a bonus to those who would shift to that type of wheat. In this situation a farmer in Grand Forks County collected $10,366 for withholding his land, but this did not prevent him from shifting to Durum wheat and increasing his production for 538 acres.

While these particular complainants cried out that there was "Too

[8] *Can We Solve the Farm Problem?* (New York, The Twentieth Century Fund, 1955), p. 275.

much sugar. Too many flies. Not enough flypaper," they admitted that "It's easy to take advantage of a prodigal Government." It always has been. From the passage of the original Homestead Act to the present, government attempts to help the American farmer by land-law modifications and other devices have met with roadblocks thrown out by some of the very people who were to be benefited. This was neither a sign of general ingratitude on the part of the tillers of the soil nor evidence that the profession was undeserving of assistance. Individual examples of human avariciousness inevitably come into play when the opportunity presents itself, and in the American experience the federal government historically has been fair game. Nor is the inclination to chisel confined to sons of the soil.

Regardless of criticisms made of the methods employed, the theory that agriculture is a sufficiently important segment of the American economy to be kept in a healthy condition has prevailed since Roosevelt tried to answer demands dating back to the day of the Populists. As a class, those engaged in agriculture have steadily declined in number and their collective voice is no longer as strong in the national clamor for attention as was once the case. But in an area such as the Great Plains they still represent a minor, if not the major, industry and the welfare of those states involved is largely dependent upon the economic health of the farmers. The government has a choice: it can either assist these people in their gamble against the climatic ups and downs they face, or abandon them.[9] The first alternative may seem expensive. The second probably would lead to a sharp drop in the plains' farm population, certainly reducing such surpluses as in wheat. The question is: Could this segment of producers safely be "mothballed" in time of plenty at the risk of shortages in time of national need? So far, the answer has been *no*.

[9] Another interesting alternative has been suggested: that the government establish "homesteads in reverse," or subsidize farm families who want to move from the farm to some nonfarming type of effort, on the theory that it would be cheaper than to follow the present course. See D. Gale Johnson, "Government and Agriculture: Is Agriculture a Special Case?" *The Journal of Law and Economics,* I (October 1958), pp. 122–136.

Chapter 14

A
LAND
IN
TRANSITION

During the booming Eighties the plains population grew twice as fast as that of the rest of the nation. Within a decade the general rush tapered off and since the turn of this century the area has consistently fallen behind national figures. Between 1920 and 1950 the seven states under consideration could show a total increase of less than seven hundred thousand people. During these years some of them were "carrying" others. In the dry Thirties the Dakotas, Nebraska, and Kansas lost population, a trend North Dakota was not able to reverse even in the prosperous wartime Forties. For the thirty-year period after 1920 only three of the states showed a steady gain in population. All of them—Montana, Wyoming, and Colorado —were mountain states whose economies did not depend as heavily as did the others upon agriculture.

In 1920 the farm population of the region stood at 2,637,316. Thirty years later a decline of nearly a million was revealed; by then only 1,734,030 were engaged in agriculture. With the exceptions of Kansas and Montana, the high point was reached in the census of

1930. The decades of the Thirties and Forties showed the farm population of every one of the states rapidly declining. In 1920 the total regional population was 6,031,968, with almost one in every three a farmer. By 1950 the total was 6,709,827, and the ratio only one to five.

During the 1920–1950 period the urban population grew steadily. In no census did it show a loss, as was the case of the farm figures. During the three decades Colorado's urban population almost doubled, outstripping that of the farm almost four to one. Wyoming's urban population almost trebled, standing in a three-to-one ratio to farmers. In Kansas the urban lead was about two to one. By 1950, only North and South Dakota could show more people on farms than in the cities and there the gap was narrowing rapidly.[1]

Yet agriculture continued to be the principal source of wealth for the region. Despite the declining number of farmers, regional productivity remained high. In 1949 the Missouri River Basin states produced thirty-six per cent of the nation's wheat and forty-six per cent of its rye. At that time it was producing a fifth of the country's meat supply. Omaha, one of the rapidly growing urban centers on the plains, did a larger volume of livestock business than any other market during most of 1952. During these years farm realty values shot upward, nearly doubling between 1945 and 1950.

The explanation for the apparent inconsistency of a farm population exodus in a time of great productivity is to be found in consolidation. As a result of the terrible times experienced in the Thirties, some revolutionary changes took place in western agriculture. Drought years and low prices triggered the movement, but wartime demands for labor that drew men and women from the region, plus the great advance in farm mechanization, resulted in larger farm units. Back in the earliest years of settlement the government prescribed a farm whose size was one hundred and sixty acres. There were attempts to modify the original homestead legislation by providing for additional acreage, laws that proved to be of more advantage to stockmen than to farmers. However, with the coming of more efficient machinery, priced to fit the need of the average landowner, extensive consolida-

[1] Figures taken from *Statistical Abstract of the United States* for the years 1921, 1935, 1944–45, and 1955.

tions took place among the wheat-raisers. By the 1950s the average size of farms along the base of the Rockies was around sixteen hundred acres with those on a broad belt of the plains to the east averaging fifteen hundred. Looking at the Missouri River Basin as a whole, which includes the area of smaller farms in parts of Minnesota, Iowa, and Missouri, the average holding in that drainage was 512 acres at midcentury.[2]

The first big boom in the Rockies, one that brought cities, transportation lines, and the usual contributions of civilization, had mineral origins. While the pick-and-pan days were fleeting, the era of hard-rock mining produced more steadily, contributing to the permanence of settlement and economic stability of a large but unexplored part of the West. As late as the turn of the twentieth century the mines were an important part of the region's annual income. The picture from that time to the present is one of steady decline, except in times of war.

In 1900 the mountain states were producing around fifty-four million ounces of silver a year, or ninety-three per cent of the national yield. By 1930 these states were producing just over forty million ounces a year, a figure that would rise sharply in World War II and then plummet downward again. At the beginning of this century more than two million ounces of gold were being taken out of the mountain area annually. By 1930 extraction of this metal had also fallen drastically, amounting to around seven hundred thousand ounces. A state like Colorado, producing nearly a million ounces of gold in 1900, could show a figure of only 122,000 in 1953. In Montana the decline was similar, and Wyoming's production was so insignificant that the Census Bureau's Statistical Abstract no longer listed a figure.

Coal production was almost stationary, rising slightly in some states, falling in others. This is not particularly significant, with regard to the region's development, because national figures show a decline between 1920 and 1955. The extensive conversion to natural gas and fuel oil, both for homes and for industrial use, as well as for

[2] *Missouri: Land and Water. The Report of the Missouri Basin Survey Commission* (Washington, 1953), pp. 43–47.

transportation, resulted in the closing of a good many coal mines in the region, thus adding to the growing list of mining ghost towns. Colorado, for example, whose available bituminous coal reserves are estimated to be the nation's largest, saw production drop from a figure exceeding ten million tons in 1925 to around three and a half million by 1953. In Montana, the story has been much the same. At the close of 1956 the Northern Pacific Railway announced the liquidation of its wholly owned subsidiary, the Northwestern Improvement Company, whose principal activity for many years had been the mining of coal for railroad use. In its day, the Improvement Company, whose principal mines were at Colstrip, Montana, and Roslyn, Washington, yielded more than a hundred million tons of coal. One hope for the Montana coal industry was the construction of such establishments as the eight-million-dollar electrical generating plant in Richland County which, when completed in 1958, would use local lignite coal as a power source. Except for government demands for such things as molybdenum, tungsten, and uranium, subsurface extractions in general declined. Unless there are radical changes in the region's economy, or great scientific advances furnishing new uses for them, the "older" mineral products probably will continue to be relatively unimportant in the years to come.

The one big exception is oil. That commodity, so well known today, was discovered in Colorado as early as 1862—just three years after Colonel Drake brought in his well at Titusville, Pennsylvania. The Colorado well, drilled near Canon City, was only fifty feet deep. Such a find, far out in a wild and unsettled area, was of limited value, although kerosene and fuel oil were sold in the mining camps and in Denver. By the time the Florence field came in during 1876, transportation facilities had been much improved and the new state of Colorado was considerably more heavily populated than it had been fourteen years earlier. Even though the Florence field was never a big producer, its output has been steady, yielding nearly fourteen million barrels of oil thus far. From 1876 to 1902 it was the only producing oil field in the state.

By the early 1920s major oil discoveries were being made in both eastern and western Colorado. The Wellington dome, near Fort Collins; the Moffat dome, south of Craig; the Tow Creek field in Routt County; and a number of others came in during that decade. Colorado's plains country saw its first major oil production in 1930 with the development of the Greasewood dome in Weld County. During the rest of that decade there were occasional profitable explorations, but from 1938 until 1943 no major discoveries were made in Colorado. In 1945, with the assurance of a pipeline outlet the Rangely field, discovered more than a decade earlier on the western slope, saw a great deal of activity. The real postwar oil activity came with a find made by the Ohio Oil Company in western Nebraska. It was sufficiently rich in commercial possibilities to touch off a wave of leasing in both Nebraska and Colorado. By the mid-1950s Colorado was producing in excess of thirty-six million barrels of oil a year. The importance of the burgeoning industry was recognized in 1953 when a severance tax was placed upon the product so that the local government might benefit from this valuable resource.

The presence of oil in Montana was known almost as early as in Colorado. In the late summer of 1864 members of an emigrant train were repairing a dried and shrinking wagon wheel along the Bozeman Trail, a few miles from the Bighorn River, and in searching for a nearby water supply some of the men came across a pool covered by a thin greasy coat. Delighted at finding both oil and water at this pioneer filling station, the men skimmed off enough of the lubricant to use on their wagons in lieu of axle grease, then presumably continued on in search of gold, leaving behind a resource that would one day be the state's real treasurehouse.

Sixteen years later a prominent cattleman, Granville Stuart, now searching for gold in the form of beef on the central Montana ranges, observed that "There are petroleum indications all through here and some day Montana will produce oil, but it is worthless now." Not until around 1900 was there any attempt at extraction and even here, in the Kintla field along the western edge of present Glacier Park, the result was disappointing. As in the case of other mineral searches, prospectors kept digging away, determined to uncover the liquid treasure. In the spring of 1902 a miner searching for copper found oil just across the continental divide from the Kintla field, near St.

Mary lake. Drilling equipment was brought in and, to the amazement of the workmen, oil was found in quantity at a mere five hundred feet. Within a short time the high slopes of the Rockies experienced Montana's first oil boom. But, like the earlier placer mining ventures, the "diggin's" began to play out; difficulties of water seepage were encountered, capital became scarce, and the excitement died.

Despite initial discouragement, oil prospecting continued. The Great Northern Railway's partial conversion from coal- to oil-burning locomotives after 1910 promised a local market for the product. Development of the Elk Basin field in northern Wyoming and in southern Montana indicated the presence of large reserves and encouraged the emigration of a number of wildcatters from other regions into the latter state. One of the best known of the early high plains fields had its origins in the discovery of petroleum in a water well drilled at the Miller ranch north of Shelby in 1912. Strangely, yet one might almost say characteristically, the obvious was ignored as the search continued elsewhere. Almost a decade later Gordon Campbell, a petroleum engineer who had gained considerable experience not only in Oklahoma, Wyoming, and Canadian fields but also in central Montana, sank a well on the Miller ranch. Early in the spring of 1922 his well came in and the Kevin–Sunburst field, for years to be one of Montana's most productive, was born.

The depression years, characterized by a scarcity of risk capital and a declining demand, meant a slackening of oil activity throughout the state. But the coming of World War II sharply stimulated this industry, just as it did all others, and production figures shot upward. After the war there was only a momentary decline. With the relaxing of price controls and a consequent price rise, oil prospecting received new impetus in undeveloped areas, while old fields were worked intensively. By 1949, Montana oil output for the first time exceeded the value of copper production. Then came the well-known Williston Basin boom. Although there had been talk of oil resources near the Montana–Dakota line for over thirty years, drilling results during that period had not been encouraging. Not until the spring of 1951 was a real producer brought in; even then the drillers had to go nearly twelve thousand feet to get a satisfactory flow.

The opening of the Beaver Lodge field at Williston in western

North Dakota was, as the management of the Northern Pacific Railroad told its stockholders, "of great importance to your company." Since the road had fee title on mineral reservations, including gas and oil, to more than three million acres in a belt crossing the basin, the company's enthusiasm over the find is understandable. The development was of importance not only to the Northern Pacific but also to the individual owners of a vast stretch of country covering parts of North Dakota and Montana. A few months later, the magnitude of the find was revealed when the Shell Oil Company brought in a heavy producer about fifty miles northwest of Glendive, Montana, followed by important discoveries south of the city that fall. During the following year the number of wells increased by twenty-four, including some in the vicinity of Baker, Montana.

By the end of 1952 it was apparent that an enormous supply of oil had been found and Montana and North Dakota were promised an important place in that industry during the years to come. The Shell Oil Company's well in the Cabin Creek area of Montana, brought in during 1953, indicated a tremendous potential. The Sun Oil and Phillips Petroleum Company went down almost thirteen thousand feet that year, near Sidney, and got a producer. A decade after World War II Montana was producing nearly twenty-two million barrels of oil yearly, a figure that was 146 per cent above the 1946 figure. Although this was by far the greatest production in the state's history, it was less than one per cent of the total United States output. That figure probably would grow. Despite the fact that the mountain West is still faced by the old transportation bugaboo of high haulage costs from a remote area, the high costs of long transmission lines, the lack of large population centers, the great risk involved in prospecting (in 1955 approximately ninety per cent of Montana's wildcat wells drilled were dry), the development goes on. The potential exists and as national petroleum and natural gas demands grow the northernmost section of the high plains will undergo even greater change.

Wyoming's oil industry, like that of Montana and Colorado, got off to a slow start because of its great distance from markets. Considerable interest was manifested in the state's petroleum capacities after 1908 when the Salt Creek dome's productivity became widely publicized, although the presence of oil in the area had been known since the days when some of the former mountain men used to mix it with flour and sell the product as axle grease to passing Oregon Trail emigrants. By 1912 the state was producing in excess of a million barrels annually, a figure that was to top thirteen million by the end of World War I, giving Wyoming sixth place in national rankings. The principal limiting factor was the high percentage of fuel oil that remained after gasoline and kerosene were extracted from the crude by normal refining practices. It amounted to nearly sixty per cent. There was no industry in the region that needed large amounts of fuel oil and it was competitively impossible to transport it into the Midwest for sale.

The Standard Oil Company of Indiana had a cracking process that was capable of extracting gasoline from the heavy fuel oil and it was not hard to induce the company, in 1913, to set up refineries at Casper. The company saw that transportation and distribution costs to its western markets could be cut by this means. Local companies, like the Franco Petroleum Company and Midwest Oil, agreed to furnish the necessary fuel oil, happy to have such an outlet.

Like many another western town blessed by sudden prosperity, Casper experienced boom times. While the local paper predicted a rise of two hundred per cent in real estate values there were other and more meaningful measures of economic well-being witnessed by the local gentry. One of them, Harry Iba, whose royalty checks had been quite large, unconsciously illustrated Casper's transition from a sheep town to one of more generous financial proportions when he complained: "The night before last the police raided one of those whorehouses down on the sand bar. They caught me and four other fellows. They fined all of them $5, but they fined me $100!" [3] Harry had made the discovery that from a monetary standpoint he was no longer just one of the boys, and that the West was changing.

The new prosperity reached out beyond Casper. Expansion of operations by Midwest (reorganized and then called the Midwest Refining Company) and by Standard Oil, as well as the increased national demands during World War I, sent exploration parties out in

[3] Harold D. Roberts, *Salt Creek Wyoming: The Story of a Great Oil Field,* Denver, 1956, p. 103.

all directions. There were promising developments in both Carbon and Albany counties, particularly in the Rock Creek field. Meanwhile, the boom continued in the original Salt Creek field, an area that in 1923 alone produced over thirty-five million barrels of oil, or just short of five per cent of the nation's total crude production. Then, as in the case of so many other fields, a decline set in. By 1927 the figure had dropped to fifteen million barrels; three years later it was just above ten million; by 1939 under five million, where it leveled off for the next two decades. However, extensive development and new explorations sent Wyoming's total crude production to new heights. It increased from just over twenty-five million barrels in 1940 to over ninety-three million in 1954,[4] a figure that again neared five per cent of a soaring national production. While this amount greatly exceeded that of neighboring mountain states, it was considerably short of that produced in Kansas, a plains state usually thought of in terms of grain-raising.

By 1957 the seven northern plains states were producing over 335 million barrels of oil a year, with Kansas and Wyoming leading, but there was some gloom in the industry. Production costs were steadily rising. New depth records were being set as drillers probed down nearly fifteen thousand feet in North Dakota and beyond seventeen thousand feet in Colorado. While these were not national records, they represented new depth figures for those states [5] and, in terms of money, meant enormous outlays. Added to this was the growing cost of prospecting. Tremendous investments had failed to develop anticipated oil and gas reserves.

So far as the mountain states of the West were concerned, two large potentials provided hope for the future. According to statisticians, the United States has produced and consumed more than fifty-five billion barrels of oil to date. For the entire world, the figure is around ninety-five billion. Oil men estimate that reserves of American oil shale and bituminous sand have a potential of many times that of ninety-five billion barrels. It is their belief that between 1957

[4] Robert W. Birch, *Wyoming's Mineral Resources* (Laramie, 1957), p. 155; *The Mineral Industry of Wyoming*, Bureau of Mines, Minerals Yearbook, 1954 (reprint), p. 8.
[5] *The Oil and Gas Journal*, Vol. 56, No. 4 (January 27, 1958), p. 153.

and 1977 crude-oil production in the United States will reach its peak and then slowly decline. At that point, provided methods of extraction are perfected, oil shale (laminated sedimentary rock) will provide a principal source of energy. At midcentury, refining costs were too high to make commercial production practicable. The deposits are nevertheless of great importance to the mountain West, for the Green River formation, particularly the Piceance Creek Basin of northwestern Colorado, has a potential of nearly one *trillion* barrels of oil.[6]

The second possibility lay in the ancient fuel, coal. Through the hydrogenation of this product, enormous amounts of petroleum products can be recovered. Another approach, being studied in the laboratories of the Denver and Rio Grande Western Railroad since 1955, is the atomic bombardment of coal particles, reducing them enough to be dispersed into oil. The BTU content of a pound of coal is approximately that of a pound of fuel oil. If the lower-cost coal could be thus utilized, mixing it with oil, a considerable price advantage would accrue to the user. The railroad estimated that if it could reduce the cost of its fuel oil only a penny a gallon, a saving of as much as four hundred thousand dollars a year could be realized. Should either or both of these methods of utilizing coal be made practical, the enormous reserves of Colorado, Wyoming, and Montana would again be very important to western economy. Here, in effect, is a new scientific frontier.

From the very beginning, the economy of the plains and Rockies was essentially extractive. Men came to trap furs, to mine gold, to graze their cattle upon free land, to cut timber, or to speculate in land. They planned to make their pile and go home. Those who came last tried to farm an arid, forbidding land. Some of them had to go home. Others couldn't afford it; they had to stay. As time elapsed, the initial excitement wore off and the country underwent a political and economic domestication, boasting of states, counties, and cities, just like the East. The westward rush lost its momentum and as the

[6] Fred L. Hartley and Claude S. Brinegar, "Oil Shale and Bituminous Sand," *The Scientific Monthly*, Vol. 84, No. 6 (June 1957), pp. 275–289.

nation's population movement sought equilibrium, the West's growth leveled off. With the inflationary aspects of furs, gold, silver, cattle, and land promotion absent, there was nothing left to do but settle down and try to live like other American farmers and burghers.

Here's where the trouble began. Capital had not been hard to attract when the mines promised great fortunes through the use of expensive machinery, or when the beef bonanza yielded a monetary return far higher than other speculative ventures around the globe. Even the early railroads sold their bonds easily in faraway money markets as investors clamored to "get in on the ground floor" in this new country. But when this excitement had passed there was great difficulty in persuading investors to participate in building up such ordinary things as commerce and industry in remote and forbidding places whose population showed little promise of continued growth.

By the middle of the twentieth century several things were obvious. For fifty years after the frontier was said to have been closed, almost no great metropolitan centers had emerged. True, the drift was from the farm to the city, or from the farm out of the country entirely, but the shift from rural to urban living did not mean the growth of large urbanized areas—cities of fifty thousand or more in population. In a spirit of near-desperation small western towns tried to attract industry, offering free land for construction sites or tempting management with stories about the depressed condition of labor and the absence of strong labor organizations. Local businessmen lost no opportunity to gain government establishments for their towns and in the period following World War II, when highly vulnerable defense plants, both governmental and private, sought remoteness, these latter-day promoters were rewarded. But even this was not enough. As before, the nation's growth outstripped that of the plains states.

There was some growth, of course. In the twenty years following 1929 the retail sales of the region trebled, but so did those of the nation. Between 1940 and 1950 only Colorado approached the national average increase in building dwelling units. Its increase was almost parallel, at twenty-three per cent. But places like Nebraska, North Dakota, and South Dakota could show increases of only between seven and eight per cent. Parts of the region fared better than others. Occasionally communities along major railroads were blessed by industrial development. In 1953, for example, construction of a distribution center for grocers and produce was commenced at Denver by a nationwide chain of retail food stores. It was to cost fourteen million dollars. The same organization planned to spend ten million for a similar plant in Omaha. The following year a million-bushel-capacity grain elevator was built at Topeka, Kansas, at a cost of about six hundred thousand dollars. At Menoken, Kansas, work was started on a battery of concrete tanks to be used for the storage of dehydrated alfalfa pellets. This would put an additional million dollars worth of industrial money into that plains state. About the same time a two-and-a-half-million-dollar aluminum rod and wire mill was under construction at Great Falls, Montana. But these were scattered instances and, while they were extremely welcome to the region, they did not—could not—create the degree of economic change the natives desired.

Perhaps some western ambitions have been false. Since the coming of white settlement the apparent desire of the young and struggling communities has been to "walk just like Daddy." Men and women brought west with them an eastern heritage, nurtured in another climate, another geography, another economy. The earliest settlements tried to look like the towns "in the States," boasted about the trappings of civilization available in remote places far west of the Missouri, struggled to copy the economic patterns cut by their forebears in Ohio, Pennsylvania, or Massachusetts. As transportation and communication facilities were perfected, bringing not only railroads, but modern highways, airlines, radio, and television, Westerners found that they were more than ever subject to the ideas, business methods, and social fads of the East. Their desires to "fit the pattern" turned into a necessity, or an apparent necessity. More than ever they tried to conform, to copy.

The result? They lost their identity. One serious student of western history has correctly called the plains region "voiceless." [7] He observes: "There is abroad in the region a general belief that when vested interests of national scope wish to test the nature and intensity of public awareness 'the thing to do is to try it out on the residents of the Plains.' Sometimes this reaches into legislative halls as at-

[7] Carl F. Kraenzel, "The Great Plains, Voiceless Region," *Montana: The Magazine of Western History,* Vol. 8, No. 1 (Winter 1958), pp. 42–49.

tempted legislation. Evidence for this is cited in the form of repeated attempts to get states to pass discriminatory tax legislation against farmer and rancher cooperatives; or to saddle 'right-to-work' laws on an unsuspecting public in predominantly agricultural states; and to petition for rate hikes in public utility enterprises." Why? Because these people are sufficiently voiceless nationally to render their complaints unimportant. The answer: the development of larger cities, places that can make their wants known. Or, sufficient cooperation on a regional plane to put force behind the needs of the "stepchild."

A century and a half after the return of Lewis and Clark to St. Louis, many residents of that country traversed by them on their way west had a feeling of lingering dissatisfaction with their historical development. The great Missouri River Valley and the millions of acres into which the fingerlike tributaries to the principal river reached, covering a fan-shaped empire extending southward from the Canadian line into central Colorado and Kansas, had in many respects failed to live up to its promise. Or to the promises white men had made for it. Few individuals, and certainly no chamber of commerce, would be willing to admit disappointment in the region's progress, for these are matters about which no loyal native would talk. Perhaps what *is* talked about is evidence that something is missing.

The nineteenth century had scarcely expired before the mourning commenced over the passing of the frontier. There were lamentations that the "good old days" were gone, that the time of high adventure and excitement in trapping, gold mining, open-range cattle raising, stagecoaching, steamboating, and railroad building were no more. It was perfectly true. What remained was the unromantic task faced by the homesteader, a drab, heart-rending lifetime of scratching at an unfriendly and treacherous soil. Or the deadening routine of small-town business in some flatland agricultural community, unrelieved by any excitement greater than defalcation by a local bank clerk whose impatience overcame him, or the maritally unblessed pregnancy of a neighbor's hired girl who suffered from the same difficulty.

Thus passed the monotonous years, brightened only briefly by the hell-raising Populists, years when the nation fought a short but exciting war with Spain, soon thereafter graduating to participation in a first-class international brawl with the Kaiser. Years when the world and the nation passed by the high plains country, no longer interested in exploiting a land from which the best had been taken. In many respects, it was a land forgotten, a land whose bright baubles had once titillated a legion of adventurers, but now a place of plows and of little towns that looked like all other little towns, except that nature's violence left them a little more faded and uninviting. It is small wonder that western communities began to talk about their glamorous past, even those which never had one.

All of America contributed to this development. Very early in the present century, at a time when much of the West was still in civilization's swaddling clothes, writers like Owen Wister and a whole school that followed him began to preach the glories of a recently demised day of the open range. From then on, first by means of the printed word, engraved upon pulp or slick paper, then through the medium of celluloid in a legion of movie palaces, and finally (and often again) through millions of television sets, the glories of "the old West"—which really wasn't old at all—were depicted. The national acceptance of this era as an integral part of its folklore fascinated Westerners to the extent that they, like retired athletes, tended to live in the past and neglect the present. And like so many of these public heroes, spoiled and pampered under a glare of publicity, they grew resentful when the material things of life were somewhat harder to come by. In short, as the days of easy gain and inflationary growth faded, the plains and mountain West became petulant over its inability to develop as fast as it had, or even as fast as the rest of the country. The petulance deepened into a feeling of neglect, discrimination, and then of defensive inferiority. The result: loud talk, conversational smoke screens, and exaggerations about the region's virtues.

Ladd Haystead, in his book *If the Prospect Pleases: The West the Guidebooks Never Mention,* had a point when he asserted that Westerners had oversold their region to the rest of the nation and to the world. Quite within the American tradition, they have advertised their part of the land as one having the biggest, the longest, the highest, the purest, the best, whether it be the size of its states, its magnificent distances, its mountains, its water, or its climate. When modern mountain men return from visiting the East, they speak long about the number of sunless days they spent there and what a contrast is the bright, cloudless sky and bracing atmosphere along the Rockies. Yet, as one promising young lawyer remarked, giving away the whole secret: "I surely wish some of my colleagues back East could come out here and enjoy this climate. Too bad there's no way for them to make a living." Or, as teachers and college professors are informed, when administrators apologetically discuss the low salary scale: "Why, you get at least fifteen hundred dollars a year in climate alone."

Western writers have gained great regional popularity by literary bulldogging of local corporate monsters, particularly those controlled by eastern interests, and decrying the fate of badly abused, down-trodden hinterland that stands in the position of a colonial appendage. The late Joseph Kinsey Howard's *Montana: High, Wide, and Handsome* made him the darling of a good many Montanans when he berated the Anaconda Copper Company (which, indeed, it needed) and the Montana Power Company (ditto). Later, when he tried to soften the blow in an article written for *Harper's,* some of his acquaintances sadly shook their heads and allowed as how "Joe must have gone over to 'the company.' " Morris Garnsey, a University of Colorado professor of economics, took a somewhat similar line in his *America's New Frontier,* entitling one of its chapters "The Betrayal of the Western Liberal Tradition," wherein he punished special interests and asked for a stronger government. Wendell Berge, an assistant attorney general in charge of the Antitrust Division of the Department of Justice, argued the case in his *Economic Freedom of the West,* published by the University of Nebraska. So did the journalist A. G. Mezerik, a lifelong resident of the East, in a work he entitled *The Revolt of the South and West.* To this list of studies might be added Bruce Nelson's *Land of the Dacotahs,* a book that struck hard at outside exploitation of a new land.

Carl Kraenzel, the Montana State College rural sociologist, after years of study, made available his thinking on these matters in an excellent volume, *The Great Plains in Transition.* He separated himself from those who merely complained by taking a hard look at the shortcomings of his region and offering some blunt advice for the future. He did not entirely escape the same feeling of maudlin sympathy for the oppressed as seen by other regional writers. He called the plains residents "pawns" and said that "Twice, in the last two world wars, the residents of the region have patriotically overextended themselves to raise bumper crops, each time with the help of more than the usual amount of rainfall. At present [1955] these residents are in the second postwar period of painful readjustment to the decline in such production, a decline made more pronounced by a reduced precipitation. Since the economy of the Plains is chiefly agricultural and without local controls to govern price or volume of production as there are in the case of many industrial areas, the residents are at the mercy of forces outside the region."

Kraenzel, however, was not content to lament the sad state of affairs arising from outside pressures. He asked his fellow plainsmen to think in terms of adjustment to their climatic situation and to work toward the development of their homeland on a regional basis, relying more upon each other rather than looking outward for help. In a nuclear and rocket age, when a good many men have not yet adjusted to the steam engine, it was, perhaps, asking too much to hope that "humid-minded" Americans could make a successful transition to life in Walter Prescott Webb's recently revived "Great American Desert," [8] but that, in all truth, is the requisite.

In short, it's time Westerners quit kidding themselves, stopped believing television "westerns," gave up the affectation of cowboy boots, abandoned ancestor worship, and took a long look at the future. If they want to read their own history, well and good, so long as they see in it a land that once had furs, minerals, and free grazing land to offer a group of hardy entrepreneurs who came, saw, conquered, and frequently got out. What was left was that which could not move, the topsoil itself—and during the days of the Dust Bowl even this was a question. Modern residents might do well to stop studying the census figures, boasting about each minute increase, trying to conceal each decrease, and to recognize the facts of economic

[8] Walter Prescott Webb, "The American West: Perpetual Mirage," *Harper's Magazine,* Vol. 214, No. 1284 (May 1957), 25–31.

life. They live in a part of the United States that is, and always has been, remote. It has no oceans, no great navigable rivers, no semitropical nor humid climate—and it won't have. It costs a lot to haul goods in and out; it always has. When the nation expands to such an extent that people are squeezed out of more economically favorable climates, or when the desperate needs of dispersion for defense dictate it, or when scientists make cornstalks grow where sagebrush now struggles for life, the region will enjoy a natural development. Not before. Meanwhile, those who live west of the 100th meridian might as well cease to "look before and after, and pine for what is not," realizing that it is up to them, not the land, to make the necessary adjustments.

BIBLIOGRAPHICAL ESSAY

IN A BOOK of this kind the material comes largely from monographic sources. The sweep is so general, and it covers so much space and time, that to burrow very deeply into original materials is to run the risk of losing the whole perspective in an avalanche of minutae. In most cases I have used the standard accounts, well known to historians, but less familiar to the general reader. Where these were lacking in detail, periodicals, newspapers, and government documents were consulted. I have also drawn upon information gathered over the years and incorporated in previous writings, such as *Westward the Briton* (1953), *William Tecumseh Sherman and the Settlement of the West* (1956), and that to be included in a forthcoming railroad volume about the Denver and Rio Grande Western. Original research done on these projects, as well as for some thirty articles about the region, found its way into parts of this study.

The following books are some of those I found useful. They will be of interest to anyone who would like to use this book as a point of departure for further investigation.

Section I

By far the most complete study of the Missouri River country prior to American occupancy is Abraham Nasatir's *Before Lewis and Clark*. Two volumes. St. Louis: St. Louis Historical Documents Foundation; 1952. The handiest reference to the Lewis and Clark expedition is Bernard DeVoto (editor), *The Journals of Lewis and Clark*. Boston: Houghton-Mifflin Company; 1953. It is a compression of

Reuben Gold Thwaites' eight volumes entitled *Original Journals of the Lewis and Clark Expedition*. The De Voto volume is useful for the reader who wants to dip into the account of the explorers. Its introduction furnishes considerable background for the account. The Pike expedition is entertainingly covered in W. Eugene Hollon, *The Lost Pathfinder: Zebulon Montgomery Pike*. Norman: The University of Oklahoma Press; 1949. There is no satisfactory study of Major Stephen Long's trek west. A number of accounts by early travelers are available. Henry Marie Brackenridge, *Brackenridge's Journal of a Voyage Up the Missouri in 1811* is found in Reuben Gold Thwaites, *Early Western Travels 1748–1846*. Cleveland: The Arthur H. Clark Company; 1904. Volume 6. Another is John Bradbury, *Bradbury's Travels in the Interior of America, 1809–1811*. Cleveland: The Arthur H. Clark Company; 1904.

Two standard general works about the fur trade are Hiram M. Chittenden, *The American Fur Trade of the Far West*. Two volumes. New York: F. P. Harper; 1902; and Charles Larpenteur, *Forty Years a Fur Trader on the Upper Missouri*. Edited by Milo Quaife. Chicago: F. P. Harper; 1898 (Lakeside Edition in 1933). Harrison C. Dale, *The Ashley–Smith Explorations and the Discovery of the Central Route to the Pacific*. Cleveland: The Arthur H. Clark Company; 1918, treats the progress of the fur trade until 1822 in the first section of his book. More general is Isaac Lippincott, *A Century and a Half of Fur Trade at St. Louis*. St. Louis: Washington University Studies, III (April 1916). W. A. Ferris, *Life in the Rocky Mountains*. Denver: The Old West Publishing Company; 1940, is a contemporary account. The best book on Astor is Kenneth Wiggins Porter's *John Jacob Astor: Business Man*. Two volumes. Cambridge, Massachusetts: Harvard University Press; 1931. See also Arthur Douglas Howden Smith, *John Jacob Astor: Landlord of New York*. Philadelphia: J. B. Lippincott Company; 1929. John G. Neihardt, *The Splendid Wayfaring*. New York: The Macmillan Company; 1924, tells of the exploits of Jedediah Smith, of the Ashley–Henry men, and of the explorations of the central route to the Pacific during the years 1822–1831. The best and most recent biography of Jedediah Smith is Dale L. Morgan, *Jedediah Smith and the Opening of the*

West. Indianapolis: The Bobbs-Merrill Company; 1953. J. Cecil Alter's *James Bridger: Trapper, Frontiersman, Scout and Guide.* Salt Lake City: Shepard Book Company; 1925, is the standard work on "Old Gabe." Charles L. Camp (editor), *James Clyman: American Frontiersman, 1792–1881.* Cleveland: The Arthur H. Clark Company; 1928, is a good companion piece for the Bridger book. Others are Burton Harris, *John Colter: His Years in the Rockies.* New York: Charles Scribner's Sons; 1952; and Stanley Vestal, *Joe Meek: The Merry Mountain Man, A Biography.* Caldwell, Idaho: The Caxton Printers, Ltd.; 1952. Vestal's *Mountain Men.* Boston: Houghton Mifflin Company; 1937, is a more general account of the trapping profession. The story of one of the more successful businessmen in the fur business is told by John E. Sunder, *Bill Sublette: Mountain Man.* Norman: University of Oklahoma Press; 1959.

Books about "The Way West" are legion. Here are some that are readable and informative: Dorothy Gardiner's *West of the River.* New York: Thomas Y. Crowell Company; 1941, is popularly written. See also Ina Faye Woestemeyer, *The Westward Movement.* New York: D. Appleton-Century Company; 1939; and Rufus Rockwell Wilson, *Out of the West.* New York: The Press of the Pioneers; 1933. Older works include James Christy Bell, Jr., *Opening a Highway to the Pacific, 1838–1846.* New York: Columbia University doctoral thesis; 1921; and Cardinal Goodwin, *The Trans-Mississippi West (1803–1853).* New York: D. Appleton-Century Company; 1922. An exceptionally fine volume, and one relied upon heavily here is Everett Dick, *Vanguards of the Frontier.* New York: D. Appleton-Century Company; 1944. LeRoy R. Hafen (editor), *Overland Routes to the Gold Fields, 1859.* Glendale, California: The Arthur H. Clark Company; 1942, describes plains travel, while the way west by water is well treated in Louis C. Hunter, *Steamboats on the Western Rivers.* Cambridge, Massachusetts: Harvard University Press; 1949. Floyd Benjamin Streeter, *The Kaw: The Heart of a Nation.* New York: Farrar & Rinehart, Incorporated; 1941, is one of the Rivers of America series and is useful for a description of early Kansas. For a contemporary account see C. B. Boynton and T. B. Mason, *A Journey Through Kansas With Sketches of Nebraska.* Cincinnati: Moore,

Wilstach, Keys & Co.; 1855. More detailed information is plentifully
supplied by the *Collections of the Kansas State Historical Society* and
the *Kansas Historical Quarterly*.

Section II

A good single volume on the gold-mining frontier of the high plains
and Rockies is yet to be written. Information has to be picked from a
number of works. Some of them are: Granville Stuart, *Forty Years
on the Frontier* (edited by Paul C. Phillips). Two volumes. Cleveland: The Arthur H. Clark Company; 1925 and 1957. The memoirs of
an early Montana pioneer and miner; a gold mine in itself. Harold
E. Briggs, *Frontiers of the Northwest*. New York: D. Appleton-Century Company; 1940, has a section on mining, taken largely from William J. Trimble, *The Mining Advance into the Inland Empire*. Madison: Bulletin of the University of Wisconsin No. 638; 1914. The
Montana mining frontier is covered in both Briggs and Trimble, but
for additional information see Merrill G. Burlingame, *The Montana
Frontier*. Helena, Montana: State Publishing Company; 1942. Hi-
larious reading is *Copper Camp: Stories of the World's Greatest Mining Town: Butte, Montana*. New York: W.P.A. Writers' Program;
1943. Some of it touches upon early Montana mining.

The financial side of western mining is ably told in Clark C.
Spence, *British Investments and the American Mining Frontier,
1860–1901*. Ithaca: Cornell University Press; 1958.

River towns in the mining country are described by Chittenden and
Hunter (see Section I), but for the best picture see Everett Dick,
The Sod-House Frontier, 1854–1890. New York: D. Appleton-Cen-
tury Company; 1937. Chapter 6, dealing with river towns of the
1850s, is excellent. See also Stanley Vestal, *The Missouri*. New York:
Farrar & Rinehart, Incorporated; 1945. More general descriptions of
Montana mining life are found in Joseph Kinsey Howard, *Montana:
High, Wide, and Handsome*. New Haven: Yale University Press; 1943.
A more recent interpretive work is K. Ross Toole, *Montana: An Un-
common Land*. Norman: University of Oklahoma Press; 1959. Regional works that touch upon the early Montana scene are W. Tur-
rentine Jackson, *Wagon Roads West*. Berkeley: The University of
California Press; 1952; and Paul F. Sharp, *Whoop-Up Country: The*

Canadian–American West, 1865–1886. Minneapolis: The University of Minnesota Press; 1955. Both of these books have won prizes. The multivolume *Contributions to the Historical Society of Montana* present a great deal of original material about Montana's gold-rush days.

The Colorado mineral frontier is discussed in LeRoy R. Hafen, *Colorado: The Story of a Western Commonwealth.* Denver: The Peerless Publishing Company; 1933; and Percy S. Fritz, *Colorado: The Centennial State.* New York: Prentice-Hall, Inc.; 1941. Don L. Griswold and Jean Harvey Griswold, *The Carbonate Camp Called Leadville.* Denver: University of Denver Press; 1951, describes one of Colorado's most spectacular mineral strikes. An early account of the Pike's Peak excitement is found in Horace Greeley, *An Overland Journey from New York to San Francisco in the Summer of 1859.* New York: C. M. Saxton, Barker and Co.; 1860. Clifford C. Hill, *Wagon Roads in Colorado, 1858–1876,* an unpublished master's thesis at the University of Colorado (1949) tells of transportation to the mines. For mining-camp justice see Wayne Gard, *Frontier Justice.* Norman: University of Oklahoma Press; 1949. *The Colorado Magazine* is filled with articles on early Colorado mining.

A great deal has been written about the American Indians. Representative of the more general studies are: Loring Benson Priest, *Uncle Sam's Stepchildren.* New Brunswick, N.J.: Rutgers University Press; 1942. William C. MacLeod, *The American Indian Frontier.* New York: Alfred A. Knopf, Inc.; 1928. Ruth Murray Underhill, *Red Man's America.* Chicago: University of Chicago Press; 1953. D'Arcy McNickle, *They Came Here First; The Epic of the American Indian.* Philadelphia: J. B. Lippincott; 1949. George Bird Grinnell, *The Story of the Indian.* New York: D. Appleton and Company; 1895. Alpheus Hyatt Verrill, *The American Indian.* New York: D. Appleton and Company; 1927, and Clark Wissler, *Indians of the United States.* New York: Doubleday, Doran and Company; 1940.

Almost all the tribes have had their biographers. Some of the better results are: George Bird Grinnell, *The Fighting Cheyennes.* New York: Charles Scribner's Sons; 1915; Norman: University of Oklahoma Press; 1956. George E. Hyde, *Red Cloud's Folk* (The Oglala Sioux). Norman: University of Oklahoma Press; 1937. Rupert N. Richardson, *The Comanche Barrier to the South Plains Settlement.*

Glendale: The Arthur H. Clark Company; 1933, and Edward E. Dale, *The Indians of the Southwest*. Norman: University of Oklahoma Press; 1949. An excellent recent study of the Blackfeet is John C. Ewers, *The Blackfeet: Raiders on the Northwestern Plains*. Norman: University of Oklahoma Press; 1958. Katharine C. Turner's *Red Men Calling on the Great White Father*. Norman: University of Oklahoma Press; 1951, is an interesting account of attempts to impress the natives by showing them the powerful and populous East.

Indian policy and its problems is well developed in Walter Prescott Webb, *The Great Plains*. New York: Ginn and Company; 1931, and Frederic Logan Paxson, *History of the American Frontier, 1763–1893*. Boston: Houghton Mifflin Company; 1924. See also James C. Malin, *Indian Policy and Westward Expansion*. Bulletin of the University of Kansas Humanistic Studies, Volume II, No. 3 (November 1921) and Robert G. Athearn, *William Tecumseh Sherman and the Settlement of the West*. Norman: The University of Oklahoma Press; 1956. The latter work deals with military–Indian relations on the high plains.

Other books that include useful descriptions of the Indians are: LeRoy R. Hafen and Francis M. Young, *Fort Laramie and the Pageant of the West, 1834–1890*. Glendale: The Arthur H. Clark Company; 1938, and Paul I. Wellman, *Death on Horseback: Seventy Years of War for the American West*. Philadelphia: J. B. Lippincott Company; 1947. Oliver LaFarge, *A Pictorial History of the American Indian*. New York: Crown Publishers; 1956, contains not only pictures but a well-written and useful text.

The "Mormon War" is treated in all major studies of the Mormon experiment in Utah. One of the older publications is William Alexander Linn, *The Story of the Mormons: From the Date of their Origin to the Year 1901*, New York: The Macmillan Company; 1923. See Chapter 12. Nels Anderson, *Desert Saints: The Mormon Frontier in Utah*, Chicago: The University of Chicago Press; 1942 treats the federal invasion in two chapters. More recent, and of a documentary nature, is LeRoy R. Hafen and Ann W. Hafen, *The Utah Expedition, 1857–1858*, Glendale: The Arthur H. Clark Company; 1958. It is the most complete work to date on this episode in western history.

The standard work on the Colorado Volunteers in the New Mexico campaign is William Clark Whitford, *Colorado Volunteers in the Civil War: The New Mexico Campaign in 1862,* Denver: The State Historical and Natural History Society; 1906. William MacLeod Raine, *Boldly They Rode,* Lakewood, Colorado: The Golden Press; 1949, is a republication of Ovando J. Hollister's *History of the First Regiment of Colorado Volunteers,* first published in 1863. Ray C. Colton, *The Civil War in the Western Territories: Arizona, Colorado, New Mexico, and Utah,* Norman: The University of Oklahoma Press; 1959, gives considerable space to the New Mexican campaign. Max L. Heyman, *Prudent Soldier: E. R. S. Canby,* Glendale: The Arthur H. Clark Company; 1959, has a chapter describing Canby's part in the same campaign. See also Robert L. Kerby, *The Confederate Invasion of New Mexico and Arizona, 1861–1862,* Los Angeles: Westernlore Press; 1958.

For a biography of Colonel Chivington, see: Reginald S. Craig, *The Fighting Parson: A Biography of Colonel John M. Chivington,* Los Angeles: Westernlore Press, 1959.

The story of the "Cow Kingdom" is one of the favorites among historians of the West. The classic work is Ernest Staples Osgood, *The Day of the Cattleman.* Minneapolis: The University of Minnesota Press; 1929 and 1954. Another standard volume is Louis Pelzer, *The Cattleman's Frontier.* Glendale: The Arthur H. Clark Company; 1936. Somewhat narrower in scope are: Ora Brooks Peake, *The Colorado Range Cattle Industry.* Glendale: The Arthur H. Clark Company; 1937, and Maurice Frink, *Cow Country Cavalcade.* Denver: The Old West Publishing Company; 1954. The latter is concerned with Wyoming.

Among the more general studies that include chapters on the cattle industry are: Harold E. Briggs, *Frontiers of the Northwest;* Walter P. Webb, *The Great Plains;* Everett Dick, *The Sod-House Frontier* and *Vanguards of the Frontier;* and Merrill G. Burlingame, *The Montana Frontier* (see above). Similarly, James Olson's *History of Nebraska:* Lincoln: The University of Nebraska Press; 1955, covers the Nebraska cattle story. Maurice Frink, W. Turrentine Jackson, and Agnes Wright Spring, *When Grass Was King.* Boulder: The University of Colorado Press; 1956, also should be consulted. It deals largely with the northern plains. Somewhat apart from the region here studied, but descriptive of the origins of the plains cattle industry, is Rupert Norval Richardson and Carl Coke Rister, *The Greater Southwest*. Glendale: The Arthur H. Clark Company; 1934.

A recent publication about those who ran the stock-raising industry is Mari Sandoz, *The Cattlemen: From the Rio Grande Across the Far Marias*. New York: Hasting House; 1958.

For those interested in the reaction of outsiders to the "Beef Bonanza," see: Robert G. Athearn, *Westward the Briton*. New York: Charles Scribner's Sons; 1953, William A. Baillie-Grohman, *Camps in the Rockies*. New York: Charles Scribner's Sons; 1882, and Isabelle Randall, *A Lady's Ranch Life in Montana*. London: W. H. Allen and Company; 1887.

Cow towns are discussed in Stanley Vestal, *Queen of the Cowtowns: Dodge City*. New York: Harper & Brothers; 1952 and Robert M. Wright, *Dodge City: The Cowboy Capital and the Great Southwest*. Wichita: Wichita Eagle Press; 1913. Norbert R. Mahnken, "Ogallala—Nebraska's Cowboy Capital," *Nebraska History*, XXVIII, No. 2 (April–June 1947), 85–110, is very well done.

In the periodical literature consult: Harold E. Briggs, "Ranching and Stock-Raising in the Territory of Dakota," *South Dakota Historical Collections*, XIV (1928), 417–465; John Bauman, "On a Western Ranche," *The Fortnightly Review*, CCXLIV (New Series) (April 1887): Frederic Logan Paxson, "The Cow Country," *The American Historical Review*, XXII, No. 1 (October 1916), 65–83; and John Rossel, "The Chisholm Trail," *Kansas Historical Quarterly*, V, No. 1 (February 1936), 3–14.

The influence of railroads upon western settlement is a subject of continuing interest to historians, but during the past thirty years no general work has appeared to supplant Robert E. Riegel, *The Story of the Western Railroads*. New York: The Macmillan Company; 1926. Most active in the field of research concerning a specific road has been Richard C. Overton. His *Burlington West*. Cambridge; Harvard University Press; 1941, is soon to be supplemented by a larger study of that railroad. The quotations by Charles Russell Lowell, used in chapter 7, were taken from this book. Joseph G. Pyle's *The Life of James J. Hill*. Two volumes. New York: Doubleday, Page & Company; 1917, contains a lot of information, but this work, too, soon will be replaced by that of Ralph Hidy. Glenn Chesney Quiett's *They Built the West: An Epic of Rails and Cities*. New York: D. Appleton-Century Company, Incorporated; 1934, is largely about the Pacific Coast and beyond the scope of this study, but the early chapters contain general information that is pertinent. Chapter 7 deals with Denver. See also James Blaine Hedges, *Henry Villard and the Railways of the Northwest*. New Haven: Yale University Press; 1930. An interesting contemporary account is Josiah Copley, *Kansas and the Country Beyond, on the Line of the Union Pacific Railway, Eastern Division, from the Missouri to the Pacific Ocean*. Philadelphia: J. B. Lippincott & Co.; 1867.

Other studies of particular railroads include George L. Anderson, *General William Palmer: A Decade of Railroad Building in Colorado* (Denver & Rio Grande). Colorado Springs: Colorado College Publication; 1936, and L. L. Waters, *Steel Trails to Santa Fe*. Lawrence: University of Kansas Press; 1950.

Chapters in books already mentioned include information about railroad building and its effect. See Harold Briggs, *Frontiers of the Northwest;* Everett Dick, *The Sod-House Frontier: 1854–1890* and *Vanguards of the Frontier;* Joseph Kinsey Howard, *Montana: High, Wide, and Handsome;* and Bruce Nelson, *Land of the Dacotahs*. Athearn, *William Tecumseh Sherman and the Settlement of the West*, dwells at length upon governmental interest in western railroad building.

Section III

Various aspects of the sodbusters' frontier are discussed in Roy M. Robbins, *Our Landed Heritage: The Public Domain, 1776–1936*. Princeton: Princeton University Press; 1942, Benjamin H. Hibbard, *A History of the Public Land Policies*. New York: The Macmillan Company; 1924, and Paul Wallace Gates, *Fifty Million Acres: Conflicts over Kansas Land Policy, 1854–1890*. Ithaca: Cornell University Press; 1954. More recent plains farm problems are treated in Carl Frederick Kraenzel's excellent *The Great Plains in Transition*. Norman: University of Oklahoma Press; 1955.

Among works previously mentioned one will find excellent chapters about the homesteaders. See Harold E. Briggs, *Frontiers of the Northwest;* Merrill G. Burlingame, *The Montana Frontier;* Everett Dick, *The Sod-House Frontier, 1854–1890;* Walter P. Webb, *The Great Plains;* and Joseph Kinsey Howard, *Montana: High, Wide, and Handsome.* Emerson Hough's *The Passing of the Frontier.* New Haven: Yale University Press; 1918, has a chapter [9] entitled "The Homesteader."

Problems of early Dakota agriculture are treated in Moses K. Armstrong, *The Early Empire Builders of the Great West.* St. Paul: E. W. Porter; 1901. More recent is Howard Roberts Lamar, *Dakota Territory, 1861–1889.* New Haven: Yale University Press; 1956. His last chapter deals with the revolt of the farmers. LeRoy Hafen's *Colorado: The Story of a Western Commonwealth,* already mentioned, gives something of the agricultural story in Colorado. James C. Olson's *History of Nebraska* is similarly useful for Nebraska. For Wyoming see Velma Linford, *Wyoming: Frontier State.* Denver: The Old West Publishing Company; 1947.

Contemporary views of plains agricultural communities can be found in John H. Blegen, "A Missionary Journey on the Dakota Prairies in 1886." *North Dakota Historical Quarterly,* I, No. 3 (April 1927), 16–29; Paul H. Giddens, "Eastern Kansas in 1869–70," *The Kansas Historical Quarterly,* IX, No. 4 (November 1940), 371–383; and "Letters of John and Sarah Everett, 1854–1864," *The Kansas Historical Quarterly,* VIII, No. 1 (February 1939), 3–34. Interesting also is Shalor W. Eldridge, *Recollections of Early Days in Kansas,* in *Publications of the Kansas State Historical Society,* II, Topeka: Kansas State Printing Plant; 1920.

The standard works on western agrarian dissent are John D. Hicks, *The Populist Revolt.* Minneapolis: University of Minnesota Press; 1931, and two books by Solon J. Buck, *The Granger Movement.* Cambridge: Harvard University Press; 1913, and *The Agrarian Crusade.* New Haven: Yale University Press; 1920. Another account of the Populists is found in Anna Rochester, *The Populist Movement in the United States.* New York: International Publishers; 1943. Chester M. Destler's *American Radicalism, 1865–1901.* New London: Connecticut College; 1946, broadens the view somewhat. Fred E. Haynes, *Third Party Movements Since the Civil War.* Iowa City: State Historical Society; 1916, is old but remains a handy and useful source. Written some forty years later is Richard Hofstadter's excellent *The Age of Reform: From Bryan to F.D.R.* New York: Alfred A. Knopf; 1955. It contains a splendid account of agrarian complaints.

Highly informative is Walter Johnson's classic study, *William Allen White's America.* New York: Henry Holt and Company; 1947. Two works by Fred Shannon ought not be overlooked: His volume *The Farmer's Last Frontier: Agriculture, 1860–1897.* New York: Farrar & Rinehart, Inc.; 1945, and *American Farmers' Movements.* D. Van Nostrand Company, Inc.; 1957. The latter is an Anvil original (paperback) dealing with general agricultural movements, the second part of which is documentary. See chapter 5, "Post-Bellum Farmers' Movements." Two articles of value are Paul R. Fossum, "The Agrarian Movement in North Dakota," *Johns Hopkins University Studies in Historical and Political Science,* Series XLIII, No. 1. Baltimore: The Johns Hopkins University Press; 1925, and Samuel P. Huntington, "The Election Tactics of the Nonpartisan League, *Mississippi Valley Historical Review,* XXXVI, No. 4 (March 1950), 613–632.

Easily available and useful are the agricultural sections of books already noted: Everett Dick, *The Sod-House Frontier, 1854–1890;* Howard Roberts Lamar, *Dakota Territory, 1861–1889;* Bruce Nelson, *Land of the Dacotahs;* James Olson, *History of Nebraska;* and LeRoy Hafen, *Colorado: The Story of a Western Commonwealth.*

No one has yet written a cultural history of the high plains. While most of the available material is to be found in the periodical literature, some books have appeared that are of use. LeRoy Hafen and Carl Coke Rister, *Western America.* New York: Prentice-Hall, Inc.; 1941, has a good chapter [35] entitled "The Evolution of Western Culture." Chapter 10 of Walter Webb's *The Great Plains* contains some interesting ideas. Colin B. Goodykoontz, *Home Missions on the American Frontier.* Caldwell: The Caxton Printers, Ltd.; 1939, is broader in scope than the title suggests. Athearn's *Westward the Briton* deals with life and labor in the post–Civil War West, as viewed by the British travelers. An older work, but one of unfailing interest, is James Bryce, *The American Commonwealth.* Two volumes. New York: The Macmillan Company; 1914.

There are a number of useful articles descriptive of early religious effort on the plains. See George W. Barnes, "Pioneer Preacher—An Autobiography," *Nebraska History,* XXVII, No. 2 (April–June 1946),

71–91; George Edwards, "Presbyterian Church History," *Contributions to the Historical Society of Montana,* VI, 1907, 290–444; C. H. Frady, "Fifty Years of Gospel Giving on the Frontier," *Nebraska History,* X, No. 4 (October–December 1927), 269–334; Russell K. Hickman, "Lewis Bodwell, Frontier Preacher, The Early Years," *Kansas Historical Quarterly,* XII, No. 3 (August 1943), 269–299, and No. 4 (November 1943), 349–365. See also John H. Blegen, "A Missionary on the Dakota Prairies in 1886," already cited. Chapter 13 of Merrill Burlingame's *Montana Frontier* is entitled "Religion on the Montana Frontier."

For short pieces about the frontier press, see William E. Connelley, *History of Kansas Newspapers.* Topeka: Kansas State Printing Plant, 1916; Henry Allen Brainerd, "Nebraska's Press History," *Nebraska History,* XIII, No. 4 (October–December 1932), 266–271; and R. L. Housman, "Pioneer Montana's Journalistic 'Ghost' Camp—Virginia City," *The Pacific Northwest Quarterly,* XXIX, (January 1938), 53–59. Very entertaining is Cecil Howes, "Pistol-Packin' Pencil Pushers," *Kansas Historical Quarterly,* XIII, No. 2 (May 1944), 115–138. Douglas C. McMurtrie wrote a number of interesting pieces on western printing. See Douglas C. McMurtrie and Albert H. Allen, *Early Printing in Colorado.* Denver: Hirschfield Press; 1935; McMurtrie, *Early Printing in Wyoming and the Black Hills.* Hattiesburg, Mississippi: Printed for the Book Farm; 1943; McMurtrie (ed.), *The History of the Frontier–Index* (*the "Press on Wheels"*), *the Ogden Freeman, the Inter-Mountains Freeman and the Union Freeman.* Evanston, Illinois; 1943; and McMurtrie, "Pioneer Printing in Kansas," *Kansas Historical Quarterly,* I, No. 1 (November 1931), 3–16.

The frontier theater is described in Melvin Schoberlin, *From Candles to Footlights: A Biography of the Pike's Peak Theater, 1859–1876.* Denver: The Old West Publishing Company; 1941. Briefer, but very informative, is Harold E. Briggs and Ernestine Bennett Briggs, "The Early Theater on the Northern Plains," *Mississippi Valley Historical Review,* XXXVII, No. 2 (September 1950), 231–264. More particularized are Robert D. Harper, "Theatrical Entertainment in Early Omaha," *Nebraska History,* XXXVI, No. 2 (June 1955), 93–104, and Hal Sayre, "Early Central City Theatricals and Other Reminiscences," *The Colorado Magazine,* VI, No. 2 (March 1929), 47–53. Also dealing with entertainment is Clifford P. Westermeier, "The Dodge City Cowboy Band," *Kansas Historical Quarterly,* XIX, No. 1 (February 1952), 1–11. Mention should be made also of Myra E. Hull's "Cowboy Ballads," *The Kansas Historical Quarterly,* VIII, No. 1 (February 1939), 36–60.

Pioneer education is the subject of E. E. Dale, "Teaching on the Prairie Plains, 1890–1900," *Mississippi Valley Historical Review,* XXXIII, No. 2 (September 1946), 293–307. Another is O. J. Goldrick, "The First School in Denver," *The Colorado Magazine,* VI, No. 2 (March 1929), 72–74. Chapter 23 of Everett Dick's *The Sod-House Frontier, 1854–1890* concerns early education on the plains.

Plains literature, in general, is considered in Levette Jay Davidson and Prudence Bostwick (eds.), *The Literature of the Rocky Mountain West, 1803–1903.* Caldwell: The Caxton Printers, Ltd.; 1939, and Ruth Hudson, *Studies in Literature of the West.* Laramie: University of Wyoming Publications, XX, No. 1; 1956.

There are a number of references to cultural attempts on the plains frontier in such contemporary accounts as: Howard Ruede, *Sod-House Days: Letters from a Kansas Homesteader, 1877–78* (edited by John Ise). New York: Columbia University Press; 1937, and Warren S. Tyron (ed.), *A Mirror for Americans: Life and Manners in the United States 1790–1870 as Recorded by American Travelers.* Chicago: University of Chicago Press; 1952. (Volume III, *The Frontier Moves West,* has some appropriate items.) See also "The Letters of John Ferguson, Early Resident of Western Washington County," *Kansas Historical Quarterly,* XII, No. 4 (November 1943), 339–348; and Thomas C. Wells, "Letters of a Kansas Pioneer," *Kansas Historical Quarterly,* V, No. 2 (May 1936), 143–179 and *ibid.,* V, No. 3 (August 1936), 381–418. Critical of cultural efforts in the West is Charles A. Beard, "Culture and Agriculture," *The Saturday Review of Literature,* V, No. 13 (October 20, 1928), 272–273. And critical of Beard is Fred A. Shannon, "Culture and Agriculture in America," *Mississippi Valley Historical Review,* XLI, No. 1 (June 1954), 3–20.

Section IV

Sources for the Fading Frontiers chapter came from widely scattered reading. A recent publication treating the impact of organized labor upon the Colorado mining camps is Stewart H. Holbrook, *The Rocky*

Mountain Revolution. New York: Henry Holt and Company; 1956. Others are David Lavender, *The Big Divide*. New York: Doubleday, Doran & Company, Inc.; 1948; and Marshall Sprague, *Money Mountain: The Story of Cripple Creek Gold*. Boston: Little, Brown and Company; 1953. Older and more particularized works include Benjamin M. Rastall, *The Labor History of the Cripple Creek District: A Study in Industrial Evolution*. Bulletin of the University of Wisconsin No. 198, Economics and Political Science Series, Vol. 3, No. 1, 1–166. Madison; 1908; and Emma F. Langdon, *The Cripple Creek Strike: A History of Industrial Wars in Colorado, 1903–4–5*. Denver: Great West Publishing Company; 1905. Mrs. Langdon was a linotype operator for the Victor (Colorado) *Record*. Her husband, one of the paper's employees, was arrested and jailed in the 1903 strike. While the book is highly biased it contains a lot of interesting information. Percy Fritz's *Colorado: The Centennial State,* already cited, has some general comments on the subject. For Montana see *Copper Camp,* also previously mentioned, and Helen Fitzgerald Sanders, *A History of Montana*. Three volumes, Chicago: The Lewis Publishing Company; 1913. Chapters 8, 9, and 10 in Ross Toole's *Montana: An Uncommon Land* treat later Montana mining.

The changing agricultural picture may be followed in several works previously cited. Carl F. Kraenzel's *The Great Plains in Transition;* Vance Johnson's *Heaven's Tableland;* and Joseph Kinsey Howard's *Montana: High, Wide, and Handsome* all contain excellent interpretations. Others are Ladd Haystead and Gilbert C. Fite, *The Agricultural Regions of the United States*. Norman: The University of Oklahoma Press; 1955; Richard Hofstadter, *The Age of Reform: From Bryan to F.D.R.* New York: Alfred A. Knopf; 1955; Grant McConnell, *The Decline of Agrarian Democracy*. Berkeley: The University of California Press; 1953; Edward Wiest, *Agricultural Organization in the United States*. Lexington: The University of Kentucky Press; 1923; Mary Wilma M. Hargreaves, *Dry Farming in the Northern Great Plains, 1900–1925*. Cambridge: Harvard University Press; 1957; E. Louise Peffer, *The Closing of the Public Domain: Disposal and Reservation Policies, 1900–50*. Stanford: Stanford University Press; 1951; and William E. Smythe, *The Conquest of Arid America*. New York: Harper & Brothers; 1900. Useful is F. H. Newell,

"Irrigation," *Annual Report of the Board of Regents, Smithsonian Institution, 1901*. Washington: Government Printing Office; 1902. Newell was the hydrographer for the United States Geological Survey. A brief but well-done account is John Lee Coulter, "Bonanza Farms and the One Crop System of Agriculture," *Collections of the Historical Society of North Dakota*, Bismarck; 1910. Volume III, 569–596.

Two articles of interest dealing with western isolationism are Ray Allen Billington, "The Origins of Middle Western Isolationism," *Political Science Quarterly*, LX, No. 1 (March 1945), 44–64; and William G. Carleton, "Isolationism and the Middle West," *Mississippi Valley Historical Review*, XXXIII, No. 3 (December 1946), 377–390.

Controversies over the disposition of "Uncle Sam's West" have provoked a good deal of writing. Among older works are George Wharton James, *Reclaiming the Arid West: The Story of the United States Reclamation Service*. New York: Dodd & Company; 1917; Fred H. Dennett, *The Public Lands of the United States*. An address of the Commissioner of the General Land Office, November 17, 1909. *Senate Document* 445, 61 Cong., 2 sess., 1–21; and Arthur P. Davis, *Irrigation Works Constructed by the United States Government*. New York: Wiley; 1917. *Theodore Roosevelt: An Autobiography*. New York: The Macmillan Company; 1913, has some outspoken comments on conservation. Forest policy is discussed in John Ise, *The United States Forest Policy*. New Haven: Yale University Press; 1920. See chapter 5 for a picture of western hostility to conservation policies. Another work is Darrell H. Smith, *The Forest Service: Its History, Activities and Organization*. Washington: U.S. Government Printing Office; 1930. It is number 58 of the Institute for Government Research Service Monographs and contains a short history of the Forest Service as well as a table of organization and the laws relating to federal forests. The most recent study of national forests is Arthur H. Carhart, *The National Forests*. New York; Alfred A. Knopf; 1959. See also the *U.S. Reclamation Service: Its History, Activities and Organization*. Institute for Government Research Service Monographs, No. 2. New York: D. Appleton and Company; 1919. Gifford Pinchot's *Breaking New Ground*. New York: Harcourt,

Brace and Company; 1947 is by the "father of forest conservation."

There is a growing body of literature about our national parks. Paul H. Buck's *The Evolution of the National Park System of the United States* is a master's thesis (1921), later published. Washington: U.S. Government Printing Office; 1946. Robert S. Yard, *The Book of National Parks.* New York: Charles Scribner's Sons; 1928 was written by the executive secretary of the National Parks Association. It is largely descriptive of the parks' physical features. His volume, *Our Federal Lands.* New York: Charles Scribner's Sons; 1928, has two chapters [7 and 8] dealing with national parks and national monuments. Jenks Cameron, *The National Park Service: Its History, Activities and Organization.* New York: D. Appleton and Company; 1922, is number 11 of the Institute for Government Research Service Monographs. It is old, but offers a concise account of the Park Service and the establishment of each park. A newer book is Nelson Beecher Keyes, *America's National Parks.* New York: Alfred A. Knopf; 1951. It tells the story of the Park Service's first director.

The western water problem is examined in Albert N. Williams, *The Water and the Power.* New York: Duell, Sloan and Pearce; 1951. Part 5 concerns the Missouri River Valley. Henry C. Hart's *The Dark Missouri.* Madison: University of Wisconsin Press; 1957, is a lively, readable account. Another popular account is Rufus Terral, *The Missouri Valley.* New Haven: Yale University Press; 1947. For more details see Missouri River Basin, Report of the Secretary of the Interior, *Senate Document* 191, 78 Cong. 2 sess. (May 1944).

For years Bernard DeVoto carried on a conservation crusade in his monthly magazine column. A sample article is his "Heading for the Last Roundup," *Harper's Magazine,* Vol. 207, No. 1238 (July 1953), 49–52. For a more moderate point of view see Warren Unna, "Republican 'Giveaways': The Charges and the Facts," *Harper's Magazine,* Vol. 212, No. 1272 (May 1956), 29–36. He concludes that neither party has a spotless record in conservation.

Finally, some of the standard books in the field contain valuable sections dealing with the public domain. Roy Robbin's *Our Landed Heritage: The Public Domain, 1776–1936* and E. Louise Peffer's superb *The Closing of the Public Domain: Disposal and Reservation Policies, 1900–50,* both previously cited, are not to be overlooked. The fight over withdrawal of public lands is discussed in chapters 22 and 23 of John Ise, *The United States Oil Policy.* New Haven: Yale University Press; 1926.

Problems of modern plains farmers ("Empire of Dust") have attracted the attention of a good many writers who are concerned by the apparent insolubility of the dilemma. James M. Shideler's *Farm Crisis 1919–1923.* Berkeley: University of California Press; 1957, is a good place to start reading. Another is Mary Wilma M. Hargreaves, *Dry Farming in the Northern Plains, 1900–1925,* previously mentioned. Gilbert C. Fite's *George N. Peek and the Fight for Farm Parity.* Norman: University of Oklahoma Press; 1954, covers the period well. Similar, but broader, works are: Lauren Soth, *Farm Trouble.* Princeton: Princeton University Press; 1957; Walter W. Wilcox, *The Farmer in the Second World War.* Ames: Iowa State College Press; 1947; and T. J. Woofter, Jr., and Ellen Winston, *Seven Lean Years.* Chapel Hill: University of North Carolina Press; 1939. Wesley McCune's *Who's Behind Our Farm Policy.* New York: Frederick A. Praeger, Inc.; 1956, and Ezra Taft Benson, *A Man with a Mission.* Washington: Public Affairs Press; 1958, should be consulted. Other works, previously referred to, are important in this field: Joseph Kinsey Howard, *Montana: High, Wide, and Handsome;* Vance Johnson, *Heaven's Tableland;* Bruce Nelson, *Land of the Dacotahs;* and James Olson, *History of Nebraska.* So is William Frank Zornow, *Kansas: A History of the Jayhawk State.* Norman: University of Oklahoma Press; 1957.

I found an enormous amount of useful information in Fred Floyd, *A History of the Dust Bowl,* unpublished doctoral dissertation, University of Oklahoma, 1950. For a personal view of the tragedy, a very appealing book is Lawrence Svobida, *An Empire of Dust.* Caldwell: Caxton Printers, Ltd.; 1940. It tells the story of a young Kansas farmer who fought drought and dust during the thirties, and gave up the struggle, just as things were about to get better on the eve of World War II. It is the best firsthand account in print of the dustbowl era.

In the periodical literature, H. H. Finnell, "Pity the Poor Land,"

Soil Conservation XII, No. 2 (September 1946), 27–32, is very good. "A Strategy for Drought," *Fortune* (April 1957) is newer and also of interest.

A view of the political aspect of the agricultural problem is found in chapter 8 of Samuel Lubell, *The Future of American Politics.* New York; Harper & Brothers, 1952. Murray R. Benedict's *Can We Solve the Farm Problem?* New York: Twentieth Century Fund; 1955, is another book touching upon this side of the problem.

Source materials for the final chapter ("A Land in Transition") are few and rather diverse. I found a good many useful facts in *Statistical Abstract of the United States.* Published annually by the Department of Commerce, Washington, D.C. Another documentary source is *Missouri: Land and Water. The Report of the Missouri Basin Survey Commission.* Washington: U.S. Government Printing Office, 1953. There is a good deal of information in *The Montana Almanac,* published annually by the Bureau of Business and Economic Research at Montana State University (1957 edition used). *The Oil and Gas Fields of Colorado.* Denver: Rocky Mountain Association of Geologists; 1954, is largely technical. Harold D. Roberts, *Salt Creek Wyoming: The Story of a Great Oil Field.* Denver: Privately published; 1956, is one of the few books on mountain states petroleum development. Don Douma, "Second Bonanza" helps to fill the gap. It was published in four parts in *Montana: The Magazine of Western History.* Autumn 1953 and Winter, Spring, and Summer issues of 1954. Taken from an M.A. thesis, Montana State University, it is probably the best and most complete history of Montana's oil industry in print. I have used it freely. More general is Paul H. Giddens, *Standard Oil Company (Indiana): Oil Pioneer of the Middle West.* New York: Appleton-Century-Crofts; 1955.

A good summary is found in William Allen White, *The Changing West.* New York: The Macmillan Company; 1939. Although it is now two decades old, its chapter 5, "How May the West Survive," is thought-provoking reading.

Abilene (Kansas), development of, 129
Adams, Andy, 131
Agrarian revolt, 211–215
Agricultural Acts (1949, 1954), 316
Agricultural Adjustment Act, 304, 305, 308, 310, 312
Agricultural Appropriation Bill, 288
Agriculture, machine, 262–264
  in mining areas, 76
  see also Farmer
Alder Gulch gold strike, 85, 86
Alexis, Grand Duke (of Russia), 161
American Fur Company, 9, 25, 34–39, 42, 43, 61
American Philosophical Society, 11
American Reform Tract and Book Society, 57
American Society for Encouraging a Settlement of the Oregon, 46
Anaconda Copper Company, 87, 332
Apollo Hall (Denver), 236
Argonauts, 205
Armstrong, Lt. John, 6
Army, U.S., Corps of Engineers, 316
  Fifth Infantry, 134
  measures against Indians, 31–32, 103–105, 110, 126
  Seventh Cavalry, 124
  Sixth Cavalry, 145
  Sixth Infantry, 31
  Twenty-second Infantry, 119
  Utah campaign (1857), 83
  see also Civil War
Ashley, Gen. William H., 29–33, 35, 38, 42, 100
Astor, John Jacob, 9, 34–39, 41–42
Atchison, Topeka and Santa Fe Railroad, 130, 131, 162

Ballad, cowboy, 249
Bannack (Montana), 85, 86, 93
Barbed wire, 151, 180, 225
Baylor, Col. John R., 109–110
Bear-that-Scatters, 103–104
Beaver trapping. See Fur trade
"Beecher's Bibles," 56
Bent, William, 54
Benton, Sen. Thomas Hart, 34, 38, 47, 54, 56

"Big die-up" [winter 1886–87], 143–145, 147–149, 208–209
Big Horn Mining Association, 86
Black Hills, 70, 96–97, 117, 139
  gold rush, 132, 164, 170
  Live Stock Association, 139
Black Kettle, 117
Bloomer, Mrs. Amelia, 237
Blue River Trail, 130
Bonanza, beef, 135–142, 146
  land, 191–193
Boomers, land, 57–60, 170–175, 198
Bozeman Road, 88, 113, 114, 322
Brackenridge, Henry M., 23–24
Bradbury, John, 24, 25
Bridger, Jim ("Old Gabe"), 28, 30, 33, 35, 37, 38, 43, 49, 137, 160
Bryan, William Jennings, 219–220
Buchanan, Pres. James, 105, 106, 206
Burlington Railroad, 161, 167, 170–172, 198
Byers, William, 242, 243

Calderwood, John, 269
California, gold rush, 51–53; see also Forty-Niners
  Joe, 139
  Trail, 137
  Volunteers, 110
Canby, Gen. E. R. S., 109
Can-can dancers, 237–238
Carey Act (1894), 279
Carrington, Col. Henry, 113–114
Carson, Kit, 19
Casement brothers, 155
Cather, Willa, 251
Catherine, Empress (of Russia), 11
Cattle industry, 127–151
Central Overland California and Pike's Peak Express Company, 82
Central Pacific Railroad, 159, 160
Charles IV, King (of Spain), 10
Cherokee Strip, 146
Cheyenne Club, 134
Cheyenne (Wyoming), as rail and cattle city, 133–134
Chicago and North Western Railroad, 91
Chisholm, Jesse, 129, 132
Chivington, Col. J. M., 109, 111–112, 272

Chouteau, Pierre, 29, 36, 38–41
Church of Jesus Christ of the Latter-
   day Saints. *See* Mormons
"Cincinnati houses," 63, 195
Cities, agricultural, 193–198
   develop respectability, 78–79, 91–92
   mining, 77–79
   railroad, 158–159, 196–197
   river, 90–92
Civil War, 106–110
Clark, George Rogers, 11, 12
Clark, William, 12, 14–17, 25, 29; *see
   also* Lewis and Clark expedition
Cleveland, Pres. Grover, 199
Clyman, Jim, 31, 43
Cody, W. F. ("Buffalo Bill"), 160–161
Colleges, frontier, 235
   land-grant, 281
Colonization societies, 171–172; *see
   also* Emigrant Aid Societies
Colorado, first school, 76
   gold rush, 53, 70, 72–75; *see also*
      Fifty-Niners
   political formation, 206–207
   Stockgrowers' Association, 144
   Volunteers, 109
Colter, John, 14
Columbia Fur Company, 35
Commerce, desert, 79–84
Communication, frontier, 82–83
Connor, Gen. Patrick E., 110, 112
Conservation, 70, 279, 280, 287; *see
   also* Reclamation
Cooke, Jay, 138, 164, 209
Cooper, James Fenimore, 114, 244
Cooperatives, cattlemen's, 142–145
Cordelling, 31
Cow kingdom, 127–151
Crazy Horse, 119
Crédit Mobilier, 158, 244
Cripple Creek (Colorado), 268–270
Crooks, Ramsay, 36, 38, 40, 41
Culture, frontier, 224–254
Custer, George Armstrong, 117–119,
   140
   Last Stand, 118–119, 193

Dakota, political formation, 206–207
Dale, Matthew, 53, 55
Davis, Jefferson, 109
Davis, Mrs. Jefferson, 86
de Bourgmont, Etienne, 4
D'Eglise, Jacques, 6–7, 9
de la Vérendrye, Pierre, 4–5
Denver (Colorado), and Civil War,
   106–107
   entertainment, 236

Denver (Colorado), first school, 232–
   233
   as railway center, 160–162, 198
   respectability, 94–95
   as trade center, 75–77
Denver, Gen. James, 72
Denver and Rio Grande Western Rail-
   road, 161, 163, 198, 327
Desert, Great American, 3, 17–23, 51,
   55–58, 63–65, 87–98, 138, 180,
   185, 191, 207, 259, 302, 333
   theory of, 19, 20, 24–26, 65, 171,
      182–183, 187
Desert Land Act (1877), 186, 279
deSmet, Father, 103, 231
DeVoto, Bernard, 250
Dime novels, 245–246
Dodge City, brass band, 238–239
   as cattle town, 130–132
Dodge, Gen. Grenville M., 113, 133,
   155, 157, 160
Drips, Andrew, 29, 37, 42
Dunbar expedition (1804), 16–17
Durum Wheat Act, 316
Dust, Empire of, 297–317
Dyer, Father, 231

Education, frontier, 76, 232–235, 281
Eisenhower, Dwight D., 295
Ekalaka (Montana), 194
Emigrant Aid Societies, 56, 62; *see
   also* Colonization societies
End-of-track cities. *See* Cities, railroad
Enterprize (river vessel), 30
Entertainment, frontier, 235–239
Evans, Sgt. Hugh, 21, 23
Excel (steamboat), 62–63

Farm Bankruptcy Act, 304
Farmer, suitcase, 301, 312, 314
   vanishing, 318–320
Farmers Alliance, 213, 217
Farmers, emigration of, 179–203
   as new pioneers, 198–203
Farming, dry, 261–263
Farnham, Thomas J., 23
Far West (steamboat), 193
Federal Reserve System, 299–300
Fencing, 199
54°40', 46
Fifty-Niners, 54, 56, 70, 78, 84, 102,
   232, 260, 269
Finlay, François (Benetsee), 84
"Firewater," 36–37; *see also* Prohibi-
   tion; Whiskey
Fitzpatrick, Thomas, 30, 35, 37, 38
Fleming, Lt. Hugh, 104

Florida, West, 12
Fontenelle, Lucien, 37
Forest Homestead Act, 288
Forest Service, U.S., 288, 289, 292, 295
Forests, National, 289, 291–293
Forty-Niners, 18, 51–53, 56, 102
Frady, Rev. C. H., 229, 230
Fraeb, Henry, 35, 37, 38
Freeman, Daniel, 183–184
Freeman, Leigh R., 243–244
Free-silver issue, 218–219
Frémont, John C., 19, 198
Frontier, mining, 75–76, 95–98, 320–321
Frontier-Index, 243–244
Fur trade, 4–10, 20, 23–24, 27–44, 64, 84, 91

Garden City (Kansas) experiment, 260–261
Garland, Hamlin, 251
Gervais, Jean, 35, 38
"Gettysburg of the West," 110
Ghost Dance (Indian religion), 123–125
Ghost towns, agricultural, 197–198
Gilpin, William, 65, 107, 108, 206
Glorieta Pass, 109, 117
Gold, effect on frontier, 50–53, 77–78
Gold, black. *See* Oil
Government, development of urban frontier, 78–79
    federal, as landgrabber, 287–296
Grand River Valley reclamation project, 282
Grange movement, 217
Grant, Gen. U. S., 97, 113, 115, 118, 119, 123, 186, 290
"Grasshoppering," 89–90
Grazing districts, 293
Great American Desert. *See* Desert
Great Dakota Boom, 170
Great Northern Railroad, 91, 92, 166–167, 200, 323
Greeley, Horace, 54, 81, 230–231
Gregory, John H., 74
Guadalupe Hidalgo, Treaty of, 49
Guide to Emigrants, 62
Gulch mining. *See* Mining, placer

Haidie, Mlle., 236
Hamilton, Alexander, 11
Hand Cart Brigade, 50
Harney, Col. William S., 104–105
Harrison, Pres. Benjamin, 145
Haywood, Big Bill, 271

"Hell on Wheels" (Wyoming), 133
Henry, Maj. Andrew, 29–30, 33, 35
Hill, James Jerome, 92, 166–167, 169, 173, 214
Homestead Acts, 136, 182, 186, 279, 280, 317
Hoover, Herbert, 285
Hudson's Bay Company, 36, 40, 84
Huffman, L. A., 165
Humor, frontier, 89, 137, 189, 225–227, 249, 307
100th Meridian, 52, 58, 160, 171, 186, 187, 259, 261, 334
Hunter, Dr. George, 16

Ickes, Harold L., 285, 286, 295
Ida Stockdale (steamboat), 91
Idaho, political formation, 207
Iliff, John W., 137
Illinois Central Railroad, 91
Immigrants, European, 172–173, 202
Indian Territory, 117, 121
Indians, American, 31–32, 99–105, 110–126
    artists' representation of, 100–101
    and buffalo, 165
    peace-pipe politics, 102–103
    and railroad construction, 156–157
    and whiskey, 36–37, 91, 101, 156
Irrigation, 198–199, 259–260, 263, 279, 280, 284–287
Irving, Washington, 23, 244
Isolationism, 277

Jackson Lake reclamation project, 282
James, Dr. Edwin, 18–19
Jefferson, Thomas, 4, 11–13, 15–17, 23
Johnson, Pres. Andrew, 206
Johnson County war (Wyoming), 144–145
Johnston, Gen. Albert Sidney, 83, 106
"Jones, Mother," 272
Joseph, Chief, 120–121
Journalism, frontier, 239–244
Julesburg (Colorado), 53, 112, 133, 243
Justice, mining-camp, 92–95

Kane, Thomas L., 106
Kansas League (Cincinnati), 57
Kansas, political formation, 205–207
    River, navigation of, 62–63
Kansas Pacific Railroad, 53, 129, 130, 159–162, 188
Kearney, Fort Phil (Wyoming), 88, 114
Kearny, Fort (Nebraska), 51, 52, 104

Keelboats, 25, 30–31
Kelley, Hall J., 45–47
King, Henry, 241, 242
Kipling, Rudyard, 165–166
Kit Carson (Colorado), 159

Labor, organization of in mines, 269–274
Land grants, railroad, 167–170; see also Boomers; Homestead Acts
Land, second-class, 259–262
Langrishe, John, 238
Laramie, Fort, 39, 40, 49, 52, 54, 82
Laramie Treaties, 103, 114, 117
Larimer, Gen. William, 53, 72, 73
Leadville (Colorado), 77, 78, 95, 163, 267, 270
Leavenworth, Col. Henry, 31–32
Leavenworth and Pike's Peak Express Company, 80, 82
Ledyard, John, 11
Lewis, Meriwether, 12–14, 16, 17, 29
Lewis and Clark expedition (1804–06), 12–16, 23, 27, 28, 89, 330
Lincoln, Pres. Abraham, 110–111
Lisa, Manuel, 10, 24, 28, 29
Little Thunder, 104
Livestock associations, 142–145
Livingston, Robert, 12
Loisel, Regis, 10, 24
Long drive, 146
Long, Maj. Stephen, 18–21, 40, 223
Long's Peak, 19, 225
Louisiana Purchase, 3, 12–14, 25, 278
    political development of, 204–223

McCoy, Rev. Isaac, 21
McDonald, Muckey, 273, 274
Mackay, James, 9
McKenzie, Kenneth, 37–41, 54
Mail service, frontier, 82
Majors, Alexander, 80
Make-believe, land of, 330–334
Manifest Destiny, 3, 47, 116, 122
Marshall, James, 51
Marshall Plan, 312
Massacres, Grattan, 103–104
    Ludlow, 272
    Plum Creek, 156–157
    Sand Creek, 111–112, 272
Masterson, Marshal Bat, 132
Maverick, Samuel, 128
Maximilian, Prince Alexander Philip, 24–25, 39
Meeker, Nathan C., 121
Mexican War, 49
Michaux, André, 11–12

Miles, Gen. Nelson A., 119–120, 134, 135, 140
Miles City (Montana), 133–135
Mining, copper, 86–87, 268–269
    gold, 69–98
    labor conditions, 74, 269–274
    lead, 78, 267
    placer, 70, 77–78
    silver, 267–268
Missouri Company (Company of Explorers of the Upper Mississippi), 7, 9, 10
Missouri Fur Company, 34, 35
Missouri Pacific Railway, 198
Missouri Republican (St. Louis), 29
Missouri River, 3–4, 6–9, 12, 15–16, 32
    early exploration of, 23–24
    irrigation and flood control, 284–287
    travel on, 64, 88–91
Missouri Valley Authority, 286
Monroe, Pres. James, 13
Montana, gold rush, 64, 70–71, 84–88
    political formation, 206–207
    Power Company, 332
Mormons, 18, 48–51, 56, 63, 102, 103, 110, 205, 260
Mormon Trail, 49
Mormon "war" (1857), 79, 105–106
Morrill Act, 281
Muckrakers, 173, 275
Mullan, Capt. John, 87
Murphy wagons, 81

Napoleon Bonaparte, 10, 12, 205
National Farmers Union, 286
National Irrigation Association, 280
National Park Service, 290–291
National Wildlife Refuges, 296
Nebraska, statehood, 207
New Deal, 22, 285, 304, 311, 312
New Orleans, 11, 13
New Zion, 49, 50, 105
Niles Weekly Register, 30
Nonpartisan League, 221–222
North Western Railroad, 192
Northern Pacific Railroad, 91, 135, 138, 162, 164–166, 170, 173, 192, 200, 209, 214, 321, 324
Nye, Bill, 137

O'Fallon, Maj. Benjamin, 25
Ogallala (Nebraska), 132–133
Oil industry, 321–327
Omaha Arrow, 241
Oregon Country, movement to, 45–48
Oregon Trail, 47, 104, 325

Overland Trail, 52–53, 56, 110, 154–
    158

Palmer, Gen. William Jackson, 160,
    162–163, 198
Panic, of 1857, 72
    of 1873, 135, 138, 140, 162, 164–
        166, 170, 190
    of 1893, 209, 218, 268
Parity, 306
Parkman, Francis, 39, 244
Parks, national, 290–291, 293
Parks, William J., 86–87
Pathfinder Dam, 283
Phillips Petroleum Company, 324
Pick, Gen. Lewis A., 285, 286
Pierre, Fort, 25, 39, 41, 61, 105
Pike, Zebulon Montgomery, 17–18,
    20, 23, 223
Pike's Peak, 17, 64, 74, 268
Pike's-Peakers, 53–55, 72–75, 109,
    196; see also Fifty-Niners
Pinchot, Gifford, 288, 294
"Pinto buffalo," 123, 127, 129
Pirogue, 8
"Plew," 27
Plummer, Henry, 93–94
Pony Express, 63, 82–83
Population, farm, decline, 318–320
Populists, 173, 211–215, 217–223, 274,
    331
Powder River road, 88
Powell, Maj. John Wesley, 139, 171,
    223, 286
Pratte, Bernard, 35, 38, 41, 42
Price, Gen. Sterling, 108
Progress, agricultural, penalties of,
    264–266
Prohibition, and grain economy, 298–
    299
Provot, Etienne, 30

Quakers, 115–117

Railroads, case for (in agrarian re-
    volt), 215–216
    development of, 152–175
    government subsidy of, 155
    Indian harassment of, 156–157
    land promotion, 216
    as political targets, 210–211
Rainmaking, experiments in, 210, 315
Range, open, 149–151
Reclamation, 263, 280–284, 287
Reconstruction Finance Corporation,
    304

Red Cloud, 114, 115
Red Stockings, 78
Refrigerator car, 140
Religion, frontier, 227–232
Respectability, civic, 78–79, 91–92
Riley, Fort, 59, 61–63
River travel, 62–64, 88–91
Rock Island Railroad, 198
Rocky Mountain Fur Company, 30,
    32–38
Rocky Mountain News (Denver), 76,
    80, 107, 108, 242–243
Roosevelt, Franklin Delano, 222, 249,
    285, 286, 295, 302–305
Roosevelt, Theodore, 248, 288, 294,
    317
    and reclamation, 281–284
Royal Canadian Mounted Police, 37,
    91
Royal Gorge (Arkansas River), 17,
    163
Ruede, Howard, 228–229, 233
Russell, Charley, 148, 200–201
Russell, Majors and Waddell, 79–83

Sacajawea, 15
St. Louis Republican, 103
Salt Lake City, 49, 50, 88, 106
Santa Fe Railway, 162, 163, 172, 198
Santa Fe Trail, 53–54, 56, 80
Shell Oil Company, 324
Sheridan, Gen. Philip, 65, 95, 117,
    118, 169–170
Sherman, Gen. William T., 53, 97,
    113–116, 118, 120, 183, 260
    and railroads, 155–157, 161–162,
        169, 174
    and reclamation, 65
Sherman Silver Purchase Act, 268
Shoshone Dam, 282
Sibley, Gen. Henry H. (CSA), 109
Sibley, Col. Henry Hastings (USA),
    110
Sitting Bull, 117–119, 123–125
Slavery issue, 56, 105, 154, 205
Smallpox, 101, 123
Smith, Rev. George G., 230–231
Smith, Jedediah, 30, 33, 35
Smith, Joseph, 48–49
Smoky Hill Trail, 53, 80, 81
Society of Friends. See Quakers
Sodbusters, 65, 133, 179–203
Soil Bank Act, 316
Soil Conservation Service, 314
Spanish-American War, 257, 331
Stage line, first, 80–81

Standard Oil Company (Indiana), 325
Steamboats, 40–41, 60–63
Stock-Raising Homestead Act (1916), 294
Stratton, Winfield Scott, 269, 270
Stuart, Granville, 84, 135, 148–149, 322
Sublette, Milton, 35, 38, 42
Sublette, William, 31, 35, 39, 42, 46
Subsidies, 310
Sun Oil Company, 324

Tabeau, Peter, 24
Talleyrand, 12, 13
Telegraph, 70, 82–83
Terry, Gen. Alfred, 117, 119
Texas fever, 133
Texas Trail, 132
Theater Comique (Cheyenne), 238
Timber Culture Act, 185–186, 309
Truteau, Jean Baptiste, 7–10
Turner, Frederick Jackson, 151, 259
Twain, Mark, 209, 244, 251

Uncompahgre project (Colorado), 282, 283
Union, Fort, 25, 37–41, 54, 61
Union Pacific Railway, 64, 88, 114, 128, 130, 132–134, 137, 138, 154–158, 160, 162, 167, 169–171, 206, 209, 241, 243, 244
United Mine Workers of America, 272
Upper Missouri Outfit, 35, 39, 42

Vanderburgh, W. H., 37
Vegetarian Kansas Emigration Company, The, 188
Virginia City (Montana), 86, 95, 230–231
Voyageurs, French, 15

Wagon freighting, 81–83
Waite, Davis ("Bloody Bridles"), 218, 269, 270
Wakefield Colony (Kansas), 188
War of 1812, 18, 34
Wars, frontier editorial, 241–243
West, and federal government, 278–296
    writing about, 227, 244–253
Western Engineer (steamboat), 40
Western Federation of Miners, 269–274
Western Pacific Railroad, 161
Whiskey, in cattle towns, 131
    and Indians, 91, 101, 156
    see also Prohibition
White, William Allen, 220–221, 252, 305
Whitman, Rev. Marcus, 47
Whitney, Asa, 164
Wilson, Pres. Woodrow, 272, 273, 294
Wislizenus, Dr., 22–23, 26
Wissler, Clark, 100
Wister, Owen, 246–248, 331
Wootton, Uncle Dick, 73, 242
Wounded Knee, "Battle" of, 125
Wovoka, 123–124
Wyeth, Nathaniel, 37, 45–46
Wyoming, political formation, 206–207
    Stock Growers Association, 134, 143–145

"Yankees, Galvanized," 100, 113
Yellow Bird (medicine man), 125
Yellowstone (steamboat), 25, 40, 41, 61
Yellowstone Packet (keelboat), 31
Yellowstone Park, 120, 282, 291
Young, Brigham, 49, 105, 106